T0305663

Law and Diplomacy in the Management of EU–Asia Trade and Investment Relations

This volume fills a gap in the literature regarding questions around the interactive dynamics between law and diplomacy on international trade and investment.

It brings together lawyers and political scientists from Europe and Asia in an interdisciplinary effort at tracing the respective roles of law and diplomacy in the relations of the European Union (EU) with its trade and investment partners in Asia. Focusing on trade and investment relations with Asia, the EU presents a particularly interesting case, as it has been a strong proponent of a rules-based international economic order for years and a frequent user of the formal procedures established in international treaties in case of disputes. At the same time, it has kept diplomatically active to adjust dispute management and international agreements to the needs and demands of the partners involved. Furthermore, not only is this region of crucial importance due to the presence of both vigorous emerging economies, like China, India and Vietnam, and more established partners, like Japan, EU–Asia relations also present a broad set of economic disputes and recent negotiation efforts analyzed in the contributions to this volume.

This book will be of key interest to scholars and students of international trade/economic law, EU politics, EU external relations (law), international relations, diplomacy and more broadly to international relations and Asian studies.

Chien-Huei Wu is associate research professor in Academia Sinica, Taipei, Taiwan.

Frank Gaenssmantel is assistant professor at the Department of International Relations and International Organisation at the University of Groningen, the Netherlands.

Routledge/UACES Contemporary European Studies

The primary objective of the new Contemporary European Studies series is to provide a research outlet for scholars of European Studies from all disciplines. The series publishes important scholarly works and aims to forge for itself an international reputation.

Series editors: **Chad Damro**, *University of Edinburgh, UK*, **Elaine Fahey**, *City University London, UK*, and **David Howarth**, *University of Luxembourg, Luxembourg*, on behalf of the *University Association for Contemporary European Studies.*

Editorial Board: *Grainne De Búrca, European University Institute and Columbia University; Andreas Føllesdal, Norwegian Centre for Human Rights, University of Oslo; Peter Holmes, University of Sussex; Liesbet Hooghe, University of North Carolina at Chapel Hill, and Vrije Universiteit Amsterdam; David Phinnemore, Queen's University Belfast; Ben Rosamond, University of Warwick; Vivien Ann Schmidt, University of Boston; Jo Shaw, University of Edinburgh; Mike Smith, University of Loughborough and Loukas Tsoukalis, ELIAMEP, University of Athens and European University Institute.*

Law and Diplomacy in the Management of EU–Asia Trade and Investment Relations

Edited by
Chien-Huei Wu and
Frank Gaenssmantel

Routledge
Taylor & Francis Group

LONDON AND NEW YORK

First published 2020 by Routledge

2 Park Square, Milton Park, Abingdon, Oxon OX14 4RN
605 Third Avenue, New York, NY 10017

Routledge is an imprint of the Taylor & Francis Group, an informa business

First issued in paperback 2021

Publisher's Note

The publisher has gone to great lengths to ensure the quality of this reprint but points out that some imperfections in the original copies may be apparent.

British Library Cataloguing in Publication Data
A catalogue record for this book is available from the British Library

Library of Congress Cataloging in Publication Data
A catalog record has been requested for this book

ISBN: 978-1-138-61746-9 (hbk)
ISBN: 978-1-03-217637-6 (pbk)
DOI: 10.4324/9780429461729

Typeset in Times New Roman
by Lumina Datamatics Limited

Contents

Figures

Tables

Contributors

Julien Chaisse is professor at the City University of Hong Kong, School of Law. He is an award-winning scholar of international law with a focus on the regulation and development of economic globalization. He has published numerous well-regarded and widely cited books and articles, and his scholarship has been cited by international courts/tribunals, as well as US courts. Dr. Chaisse's teaching and research include international trade/investment law, international taxation, contract law, international arbitration and Internet law. Dr. Chaisse served as a senior fellow at the World Trade Institute (Switzerland), and as a diplomat for the Embassy of France in New Delhi, India. As a leading scholar in the field of international economic law, Dr. Chaisse sits on the editorial board of several high-impact international journals. He is also an experienced arbitrator and a sought-after consultant/expert to international organizations, governments, multinational law firms and private investors. Dr. Chaisse is an active member of the World Economic Forum ("Global Future Council on International Trade and Investment" and "Tax and Globalization Working Group"). Dr. Chaisse is also an advisor and partner to the United Nations ARTNET on FDI, member of the Academic Forum on ISDS and Advisory Board member of the Asian Academy of International Law (AAIL).

Shaofeng Chen is associate professor at the School of International Studies, Peking University (PKU), Beijing, China. Before joining in PKU, he used to work at the East Asian Institute, National University of Singapore. Currently, he serves as an editorial board member of *Korean Journal of Policy Science*. He was a visiting professor at Hong Kong University in 2014 and New York University in 2015. His research interests cover energy security, regional integration in Asia, and global economic governance. He has published for more than 30 papers and book chapters, and his works appear in both English and Chinese journals, such as the *China Quarterly*, *Journal of Current Chinese Affairs*, *China: An International Journal*, *Copenhagen Journal of Asian Studies*, *Policy and Society*, *Journal of Chinese Political Science*, *International Politics Quarterly*, *International Journal of China Studies*, *American Study* and so on.

Leïla Choukroune is professor of International Law and director of the University of Portsmouth Thematic Area in Democratic Citizenship. Her research focuses on the interactions between international trade and investment law, human rights, development studies, jurisprudence and social theory. It is also applied to emerging countries, India, China and East Africa in particular.

Professor Choukroune has published numerous scientific articles, book chapters and special issues in English, French, Spanish or Chinese and authored six books, including recently, *Judging the State in International Trade and Investment Law* (2016) and *Exploring Indian Modernities* (2018). She is the editor of the Springer book series *International Law and the Global South*; and the Routledge Series in *Human Rights, Citizenship and the Law*. She is also associate editor of *the Manchester Journal of International Economic Law* and member of the editorial boards of the leading peer-reviewed journals *China Perspectives* and *Perspectives Chinoises*. She regularly publishes in the global media and has given a large number of interviews about her research and its impact. Together with Professor James Nedumpara, she is the co-chair of the South Asia International Economic Law Network (SAIELN) a learned society, which endeavours to foster research and publication in international economic law.

Andrés Delgado Casteleiro is assistant professor at the Law Faculty of Universidad Autónoma de Chile. Previously, he was senior research fellow at the Max Planck Institute of Procedural Law, Luxembourg and a lecturer at Durham Law School, United Kingdom where he also co-directed its European Law Institute. Andrés has a PhD in law from the European University Institute, Florence, Italy and is the author of *The International Responsibility of the European Union: From competence to normative control* (Cambridge University Press, 2016). His research interests include EU external relations law, international economic law and international dispute settlement.

Jappe Eckhardt is a senior lecturer in International Political Economy at the University of York, United Kingdom. His research focuses on the political economy of trade, the role and influence of non-state actors in global governance and the politics of global value chains. He is the author of more than 20 peer-reviewed journal articles, 2 edited volumes and the monograph *Business Lobbying and Trade Governance: The Case of EU-China Relations* (Palgrave 2015).

Frank Gaenssmantel is assistant professor at the Department of International Relations and International Organisation at the University of Groningen since 2010. He previously held a position as research fellow at the Centre for Advanced Studies on Contemporary China (Centro di Alti Studi sulla Cina Contemporanea, CASCC) in Turin and taught at the School of Advanced International and Area Studies at East China Normal University in Shanghai. His research interests include European and Chinese foreign policies, China–EU relations, foreign policy analysis, and international trade relations. He received his PhD from the European University Institute (EUI) in Florence.

Ching-Wen Hsueh is associate professor at National Chengchi University, Department of International Business. In 2012–2016, she was assistant professor at National Chiao-Tung University, School of Law. She served an assistant professor at Graduate Institute of Financial and Economic Law, Feng Chia University in 2012. In 2011, she worked for Institutum Iurisprudentiae, Academia Sinica as a post-doc researcher. During her study in Germany, she completed an internship at in the Legal Division of the World Trade Organization. She received a scholarship of the Ministry of Education, Taiwan, and a scholarship of the University of Cologne, Germany, for international doctoral candidates. She earned her Dr. iur. from the University of Cologne in 2011. Her doctoral dissertation "Direct Effect of the WTO Agreements: Practices and Grounds" was published in 2012.

Xueliang Ji is currently a PhD candidate at the University of Macau, Faculty of Law. His doctoral research deals with international taxation dispute resolution, including international arbitration, OECD/G20 base erosion and profit shifting (BEPS) project and broader issues of international economic law. Xuliang's academic publications include "'Soft Law' in International Law-Making: How Soft International Taxation Law is Reshaping International Economic Governance" 13 *Asian Journal of WTO Law and Health Policy* (2018); "China, Special Economic Zones, and Tax Dispute Resolution" *GLOBTAXGOV* (2018); "The Internationalization of Tax Disputes: Issues and Options of a Standing International Tax Court" *Cardozo Public Law, Policy and Ethics Journal* (2019). He holds a BA from Shenyang Normal University, China (2014), and a BA from Fort Hays State University, US (2014). He also holds an LLM in international economic law from The Chinese University of Hong Kong (2015). He is a member of the Asian Academy of International Law (AAIL).

Yumiko Nakanishi is professor of European Union Law at the Graduate School of Law, Hitotsubashi University, Tokyo. She received her master of law at Hitotsubashi University and University of Münster, Germany, and doctor of law at University of Münster. She is the chief editor of *Review of European Law* (EU ho kenkyu) (shinzansha). She is a member of the Board of Directors of the EUSA-Japan. Main works include: "The Economic Partnership Agreement and the Strategic Partnership Agreement between the EU and Japan", *Hitotsubashi Journal of Law and Politics*, 47 (2019); Yumiko Nakanishi (ed.), *Contemporary Issues in Human Rights Law: Europe and Asia*, Springer, 2018; "Characteristics of EU Free Trade Agreements in a Legal Context: A Japanese Perspective," *European Yearbook of International Economic Law*, 2017; Yumiko Nakanishi (ed.), *Contemporary Issues in Environmental Law*, Springer 2016; *Case law of EU competences*, Shinzansha 2015 (in Japanese); *Legal Structure of EU Competences,* Shinzansha 2013 (in Japanese) and *European Union Law,* Shinseisha 2012 (in Japanese).

Gerda van Roozendaal graduated from the University of Amsterdam in political science (with a specialization in international relations) in 1993. After her graduation, she worked for several research projects at the University of Amsterdam. In 2001, she received her PhD from the University of Amsterdam, Amsterdam School for Social Science Research for her research on the influence of trade unions on the debate related to trade and labour standards. She moved to Curaçao in 2001 where she worked as a researcher and consultant. In 2003 and 2004 she was the policy advisor at the Foreign Relations Department of the Dutch Antilles. Between 2005 and 2016 she worked as an assistant professor at the Department of IRIO at the University of Groningen, and since November 2016 as associate professor. Her research focus is on trade-related policy issues and on institutional change.

Herman H. Voogsgeerd holds degrees in public international and EU law and in contemporary history. His PhD from 2000 is in EU internal market law. He is assistant professor at the University of Groningen and researches and lectures on international political economy at the department of International Relations and International Organization (Faculty of Arts) and on labour law in the Department of Business Law and European Law (Faculty of Law). His research interests focus on balancing social and economic rights, corporate governance of large firms and the rise of Asia.

Chien-Huei Wu is currently associate research professor in Academia Sinica, Taipei, Taiwan. He received his PhD degree in European University Institute, Florence in 2009. Since then, he worked as assistant professor in National Chung Cheng University, Chiayi, Taiwan for a short period. Before pursing his doctoral degree in Florence, he worked for the Ministry of Justice in Taiwan as a district attorney. In 2011–2012, he advised the Ministry in drafting prisoner transfer legislation in Taiwan with a view to facilitating the prisoner transfer between Taiwan and China, and Taiwan and Germany. He also regularly advises the Ministry of Economic Affairs and the Ministry of Health and Welfare on health-related trade issues. His research interests cover EU external relations law and international economic law. He follows closely EU–China and EU-ASEAN relations and pays particular attention to Asian regionalism and WTO-IMF linkage. He has just published a new book by Martinus Nijhoff entitled *WTO and the Greater China: Economic Integration and Dispute Resolution*. In 2014, he was awarded the Ta-You Wu Memorial Award, an award set up by the Ministry of Science and Technology in memorial of the renowned physicist Ta-You Wu for his academic achievement and contribution. Every year, each discipline may appoint one candidate for this award.

Qian Xu's doctoral project examines the international governance and regulation of global sanitation and water services. Her PhD research verges on both international investment law and human rights law, with a focus on the interplay between these bodies of law in the context of international arbitration. Xu's PhD thesis seeks to provide the first exhaustive analysis of international disputes in the increasingly globalized challenges of water resource allocation. The stakes in arriving at a rational and effective normative regime for international water governance are considerable given the potential for high profits, the development of new technologies and the basic need of all human populations for water access. Her objective is to suggest legal developments that might enable states to better manage the privatization of water services. Xu's academic publications include "Is It Finally Time for India's Free Trade Agreements? The ASEAN 'Present' and the RCEP 'Future'" *Asian Journal of International Law* (2019); "Challenges of Water Governance (and Privatization) in China" 47 *Georgia Journal of International and Comparative Law* (2018); "Trans-Pacific Partnership: A World Trade Revolution?" *APEC Currents* (2016). She is also a contributor to the Asia Law Portal, which is the leading source of information and insights on the practice of law in the vast Asia-Pacific region. Xu is currently working on a new article that critically examines the application of the proportionality principle across two decades of investment disputes. Qian Xu holds a BA from Heilongjiang University (2012), an LLM from CUHK Law (2014) and a post-graduate diploma from the Academy of International Trade and Investment Law (2015). She is a member of the Asian Academy of International Law (AAIL).

Acknowledgements

This volume is the outcome of a project that started as a research cooperation between scholars from Taiwan and the Netherlands, coordinated by Academia Sinica in Taipei and the University of Groningen, and grew over time to include further academics of different origins and institutional affiliations. The intention was from the outset to approach an issue that by its nature crosses the boundaries of academic disciplines, from an interdisciplinary perspective. In order to explore why and how EU policymakers choose between, or combine, legal and diplomatic strategies in their efforts at managing economic relations with international partners, it was indispensable to include both lawyers and political scientists and to create space for discussion and exchange amongst them. For this purpose, the involved scholars gathered on two occasions, first for a research workshop at the University of Groningen and then for a larger conference at Academia Sinica. Disciplinary conventions and perspectives, and to some extent also limitations, remained a challenge throughout the project, but we believe that we managed in the end, through the debates, mutual feedback and the editorial process involving various rounds of paper revisions, to construct bridges across the disciplines that allow for synergies in terms of research findings. We hope this will make it an enriching read for other scholars, in these two disciplines and beyond, policymakers, consultants and, more broadly, anyone interested in questions related to international economic governance.

On its trajectory from a simple idea for research and academic cooperation to an edited volume, this project has benefitted from support from many sides, without which it would not have been possible. This concerns first and foremost all involved scholars, whom we would like to thank for their commitment and contributions. We also feel extremely grateful towards the many academics and practitioners who kindly agreed to serve as hosts, keynote speakers, session chairs or discussants during the workshop and the conference, and also supported the project in many other ways. They include the former Director of the Institute of European and American Studies, Academia Sinica, Dr. Chyong-fang Ko; the former Deputy Head of the European Economic and Trade Office, Viktoria Lovenberg; the former Representative of the British Office Taipei, Dr. Michael Reilly; the Justice of the Constitutional Court of Taiwan and WTO panellist Prof. Chang-Fa Lo; Prof. Tai-Lin Chang and Minister without Portfolio John

Chen-Chung Deng in Taiwan; and in Groningen, Prof. Jan van der Harst, Prof. Herman Hoen, Prof. Jaap de Wilde, Prof. Tjalling Halbertsma and Dr. Francesco Giumelli. Various institutions contributed to the project as well. It received funding from the Taiwanese Ministry of Science and Technology (MOST) and the Netherlands Organization for Scientific Research (NWO). We are most grateful for this support, as without it the scholarly gatherings, which are essential for this kind of project, could not have been organized. Academia Sinica and the University of Groningen also made crucial contributions to these events, through the vital support provided by administrative staff, by making venues available and again through generous funding for many additional expenses related to the organization of international scholarly cooperation.

Finally, we would like to express our gratitude to the persons who played a crucial role in transforming the text into a book manuscript ready for publication. Esther Liao at Academia Sinica did an outstanding job in adjusting the very diverse referencing conventions of the two disciplines into a coherent system that matched the expectations of the publisher. The editorial team at Routledge, in particular the copyeditor, also performed extremely well on the final steps towards publication. We feel particularly indebted to Sophie Iddamalgoda, both for her guidance through the entire editing and publication process and for her patience in the face of the many delays and issues that we (and she) had to grapple with.

Chien-Huei Wu and Frank Gaenssmantel
Taipei and Groningen

Introduction

Chien-Huei Wu and Frank Gaenssmantel

Contemporary international economic relations develop in a highly legalized and institutionalized setting. Nevertheless, in their management, diplomatic consultation and political compromise continue to play crucial roles. In case of disputes, policymakers oftentimes prefer to negotiate rather than refer the cases to judicial or quasi-judicial institutions, or they may opt for some combination of diplomatic and legal approaches, with the latter often serving as a backup option or possibly even as a threat scenario. In negotiations towards future agreements they have to decide which issues to legalize and in what way, and which issues to keep in the realm of diplomacy. This leads to the question of why and how policymakers make these choices, and with what implications and effects. Are there any political, legal or institutional factors that promote either legal or diplomatic approaches to disputes, or specific combinations of the two? Is there any evidence on their respective effectiveness? What are the institutional venues for dispute management available and the specific features of each, and what does this imply for their use by policymakers? What are the roles of private actors in determining the nature and venue of dispute settlement? Has the trend towards legalization changed in recent or ongoing international economic negotiations? Which types of issues are legalized, which not? Is there any new pattern in terms of the degree of obligation and precision of the rules and the nature of dispute settlement provisions?

These questions point to the core of current developments in international trade and investment relations and the answers are crucial for understanding them. Surprisingly, they have received limited scholarly attention. While trade and investment policies, related domestic laws, international agreements and in particular the system of the World Trade Organization (WTO) have been studied extensively by both political scientists and lawyers, interactive dynamics between law and diplomacy have been largely neglected, with some rare and rather limited exceptions. For example, Christina Davis has argued that in trade disputes governments use litigation at the WTO dispute settlement mechanism (DSM) to demonstrate commitment to mobilized domestic industries, while negotiation is preferred in the absence of interest group pressure (Davis 2008, 2012). This is an insightful analysis, but her focus on explaining litigation leaves the advantages of negotiation somewhat underexplored, and more generally, she disregards almost entirely dynamics at the international level, which are an important dimension of the contributions to this book. Other scholars have analyzed the conditions under which negotiated settlements can be reached after cases have been filed with the WTO DSM but before a panel is established (Busch and Reinhardt 2000; Reinhardt 2001; Guzman and Simmons 2002). Lastly, the impact of the legalization of the WTO trade regime on further multilateral negotiations has been studied (Goldstein and Martin 2000; Poletti 2011; De Bièvre and Poletti 2015). While these studies contribute significantly to our understanding of international economic relations, they remain limited in that they focus only on very specific aspects of the WTO system.

This volume proposes to fill this gap in the literature on international trade and investment. It brings together lawyers and political scientists from Europe and Asia in an interdisciplinary effort at tracing the respective roles of law and diplomacy in the relations of the European Union (EU) with its trade and investment partners in Asia. The contributions explore how policymakers choose between diplomatic, legal and mixed approaches in managing international economic relations and with what effects. We will pay particular attention to aspects like policymaking dynamics, the preferences and perceptions of policymakers, the role of private actors, the institutional and legal environment in which a specific case unfolds, the nature of formal procedures available and the characteristics of the cases in question.

The European Union and Asia

The EU presents a particularly interesting case for this project, as it has been a strong proponent of a rules-based international economic order for years and a frequent user of the formal procedures established in international treaties in case of disputes, while at the same time remaining very active diplomatically to adjust dispute management and international agreements to the needs and demands of all partners involved. The EU's role as promoter of a rules-based system is visible, for example, in its regular use of the WTO DSM or of trade defence mechanisms in a manner consistent with the WTO rules. Beyond the trade regime, through bilateral negotiations with Singapore, Vietnam, Canada and other countries, the EU has been trying to replace the established investor–state dispute settlement (ISDS) with an investment court system and thereby resolve the legitimacy deficit plaguing the ISDS. In the context of substantial rule-making, the EU strives to bring non-trade issues, such as environmental provisions or human rights, into the scope of trade agreements, to subject them to the same degree of scrutiny, and to fill the gap of the trade rules in regulating export restrictions and redefine the concept of "right to regulate" in the investment law context.

To illustrate, data from the WTO DSM, the single most important mechanism to address disputes in the commercial field, show that the EU accounts for the lion's share of complaints, taking into consideration all cases where it acts as either complainant or respondent, as illustrated in Figure I.1. On average, the EU is involved in around 40 per cent of WTO disputes. It is difficult to say whether the EU is more active in complaining or responding in the WTO DSM since the trend

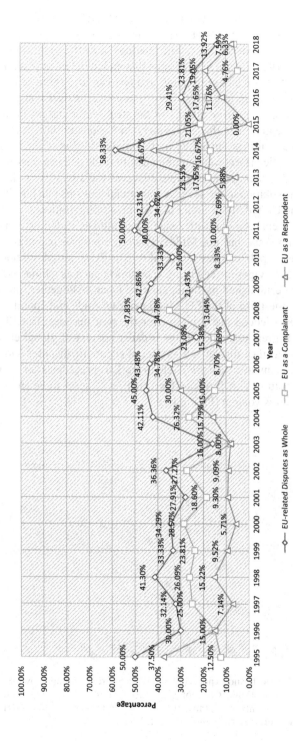

Figure I.1 EU-related disputes in the WTO (from 1995 to 2018). Source: Compiled by the authors based on WTO, Chronological List of Disputes Cases, retrieved from https://www.wto.org/english/tratop_e/dispu_e/dispu_status_e.htm; https://www.wto.org/english/tratop_e/dispu_e/dispu_by_country_e.htm.

varies from time to time. There are two peaks, in 1998 and 2014. In these 2 years, EU-related disputes account for about 60 per cent of the total WTO disputes.

Other instances of EU external economic relations show the continuing importance of diplomacy. The bilateral negotiations that ended the dispute with China on textile trade in 2005 are a case in point, and one can also think of the many requests in the past to Japan to address European concerns over non-tariff barriers. More recently, China's overcapacity in the steel sector and resulting commercial tensions have also seen the EU involved in various initiatives at finding mutually acceptable solutions, including in the broader setting of the G20, even though these diplomatic efforts were combined with trade defence measures and WTO DSM cases. Another recent example concerns the attempts by the EU at finding a diplomatic solution to the severe commercial tensions that have built up in relations with the United States under the Trump administration.

Trade and investment relations with Asia (understood as including Northeast, Southeast and South Asia, but not Middle Eastern countries, Central Asia or other former Soviet Republics) play a crucial role in EU external relations, due to the presence of both vigorous emerging economies, such as China, India and Vietnam, and more established partners, such as Japan. Altogether, the region accounts for about one-third of the EU's total external trade and contains economies that have experienced fast growth over the past decades. But EU–Asia relations are also of great relevance in the broader context of global economic exchanges, not least as they display a broad set of economic disputes and recent negotiation efforts, many of which are likely to work as precedents for economic interactions in the future. This provides for a rich set of cases to be analyzed in the contributions to this volume (Figure I.2).

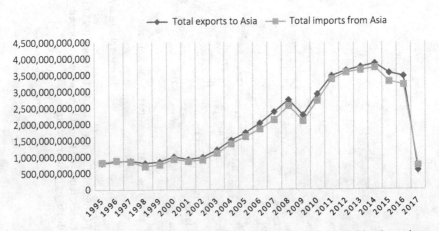

Figure I.2 Asia, total imports and exports (1995–2017). Source: Compiled by the authors based on World Bank, Chronological List of imports and exports of Asia, retrieved from https://data.worldbank.org/indicator/NE.IMP.GNFS.CD; https://data.worldbank.org/indicator/NE.EXP.GNFS.CD.

If we take the WTO DSM as a reference once again, it becomes apparent that of the EU's trade disputes, a large proportion is related to Asia, as visible in Figure I.3. A closer look at the graph reveals a growing general trend in the ratio of EU–Asia trade disputes to total EU-related trade disputes, with a peak in 2008 when the global financial crisis took off.

Relevant literature: a broader view

Aside from the limited existing literature that addresses specific dimensions of the diplomacy vs. law *problématique*, naturally there is a broader set of writings that bear relevance for this collective research project. In the first place, this includes the many publications on the WTO DSM, the most important legal procedure with a court-like body in international economic relations, including between the EU and Asia. Contributions to this volume have built on earlier research on the origins and function of this institution, both by lawyers and political scientists (Davey 2014; Petersmann 1994; Petersmann and Pollack 2003; Trachtman 2006; Elsig and Eckhardt 2015). Literature on the political dynamics around the WTO DSM has also been helpful. This includes the work on diplomatic settlement of a dispute before a panel is established, already mentioned above, but also issues like the impact of the relative power of parties to a dispute, the role of third party submissions, and industry-specific submission strategies of WTO members (Sattler and Bernauer 2011; Busch and Pelc 2010; Davis and Shirato 2007).

Another huge body of literature that has played a crucial role in the preparation of the contributions to this volume regards the formal procedures and political dynamics of decision-making, especially in the highly complex polity of the EU. This concerns first and foremost the relevant legal and institutional provisions and how they play out in practice, in particular regarding the central role of the European Commission and its interaction with member states (Cremona and de Witte 2008; Eeckhout 2011; Koutrakos 2015; De Bièvre and Dür 2005; Woolcock 2011; Heron 2007; Gaenssmantel 2012). Such institutional dynamics have also been linked to the EU's behaviour in international trade negotiations, along with certain external factors that impact positions within the EU (Meunier 2000; Dür and Zimmermann 2007; Frennhof Larsén 2007; Damro 2007; Young 2007; da Conceição-Heldt 2011; Woolcock 2011). This literature, in combination with work on the choice between bilateral and multilateral negotiation strategies (Elsig 2007), has fed into the contributions to this volume that focus on international negotiation and law creation (see especially Part 3). The fact that legal provisions disciplining trade and investment relations, and related DSMs, may exist at bilateral, regional and global levels, has also led to links between these institutions and even the possibility of choosing preferred venues for the management of economic relations (Flett 2015; Busch 2007).

In looking at EU trade and investment policymaking, and also EU–East Asia economic relations more broadly, this project has been particularly sensitive to the

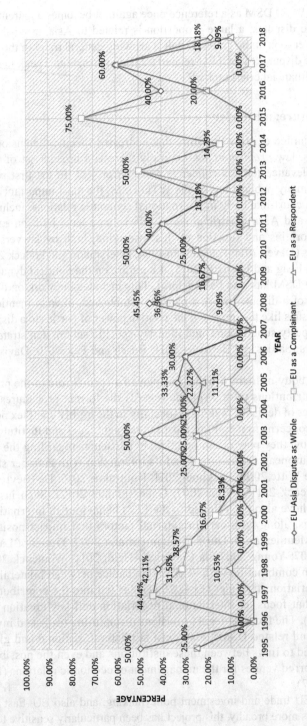

Figure I.3 EU–Asia disputes in the WTO (from 1995 to 2018), Source: Compiled by the authors based on WTO, Chronological List of Disputes Cases, retrieved from https://www.wto.org/english/tratop_e/dispu_e/dispu_status_e.htm; https://www.wto.org/english/tratop_e/dispu_e/dispu_by_country_e.htm.

multiple levels and multiple types of actors involved in contemporary regional and global economic governance. In this context, studies on new dynamics involving interest groups and business actors have also been relevant (Dür 2007; De Bièvre and Eckhardt 2011; Eckhardt 2011; Curran 2015; Liu and Peng 2016). A last group of publications that is relevant for this project analyzes the characteristics of specific issues on the bilateral economic agenda, their perception by the public and by policy elites and how this impact international interaction. Whether or not foreign policy in general is salient to the population, and how specific issues are perceived, oftentimes conditions available policy options (Oppermann and Viehrig 2008, 2009; Oppermann and Spencer 2013). Also, the way policymakers view a certain issue at stake may constrain their approach to managing it in their relations with international partners, including the choice between diplomatic and legal strategies (Sylvan and Voss 1998; Gaenssmantel and Liu 2017).

Naturally, many more sources have been used by the contributors, and these will be mentioned in the chapters and listed in their respective bibliographies. However, most of the groups of literature or analytical traditions that have had a broader influence on the project as a whole have been listed here.

Overview of the contributions

One of the main challenges of this undertaking has been its interdisciplinary nature. Political scientists and lawyers identify and analyze problems in very different ways. It was simply impossible to force each contributor to familiarize herself or himself with the concepts and methods of the respective other discipline to arrive at truly interdisciplinary individual contributions. What was asked of all participants, however, was to keep the overall purpose in mind when designing and orienting their individual research and to develop results that are not only relevant for their own discipline but can contribute to building a relevant set of conclusions for the project as a whole. A general framework was provided as a reference point for the contributors to draft their contributions to this project, which with revision and further elaboration has become Chapter 1 of this volume. Frank Gaenssmantel and Chien-Huei Wu propose a systematic approach to the various dimensions that influence the choice between diplomatic and legal approaches in the EU's external economic policy. The discussion starts from fundamental comments on law and diplomacy in the EU's external economic policy and on the context of multilevel and multi-actor governance in which it unfolds. The authors then discuss legal and diplomatic options available to EU policymakers, reflect how the two may be combined and examine the implications of these various strategies. The chapter addresses both economic disputes and negotiations towards international agreements, and it includes comments on institutional rules and policymaking practice in the EU's external economic relations as well as a thorough review of legal mechanisms available. The last section explicitly identifies factors that promote legal and diplomatic strategies respectively.

After the framework chapter, Part 1 of the volume continues with a focus on recent developments of the legal and institutional context in which economic relations between the EU and Asia unfold and analyzes some specific political dynamics that can be observed in these settings. Andrés Delgado Casteleiro, in Chapter 2, addresses the decreasing influence of the Court of Justice of the EU (CJEU) in external trade relations. The chapter first examines the extent to which the European institutions can be criticized for allowing trade disputes to be litigated in Luxemburg. It then looks at the substance of the CJEU's approach to trade disputes so far. In a last step, the chapter discusses whether and how the newly concluded EU trade agreements are downsizing the role of the CJEU in external trade relations through the exclusion of direct effects and limitation of exceptions. A key argument of this chapter is that the EU is moving away from domestic judicialization of trade disputes, and with two driving forces. The EU political institutions, when negotiating trade agreements, explicitly exclude trade disputes arising therefrom, from the realm of the CJEU, which, itself, also prefers the disputes be dealt with at an international level. Chapter 3 by Jappe Eckhardt provides a historical analysis of EU–China trade disputes and of how the use of diplomatic and legal tools has developed over time. Eckhardt identifies three phases. The first phase, from 1978 until the Tiananmen Square massacre in 1989, was dominated by EU protectionism against Chinese imports and a relatively powerless China, which lacked the legal and political means to stop the EU from imposing protectionist measures. During the second phase, from 1989 until 2002, trade relations where increasingly driven by China's economic pull, yet the EU still had plenty of leeway to adopt protectionist measures against China. The third and final phase, which started with China's WTO accession in 2002 and is still ongoing, can be characterized by increased politicization of trade disputes between the EU and China but also among EU member states. Eckhardt argues that China's WTO membership and its increased trade law capacity enable China to defend its trade interests. He also observes that with China's central position in global value chains, import-dependent firms in the EU have started to play a more vocal role in intra-EU politics.

Closing Part I, Leïla Choukroune in Chapter 4 delves into the larger question of how Asian governments have mixed legal and diplomatic approaches in their international economic relations, and in the context of their own development strategies. Through an in-depth analysis of China's and India's record of trade and investment dispute settlement, the author shows that these two countries have been active but selective in their approach to (and acculturation in) the structures of international trade and investment dispute settlement. She argues that in this domain China and India (and also a number of other Asian countries) have deployed heterodox economic strategies backed by normative autonomy in the service of development. The idea of normative autonomy has implications for the readiness to further legalize trade, investment or more or less directly related issue-areas in future agreements. With a view to preserving such autonomy, some countries thus decide to terminate such BITs that contain investor–state dispute settlement mechanisms. Choukroune's analysis points to the reversing trend of investment disputes. BITs, which were originally an instrument invented by European countries to protect their investors, come back to "bite" European countries themselves.

In Part II, the discussion turns to diplomatic and legal strategies in handling specific disputes. In Chapter 5, Frank Gaenssmantel traces legal and diplomatic elements in the European Commission's approach to the China–EU solar panel dispute, from the start of trade defence investigations in 2012 to the bilateral negotiations on a minimum price undertaking in 2013. It shows that initially the European Commission had virtually no diplomatic options, and the conditions for it to engage successfully in diplomacy were also not given. Amongst legal options, trade defence procedures had a number of advantages, both *vis-à-vis* China and in the EU context. Towards third countries they are powerful tools due to their unilateral nature and for the fact that the burden of proof lies with the targets. Within the EU, treaties and relevant regulations unambiguously establish Commission authority in trade defence measures, thus strengthening its position towards member states. Since the procedure is started by a complaint from the private sector, the Commission can avoid criticism for excessive activism. Nevertheless, the opposition of a significant number of member states made this approach untenable, and the Commission was forced to envisage a diplomatic approach. It relied again on the formal rules to turn this adverse situation somewhat more to its favour. It did so firstly, by using preliminary anti-dumping duties to construct a threat scenario, and secondly by making use of the provisions in the relevant regulations on negotiating minimum price undertakings. The outcome was still criticized as more favourable to China than to EU industries, but the exercise of "legally embedded diplomacy" allowed the Commission to avoid the worst.

Shaofeng Chen in Chapter 6 analyzes the same dispute but from a different angle, in that he develops an explanation of the very different reactions amongst EU member states to the trade defence investigations targeting imports of Chinese solar panels. He first discusses the role played by member states in the decision-making process on trade defence and then presents a framework for explaining member state preferences based on both values, i.e. underlying preferences regarding free trade vs. protectionism, and economic interests in relation to China. Case studies of German, Italian and Polish positions on solar panel trade defence show that these two variables can indeed explain member state position to a large extent. The chapter shows that different preferences on economic policies towards third states are structurally embedded in the political economies of member states. The challenges this implies for the Commission in the management of external economic relations are therefore unlikely to disappear any time soon.

Chapter 7 by Chien-Huei Wu then examines the EU's trade dispute management strategy with regard to export restrictions by looking at the interaction between negotiation and litigation. Wu first explores the role of export restrictions in the GATT/WTO regime and traces both, negotiation efforts at disciplining export restrictions during China's accession process, and attempts by the

EU to secure enforcement of such obligations and commitments through WTO litigation. As China could comply with WTO rules by switching from export taxes to production quota, he then asks whether the EU may have to return to diplomatic tools to resolve its differences with China. He then concludes the chapter by investigating how the EU globalizes China-specific rules to all WTO members, or at least to the new WTO members during the accession negotiations and to its counterparts in FTA negotiations.

In the concluding chapter of Part II, Ching-Wen Hsueh studies difficulties of finding a legal solution to EU–China disputes over China's treatment as a non-market economy (NME). She first looks at the origin of the NME concept and its problematic legal definition, and then turns to the specific provisions for NME treatment under the EU's anti-dumping regime. In a further step she analyzes EU–China anti-dumping cases to show the limits, if not impossibility, of solving the NME disputes through legal means. The limited role of a legal approach in resolving the dispute on NME lies in the lack of a clearly defined concept that prevents the judiciary from adjudicating the case. Moreover, given that political and economic complexity surrounding the NME, the judiciary tends to take a lenient approach and endorses a broader scope of manoeuvre for the political branches.

The third and last part of the volume analyzes the creation and development of law in relations between the EU and Asian partners. This concerns the ongoing negotiations on a bilateral investment treaty, but also how non-trade issues are treated in bilateral negotiations and agreements. In Chapter 9, Julien Chaisse, Qian Xu and Xueliang Ji probe the future of the EU–China economic relations and explore how the EU and China are rearranging their investment relations by negotiating a new investment treaty that will replace the 26 investment treaties concluded by China and 27 member states, except Ireland. By concluding a new investment treaty, the EU may shield itself from investment disputes arising from various investment treaties as investors may rely upon treaties favourable to them and sue the EU. In response, China, by reviewing and modernizing its investment treaties, aims to pursue a better balance between the foreign investors' rights and the host state's ability to regulate in the public interest. Against the backdrop of other negotiations of investment treaties or FTAs with investment chapters, Chaisse, Xu and Ji show how the EU and China use their BIT negotiation as an effort to set global norms on international investment regimes.

In Chapter 10, Herman Voogsgeerd analyzes the treatment of non-trade issues in free-trade negotiations between the EU and major commercial partners. First, the author discusses the implications of the EU's institutional structure and EU law, and then he turns to the international legal context under the WTO. In a last step he uses the recently closed EU–Japan negotiations as a case study for how negotiations develop between two similarly advanced economies. The author argues that due to the political context surrounding bilateral free-trade negotiations, non-trade issues are unlikely to be included with a high degree of precision and obligation. Instead, related provisions mostly serve as focal points for further diplomatic consultations. Chapter 11 by Gerda van Roozendaal studies the role of labour standards in the negotiations towards a free-trade agreement between the EU and India. She examines normative and rational considerations from both the EU and the Indian side, and she adds an extensive discussion on legal and institutional options for labour standards in a future EU–India free-trade agreement. Normative differences between the two sides have created particular tensions in the negotiation process. While for the EU the inclusion of labour standards follows international norms and practice, from the Indian perspective this would represent interference in its sovereignty. The author argues that even if negotiators eventually agree on the inclusion of labour standards in the treaty, one should expect them to serve as reference for further diplomatic consultation, while enforceable legal provisions are highly unlikely.

In the last chapter of Part III, and the volume as a whole, Yumiko Nakanishi looks at trade and sustainable development (TSD) chapters in EU–Asia trade agreements and examines how environmental issues are regulated in the context of trade and investment relations. She first traces the development of sustainable development within the EU and investigates how the EU introduces this issue into the scope of trade negotiations. She uses TSD chapters as an example to show how the EU, through bilateral FTA negotiations, legislates new trade rules focusing especially on dispute settlement in the TSD chapters, as opposed to a general dispute settlement mechanism, and on the right to regulate in the investment context. A core argument of this chapter is that environmental issues constitute a particular challenge in the context of both negotiations and dispute management, as they go to the heart of each side's right to regulate in the name of public interest and related domestic policies.

Conclusion

The contributions to this volume cover a wide array of instances where law and diplomacy interact and lead to conclusions that allow us to provide some solid answers to the questions laid out at the beginning of this introduction. In the conclusion of the volume the editors will bring together the findings from the individual chapters in the context of the conceptual framework. This will allow us not only to show the insights added by this collective project, but also to point to some persisting gaps, which we hope can inspire further academic research.

References

Busch, M.L. (2007) 'Overlapping Institutions, Forum Shopping, and Dispute Settlement in International Trade', *International Organization*, 61(4), pp. 735–761.

Busch, M.L. and Pelc, K.J. (2010) 'The Politics of Judicial Economy at the World Trade Organization', *International Organization*, 64(2), pp. 257–279.

Busch, M.L. and Reinhardt, E. (2000) 'Bargaining in the Shadow of the Law: Early Settlement in GATT/WTO Disputes', *Fordham International Law Journal*, 24(1), pp. 158–172.

Curran, L. (2015) 'The Impact of Trade Policy on Global Production Networks: The Solar Panel Case', *Review of International Political Economy*, 22(5), pp. 1025–1054.

Cremona, M. and de Witte, B. (eds.) (2008) *EU Foreign Relations Law: Constitutional Fundamental*, Oxford, UK: Hart Publishing.

da Conceição-Heldt, E. (2011) 'Variation in EU Member States' Preferences and the Commission's Discretion in the Doha Round', *Journal of European Public Policy*, 18(3), pp. 403–419.

Damro, C. (2007) 'EU Delegation and Agency in International Trade Negotiations: A Cautionary Comparison', *Journal of Common Market Studies*, 45(4), pp. 883–903.

Davey, W.J. (2014) 'The WTO and Rules-Based Dispute Settlement: Historical Evolution, Operational Success, and Future Challenges', *Journal of International Economic Law*, 17(3), pp. 679–700.

Davis, C.L. (2008) 'The Effectiveness of WTO Dispute Settlement: An Evaluation of Negotiation Versus Adjudication Strategies', Paper presented at the *Annual Meeting of the American Political Science Association*, Boston, MA, August 2008.

Davis, C.L. (2012) *Why Adjudicate? Enforcing Trade Rules in the WTO*, Princeton, NJ: Princeton University Press.

Davis, C. and Shirato, Y. (2007) 'Firms, Governments, and WTO Adjudication: Japan's Selection of WTO Disputes', *World Politics*, 59(2), pp. 274–313.

De Bièvre, D. and Dür, A. (2005) 'Constituency Interests and Delegation in European and American Trade Policy', *Comparative Political Studies*, 38(10), pp. 1271–1296.

De Bièvre, D. and Eckhardt, J. (2011) 'Interest Groups and EU Anti-Dumping Policy', *Journal of European Public Policy*, 18(3), pp. 339–360.

De Bièvre, D. and Poletti, A. (2015) 'Judicial Politics in International Trade Relations: Introduction to the Special Issue', *World Trade Review*, 14(S1), pp. S1–S11.

Dür, A. (2007) 'EU Trade Policy as Protection for Exporters: The Agreements with Mexico and Chile', *Journal of Common Market Studies*, 45(4), pp. 833–855.

Dür, A. and Zimmermann, H. (2007) 'Introduction: The EU in International Trade Negotiations', *Journal of Common Market Studies*, 45(4), pp. 771–787.

Eckhardt, J. (2011) 'Firm Lobbying and EU Trade Policy Making: Reflections on the Anti-Dumping Case against Chinese and Vietnamese Shoes (2005–2011)', *Journal of World Trade*, 45(5), pp. 965–991.

Eeckhout, P. (2011) *EU External Relations Law*, Oxford: Oxford University Press.

Elsig, M. (2007) 'The EU's Choice of Regulatory Venues for Trade Negotiations: A Tale of Agency Power?' *Journal of Common Market Studies*, 45(11), pp. 927–948.

Elsig, M. and Eckhardt, J. (2015) 'The Creation of the Multilateral Trade Court: Design and Experiential Learning', *World Trade Review*, 14(S1), pp. S13–S32.

Flett, J. (2015) 'Referring PTA Disputes to the WTO Dispute Settlement System' in A. Dür, and M. Elsig (eds.), *Trade Cooperation: The Purpose, Design and Effects of Preferential Trade Agreements*, Cambridge: Cambridge University Press, pp. 555–579.

Frennhof Larsén, M. (2007) 'Trade Negotiations between the EU and South Africa: A Three-Level Game', *Journal of Common Market Studies*, 45(4), pp. 857–881.

Gaenssmantel, F. (2012) 'EU-China Relations and Market Economy Status: EU Foreign Policy in the Technical Trap', *Journal of European Integration History*, 18(1), pp. 51–66.

Gaenssmantel, F. and Liu, F. (2017) 'Same Name, Different Substance? Exploring the Impact of Issue Perceptions on China-EU Relations', in T. Halbertsma and J. van der Harst (eds.), *China, East Asia and the European Union: Strong Economics, Weak Politics?* Leiden: Brill.

Guzman, A. and Simmons, B.A. (2002) 'To Settle or Empanel? An Empirical Analysis of Litigation and Settlement at the World Trade Organization', *The Journal of Legal Studies*, 31(S1), pp. S205–S235.

Goldstein, J. and Martin, L.L. (2000) 'Legalization, Trade Liberalization, and Domestic Politics: A Cautionary Note', *International Organization*, 54(3), pp. 603–632.

Heron, T. (2007) 'European Trade Diplomacy and the Politics of Global Developments: Reflections on the EU-China "Bra-Wards" Dispute', *Government and Opposition*, 42(2), pp. 190–214.

Koutrakos, P. (2015) *EU International Relations Law*, London, UK: Bloomsbury Publishing.

Liu, H.-W. and Peng, S.-Y. (2016) 'Managing Trade Conflicts in the ICT Industry: A Case Study of EU–Greater China Area', *Journal of International Economic Law*, 19(3), pp. 629–656.

Meunier, S. (2000) 'What Single Voice? European Institutions and EU-US Trade Negotiations', *International Organization*, 54(1), pp. 103–135.

Oppermann, K. and Viehrig, H. (2008) 'Issue Salience and the Domestic Legitimacy Demands of European Integration: The Cases of Britain and Germany', *European Integration Online Papers*, 12(2), available at http://eiop.or.at/eiop/pdf/2008-002.pdf

Oppermann, K. and Viehrig, H. (2009) 'The Public Salience of Foreign and Security Policy in Britain, Germany and France', *West European Politics*, 32(5), pp. 925–942.

Oppermann, K. and Spencer, A. (2013) 'Thinking Alike? Salience and Metaphor Analysis as Cognitive Approaches to Foreign Policy Analysis', *Foreign Policy Analysis*, 9(1), pp. 39–56.

Petersmann, E.U. (1994) 'The Dispute Settlement System of the World Trade Organization and the Evolution of the GATT Dispute Settlement System since 1948', *Common Market Law Review*, 31(6), pp. 1157–1244.

Petersmann, E.U. and Pollack, M.A. (eds.) (2003) *Transatlantic Economic Disputes: The EU, The US and the WTO*, Oxford: Oxford University Press.

Poletti, A. (2011) 'World Trade Organization Judicialization and Preference Convergence in EU Trade Policy: Making the Agent's Life Easier', *Journal of European Public Policy*, 18(3), pp. 361–382.

Reinhardt, E. (2001) 'Adjudication without Enforcement in WTO Disputes', *Journal of Conflict Resolution*, 45(2), pp. 174–195.

Sattler, T. and Bernauer, T. (2011) 'Gravitation or Discrimination? Determinants of Litigation in the World Trade Organisation', *European Journal of Political Research*, 50(2), pp. 143–167.

Sylvan, D.A. and Voss, J.F. (eds.) (1998) *Problem Representation in Foreign Policy Decision Making*, Cambridge: Cambridge University Press.

Trachtman, J.P. (2006) 'The Constitutions of the WTO', *European Journal of International Law*, 17(3), pp. 623–646.

Woolcock, S. (2011) 'EU Economic Diplomacy: The Factors Shaping Common Action', *The Hague Journal of Diplomacy*, 6(1), pp. 83–99.

Young, A. R. (2007) 'Trade Politics Ain't What It Used to Be: The European Union in the Doha Round', *Journal of Common Market Studies*, 45(4), pp. 789–811.

Part I

Conceptual discussion and historical evolution

1 Managing international economic relations through diplomacy and law

Towards a framework for understanding the external policies of the European Union

Frank Gaenssmantel and Chien-Huei Wu

In an interdisciplinary project as the one we present in this volume, some theoretical and conceptual considerations are necessary to bridge the gap between the involved disciplines and bring the involved scholars closer together in their analytical efforts. Given the considerable differences between law and political science, and also between the approaches and methods adopted by the participants of this project, our purpose here is not to present a theoretical framework in the narrow sense, with concrete hypotheses or observable implications, which can be assessed or tested in subsequent chapters. Instead, we aim at exploring the various dimensions of the topic and problem at hand, and at structuring the field of investigation, in order to show the conceptual connections between the contributions and to set the stage for presenting a set of conclusions at the end of the volume.

The conceptual framework developed here will thus present the characteristics of diplomatic and legal approaches in the management of external economic relations by the European Union (EU), discuss the role of policymaking processes in this connection and elaborate on the governance and institutional environment within which economic relations are managed. It will also point to various factors that we expect to make diplomatic or legal approaches, or specific combinations thereof, more or less likely, and with what effect.

The chapter starts with a discussion of diplomacy and law in EU external relations and the issue of choosing between different approaches in a highly diversified, yet legalized and institutionalized context of governance. The two subsequent sections comment respectively on diplomatic dynamics and legal tools for managing commercial disputes. We close the chapter by bringing these two aspects together and discussing conditions that favour either diplomatic or legal approaches, or combinations of the two.

Diplomacy and law as alternatives for the EU

Diplomacy and law are fundamentally different ways of managing international relations, including economic relations; in the following paragraphs, we discuss

some of the specific features of each. Before doing so, it is important to emphasize a crucial commonality of diplomacy and law: the fact that both are means
to solve disputes (Laswell and McDougal 1991). Therefore, both can be seen as
essentially political processes in the famous Eastonian sense of an "authoritative
allocation of values" (Easton 1965). But while the legal approach to this allocation of values is based on a system of binding rules and procedures, and oftentimes delegation of the authority to interpret the rules and adjudicate (typically
to a court or court-like body), diplomacy steers clear of general rules, formal procedures and delegation and instead seeks compromise on the basis of the specific
character of the issue at hand.

Diplomacy and the EU

Going a step further, diplomacy can be understood in two different senses.
Firstly, it is one of the techniques available to policymakers pursuing their foreign policy (Baldwin 1985), a concept that we understand as "the sum of official
external relations conducted by an independent actor (usually a state) in international relations," (Hill 2003, p. 3) and which therefore comprises commercial
and other external economic policies. More specifically, diplomacy "consists of
communication between officials designed to promote foreign policy either by
formal agreement or tacit adjustment" (Berridge 2010). This is a broad definition
and includes, but is not limited to, international negotiations, which have been
the focus of some classical discussions of diplomacy (see for example Nicolson
1961). Secondly, taking representation as a central element of diplomacy (Sharp
1997), diplomacy is not only about the pursuit of specific goals but also a "state
of affairs," in that communication is regular and ongoing through embassies,
representative offices and the like. This differs from the idea of a tool that is
deployed whenever deemed necessary in the pursuit of a specific foreign policy
goal. Considering diplomacy as a state of affairs, the use of diplomatic channels
to raise an issue with the concerned counterpart to "sound out" their interests and
disposition, and possibly start working towards a mutually agreeable arrangement, is typically the most immediate approach when any kind of questions or
tensions arise in international relations.

Who are the actors of diplomacy? The trained diplomats from foreign ministries
certainly remain the principle agents of diplomacy, as they are typically in charge
of negotiations and representation. But their field of activity has been progressively constrained by competition from various other levels of social organization
and different types of actors, including other branches of their own governments
(Devin 2002), but also the administrative services of international organizations.
On the one hand, most departments of the executive now maintain their own contacts with international counterparts, often with only marginal involvement of
professional diplomats, and sometimes none at all. In the field of commercial
diplomacy, trade ministries lead negotiations and typically second their own staff

to embassies abroad, thus frequently side-lining their colleagues from the foreign ministry. On the other hand, the increasingly active summit diplomacy of top leaders also complicates the work of trained diplomats who are better prepared for international interaction but less authoritative in the politico-administrative hierarchy. At the same time, international organizations have their own staff involved in diplomatic interactions (among member states and with respect to outsiders), with interests and ideas that may diverge from national officials and thus further constrain the activities of foreign ministries. Lastly, one should not forget that the international activities and interests of transnational private actors, like business corporations or nongovernmental organizations, also bring pressure to bear on diplomats and condition their scope for action.

If we say, as quoted above, that foreign policy is "usually" related to a state, then how does the EU fit into a discussion of diplomacy? In the form of its common commercial policy (CCP), as well as development policies to a certain extent, the European integration project has had a foreign policy dimension since the Treaty of Rome. The European Commission has provided, for a long time already, a pool of officials ready to engage in diplomacy as a tool of foreign policy, for example, in the negotiation rounds of the General Agreement on Tariffs and Trade (GATT). Through its delegations in virtually all countries of the world it also takes part in diplomacy as a state of affairs. Over the past decades, the EU has progressively broadened the ambition and scope of its foreign policy activities, and with the High Representative of the Union for Foreign Affairs and Security Policy and the European External Action Service (EEAS), it has even created a *de facto* foreign minister and a diplomatic service. This means it has developed an outward-facing diplomatic profile that looks surprisingly similar to that of states.

Nevertheless, EU diplomacy displays a series of particular features that distinguish it from that of states. First, the scope of competence is limited by its nature as an international organization. Without a basis in the European treaties, EU legislation or court decisions, EU officials cannot authoritatively talk to international counterparts. Second, all member states maintain their own foreign policy and diplomatic services, which means that we can oftentimes observe parallel, and possibly even competing, claims for (and efforts at) external representation, at EU and member state levels. Third, the EU's foreign policy process and its diplomacy are subject to an unusually wide array of constraints. This includes, first and foremost, pressure from the member states but also lobbying by private actors. In the trade policy field, the European Commission and the Trade Policy Committee (TPC, formerly 133 Committee) in the Council have long been important targets for private actors in their efforts to influence decision-making in their favour (Woll 2009). Since the Treaty of Lisbon, with the CCP now subject to the EU's "ordinary legislative procedure,", and thus scrutiny by the European Parliament (EP), the parliamentary International Trade Committee (INTA) has also attracted lobbyists' attention (Marshall 2010).[1]

International law and the EU

In parallel to diplomacy, international law plays a key role in the management of international frictions. On the one hand, it provides a set of procedures that public and private actors can follow when they feel disadvantaged by violations of shared rules. On the other hand, law defines the boundaries of discretion, or policy space, available to decision makers and diplomats. In international economic relations, there has been a trend towards legalization over the past few decades, with the key development being the coming into being of the World Trade Organization (WTO) in 1995 (Petersmann 1994; Weiler 2001; Reich 1996). With its compulsory jurisdiction, the establishment of a permanent Appellate Body and quasi-automatic adoption of panel/Appellate Body reports by virtue of negative consensus, the WTO dispute settlement mechanism (DSM) significantly contributes to this legalization process (Petersmann 1997; Palmeter and Mavroidis 2004).

The term "legalization" has been used both by scholars of international law and international relations. According to Kenneth Abbott, Robert Keohane, Andrew Moravcsik, Anne-Marie Slaughter and Duncan Snidal (Abbott et al. 2000), legalization refers to "a particular form of institutionalization characterized by three components: obligation, precision and delegation." According to them, "*[o]bligation* means that states or other actors are bound by a rule or commitment or by a set of rules or commitments. [...] *Precision* means that rules unambiguously define the conduct they require, authorize, or proscribe. *Delegation* means that third parties have been granted authority to implement, interpret, and apply the rules; resolve disputes; and (possibly) to make further rules" (Abbott et al. 2000, p. 401). In applying this definition to the WTO agreements, it can be concluded that such agreements can be characterized by a high degree of legalization given the binding nature of international obligations and commitments, precise and detailed regulation of trade rules and the compulsory third-party DSM. Similar phenomena of legalization, to a various extent, can also be observed in the bilateral agreements concluded by the EU. The most illustrative examples are free trade agreements (FTAs), which provide for clearly defined obligations and compulsory DSMs. Some investment chapters of the EU FTAs and EU bilateral investment treaties (BITs) move a step forward by providing individuals an option for resorting to investor–state dispute settlement (ISDS).

This broader context of the legalization of international trade law, especially under the auspices of the WTO, inevitably affects the legal regulatory framework of the EU's trade dispute management. On the inward-looking (defensive) side, the EU has strengthened its trade defence mechanisms, which cover anti-dumping, countervailing and safeguard measures, while emphasizing WTO conformity. On the outward-looking (offensive) side, the EU has developed tools to expand its markets abroad, in particular the Trade Barriers Regulation (TBR),[2] but also a broader "market access strategy."[3] Private actors, individuals or enterprises may refer to the TBR with petitions to request the European Commission to bring a legal challenge in the WTO DSM or DSMs under the bilateral agreements to address trade barriers in third countries (Bronckers 1996).[4]

It is thus clear that boundaries set by law that constrain the discretion of diplomats and policymakers also arise from the EU's internal legal order. Whereas the Anti-Dumping Agreement (ADA), the Agreement on Subsidies and Countervailing Measures (ASCM) and the Agreement on Safeguards (ASG) set out the rules to be followed when the EU initiates a trade defence measure, which would be subject to the scrutiny of the WTO DSM, the EU domestic counterparts of these three WTO agreements, namely the Anti-Dumping Regulation, Anti-Subsidy Regulation and Safeguards Regulation also dictate the policymakers' behaviour within the EU legal order, which could be reviewed by the Court of Justice of the EU (CJEU). Law governing the EU's trade dispute management can therefore be located at two levels: EU law at the domestic level and international trade law, including both the multilateral WTO DSM and bilateral FTAs with the DSMs they set up. Between these two levels, a linkage may be found through the resort to the TBR.

Just as for diplomacy, the competence of the EU also plays a pivotal role with regards to legal tools for managing economic external relations, naturally along with the jurisdiction of the pertinent DSM, if applicable. With various treaty revisions, from Amsterdam to Lisbon, the EU has gradually obtained exclusive competence on almost every aspect of trade relations, including also international investment (Herrmann 2002; Krajewski 2005, 2012; Young 2000; Wu 2011). The EU, and only the EU, is supposed to argue for, and defend, the EU and its member states before the DSMs as provided by the WTO and bilateral agreements. However, it happens from time to time that third countries identify both the EU, and at the same time some of its member states, as defending parties (see most famously *European Communities – Selected Customs Matters* 2006, and most recently *EU – Feed-in-Tariffs [China]*, which included a consultation request but not a request for the establishment of a panel). This may complicate the EU's trade dispute management strategy, especially when it comes to sectors that member states consider sensitive, such as public health or cultural areas. When representing the EU at the WTO DSM, the European Commission, in particular its legal service, takes the lead; nonetheless, the influence of private interests in shaping the course of disputes is also apparent. A "public-private partnership" in advancing the EU's interests before the WTO DSM can often be registered in the sense that EU institutions, through policy instruments such as trade defence mechanisms and TBR, cooperate with enterprises in challenging WTO-inconsistent measures of third countries and defending the legality of EU measures (Shaffer 2006).

Choice and constraints

One ambition of this project is to account for choice by policymakers, i.e. between diplomatic or legal approaches to the management of trade disputes, or otherwise any combination of the two. Given the fact that there are different strategies for managing relations with trade partners, exploring how policymakers decide between these alternatives will significantly enhance our understanding of international commercial relations. This recalls the "logic of choice," proposed by David Baldwin (1999/2000), as well as his earlier work in which he compares "techniques of statecraft" (Baldwin 1985, pp. 12–18). Following Baldwin, our purpose is to move a step beyond the common tendency of looking only at single tools of external relations and their effectiveness, as for example either the WTO's DSM or commercial negotiations, and to view them as alternatives and in terms of respective advantages and disadvantages.

In Baldwin's discussion, choice results from a rational process of comparing costs and expected benefits. In this respect our approach differs from the original logic of choice. The process of choosing between diplomacy and law in the context of a specific interaction with a commercial partner, as well as the definition of concrete diplomatic or legal strategies, may reveal a variety of features of social interaction. It is true of course that typically we think in terms of a rational process, both in the choice between law and diplomacy and in the ensuing interactions with the representatives of the concerned partner economy. However, in addition to rationality, issues falling under the so-called "logic of appropriateness" may also play a role (March and Olsen 2009), for example, when the decision to use legal procedures is based on the profound conviction that a certain behaviour by the counterpart is in violation of shared norms or in the case of disagreement on the extent to which non-trade norms, like labour rights, can be invoked in relation to trade issues. Lastly, both the decision and the interaction are subject to the "logic of arguing" and "rhetorical action," i.e. put simply, how effectively a specific argument is presented and whether one side can make strategic use of prior normative commitments of the counterpart (Risse 2000; Schimmelfennig 2001).

"Choice" in this context does not necessarily mean "freedom." Although the very existence of alternatives implies a minimum of freedom, policymakers are subject to myriad constraints when deciding how to deal with a commercial dispute. First of all, in many situations, institutional procedures reduce *de facto* the number of alternatives. For example, when private actors launch an anti-dumping investigation, the European Commission has to follow established procedures, even if it might favour solving the issue through diplomatic consultations with the concerned government. Second, numerous factors condition the diplomatic or legal dispute management. Diplomatic action may be constrained by the activities of other actors, like EU member states, while legal strategies crucially depend on formal institutional structures of international trade law.

Therefore we propose a "logic of constraints" as a necessary counterpart to the logic of choice. The constraints that EU policymakers face when managing commercial disputes are rooted in the multilevel and multi-actor nature of contemporary governance (Hooghe and Marks 2003; Kahler and Lake 2004; Dingwerth and Pattberg 2006), whereby governance is understood in a very broad sense "to refer to all coexisting forms of collective regulation of social affairs, including the self-regulation of civil society, the coregulation of public and private actors, and authoritative regulation through government" (Dingwerth and Pattberg 2006, p. 188). The emphasis on multiple levels points to the fact that processes

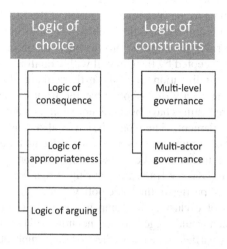

Figure 1.1 The different influences on policy-maker decisions.

of governance unfold around venues at different levels of social organization, meaning that constraints on policymakers may come from both the bottom and the top. Concretely, EU policymakers must take the state and substate level into account, but also other regional organizations and bilateral or multilateral dynamics towards the outside. Multi-actor governance implies that governance processes at all levels are not limited to public entities but crucially include private actors, whereby their interests, expectations or formal initiatives constitute constraints for policymakers. The factors shaping the logic of choice and the logic of constraints are summarized in (Figure 1.1).

The EU and the diplomatic approach to external economic relations

The CCP of the EU stands out as "by far the most integrated of the EU's external policies" (Marsh and Mackenstein 2005, p. 57). It is an exclusive competence of the EU, meaning that member states cannot make their own commercial policy (unlike, say, in the field of development cooperation) and have a rather limited influence on formal decision-making (unlike, for example, under the Common Foreign and Security Policy). The CCP goes back to the Treaty of Rome, but its scope has been growing over the decades as new policy areas have been progressively integrated, like trade in services, intellectual property rights and foreign direct investment.

EU trade policymaking and commercial diplomacy

If we look at who designs the EU's commercial policy, the European Commission plays such a crucial role that the EU's foreign service, the EEAS, may appear to be yet another body of professional diplomats crowded out by institutional competition. This is misleading though, as the explanation for the Commission's influence lies in its long history as a central player of EU policymaking, which stands in stark contrast to the very recent creation of the EEAS. Since the Treaty of Rome, the Commission has had the exclusive right of initiative with regards to the definition of rules for imports into the customs union.[5] In the past, such initiatives could be accepted by the Council with a qualified majority but would need unanimity for modification, and this further enhanced the influence of the Commission.[6] As the Treaty of Lisbon subjected trade policy to the "ordinary legislative procedure," things have become more complex due to the involvement of the European Parliament.[7] The Commission is also central to the core business of diplomacy: communication. The Treaty of Rome made the Commission the sole negotiator in international commercial negotiations,[8] and officials of the Directorate-General (DG) for Trade are ensuring proper representation and communication with third parties in the trade policy field.

The combination of exclusive EU competence and a central position for the European Commission would suggest strong and unified EU commercial diplomacy. However, this is only partially true due to the growing complexities of diplomacy in general and EU external diplomacy in particular. More specifically, member states exert strong pressure on the Commission despite the high level of integration. The latter also has to keep in mind the role of both the Council and the European Parliament in formal decision-making, while private actors engage in lobbying and make frequent use of formal procedures available to them, like anti-dumping complaints.

These constraints can be illustrated by taking a closer look at how the Commission uses diplomacy in its pursuit of EU commercial policy, and in particular in commercial disputes. Fundamentally, officials of the Commission's DG Trade have two diplomatic options when tensions arise with trade partners. The first is to attempt to solve the issue in the context of regular diplomatic consultations, i.e. based on diplomacy as "state of affairs." The second involves asking the member states in the Council of the EU to approve a mandate to engage in formal negotiations towards an agreement that would resolve the dispute, in the sense of diplomacy as a tool of foreign policy.

The first of these options has the advantage of low visibility: what happens in the regular consultations of the Commission's trade officials with their international counterparts can hardly be scrutinized by member states, members of the European Parliament or lobby groups, which leaves space for informal and indirect approaches, including through "friendly" officials on the other side, as well as for issue linkage if possible and expedient. The disadvantage, of course, is that if the consultations go public, the Commission risks considerable pressure from interested parties within the EU. Oftentimes, member states do not fully trust the Commission and are fearful of the Commission engaging in "horse-trading" in pursuit of its own agenda (interview with Council Secretariat officials, 2008). Such an impression may impose a heavy burden on an agent like the Commission. In a huge and complex polity like the EU, building an agreement among all necessary players is a challenging task and requires a significant level of confidence among the member states. This is particularly important if consultations lead to an agreement that includes concessions on the part of the

EU; as for changes to import rules, the Commission needs the approval of the European Parliament and the member states in the Council.

In the second hypothesis, the Commission has to propose a negotiating mandate, have it accepted by the Council of the EU and then engage in international negotiations under the close scrutiny of the TPC. This is a rather lengthy undertaking and therefore not adequate to address new and possibly urgent issues within a tight time frame. The formal mandate and regular reporting to the TPC also create awareness and visibility among member states and lobbies (even though the contents of the mandates are secret), and this reduces much of the flexibility in terms of channels of communication and issue linkage. At the same time, with the "red lines" of member states defined in advance, it is easier to keep them on board, which is particularly important for ambitious long-term projects, like trade agreements, where failure is simply too costly. This means that this scenario is of particular relevance in cases of law creation through diplomatic negotiation, but less relevant for managing current developments in the relationship, including disputes.

Diplomatic interaction between the EU and its trading partners

So despite the comparatively deep integration of commercial policy, the internal politics of the EU, and in particular member states and their positions, remain a key factor in EU trade diplomacy. This recalls the logic of two-level games, as first proposed by Robert Putnam, and the notion of "win-set," i.e. the group of outcomes of a diplomatic interaction that are acceptable to both the international counterpart and the domestic constituency (Putnam 1988). Of course, two levels are not sufficient to adequately depict the numerous constraints that weigh on EU trade diplomacy in a multilevel and multi-actor system of governance, as described above. Still, in comparison to later adaptations to processes that stretch across more than two levels (Collinson 1999; Patterson 1997), the clarity of Putnam's original discussion allows us to focus on the core mechanism of interaction at various levels, which can be flexibly adapted to the specific needs of a diversity of cases.

Elaborating on Putnam, one should expect that the following factors enhance the capacity of EU commercial diplomacy to find solutions to trade disputes:

- A big win-set on the EU side. This presupposes a wide agreement within the EU on the range of outcomes that would be acceptable. However, the multitude of players participating in the EU's policy process and their diverging interests typically tend to restrain the win-set (Putnam 1988, pp. 437–438).
- In case of a narrow win-set, the ability to turn this into bargaining power on the basis of the "tied hands" argument (or Schelling conjecture) (Putnam 1988, pp. 440–441; Schelling 1956). This has been considered a strong tool in the hands of EU negotiators (Meunier 2000). At the same time though, the fact that member states (who are supposed to be "tying the hands" of Commission officials) are themselves in diplomatic contact with the commercial counterparts and often voice their positions directly to the counterparts, despite the delegated competence, tends to counter this effect.[9]

But aside from the dynamics "at home": how do EU trade diplomats interact with their counterparts? As a first step we can say that this depends on whether they are able to develop a common understanding of the dispute. This has to do with psychological and ideational factors. Psychology is relevant insofar as the compatibility of diplomats' characters, the right personal "chemistry," may play an important role. Ideational factors refer to the compatibility of worldviews on the one hand and perceptions about the nature of the issue at stake on the other. Worldviews form the general ideational background within which diplomats' words and deeds acquire meaning and which also comprise normative notions of what is right or wrong. Similar issue perceptions do not necessarily imply agreement on what to do, but they may facilitate cooperation in managing commercial tensions (Gaenssmantel and Liu 2017).

Classical bargaining tools, such as threats and side payments, also play a role in direct diplomatic interaction. EU commercial diplomats can develop threat or reward scenarios in the context of the EU's rules on imports. WTO tariff schedules constitute a binding constraint of course, but they often leave some flexibility to design implementation in a way more or less beneficial for specific partners. Another example is China's market economy status: recognition would have required adjustment of the Anti-Dumping Regulation, and the EU tried, without success, to use this as a reward for market opening in China (Gaenssmantel 2012).

Apart from the rules on imports, diplomats may also use legal mechanisms as threat scenarios, or the cessation thereof as rewards (Busch and Reinhardt 2000; Reinhardt 2001). Beyond the classical idea of "carrots and sticks," legal mechanisms can also serve to alter the status quo and thus make the concerned trade partner more amenable to the diplomatic agreement preferred by the EU. If the expected legal settlement appears worse than what can be achieved through consultation, this can be a winning strategy. This can be read in parallel to the "lesser evil strategy" in intra-EU politics, as described by Susanne K. Schmidt (2000), in which the Commission forces member states to converge on its preferred policy through the use of the CJEU.

Negotiations to create law constitute a particular category in this discussion. Rather than an effort at managing current developments between various diplomatic and legal options, they aim at structuring and facilitating the future management of economic relations through concerted yet selective legalization. "Concerted" points to the fact that law is purposefully created by unanimous agreement amongst all parties to the negotiations. "Selective" indicates that, even in bilateral or multilateral negotiations towards new agreements, the parties have to choose between more or less legalization, and conversely less or more room for diplomatic activity, in the treaty text. This is visible, for example, in trade-related non-trade issues, for which in most agreements we find less precision, fewer obligations and special DSM provisions.

This means that when we talk about negotiations towards new treaties or treaty changes, the choice between law and diplomacy concerns the nature of the provisions in the future agreement rather than the method of, or approach to, interaction between the parties involved. Still, the above considerations on factors facilitating diplomatic interaction between the EU and third parties apply also in this situation. The negotiation mandate pre-conditions the win-set, and the option of using the "tied-hands" strategy in order to push through a specific agenda depends on discipline on the part of the member states. Psychological and ideational factors can also be decisive. The quality of personal relations may play an important role in a lengthy negotiation process, and worldviews and issue perceptions may crucially predetermine whether an agreement is possible and of what kind. For example, divergent worldviews regularly complicate negotiations between the EU and their former colonies amidst concerns about post-colonial attempts to infringe on the sovereignty of developing countries.

The EU and the legal approach to external economic relations

Like diplomacy, the EU's legal approach to managing economic relations is conditioned by the distribution of competences and the rules and procedures of the CCP. At the same time, though, it also depends on the available legal instruments, and in particular related DSMs. The choice of the forum for dispute settlement is indeed one of the factors – along with the nature of this forum and the involved actors – determining whether or not a legal approach can be successful.

The fora of dispute settlement mechanisms: multilateral, bilateral and domestic

At the international level, the EU may refer a trade dispute to the multilateral WTO DSM. In addition, given that most FTAs to which the EU is a contracting party set up distinct DSMs, such bilateral DSMs may also be available to the EU. Moreover, such FTAs may contain ISDS and thus create opportunities for foreign investors to refer investment disputes to arbitral tribunals. In this case, the DSM is no longer state-to-state, but investor–state, in nature. Therefore, international DSMs available to the EU and its nationals may be summarized as shown in Table 1.1.

The multilateral WTO DSM is the prime forum for the EU to settle trade disputes with its trading partners. The strength of the WTO DSM lies in its compulsory jurisdiction, permanent Appellate Body and quasi-automatic adoption of panel and Appellate Body reports. However, the jurisdiction of the WTO DSM

Table 1.1 Legalized dispute settlement mechanisms and their forms

	State-to-state	Investor–state
Multilateral	WTO DSM	N/A
Bilateral	FTAs	FTAs (investment chapters) and BITs[a]

a Bilateral Investment Treaty

is limited to the WTO agreements and does not extend to "WTO-plus" issues, oftentimes regulated in FTAs, or investment disputes.[10] Therefore, when a pertinent dispute concerns a subject matter falling outside the scope of WTO agreements, either legal resort has to be sought in bilateral DSMs as set out in the FTAs, or, alternatively, diplomatic approaches may be relied upon.

Bilaterally, the EU has woven a dense web of agreements with its Asian trading partners, ranging from partnership and cooperation agreements (PCAs) with broader political and security implications to FTAs and bilateral investment treaties (BITs) with a specific trade and investment focus. In some cases both PCAs and FTAs have been concluded, for example, with Vietnam and Singapore. These agreements also provide a different set of DSMs. In the trade area, FTAs are most relevant to this chapter. Currently, the EU has concluded FTAs with South Korea, Singapore, Vietnam and Japan and it is still negotiating an FTA with India. Moreover, the EU is negotiating a stand-alone BIT with China (Sally 2007; Wu 2015a) and investment issues between the EU and Singapore and Japan will be dealt with through agreements distinct from the FTAs.

These bilateral agreements set out three types of DSMs with varying degrees of legalization. Firstly, the DSMs provided in PCAs have the broadest coverage with the least legalization, with general obligations, oftentimes imprecise commitments, and no delegation. Such mechanisms largely take the form of joint committees with consensus-based decision-making.[11] One of the main tasks of the joint-committees is to resolve differences arising from the infringement of so-called "essential elements," a notion that refers to general EU external relations policy objectives, such as democracy, human rights and rule of law.[12] Suspension of trade preferences may be used as a sanction for the violation of such principles. The second type of DSMs is state-to-state arbitral proceedings, which may cover trade or investment issues. The EU and its trading partners agree to refer the dispute to a third party, i.e. arbitral tribunals, to find a resolution. This type of DSM demonstrates a certain degree of legalization as procedures are obligatory for involved members, rules tend to be precise and settlement is delegated to a third party. However, the scope of jurisdiction is limited to trade or investment (see for example EU–Korea, EU–Canada, EU–Vietnam and EU–Japan FTAs). A third type of DSM is ISDS, or the EU's proposal for an investment court system, which allows private actors, individuals or enterprises, with their status of foreign investors, to resort to investment arbitral tribunals. Such DSMs, in offering private actors access to arbitral tribunals, and thus extending the range of actors for whom they are creating obligations, demonstrate the highest degree of legalization (see for example, investment chapters in EU–Canada and EU–Vietnam FTAs.[13] The characteristics of these three categories of DSMs can be summarized as shown in Table 1.2.

Within the EU's domestic legal setting, management of economic relations, and in particular trade disputes, can be perceived from two perspectives: inward-looking (defensive) and outward-looking (offensive). From an inward-looking perspective, the EU shields its domestic industries from unfair trade practices (dumping and subsidization) and relieves serious injury, or the threat of serious

Table 1.2 A typology of dispute settlement mechanisms and their characteristics

	Joint committee	*State-to-state arbitral tribunals*	*Investor–state arbitral tribunals*
Genre of agreements	PCAs	FTAs (trade and investment)	FTAs (investment chapters), BITs
Scope of coverage of the agreement	Broad and general	Narrow and specific	Narrow and specific
Jurisdiction	Optional	Compulsory	Compulsory
Degree of legalization	Low	Medium	High

injury, arising from an increase in the quantity of foreign imported products by means of trade defence measures, including anti-dumping, countervailing and safeguard measures. The CJEU plays a gatekeeping role in ensuring EU institutions' due exercise of trade regulatory power and providing resort to affected European and foreign enterprises. From an outward-looking perspective, the EU helps its industries to access foreign markets by minimizing trade barriers. The primary legal tool employed in achieving this objective is the TBR.[14]

From an inward-looking perspective, during trade defence investigations, EU domestic industries play a key role. In fact, most investigations are initiated in response to petitions from domestic industries. In this context, the importers of the subject products and their downstream producers, and even consumers, share an interest that differs from that of EU domestic producers. In order to ensure that these divergent interests are taken into due account during investigations, the CJEU plays the role of a final arbiter. Private actors, regardless of whether they are importers or exporters, domestic or foreign industries, are offered an opportunity to challenge the decisions of EU institutions. This stands in stark contrast to international-level WTO DSM, or bilateral DSMs, as set out in the FTAs (except for ISDS), where only states have the standing to sue. That being said, the CJEU has long taken a deferential approach in reviewing trade defence measures and largely respected the decisions of the political branches.[15]

From an outward-looking perspective, the EU explores ways and means to obtain access to foreign markets, in particular with a view to reaping the fruits of the Uruguay Round negotiations. European private actors, individuals and enterprises, may opt for the legal instrument of the TBR, a more political strategy based on lobbying, or a combination of both. The virtue of the legal instrument approach is that even weak private actors may rely on the TBR to petition for launching a WTO complaint, regardless of the attitude of the European Commission. Resort may be had to the General Court or the CJEU when such a petition is rejected. This legal recourse is especially appealing should member states block the decision; also, private enterprises may thus challenge Council decisions before the CJEU if the criteria for standing are satisfied. The disadvantage of such an approach is nonetheless the exposure of the individuals and enterprises in the spotlight and the related risk of facing potential retaliation by foreign industries or governments. By contrast, powerful private actors may wish to exercise influence through political mobilization and lobbying. This can be done directly before the European Commission or indirectly through the TPC of the Council of the EU or the INTA in the European Parliament. Via this political approach, private actors may hide behind European institutions.

As an outward-looking domestic instrument, the TBR constitutes a linkage between international and domestic levels of DSMs. It was adopted on the eve of the coming into being of the WTO with a view to providing a transparent and effective legal mechanism for the EU to react to obstacles to trade adopted by third countries which cause injury or adverse trade effects.[16] The objective of the TBR is to offer EU enterprises an opportunity to file a complaint before the European Commission when a Union industry considers that "it has suffered injury as a result of obstacles to trade that have an effect on the market of the [Union]"[17] or a Union enterprise considers "it has suffered adverse trade effects as a result of obstacles to trade that have an effect on the market of a third country."[18]

When the injury and adverse trade effects are found to exist, and when it is in the interests of the Union to exercise the EU's rights under the international trade rules, three main possible measures may be adopted:

- Suspension or withdrawal of any concession resulting from commercial policy negotiations
- Raising of existing customs duties or the introduction of any other charge on imports
- Introduction of quantitative restrictions or any other measures modifying import or export conditions or otherwise affecting trade with the third country concerned[19]

Nonetheless, the adoption of such CCP measures can only be made in conformity with relevant international obligations, in particular the WTO agreements.[20] Therefore, with the affirmative finding of injury or adverse trade effect, the European Commission will adopt a formal decision on commencing the dispute settlement procedures either under bilateral agreements or multilateral WTO agreements. Only with authorization from the relevant DSMs can the aforementioned three types of measures be referred to. Therefore, the TBR serves as a linkage between international and domestic levels of DSMs by offering an opportunity in the EU legal order for private actors to petition before the European Commission and urge the Commission to seek redress in the international legal order.

When and how do legal approaches work: actors and forum?

We now need to examine whether these mechanisms, operating at the multilateral, bilateral or domestic level, can solve the problems they are supposed to – that is, whether they are effective (Young and Levy 1999; Iida 2004). In examining whether institutions and their related procedures function effectively in resolving disputes between the EU and its Asian partners, several factors must be taken into account: the nature and characteristics of DSMs in question and their reach; the actors within such DSMs; and the choice between multiple fora. Note that institutional effectiveness does not necessarily imply attractiveness to policymakers, as will be discussed in the following section.

From the outset, the institutional design of a given DSM, notably, its jurisdictional exclusivity and compulsoriness, matters in resolving EU–Asia trade disputes through legal approaches. The CJEU enjoys exclusive jurisdiction on the interpretation and application of EU law whereas the WTO DSM reserves exclusive jurisdiction in resolving disputes arising from the implementation of WTO agreements. This exclusivity precludes EU institutions, EU member states and EU nationals from subjecting EU disputes to fora other than EU courts, and WTO members from referring to international courts or tribunals other than the WTO DSM. Such exclusive jurisdiction may contribute to the effectiveness of a given DSM at the expense of other DSMs, such as at the regional or bilateral level (Busch 2007; Hillman 2009; Qin 2010). By contrast, the state-to-state DSM provided in FTAs is normally complementary to the WTO DSM with the common drafting technique of a choice of forum clause. States may thus refer to bilateral mechanisms to resolve their dispute arising from FTAs; nonetheless, they may still seek recourse to the WTO DSM, wherever a dispute relating to a WTO agreement arises.

The compulsoriness of a given DSM relates to the question of whether the respondent party is obliged to present itself in the proceedings. If an *ad hoc* agreement between the complainant and respondent is necessary for the DSM to exercise its jurisdiction, its effectiveness is definitely undermined. The WTO DSM and the CJEU enjoy compulsory jurisdiction; a complaint before these two DSMs is not contingent on the consent of the respondent party. Similarly, in DSMs under bilateral FTAs, the EU and its trading partners have agreed to refer the disputes resulting from the pertinent FTAs to arbitral tribunals. The request by the complaining party is sufficient for the establishment and composition of an arbitral tribunal. In the context of ISDS, the consent of the state to refer to an arbitral tribunal is given previously; therefore, whenever an investor–state dispute arises, the investor can initiate the proceedings without depending on the consent of the respondent state. Overall, it may be said that DSMs available to the EU and its trading partners generally enjoy compulsory jurisdiction. The respondent state is unable to block unilaterally the gate to such DSMs.

Finally, the breadth and width of a given DSM also affects legal approaches in managing EU–Asia trade disputes. Whereas the WTO DSM has general jurisdiction over the WTO agreements, its jurisdiction does not extend to "WTO-plus" obligations in bilateral FTAs between the EU and its trading partners. When a dispute relates to subject matters falling outside the scope of the jurisdiction of the WTO DSM, the EU may have to refer to other fora to settle trade disputes. A similar observation can be made regarding investment disputes, which have to be dealt with by state-to-state DSMs or ISDS. Moreover, for disputes in certain sensitive service sectors, the EU and its trading partners may choose to set up a special DSM in their FTAs with less legalized characteristics (in particular concerning delegation).

An illustrative example for this is the Protocol on Cultural Cooperation annexed to the EU–Korea FTA of 2011, which addresses such sensitive areas as audio-visual services, otherwise excluded in the agreement, and other cultural services. Art. 3.6 of the protocol underlines the importance of mutually satisfactory agreements and instructs the Committee on Cultural Cooperation to "make every attempt to arrive at a mutually satisfactory resolution of the matter."[21] In case of failure to reach such agreement, the protocol excludes disputes arising therein from the general DSM but establishes a distinct DSM where the Committee on Cultural Cooperation plays a key role.[22] The establishment of an arbitral panel is possible only in case the matter "has not been satisfactorily addressed through the consultation procedure."[23]

The spirit of the Protocol on Cultural Cooperation demonstrates the resistance to delegation in negotiations on certain matters considered sensitive. This special arrangement indicates that DSM design depends to a large extent on the subject matter at stake, which thus also determines how the EU and its trading partners subsequently resolve their disputes.

Different actors, governments and private litigants may have a role to play in resolving trade disputes through legal approaches, which in turn depend on the standing of the DSM in question. The WTO DSM and DSMs provided in FTAs remain largely state-to-state in nature whereas domestic courts and ISDS provide access to judicial remedies for private litigants. The breadth and width of the gate to such DSMs heavily impact on their success.

One is tempted to endorse such a view that private access to dispute settlement mechanisms would contribute to its effectiveness, which can be evidenced by the cases of the CJEU and ISDS. The virtue of granting standing to individuals and enterprises and opening the door for private access to the DSMs lies in the possibility of resolving disputes directly at their origin, for private actors can then activate legal dispute resolution independent from their home states and their broader interests and decision-making procedures. Nonetheless, we should remember that the WTO DSM, which is limited to states and not available to private litigants, is also widely hailed as a great success. The reputation of the WTO DSM may be attributed to the fact that in major economies, such as the EU and US, there is a mechanism that links DSMs at the international and domestic level (like the TBR in the case of the EU) and opens the door for public-private partnership in defending trade interests. Moreover, the success of the WTO DSM is relative to other international tribunals and courts, which are limited to states as well, with the exception of the International Centre for the Settlement of Investment Disputes (ICSID). The least effective DSMs turn out to be the bilateral state-to-state DSMs provided in FTAs. On the one hand, they suffer from the weakness of being state-to-state in nature; on the other hand, it is difficult to compete with multilateral WTO DSM in terms of resources, secretariat support as well as the rich body of WTO jurisprudence.

When developing a legal approach to managing trade disputes, the EU may have a certain degree of freedom over the choice of forum, except of course in cases of exclusive jurisdiction and/or if the respondent is subject to compulsory jurisdiction. In fact, resort may be sought in different fora with different considerations being factored in. Governments and individuals may have different legal strategies in choosing their forum. When faced with unfair trade practices, such as anti-dumping, subsidization and safeguard measures, a state may either impose trade defence measures in response or challenge the foreign measures in the WTO DSM. The choice of resort sought will depend greatly on where the burden of proof lies in the possible fora.

To be more specific, in cases of unfair trade practice such as subsidization, a state (or the EU) has two options. In the first scenario, it may opt to start an investigation with the goal of imposing countervailing duties against the foreign subsidized products. In this case, the investigated industry will have to prove the absence of subsidies or, if measures are imposed, prove their illegality before the domestic courts of the investigating country (i.e. go to the CJEU in the case of the EU). At the same time, the investigated industry may also request its home country to file a complaint in the WTO DSM and challenge the WTO consistency of such countervailing measures. Then the investigated industry or its home country bears the burden of proof for EU illegality or a *prima facie* case for WTO inconsistency. Under the alternative scenario, the state (or the EU) that feels disadvantaged by the subsidy policy may bring the case to the WTO DSM. Yet it then bears the burden of proof to make a *prima facie* case.

The choice between trade defence measures and a direct WTO challenge depends not only on the burden of proof but also on the nature of the subject matter. A countervailing investigation against foreign subsidized products focuses on foreign products rather than the foreign subsidy policy that is at the origin of the issue; by contrast a legal challenge in the WTO directly confronts the foreign country that imposes such a policy. A similar observation may be applicable to safeguard measures. When a foreign country imposes safeguard measures, a state may respond either with its own domestic safeguard measures (against the concerned products) or legal challenges in the WTO (against the state policy). Of course, a state may opt for both approaches simultaneously. The best example illustrating this option is *US – Steel Safeguards Measures (2003)* where the EU responded to US safeguard measures on steel products with domestic steel safeguard measures and with a legal challenge in the WTO.

The case of anti-dumping measures is slightly different. As dumping is a business strategy rather than a state policy, a challenge at the WTO DSM is not an option. When faced with dumping from foreign industries, a state can only impose anti-dumping measures against the products in question. In response, the investigated industry has two options: it may seek judicial remedies in the domestic courts of the country that imposes such anti-dumping measure; otherwise, it has to request that its home country refer the dispute to the WTO DSM to rule on their WTO consistency.

Moreover, commercial disagreements may go beyond trade defence measures or trade disputes, investment disputes being the prime example. When an investment dispute arises, the investor is entitled to launch a complaint before the investment arbitral tribunal without relying on its home state. Given the public discontent about the ISDS, the EU has recently strived to reform the ISDS with an investment court system. This attempt has been successful in the EU's FTAs with Vietnam and Canada, which establish investment and appeal tribunals to hear investment disputes. In addition, the EU has concluded with Singapore a separate investment protection agreement that contains similar dispute settlement mechanisms. Such practices may be also appearing in EU–Japan negotiations in the context of investment protection. Therefore, the fora for resolving the commercial disputes between the EU and its Asian trade partners are even more diversified.

Towards a new framework: choosing between or combining diplomatic and legal tools

After looking separately at diplomatic and legal approaches, how can we make sense of the EU's choice between them, or of a combination of both? On the basis of diplomacy as a "state of affairs," in the sense of continuous communication and representation, one should expect informal diplomatic consultations to be the initial, or "default," approach for virtually all issues that arise in relations with a partner economy. Still, the question remains how far the Commission can go with this approach. The discussion in the section on diplomacy allows us to identify a series of conditions that facilitate successful informal consultations.

First, if there is broad agreement within the EU on its goals with respect to the trade partner in question, i.e. a large win-set, this will allow for greater flexibility on the part of EU trade diplomats and therefore make an informal diplomatic solution more likely. Second, if the commercial issues at stake are contested within the EU, the "tied hands" argument may afford considerable bargaining power to EU diplomats, but only if member states do not use their own diplomatic channels to communicate their diverging preferences (which they are free to do despite exclusive EU competence) and thus influence the consultation process.

So, the broader the agreement among member states and the more disciplined they are, the higher the probability that the Commission's trade negotiators will manage to resolve a disagreement with a trading partner through informal consultations. However, generally speaking, both conditions are rather daring, and one should assume that in the majority of cases trade diplomats have to deal with a very narrow win-set and active communication on the part of member states with the concerned trading partner. Of course, the low visibility of such an informal diplomatic process may strengthen the hand of the Commission, as it will face less scrutiny during the consultations and member states will have fewer incentives to get in touch directly with the concerned trading partner. At the same time, the other factors discussed above, namely matching psychological and ideational dispositions among the involved diplomats, as well as the ability to make use of classical bargaining tools, can also promote diplomatic approaches.

In contrast to informal consultations, formal negotiations, in line with the idea of diplomacy as a tool to pursue broader foreign policy goals, are far less likely in reaction to specific episodes of commercial tension. Instead, this type of EU diplomacy, with a Council mandate and under the scrutiny of the TPC, should be expected in the context of law creation through international agreements, as for example in FTAs, where the stakes are sufficiently high to justify the lengthy and burdensome procedures. Nevertheless, the factors that facilitate diplomacy are at work also in this context. In particular, a broad win-set is related to a flexible negotiation mandate for the Commission, and the formal role of the Commission as the sole negotiator strengthens its ability to make use of the tied hands argument, under the condition that member states keep a low profile.

With regard to legal tools, the previous section has presented a series of factors that can be expected to influence whether EU trade policymakers choose to employ them rather than diplomacy. First, while compulsory jurisdiction enhances the effectiveness of a DSM in terms of rule enforcement, it also makes recourse to this mechanism a double-edged sword: if the EU's case is not watertight, policymakers may not want to run the risk of having to implement a verdict that is not in their favour. More generally, one can say here that legalization may also work to the disadvantage of the party who initiates the claim, as the process has been delegated, and therefore it cannot be controlled by the European Commission, and the decisions at its end are precise and obligatory. This means that recourse to the WTO DSM is not an easy alternative to a diplomatic settlement and subject to extensive checks by the EU's legal services. By contrast, joint committees of PCAs or some of the special DSMs for "WTO plus" issues may present an attractive alternative to purely diplomatic approaches, as they display some characteristics of delegation but at the same time the diplomats retain some control over the case in question. Moreover, "WTO-plus" issues tend to be broad and general in nature, more political and less legal, which means the obstacles to break through in terms of legal preparation are lower.

Second, the discussion on private actors has shown the limits of choice and the importance of constraints in a context of multi-actor governance. In procedures that allow for private actor involvement, public officials are indeed limited in their freedom of choice between diplomatic and legal approaches. This is most obviously the case in investor–state arbitral tribunals or when private actors make use of the domestic court system. But it is also visible in the EU's trade defence and TBR procedures: it is private actors who lodge anti-dumping, anti-subsidy or safeguards petitions, thus forcing the European Commission to open formal procedures, and they are also the ones who initiate proceedings under the TBR. What is interesting here is that the procedures under EU law include their own "safeguards": when verifying a trade defence claim, the Commission has the somewhat flexible tool of assessing whether defensive measures would be in the interest of the EU as a whole. In case of anti-dumping and anti-subsidy procedures, the Commission can also bring diplomacy back in by opting to negotiate a minimum price undertaking, if the concerned exporters agree to do so.

Similarly, under the TBR the Commission may initially attempt to use diplomatic consultations rather than going directly to the WTO's DSM. In other words, whereas the TBR aims to establish a legal mechanism for private actors to file a complaint against barriers to access to foreign market, it retains a strong diplomatic dimension, visible also in a close link with political bodies through consultation with advisory committees comprised of representatives from member states. In some cases, the Council of the EU may also revise the proposed decisions of the European Commission, which brings politics back into a legal mechanism. While legal challenges and subsequently retaliation are envisaged by the TBR, it nonetheless underlines the importance of a mutually satisfactory agreement through negotiations. Therefore, the negotiations between the EU and its trade partners can be best termed as "negotiations in the shadow of WTO legal challenges" (Shaffer 2006). Obviously, private actors may also create constraints outside formal procedures, for example by lobbying through political venues to lodge a legal complaint against the EU's trading partners or request the EU to consult with them.

Lastly, even in the context of legal approaches based on formal procedures in resolving the disputes between its partners, the EU still has a certain latitude between unilateral measures or international complaints, which may in turn shift the burden of proof, or more broadly the costs, to the investigated industry or counterpart country. In choosing between unilateral measures or international complaints, the EU is also able to target either particular enterprises or engage with a specific country. Such a calculation is most salient in the context of subsidy as domestic anti-subsidy investigations target subsidized products while international complaints provoke foreign governments.

With regards to the issue of choice between diplomatic and legal approaches, this still leaves us with a complex picture, as shown in Table 1.3. Generally speaking, the stronger the impact of factors that facilitate a diplomatic solution, the more likely EU trade policymakers will continue with informal consultations. By contrast, the more factors that facilitate legal approaches are in place, the stronger the incentive to make use of them. Given that both a broad win-set and disciplined member states are rare in the EU's commercial policy, one should expect a consistent tendency towards formal legal approaches.

Of course, the choice for one rarely excludes the other, and combinations are likely to be the rule rather than the exception. In particular, legal mechanisms can be used as parts of a broader diplomatic bargaining strategy. For example, the outlook of an anti-dumping procedure can be used as a threat, and the same is true for bringing a case to the WTO DSM. Similarly the interruption of such procedures can be a reward, also through issue linkage in the context of a different dispute. As mentioned above, in this sense legal procedures can serve negotiators to alter the status quo for the counterpart and make a diplomatic agreement a better option than no agreement and a legal procedure.

So the use of legal mechanisms may often be strategic. But aside from that, the decision by EU trade policymakers to use either diplomatic or legal tools does not necessarily depend only on the feasibility or opportunity of each of the two.

Table 1.3 Factors facilitating/promoting diplomatic and legal approaches in resolving EU–Asia disputes

Factors facilitating/promoting a ...	
... diplomatic approach	*... legal approach*
• Broad win-set • Ability to use tied-hands argument/ disciplined member states • Psychological factors: good personal relations between diplomats • Ideational factors: similar world views and perceptions about issues at stake • Ability to use bargaining tools (threats and side payments)	• Nature of the dispute settlement mechanism: • Exclusive and/or compulsory jurisdiction implies greater effectiveness in rule enforcement but policymakers submit complaints only if they are positive to have a strong case • Nonexclusive and/or noncompulsory jurisdiction makes for less effectiveness in rule enforcement but more control for policymakers and hence less caution in making use of such fora • Availability for private actors to initiate formal proceedings • Burden of proof with defendant who is nonstate actor • Ideational factors: profound conviction that legal or formal mechanisms are the right options in rules-based international order and given the relevant legal culture • Strategic use of legal or formal mechanisms to support diplomatic approaches

A last set of factors has to do with non-rational aspects of trade policymaking in the EU. This is to say that the decision to use a legal mechanism may also be the result of a profound conviction among the involved officials that this is the right thing to do: someone else has violated the rules, so the correct reaction is to use the procedures available for the defence of those rules. This argument refers to norms and values and is in line with the logic of appropriateness. At the same time, though, a logic of arguing may be at work, i.e. the question of who in the policymaking process makes the most effective use of arguments, be they norm- or value-based or purely rational.

A final point of attention relates to law creation, where there is no legal alternative to diplomatic negotiation. Instead, the choice between law and diplomacy concerns the contents of the agreement, in particular the degree of legalization versus the space kept for diplomatic solutions. Here, we typically find a divergence between highly legalized provisions on trade issues and less legalization for trade-related non-trade issues. This concerns both the degree of obligation and precision of rules and the nature of dispute settlement, including also whether or not there is delegation.

Conclusion

This chapter set out to present diplomacy and law as alternatives in EU external economic relations in such a way as to structure the research, show the connections between the various contributions to this volume and facilitate the development of final conclusion at its end. With this goal we first discussed diplomacy and law in the context of EU rules and institutions related to external economic relations. This also led to reflections on the importance of viewing policymaker decisions as output from both a logic of choice and a logic of constraints. Secondly, the chapter devoted two sections to the EU's diplomatic and legal options for managing economic relations. For the former, a central point that emerged was that the Commission's diplomatic efforts tend to be complicated by internal divisions (small win-sets) and member states' own diplomatic contacts with external partners (weakening of the tied-hands argument). For legal options, it was developed how relevant rules and DSMs extend from domestic EU settings to bilateral or multilateral venues. Furthermore, the relevance of various specific features was discussed, such as in particular exclusivity and compulsoriness of jurisdiction, whether or not settlement is delegated, and where the burden of proof lies in a specific procedure.

At the end of the chapter these two perspectives were brought together to develop a set of conditions that promote diplomatic or legal approaches to the management of economic relations, or a combination thereof. Overall, it seems likely that in many instances the use of legal procedures is embedded in broader diplomatic strategies. For negotiations towards new agreements, the choice between diplomacy and law concerns the degree of legalization of their contents and, conversely, the room afforded to (future) diplomatic efforts.

These considerations will inform and structure the discussion and conclusions in the following chapters, even though disciplinary differences and the particularities of the chosen topics imply that the way in which the points from this opening chapter are used differs for each author. At the end of the volume the conceptual points will then play a core role for the development and presentation of general conclusions to the project as a whole.

Notes

1 While the emphasis here has been on the role of the European Commission as the most actively and directly involved body in EU trade diplomacy, the Council also plays a role and so does the EP, especially since the entry into force of the Treaty of Lisbon; see Smith and Woolcock (1999); den Putte, De Ville and Orbie (2014) and Richardson (2012).
2 Council Regulation (EC) No 3286/94 of 22 December 1994 laying down Community procedures in the field of the common commercial policy in order to ensure the exercise of the Community's rights under international trade rules, in particular those established under the auspices of the World Trade Organization, OJ L 349/71, 31 December 1994.
3 The EU's market access strategy is continuously updated, most famously in the context of the Lisbon Agenda at the Lisbon European Council in 2000 and with the Global Europe strategy in 2006. The EU's updated market access strategy emphasizes "a partnership between the Commission, Member States, and business, based on extensive

public consultation"; see European Commission, Communication from the Commission to the Council, the European Parliament, the Economic and Social Committee and the Committee of the Regions: The Global Challenge of International Trade: A Market Access Strategy for the European Union, COM(96) 53 final, 14 February 1996.

4 For a critique of the lack of participation of private sectors in the WTO, see Bown and Hoekman (2005).

5 Treaty of Rome, Art. 113(2).

6 This has been referred to as "formal agenda-setting" by the European Commission; see Pollack (1997).

7 Treaty on the Functioning of the European Union (TFEU), Art. 207(2).

8 Treaty of Rome, Art. 113(3), TFEU, Art. 207(3–4). Moreover, the Treaty of Rome provided for a similarly central role for non-commercial negotiations as well (Art. 228(1)), but this provision has been loosened by the Treaty of Lisbon; see TFEU, Art. 218.

9 Schelling recognizes that if the third party to which a binding commitment is made is brought to the negotiating table, the effect of the commitment is nil; see Schelling (1956, p. 284); see also Meunier (2000, p. 132).

10 The TRIMS agreement includes some regulation on investment issues but does not touch upon investment protection, nor does it include anything regarding state-to-state or investor–state investment dispute settlement.

11 E.g., EU–Indonesia PCA, arts. 44 and 41.

12 Treaty on European Union, TEU, Art. 21.

13 The EU–Korea FTA does not contain ISDS but only state-to-state dispute a settlement mechanism on investment matters. As regards EU–Singapore and EU–Japan FTAs, they do not cover investment issues, which will be dealt with separately by another agreement.

14 In addition to the formal procedure of the TBR, this objective may also be achieved by political lobbying directly at the European Commission or indirectly in the TPC and INTA.

15 In reviewing trade defence measures cases, in particular on such sensitive issues as non-market economy status, non-market economy treatment or the selection of analogue countries, the CJEU in principle limits its review to "establishing whether the relevant procedural rules have been complied with, whether the facts on which the contested choice is based have been accurately stated and whether there has been a manifest error of assessment of the facts or a misuse of power" (*Shanghai Teraoka Electronic Co. Ltd. v. Council of the European Union* 2004, para. 49; for further discussion, see Wu, 2015b).

16 Trade Barrier Regulation (TBR), recitals 10-11.

17 TBR, Art. 3.1.

18 TBR, Art. 4.1.

19 TBR, Art. 12.3.

20 TBR, Art. 12.3.

21 EU–Korea FTA, Protocol on Cultural Cooperation, Art. 3.6.

22 EU–Korea FTA, Protocol on Cultural Cooperation, Art. 3bis.

23 EU–Korea FTA, Protocol on Cultural Cooperation, Art. 3bis (c).

References

Abbott, K.W., Keohane, R.O., Moravcsik, A., Slaughter, A.-M. and Snidal, D. (2000) 'The Concept of Legalization', *International Organization*, 54(3), pp. 401–419.

Baldwin, D. A. (1985) *Economic Statecraft*, Princeton University Press.

Baldwin, D.A. (1999/2000) 'The Sanctions Debate and the Logic of Choice', *International Organization*, 24(3), pp. 80–107.

Berridge, G.R. (2010) *Diplomacy: Theory and Practice*, 3rd edn, Palgrave Macmillan.

Bown, C.P. and Hoekman B.M. (2005) 'WTO Dispute Settlement and the Missing Developing Country Cases: Engaging the Private Sector', *Journal of International Economic Law*, 8(4), pp. 861–890.

Bronckers, M.C.E.J. (1996) 'Private Participation in the Enforcement of WTO Law: The New EC Trade Barriers Regulation', *Common Market Law Review*, 33(2), pp. 299–318.

Busch, M.L. (2007) 'Overlapping Institutions, Forum Shopping, and Dispute Settlement in International Trade', *International Organization*, 61(4), pp. 735–761.

Busch, M.L. and Reinhardt, E. (2000) 'Bargaining in the Shadow of the Law: Early Settlement in GATT/WTO Disputes', *Fordham International Law Journal*, 24(1), pp. 158–172.

Collinson, S. (1999) '"Issue-Systems", "Multi-Level Games", and the Analysis of the EU's External Commercial and Associated Policies: a Research Agenda', *Journal of European Public Policy*, 6(2), pp. 206–224.

den Putte, L.V., De Ville, F. and Orbie, J. (2014) 'The European Parliament's New Role in Trade Policy: Turning Power into Impact', *CEPS Special Report*.

Dingwerth, K. and Pattberg, P. (2006) 'Global Governance as a Perspective on World Politics', *Global Governance*, 12(2), pp. 185–203.

Easton, D. (1965) *A Framework for Political Analysis*, Prentice Hall.

Gaenssmantel, F. (2012) 'EU-China Relations and Market Economy Status: EU Foreign Policy in the Technical Trap', *Journal of European Integration History*, 18(1), pp. 51–65.

Gaenssmantel, F. and Liu F. (2017) 'Same Name, Different Substance? Exploring the Impact of Issue Perceptions on China-EU Relations', in T. Halbertsma and J. van der Harst (eds.), *China, East Asia and the European Union: Strong Economics, Weak Politics?* Leiden: Brill, pp. 91–112.

Goldstein, J. and Martin, L.L. (2000) 'Legalization, Trade Liberalization, and Domestic Politics: A Cautionary Note', *International Organization*, 54(3), pp. 603–632.

Devin, G. (2002) 'Les diplomaties de la politique étrangère', in F. Charillon (ed.), *Politique étrangère: Nouveaux regards*, Les Presses de Sciences Po, pp. 215–233.

Herrmann, C.W. (2002) 'Common Commercial Policy after Nice: Sisyphus Would Have Done a Better Job', *Common Market Law Review*, 93(1), pp. 7–29.

Hill, C. (2003) *The Changing Politics of Foreign Policy*, Palgrave Macmillan.

Hillman, J. (2009) 'Conflicts Between Dispute Settlement Mechanisms in Regional Trade Agreements and the WTO—What Should WTO Do?' *Cornell International Law Journal*, 42(2), pp. 194–208.

Hooghe, L. and Marks, G. (2003) 'Unraveling the Central State, but How? Types of Multi-Level Governance', *The American Political Science Review*, 97(2), pp. 233–243.

Iida, K. (2004) 'Is WTO Dispute Settlement Effective', *Global Governance*, 10(2), pp. 207–225.

Kahler, M. and Lake, D.A. (2004) 'Governance in a Global Economy: Political Authority in Transition', *Political Science and Politics*, 37(3), pp. 409–414.

Krajewski, M. (2005) 'External Trade Law and the Constitutional Treaty: Towards a Federal and More Democratic Common Commercial Policy?', *Common Market Law Review*, 42(1), pp. 91–127.

Krajewski, M. (2012) 'The Reform of Common Commercial Policy', in A. Biondi, P. Eeckhout, and S. Ripley (eds.), *EU Law after Lisbon*, Oxford University Press, pp. 292–311.

Laswell, H.D. and McDougal, M.S. (1991) *Jurisprudence for a Free Society: Studies in Law, Science, and Policy*, vol. 1, Nijhoff.

March, J.G. and Olsen, J.P. (2009) 'The Logic of Appropriateness', *ARENA Working Paper 04/2009*.

Marsh, S. and Mackenstein, H. (2005) *The International Relations of the European Union*, Pearson Longman.

Marshall, D. (2010) 'Who to Lobby and When: Institutional Determinants of Interest Group Strategies in European Parliaments Committees', *European Union Politics*, 11(4), pp. 553–575.

Meunier, S. (2000) 'What Single Voice? European Institutions and EU-US Trade Negotiations', *International Organization*, 54(1), pp. 103–135.

Nicolson, H. (1961) 'Diplomacy Then and Now', *Foreign Affairs*, 40(1), pp. 39–49.

Palmeter, D. and Mavroidis, P.C. (2004) *Dispute Settlement in the World Trade Organization: Practice and Procedure*, 2nd edn, Cambridge University Press.

Patterson, L.A. (1997) 'Agricultural Policy Reform in the European Community: A Three-Level Game Analysis', *International Organization*, 51(1), pp. 135–165.

Petersmann, E.U. (1994) 'The Dispute Settlement System of the World Trade Organization and the Evolution of the GATT Dispute Settlement System since 1948', *Common Market Law Review*, 31(6), pp. 1157–1244.

Petersmann, E.U. (1997) *The GATT/WTO Dispute Settlement System: International Law, International Organizations, and Dispute Settlement*, Kluwer Law International.

Pollack, M.A. (1997) 'Delegation, agency, and agenda setting in the European Community', *International Organization*, 51(1), pp. 99–134.

Putnam, R.D. (1988) 'Diplomacy and Domestic Politics: The Logic of Two-Level Games', *International Organization*, 42(3), pp. 427–460.

Qin J.Y. (2010) 'Managing Conflicts Between Rulings of WTO and Regional Trade Tribunals: Reflections on the Brazil-Tyres Case', in P.H.F. Bekker, R. Dolzer and M. Waibel (eds.), *Making Transnational Law Work in the Global Economy: Essays in Honour of Detlev Vagts*, Cambridge University Press, pp. 601–629.

Reich, A. (1996) 'From Diplomacy to Law: The Juridicization of International Trade Relations', *Northwestern Journal of International Law & Business*, 17(1), pp. 775–849.

Reinhardt, E. (2001) 'Adjudication without Enforcement in WTO Disputes', *Journal of Conflict Resolution*, 45(2), pp. 174–195.

Richardson, L. (2012) 'The post-Lisbon Role of the European Parliament in the EU's Common Commercial Policy: Implications for Bilateral Trade Negotiations', *EU Diplomacy Paper 05/2012*.

Risse, T. (2000) '"Let's Argue!" Communicative Action in World Politics', *International Organization*, 54(1), pp. 1–39.

Sally, R. (2007) 'Looking East: The European Union's New FTA Negotiations in Asia', *Jan Tumlir Policy Essays*, paper No. 03/2007.

Schelling, T.C. (1956) 'An Essay on Bargaining', *The American Economic Review*, 46(3), pp. 281–306.

Schimmelfennig, F. (2001) 'The Community Trap: Liberal Norms, Rhetorical Action, and the Eastern Enlargement of the European Union', *International Organization*, 55(1), pp. 47–80.

Schmidt, S.K. (2000) 'Only an Agenda Setter? The European Commission's Power over the Council of Ministers', *European Union Politics*, 37(1), pp. 37–61.

Shaffer, G. (2006) 'What's new in EU trade Dispute Settlement? Judicialization, Public–Private Networks and the WTO Legal Order', *Journal of European Public Policy*, 13(6), pp. 832–850.

Sharp, P. (1997) 'Who Needs Diplomats? The Problems of Diplomatic Representation', *International Journal*, 52(4), pp. 609–634.

Smith, M. and Woolcock, S. (1999) 'European Commercial Policy: A Leadership Role in the New Millennium?' *European Foreign Affairs Review*, 4(4), pp. 439–462.

Weiler, J.H.H. (2001) 'The Rule of Lawyers and the Ethos of Diplomats: Reflections on the Internal and External Legitimacy of WTO Dispute Settlement', *Journal of World Trade*, 35(2), pp. 191–207.

Woll, C. (2009) 'Trade Policy Lobbying in the European Union: Who Captures Whom?' in D. Coen and J. Richardson (eds.), *Lobbying the European Union: Institutions, Actors and Issues*, Oxford University Press, Oxford, pp. 277–297.

Wu, C.H. (2011) 'Foreign Direct Investment as Common Commercial Policy: EU External Economic Competence after Lisbon' in P.J. Cardwell (ed.), *EU External Relations Law and Policy in the Post-Lisbon Era*, Asser Press 2011, pp. 375–400.

Wu, C.H. (2015a) 'A Mismatch between Ambition and Reality: the EU's Efforts to Counterbalance China and the EU in East Asia', in C. Herrmann, M. Krajewski and J.P. Terhechte (eds.), *European Yearbook of International Economic Law*, vol. 6, Springer, pp. 251–272.

Wu, C.H. (2015b) 'Key Issues regarding the EU's Concurrent Imposition of Anti-Dumping and Countervailing Duties on Chinese Coated Fine Papers: Analogue Country, Market Economy Treatment, Individual Treatment and Double Remedy', *Asian Journal of WTO & International Health Law and Policy*, 10, pp. 263–305.

Young, O.R. and Levy, M.A. (1999) 'The Effectiveness of International Environmental Regimes' in O.R. Young (ed.), *The Effectiveness of International Environmental Regimes: Causal Connections and Behavioral Mechanisms*, MIT Press, pp. 1–32.

Young, A.R. (2000) 'The Adaptation of European Foreign Economic Policy: From Rome to Seattle', *JCMS: Journal of Common Market Studies*, 38(1), pp. 93–116.

2 Judicial diplomacy?

The role of the CJEU in EU–Asia trade disputes*

Andrés Delgado Casteleiro

Different factors need to be taken into consideration in managing trade disputes. If a legal approach is followed, the judicial forum where the dispute is going to be dealt with becomes a fundamental issue.[1] Among the different considerations that the actors might take into account, we might find issues having to do, among others, with the access of individuals to the forum or the flexibility that the said forum would give to non-legal solutions. When speaking about the extent to which the Court of Justice of the European Union (CJEU) can be a suitable forum to deal with EU–Asia trade disputes, deep constitutional questions of separation of powers explain the role (or lack of) that the Court plays. The CJEU seems to strike a balance between the separations of powers and the rule of law and the necessary flexibility that the EU institutions need when conducting complex international trade negotiations.

By now, it might be commonplace to highlight the important role that the CJEU plays in the realm of EU external economic relations (Cremona 2014; de Witte 2014; Hillion 2014). The traditional understanding of foreign affairs as strict political questions has been challenged on a constant basis by the CJEU's case law (Mendez 2013). As the common narrative goes, only on issues regarding WTO law has the CJEU taken the backseat, leaving EU political institutions in the driving seat (Klabbers 2012, p. 89). However, this paper shows an emerging shift in the current paradigm by which the CJEU is going to have a much more limited role in EU external relations and specially in the articulation of the effects of the EU's trade policy. This chapter argues that both the institutional and judicial structures set up to articulate the internal facet of the EU's trade dispute management responds not so much to a logic of constraints but more to a logic of choices, as the CJEU is creating a wide policy space where the other institutions can choose appropriately between diplomacy and law in the context of specific interactions with a commercial partner, as well as the definition of concrete diplomatic or legal strategies (Gaenssmantel and Wu 2019).

* Part of the research on which this chapter is built has been previously published in: A. Delgado Casteleiro, "The Effects of International Dispute Settlement Decisions in EU Law," in M. Cremona, A. Thies and R.A. Wessel (eds.), *The European Union and International Dispute Settlement* (Hart 2017), pp. 191–211.

This chapter is divided into three sections. The first section deals with the current understanding on the role the CJEU plays in giving effect to the EU's foreign policy. The second section touches upon how the current treaty-making practice with Asian countries is challenging an important aspect of the CJEU's role as an international actor. The third section of the chapter revisits the role of the CJEU in the establishment of the effects of the WTO and shows how the exceptions to the Court's case law are narrower than previously thought, further limiting the CJEU's impact on the EU–Asia trade disputes in multilateral settings.

The CJEU and the effects of trade agreements

Like any other legal system, it is for the EU to determine what is "the law of the land" and what effects this law has within the EU's legal order (Eeckhout 2011, p. 324; Klabbers 2012, p. 71).[2] Yet, as with many other fundamental principles governing the EU, the EU treaties do not contain much guidance on the role that international law and, by extension, its different sources would play within the EU legal order (Holdgaard 2006; Wessel 2013, p. 30). Art. 216(2) TFEU gives very little information, as it merely provides that agreements concluded by the EU will be binding on the institutions and the member states. Thus, the exact scope and implications of this and whether this provision applies to other sources of international law[3] have been left for the CJEU to decide.

The CJEU has established the scope of this provision in numerous cases (Mendez 2013) since its inception in *Haegeman*. In this case, the CJEU argued that "the provision of [an] agreement [...] form[s] an integral part of [EU] law." By taking a monistic approach, the CJEU established that the provisions of a Union agreement do not need be incorporated into a Union act in order to be part of the EU legal order and to be implemented within the EU (Eeckhout 2011, p. 328). The incorporation and assimilation of international dispute settlement (IDS) decisions to EU acts[4] would entail the extension of the main characteristics of an EU act to IDS decisions: primacy and direct effect. Whilst primacy inasmuch as it does not determine whether the CJEU can hear a case is not the object of this chapter, direct effect, on the other hand, opens the way for EU–Asia trade disputes to be judicialized in the CJEU. Otherwise put, the primacy of an international agreement would act as a conflict rules vis-à-vis EU law (Schütze 2006) whereas direct effect would allow for the dispute to reach the CJEU.

The Court has not been blind to the special nature of EU external relations law and more specifically the inherent political nature of this field (Franck 1992). The establishment of the effects of international agreements might be seen as a task to be allocated to the legislative and not to be determined via case law. The Court has always favoured self-restraint in this regard (Gaja 2002, p. 133). This is especially clear in relation to the question of the direct effect of international agreements. As Kuijper recognizes, there is an element of institutional balance in the reasoning of the Court that is necessary given the interests that the other political actors have in the issue of direct effect of international agreements (Kuijper and Bronckers 2005, p. 1321). The institutional balance considerations mean that the Court limits the extent to which international agreements might be invoked by any applicant (Klabbers 2001) besides the EU institutions.

The first part of the two-stage test by which the Court decides whether an international agreement[5] reflects that political nature (Schütze 2014, p. 52). The analysis of the nature and the broad logic of the agreement[6] boils down to consider two main factors; on the one hand, whether the EU institutions have agreed with the third States concerned what effect the provisions of the agreement are to have in the internal legal order of the contracting parties.[7] On the other hand, whether the agreement as a whole was designed to establish rules intended to apply directly and immediately to individuals and to confer upon them rights or freedoms capable of being relied upon against States.[8] In other words, the Court will look into whether contracting parties of an agreement decided either expressly or implicitly that it confers rights to other subjects besides the contracting parties.

Traditional accounts of how the Court has approached the issue of the direct effect of international agreements argued that direct effect of international agreements was the general rule under EU law and its lack an exception (Lenaerts and Corthaut 2006; Jacobs 2011). This narrative relied on the fact that the Court was eager to recognize that the provisions of bilateral association agreements had direct effect[9] while it was not as eager to recognize the direct effect of the WTO.[10]

Furthermore, the Court has linked the effects of dispute settlement decisions to the effects of the international agreement that established the dispute settlement mechanism. In Opinion 1/91, the Court established that:

> Where, however, an international agreement provides for its own system of courts, including a court with jurisdiction to settle disputes between the Contracting Parties to the agreement, and, as a result, to interpret its provisions, the decisions of that court will be binding on the [Union] institutions, including the Court of Justice. Those decisions will also be binding in the event that the Court of Justice is called upon to rule, by way of preliminary ruling or in a direct action, on the interpretation of the international agreement, in so far as that agreement is an integral part of the [Union] legal order.[11]

Thus, insofar as the agreement is not capable of having direct effect as a whole, the decisions of its dispute settlement mechanism will not have direct effect either. So far, the Court has only approached the issue of the direct effect of dispute settlement decisions in relation to the decisions of the WTO dispute settlement mechanism (WTO DSM). For instance, in *FIAMM* the Court was clear when it held that:

> A [WTO DSM] decision, which has no object other than to rule on whether a WTO member's conduct is consistent with the obligations entered into by it within the context of the WTO, cannot in principle be fundamentally distinguished from the substantive rules which convey such obligations and by reference to which such a review is carried out, at least when it is a question

of determining whether or not an infringement of those rules or that decision can be relied upon before the Community courts for the purpose of reviewing the legality of the conduct of the Community institutions.[12]

While traditional accounts argued that direct effect of international agreements is the general rule (Klabbers 2001; Lenaerts and Corthaut 2006; Jacobs 2011; Mendez 2013), when it comes to dispute settlement decisions the opposite picture seems to emerge. For instance, in *Intertanko* the CJEU recognized that the United Nations Convention of the Law of the Seas (UNCLOS) does not establish rules intended to apply directly and immediately to individuals (Eeckhout 2009, p. 2055). Therefore, applying the rationale that the CJEU used in *FIAMM*, the decisions from any of the IDS mechanisms envisaged in Part XV of UNCLOS, including the decisions of the International Tribunal for the Law of the Seas (ITLOS), are not capable of having direct effect in the EU.

In principle, as a general rule, only if a trade dispute comes within the scope of association agreement with an Asian country, the CJEU would have a role to play in dealing with the consequences of such a dispute. In any other issues, especially those falling within the WTO, the CJEU has been quite clear: it does not want to play a role in them. Yet it must not be forgotten that in recent years the CJEU has established that more and more international agreements are not susceptible of having direct effect under EU law. In fact, it appears that the narrative seems to be reversing. Since it appears that the Court is becoming more reluctant to accept the direct effect of multilateral international agreements one way or another,[13] the direct effect of international agreements might be the exception to the general rule of their lack of direct effect (Klabbers 2012, p. 89).

The effects of the new FTAs as paradigm shift

Embedding the exception as the new general rule

The new free trade agreements (FTAs) concluded by the EU would seem to further anchor this new understanding of the Court's case law. Whereas there have not been any cases on whether their provisions can be invoked by individuals, they nonetheless can be considered a challenge to the traditional thinking on the intersection between direct effect and international law. There are two main reasons to understand that the new FTAs have the potential of altering the common narratives on the direct effect of international law.

First, these FTAs put great weight to what the parties intended and are explicit in precluding the direct effect of their provisions. For instance, the EU–Singapore FTA provides in its Art. 17.15 concerning the rights and obligations under the agreement that:

> For greater certainty, nothing in this Agreement shall be construed as conferring rights or imposing obligations on persons, other than those created between the Parties under public international law.

Similarly, the EU–Japan FTA establishes in its Art. 23.5 entitled "No direct effect on persons" that:

> Nothing in this Agreement shall be construed as conferring rights or impos-
> ing obligations on persons, without prejudice to the rights and obligations of
> persons under other public international law.

These provisions clearly show that the parties intended to exclude the direct effect of the agreement. Moreover, as Semertzi rightly shows, it is not only the fact that the new FTAs explicitly preclude the direct effect but also that those FTAs incorporate to varying degrees WTO provisions (2014, p. 1126) (which by their nature exclude their direct effect)[14] what explains why these agreements would not confer rights. However, in the past the fact that the decision conclud-ing the WTO agreements mentioned that the WTO could not have direct effect, or that the WTO itself ruled it out, was not an obstacle to argue that the Court should disregard the will of parties to the WTO and grant direct effect to its pro-visions (Griller 2000; Petersmann 2000, p. 1375).

Second, the new FTAs envisage IDS chapters and, in some cases, could be seen as a confirmation of the lack of direct effect of international agreements as the new general rule. These chapters create quasi-judicial dispute settlement mechanisms for trade disputes that are largely based on the WTO Dispute Settlement Understanding (Semertzi 2014, p. 1126). Therefore, given the explicit linkage made by the Court between the lack of direct effect of an international agreement and the fact that some of these explicitly exclude the direct effect of the ruling of the panels,[15] the argu-ments in favour of decoupling the direct effect of IDS decisions from the (lack of) direct effect of an agreement would be more difficult to be accepted by the Court.

Third, the lack of direct effect of the new FTAs like those signed with South Korea, Singapore and Japan further moves away from Luxembourg any dispute that might arise within the framework of those agreements.

Investor–State Dispute Settlement (ISDS) and the no-direct effect rule

Yet, the exact scope of the no-direct effect rule will most likely be challenged in relation to the most recent FTAs, as these agreements also include provisions excluding the direct effect of any provision of the agreement[16] while also envis-aging investment chapters with a separate Investor–State Dispute Settlement (ISDS)[17] applying only to that chapter. Inasmuch as those investment chapters cover the treatment to be afforded to foreign investors, those provisions in sub-stance apply directly and immediately to individuals and confer upon them rights or freedoms capable of being relied upon against States (Dimopoulos 2011, p. 304). Therefore, would an arbitral award interpreting the obligations contained in the said investment chapter have direct effect? It is submitted that the no-direct effect provisions of these FTAs would apply regardless of the actual substance of the agreements. Two main reasons would back this point view.

On the one hand, as mentioned before, the Court's case law on direct effect gives great weight to the will of the parties. Thus, it would be rather unlikely that the CJEU would disregard the explicit and unequivocal will of the parties and establish the direct effect of an arbitral award.

On the other hand, the nature of awards would make it rather unlikely for the awards to be considered as having direct effect in the sense that it would also entail assessing the validity of the norm that breached a provision of the investment chapter of an FTA.[18] The Investment Court System established under either the EU–Singapore FTA or the EU–Vietnam FTA would only deal with the liabilities stemming from the breach.[19] The arbitral awards adopted under the ISDS of these FTAs would not deal with the validity of the act being reviewed but just with the pecuniary damage that the foreign investor has suffered (van Aaken 2010, p. 747). Therefore, the effects of that award would not be capable of conferring rights to other individuals besides the actual foreign investor who succeeded in obtaining a remedy from the arbitral tribunal inasmuch as the investor would be the only one entitled to liability. Even more, the "right" that this award would recognize would only entail the payment of compensation or restitution of property, not the general disapplication of the act or its eventual annulment.

Moreover, the provisions on enforcement of awards contained in the FTAs with Singapore and Vietnam would further reinforce the limited effects of those arbitral awards. The new FTAs establish that those awards will be subject to the specific rules of either ICSID and/or the New York Convention on the Recognition and Enforcement of Arbitral Awards.[20] While both of these regimes provide for venues for the award to be enforced at a national level, they are mainly concerned with the pecuniary aspects of the award (Dolzer and Schreuer 2012, p. 310). For instance, Art. 54 of ICSID limits the enforcement of ICSID arbitral awards to its pecuniary obligations (Alexandrov 2009, p. 336).

Overall, it appears that it would be rather unlikely that the CJEU would recognize the direct effect of IDS decisions. First, the CJEU has consistently held that the decisions of the WTO DSM do not have direct effect. Second, even though the new FTAS contain IDS, they are tailored following the WTO DSM template. Third, those FTAs explicitly exclude the possibility of direct effect even for IDS decisions. Finally, even in those situations (ISDS) where a stronger case for direct effect could be made (arbitral awards in ISDS scenarios), the nature of the award (dealing only with liability award) would preclude that possibility.

The exceptions to the lack of direct effect of the trade agreements

A narrow reading of the Nakajima exception

In any case, the Court has carved certain exceptions to the lack of direct effect that prove fundamental when considering the future of the EU–Asia trade disputes and the role of the CJEU within it. In the *Nakajima* case,[21] the CJEU dealt with the issue of the compatibility of the anti-dumping regulation with the WTO's Anti-Dumping Agreement (ADA). Following the approach explained before,

Nakajima would not have been able to rely on the ADA to challenge the validity of the EU's anti-dumping regulation inasmuch as the ADA is part of WTO law and thus should not have direct effect. Yet the Court understood that Nakajima was not relying on the direct effect of the ADA.[22] Nakajima was in fact questioning the legality of that regulation vis-à-vis the ADA. Inasmuch as the ADA was a part of WTO law, the no-direct effect rule would have also applied to the ADA. However, since the second and third recitals in the preamble to the anti-dumping regulation showed that the regulation was adopted in accordance with existing international obligations, mainly the ADA, the validity of the regulation could be examined in light of the ADA. In the Court's own words:

> It follows that the [anti-dumping] regulation, which the applicant has called in question, was adopted in order to comply with the international obligations of the [Union], which, as the Court has consistently held, is therefore under an obligation to ensure compliance.... In those circumstances, it is necessary to examine whether the Council went beyond the legal framework thus laid down, as Nakajima claims, and whether, by adopting the disputed provision, it acted in breach [ADA].[23]

The anti-dumping regulation has been one of the main vehicles through which some of the most pressing trade issues in the EU–Asia relations have been channelled. This is specially true with regards to China, as AG Kokott highlighted in *Zhejiang Xinan Chemical Industrial Group* case:

> The present anti-dumping case is of fundamental importance for future trade relations between the European Union and a number of dynamic emerging countries, such as the People's Republic of China, which are currently in transition from a planned economy to a market economy, but are still classified as 'non-market economy countries.[24]

China's status as a Non-Market Economy (NME) has been a central structuring factor in its trade relations with the EU (Hsueh 2019). In practice this has been translated in a gradual erosion of China's NME status. Since companies importing goods from China are the ones bringing the claims, this has led to a case-by-case analysis of the extent to which a certain company is operating under "normal" market conditions within China. Recognition of such market economy status means that the companies concerned are given preferential treatment over other producers since the anti-dumping duties will not be calculated on the basis of an analogous market but on the basis of their own economic figures.[25]

The recent adaptation of the trade defence instruments[26] seems to codify the Court's approach. Art. 2(7)(b) of the anti-dumping regulation establishes that for and any non-market-economy country that is a member of the WTO (like China or Vietnam) the normal value shall be determined in accordance with the general rules on the basis of properly substantiated claims by one or more companies subject to the investigation that market-economy conditions prevail for them in respect of the product concerned. When that is not the case, the rules for NMEs enshrined in Art. 2(7)(a) will apply instead.

There is no doubt that the wording of this provision would clash with the view that China should be considered as an ME since 11 of December 2016, as provided in Section 15(d) of China's Accession Protocol to the WTO.[27] Leaving aside whether the EU has an obligation to accept that the ME status of China regardless of the facts in the ground (de Kok 2016; Kleimann 2016), an eventual disregard of the WTO panel or Appellate Body ruling(s) on the issue by the EU would open the possibility of claims within the scope of the Nakajima exception. Yet it is unclear to what extent this claim would be successful.[28]

In *Petrotub*, the Nakajima exception was worded in a broad sense so as to establish that:

> where the [Union] intended to implement a particular obligation assumed in the context of the WTO, or where the [Union] measure refers expressly to precise provisions of the agreements and understandings contained in the annexes to the WTO Agreement, it is for the Court to review the legality of the [Union] measure in question in the light of the WTO rules.[29]

A certain reading of this paragraph of *Petrotub* would favour the idea that the WTO law on anti-dumping would serve as a benchmark to review the legality of EU acts (Thies 2013, p. 26; Koutrakos 2015, p. 306). Thus, in principle, if a case on the non-compliance with an eventual WTO ruling declaring that the EU breached China's Accession Protocol by not granting automatic MES to China, would the Nakajima exception apply? To the extent that the discussion on whether the shift between MES and NME is a discussion on how anti-dumping duties should be calculated to those companies importing goods into the EU, there is a case to be made that the eventual WTO decision on the MES of China would fall within the Nakajima exception.

However, in 2015 the Court called into question the scope of the Nakajima exception. In *Rusal Armenal*[30] the Court was confronted with an appeal from the Commission on a General Court judgment that assessed the validity of Art. 2(7) of the anti-dumping regulation[31] in light of Art. 2 of the ADA. Rusal Armenal was a manufacturer and exporter of aluminium products and has been established in Armenia, a country considered an NME by the EU. As a consequence of Armenia's accession to the WTO in 2003, Rusal Armenal considered that the anti-dumping duties on its aluminium imports breached the ADA. These duties had been calculated on the basis of the analogue country system enshrined in Art. 2(7) of the anti-dumping regulation for NME states.

Whilst reasserting the relevance of the Nakajima exception, the Court recalled that

> it has in certain cases acknowledged that the WTO's anti-dumping system could constitute an exception to the general principle that the EU Courts cannot review the legality of the acts of the EU institutions in light of whether they are consistent with the rules of the WTO agreements.[32]

However, the Court moved the benchmark for the assessment of the legality of the anti-dumping regulation. In *Rusal Armenal* it was not enough to meet the *Petrotub* dictum.[33] The CJEU understood that *"it is necessary to be able to deduce from the specific provision of EU law contested that it seeks to implement into EU law a particular obligation stemming from the WTO agreements."*[34] Insofar as Art. 2(7) of the anti-dumping regulation introduces a special regime laying down detailed rules for the calculation of normal value for imports from NME states, and that there are no specific rules relating to such a category of countries in ADA, a correlation could not be established between Art. 2(7) of the anti-dumping regulation and the rules set out in the ADA.[35] This narrow reading seems almost to equate implementation with transposition and that only the incorrect transposition of the ADA could trigger the *Nakajima* exception. The impact that *Rusal Armenal* will have cannot be overstated (Hsueh 2019). This narrow reading of Nakajima will leave the question of the consequences of China's transition into a market economy out of Luxembourg, since Art. 2(7) of the basic regulation continues to establish a special procedure for NMEs. Yet, the extent to which this procedure is in violation of WTO obligations and the ADA will be something left for Geneva to establish and for the political institutions of the EU to decide how they comply (Tietje and Sacher 2018).

Giving effect to international decisions through the political process

Having shown how, as currently the EU's practice stands, that it would seem rather unlikely the CJEU would recognize the direct effect of the decisions of any of international bodies responsible for dealing with EU–Asia trade disputes, this section shows that there are other ways for those decisions to be given effect in the EU legal order. Whereas the respect for institutional balance and the democratic legitimacy that EU institutions have would further justify the approach of the Court to the issues of direct effect (Kuijper and Bronckers 2005, p. 1321), the main consequence of the Court's attitude seems to run contrary to judicialization of the question. In fact, if the Court's practice would remain the same, the other EU institutions would be the main gatekeepers of how decisions of international disputes bodies enter into the EU (Snyder 2003). In a nutshell, only inasmuch as the EU institutions agree to implement those decisions they will become the law of the EU land.

So far the trend has been on an *ad hoc* basis and following to a certain extent the logic of the exceptions to the no-direct effect rule of WTO law.[36] For instance, the recent modifications to the Seals regulation (European Commission 2015; European Union 2015)[37] were adopted to comply with the WTO panel report on the *EC-Seals* product dispute and the relevant DSB reports.[38] The explanatory memorandum of the Commission proposal mentioned that:

> The purpose of this legislative proposal is to implement the DSB recommendations and rulings with regard to the [Seals] Regulation. It also creates the legal basis for bringing Regulation (EU) No 737/2010 in compliance with the said rulings.

Consequently, in the event that either a member state or an individual considers that this regulation, once it is adopted, does not correctly comply with the WTO rulings and recommendations, that member state or individual should be able to question the validity of the regulation by invoking the relevant WTO reports and rulings.

Whereas the *ad hoc* basis to comply with WTO DSM decisions is not exempt from problems,[39] a permanent internal legal framework designed to give effect to the arbitral awards adopted under the investment chapters of the new FTAs has already been put in place. As mentioned above, if the new FTAs and the decisions adopted therein do no create rights for individuals to enforce at the EU level, is there any other way those rights could be recognized at an EU level? It is submitted that Regulation 912/2014 (European Union 2014)[40] enables for the compensation stemming from an award adopted by under the investment chapter (such as those enshrined in the EU–Singapore and EU–Vietnam FTAs) to be paid. Art. 18 provides that *"Where an award has been rendered against the Union, that award should be paid without delay. The Commission should make arrangements for the payment of such awards, unless a Member State has already accepted financial responsibility."* Moreover, given the pecuniary nature of the award, it seems consistent that Regulation 912/2014 would limit its scope as to only create an EU obligation to compensate the investor while leaving the validity of the rule that gave rise to the compensation untouched.

The new arrangements currently being put in place in the EU's treaty-making practice in relation to the (lack of) direct effect of its provisions have two interrelated consequences. On the one hand, it institutionalizes the issue of the effects of the agreement. By establishing that the agreement does not have direct effect, the parties are giving plenty of room for the EU institutions (mainly the Council and the Commission) to decide how the agreement will be implemented in the EU. On the other, the lack of direct effect of FTAs does not only preclude individuals and member states from challenging the validity of EU acts in light of an IDS decision; it also would move the issue away from the CJEU. Inasmuch as those agreements do not have direct effect, the Court's role in dealing with the EU's compliance with IDS would be more limited than nowadays.

Conclusion

The paradigm shift that international trade relations are experiencing at the moment with the move (and collapse) of mega regionals (Tzouvala 2018) reveals that the sidelining of the WTO also includes the reduction of the role that domestic courts such as the CJEU are going to have in shaping those relations.

This chapter has identified two main sources for moving away from the domestic judicialization of trade disputes. On the one hand, the EU political institutions when negotiating the new FTAs have favoured the inclusion of strong dispute settlement provisions within the agreement and explicitly excluded the possibility for domestic courts to adjudicate on trade issues. On the other hand, the chapter has shown how also the CJEU considers that those disputes should not be dealt at the domestic judicial level. The extension of the lack of direct effect to other agreements besides the WTO and the increasing narrow scope of the exceptions to that lack of direct effect demonstrate how the Court is exercising an increasing deference and self-restraint towards the other EU institutions when dealing with trade disputes.

The CJEU is well aware that it can influence and impinge upon the different ways in which the other EU institutions manage the different aspects of the EU external economic relations. The judicial restraint exercised by the CJEU has the logical consequence of giving more freedom to the Commission and the Council on how to deal with EU–Asia trade disputes. Otherwise put, the EU institutions do not have to worry about other actors, i.e. undertakings advancing their own interests through the CJEU. The EU political institutions do not only enjoy a greater procedural flexibility on how to manage trade disputes but also a greater flexibility as to the objectives to achieve in international trade negotiations. The explicit exclusion of the direct effect from the new FTAs can be seen as the logical corollary of that practice. By explicitly providing in the text of the agreement that direct effect is excluded, both the EU and the Asian country are making an explicit choice on where the disputes should be brought and consequently which actors will participate in the management and solution of disputes.

Notes

1 See introduction to this volume.
2 Case C-402/05 P and C-415/05 P *Yassin Abdullah Kadi, Al Barakaat International Foundation v. Council*, [2008] ECR I-6351, para. 21; Case C-149/96 *Portugal v. Council* [1999] ECR I-8395, para. 34 (hereinafter *Portugal v. Council*).
3 Art. 38 (1) Statute of the International Court of Justice: The Court, whose function is to decide in accordance with international law such disputes as are submitted to it, shall apply:

   a. international conventions, whether general or particular, establishing rules expressly recognized by the contesting states;
   b. international custom, as evidence of a general practice accepted as law;
   c. the general principles of law recognized by civilized nations;
   d. subject to the provisions of Art. 59, judicial decisions and the teachings of the most highly qualified publicists of the various nations, as subsidiary means for the determination of rules of law."

4 Case C-104/81 *Hauptzollamt Mainz v. Kupferberg & Cie* [1982] ECR 3641, para. 13 (hereinafter *Hauptzollamt Mainz v. Kupferberg & Cie*).
5 The first part of the test focuses on the analysis of the international agreement as a whole, whereas the second part of the test applies the classical criteria for direct effect under EU Law to the provision of the international agreement being invoked. See: Case 22-24/72 *International Fruit Company NV and others v. Produktschap voor Groenten en Fruit* [1972] ECR J-0021 (hereinafter *International Fruit Company NV and others v. Produktschap voor Groenten en Fruit*). For a more recent application of the test to a wider range of sources of international law see: Case C-366/10 *Air Transport Association of America and Others* [2011] ECR I-13755 (hereinafter *Air Transport Association of America and Others*).
6 Case C-308/06 *The Queen on the application of Intertanko and Others v. Secretary of State for Transport* [2008] ECR I-4057, para. 45 (hereinafter *The Queen on the application of Intertanko and Others v. Secretary of State for Transport*).

7 Case C-366/10 *Air Transport Association of America and Others* [2011] ECR I-13755, para. 51 (hereinafter *Air Transport Association of America and Others*).

8 *The Queen on the application of Intertanko and Others v. Secretary of State for Transport*, para. 66.

9 See *Hauptzollamt Mainz v. Kupferberg & Cie*; Case C-12/86 *Demirel v. Stadt Schwäbisch Gmünd* [1987] ECR 3719 (hereinafter *Demirel v. Stadt Schwäbisch Gmünd*); Case C-265/02 *Frahuil SA v. Assitalia SpA* [2004] ECR I-1543 (hereinafter *Frahuil SA v. Assitalia SpA*).

10 See *Portugal v. Council*.

11 Opinion 1/91 *Re: European Economic Area Agreement* [1991] ECR I-6079, para. 39.

12 Joined Cases C–120/06 P and 121/06 P *Fabbrica italiana accumulatori motocarri Montecchio SpA (FIAMM) and Others v. Council and Commission and Giorgio Fedon & Figli SpA and Others v. Concil and Commission* [2008] ECR I-6513, para. 128. See also, Case C-94/02 P *Établissements Biret et Cie SA* [2003] ECR I-10565, para. 77; Case C-377/02 *Léon Van Parys NV v. Belgisch Interventie- en Restitutiebureau (BIRB)* [2005] ECR I-01465; Case C-306/13 *LVP NV v. Belgische Staat* [2014] ECLI:EU:C:2014:2465.

13 UNCLOS: *The Queen on the application of Intertanko and Others v. Secretary of State for Transport*; Aarhus Convention: C-240/09 L: Case C-401/12 P, C-402/12 P, C-403/12 P *Vereniging Milieudefensie and Stichting Stop Luchtverontreiniging Utrecht* [2015] EU:C:2015:209; Case C-404/12, C-405/12 *Council and Commission v. Stichting Natuur en Milieu and Pesticide Action Network Europe* [2015] EU:C:2015:5. UN Convention on the Rights of the Child: Case C-363/12 *Z v. A Government department and The Board of management of a community school* [2014] ECLI:EU:C:2014:159. Kyoto Protocol: C-366/10 *Air Transport Association of America and Others*.

14 Panel Report on *United States-Sections301-310 of the Trade Act 1974*, WT/DS152/R of 22 December 1999, (hereinafter Panel Report on *United States-Sections 301–310 of the Trade Act 1974*) paras. 7.72. "Neither the GATT nor the WTO has so far been interpreted by GATT/WTO institutions as a legal order producing direct effect; the GATT/WTO did *not* create a new legal order the subjects of which comprise both contracting parties or Members and their nationals."

15 Art. 14.17 (2) EU–South Korea FTA: "*Any ruling of the arbitration panel shall be binding on the Parties and shall not create any rights or obligations for natural or legal persons.*"

16 For instance, the EU–Singapore FTA in its Art. 17.15 entitled "No Direct Effect" emphasizes that: "*For greater certainty, nothing in this Agreement shall be construed as conferring rights or imposing obligations on persons, other than those created between the Parties under public international law.*"

17 So far only the FTAs with Singapore and Vietnam include some sort of ISDS.

18 The link between direct effect and validity of an EU norm can be easily seen in *Portugal v. Council*.

19 See Art. 8.39 CETA, Art. 9.24 EU–Singapore FTA, Art. 28 of the EU's proposal for Investment Protection and Resolution of Investment Disputes, available at http://trade.ec.europa.eu/doclib/docs/2015/november/tradoc_153955.pdf

20 See Art. 9.27 EU–Singapore FTA and Art. 27 of Chapter II of Chapter of EU–Vietnam FTA.

21 Case C-69/89 *Nakajima All Precision Co. Ltd v. Council* [1991] ECR I-2069 (hereinafter *Nakajima All Precision Co. Ltd v. Council*).

22 *Ibid.*, para. 28.

23 *Ibid.*, paras. 31–32.

24 Case C-337/09 *Zhejiang Xinan v. Chemical Industrial Group Co. Ltd* [2012] ECR I-77, Opinion of AG Kokott para. 1 (hereinafter *Zhejiang Xinan v. Chemical Industrial Group Co. Ltd*).

25 *Ibid.*, para. 2.
26 Regulation (EU) 2017/2321 of the European Parliament and of the Council amending Regulation (EU) 2016/1036 on protection against dumped imports from countries not members of the European Union and Regulation (EU) 2016/1037 on protection against subsidised imports from countries not members of the European Union. OJ L 338, 19 December 2017 (hereinafter Regulation 2017/2321).
27 "*Once China has established, under the national law of the importing WTO Member, that it is a market economy, the provisions of subparagraph (a) shall be terminated provided that the importing Member's national law contains market economy criteria as of the date of accession. In any event, the provisions of subparagraph (a)(ii) shall expire 15 years after the date of accession. In addition, should China establish, pursuant to the national law of the importing WTO Member, that market economy conditions prevail in a particular industry or sector, the non-market economy provisions of subparagraph (a) shall no longer apply to that industry or sector.*"
28 *European Union – Measures Related to Price Comparison Methodologies.* DS516. A panel was established in 2017 but no decision has been reached at the time of writing.
29 Case C-76/00P *Petrotub SA and Republica SA v. Council* [2003] ECR I-79.
30 Case C-21/14 P *Commission v. Rusal Armenal,* [2015] ECLI:EU:C:2015:494 (hereinafter *Commission v. Rusal Armenal*).
31 Art. 2(7) of Council Regulation (EC) 384/96 of 22 December 1995 on protection against dumped imports from countries not members of the European Community, OJ L 56, 6 March 1996, p. 1, amended by Council Regulation (EC) 2117/2005 of 2 amending Regulation (EC) No 384/96 on protection against dumped imports from countries not members of the European Community, OJ L 340, 23 December 2005, p. 17. Now replaced by Regulation (EU) 2016/1036 of the European Parliament and of the Council on protection against dumped imports from countries not members of the European Union, OJ L 176, 30 June 2016, pp. 21–54.
32 *Commission v. Rusal Armenal,* para. 44.
33 See *Zhejiang Xinan v. Chemical Industrial Group Co.*
34 *Commission v. Rusal Armenal,* para. 46.
35 *Commission v. Rusal Armenal,* para. 50.
36 Case 70/87 *Fediol v. Commission* [1989] ECR I-1781; C-69/89 *Nakajima v. Council* [1991] ECR I-2069.
37 Regulation (EU) 2015/1775 of the European Parliament and of the Council of 6 October 2015 amending Regulation (EC) 1007/2009 on trade in seal products and repealing Commission Regulation (EU) 737/2010, OJ L 262/1, 6 October 2015 (hereinafter Regulation 2015/1775).
38 Panel Report on *EC – Measures Prohibiting the Importation and Marketing of Seal Products,* WT/DS400/R of 25 November 2013, Appellate Body Report of 22 May 2014.
39 C-306/13 *LVP NV v. Belgische Staat* [2014] ECLI:EU:C: 2014:2465.
40 Regulation (EU) 912/2014 of the European Parliament and of the Council establishing a framework for managing financial responsibility linked to investor-to-state dispute settlement tribunals established by international agreements to which the European Union is party, OJ L 257, 23 July 2014 (hereinafter Regulation 912/2014).

References

Alexandrov, S.A. (2009) 'Enforcement of ICSID Awards: Articles 53 and 54 of The ICSID Convention', in C. Binder, U. Kriebaum, A. Reinisch and S. Wittich (eds.), *International Investment Law for the 21st Century: Essays in Honour of Christoph Schreuer,* Oxford: Oxford University Press, pp. 322–337.

Cremona, M. (2014) 'A reticent court? policy objectives and the Court of Justice', in M. Cremona and A. Thies (eds.), *The European Court of Justice and External Relations Law: Constitutional Challenges*, Oxford: Hart Publishing, pp. 15–32.

de Kok, J. (2016) 'The future of EU trade defence investigations against imports from China', *Journal of International Economic Law*, 19(2), pp. 515–547.

de Witte, B. (2014) 'A selfish court? The Court of Justice and the design of international dispute settlement beyond the European Union', in M. Cremona and A. Thies (eds.), *The European Court of Justice and External Relations Law: Constitutional Challenges*, Oxford: Hart Publishing, pp. 33–46.

Dimopoulos, A. (2011) *EU Foreign Investment Law*, Oxford: Oxford University Press.

Dolzer, R. and Schreuer, C. (2012) *Principles of International Investment Law*, Oxford: Oxford University Press.

Eeckhout, P. (2009) 'Case C-308/06, The Queen on the application of Intertanko and others v. Secretary of State for Transport, judgment of the Court of Justice (Grand Chamber) of 3 June 2008, nyr', *Common Market Law Review*, 46(6), pp. 2041–2057.

Eeckhout, P. (2011) *EU External Relations Law*, Oxford: Oxford University Press.

European Commission (2015) 'Proposal for a Regulation of the European Parliament and of the Council' amending Regulation (EC) No 1007/2009 on trade in seal products, COM (2015) 45 final.

Franck, T.M. (1992) *Political Questions/Judicial Answers: Does The Rule of Law Apply to Foreign Affairs?* Princeton, NJ: Princeton University Press.

Gaja, G. (2002) 'Trends in judicial activism and judicial self-restraint relating to community agreements', in E. Cannizzaro (ed.), *The European Union as an Actor in International Relations*, The Hague, the Netherlands: Kluwer, pp. 117–134.

Griller, S. (2000) 'Judicial enforceability of WTO law in the European Union', *Journal of International Economic Law*, 3(3), pp. 441–472.

Hillion, C. (2014) 'A powerless court? The European Court of Justice and the common and foreign security policy', in M. Cremona and A. Thies (eds.), *The European Court of Justice and External Relations Law: Constitutional Challenges*, Oxford: Hart Publishing, pp. 47–72.

Holdgaard, R. (2006) 'Principles of reception of international law in community law', *Yearbook of European Law*, 25(1), pp. 263–314.

Hsueh, C. (2019) 'The limits of a legal approach in resolving EU-China trade disputes on non-market economy status', in F. Gaenssmantel and C. Wu (eds.), *Law and Diplomacy in the Management of EU-Asia Trade and Investment Relations*, London: Routledge, pp 153–172.

Jacobs, F.G. (2011) 'Direct effect and interpretation of international agreements in the recent case law of the European Court of Justice', in A. Dashwood and M. Maresceau (eds.), *Law and Practice of EU External Relations: Salient Features of a Changing Landscape*, Cambridge: Cambridge University Press, pp. 13–33.

Klabbers, J. (2001) 'International law in community law: The law and politics of direct effect', *Yearbook of European Law*, 21(1), pp. 263–298.

Klabbers, J. (2012) *The European Union in International Law*, Paris: Pedone.

Kleimann, D. (2016) 'The vulnerability of EU anti-dumping measures against China after December 11, 2016', *EUI Working Paper RSCAS*, paper No. 2016/37.

Koutrakos, P. (2015) *EU International Relations Law*, 2nd edn, Oxford: Hart Publishing.

Kuijper, P.J. and Bronckers, M. (2005) 'WTO law in the European Court of Justice', *Common Market Law Review*, 42, pp. 1313–1355.

Lenaerts, K. and Corthaut, T. (2006) 'Of birds and hedges: The role of primacy in invoking norms of EU law', *European Law Review*, 31(3), pp. 287–315.

Mendez, M. (2013) *The Legal Effects of EU Agreements*, Oxford: Oxford University Press.

Petersmann, E.U. (2000) 'From "negative" to "positive" integration in the WTO: Time for "mainstreaming human rights" into WTO law?' *Common Market Law Review*, 37(6), pp. 1363–1382.

Schütze, R. (2006) 'Supremacy without pre-emption? The very slowly emergent doctrine of community pre-emption', *Common Market Law Review*, 43(4), pp. 1023–1048.

Schütze, R. (2014) *Foreign Affairs and the EU Constitution*, Cambridge: Cambridge University Press.

Semertzi, A. (2014) 'The preclusion of direct effect in the recently concluded EU free trade agreements', *Common Market Law Review*, 51(4), pp. 1125–1158.

Snyder, F. (2003) 'The gatekeepers: The European courts and WTO law', *Common Market Law Review*, 40, pp. 313–367.

Thies, A. (2013) *International Trade Disputes and EU Liability*, Cambridge: Cambridge University Press.

Tietje, C. and Sacher, V. (2018) 'The new anti-dumping methodology of the European Union—A breach of WTO law?' *European Yearbook of International Economic Law*, Springer, pp. 89–105.

Tzouvala, N. (2018) 'Not letting go: The academic debate about mega-regionals and international lawyers', *London Review of International Law*, 6(2), pp. 189–209.

van Aaken, A. (2010) 'Primary and secondary remedies in international investment law and national state liability: A functional and comparative view', in S.W. Schill (ed.), *International Investment Law and Comparative Public Law*, Oxford: Oxford University Press, pp. 721–754.

Wessel, R.A. (2013) *Close Encounters of the Third Kind: The Interface between the EU and International Law after the Lisbon Treaty*, Stockholm, Sweden: SIEPS.

3 Law and diplomacy in EU–China trade relations

A historical overview

Jappe Eckhardt

Up until the early 1970s diplomatic and economic relations between the European Union (EU) and China were limited. This changed when, in 1973, China invited the then European Commissioner for Foreign Affairs Christopher Soames to visit China. The visit was a success and the European Commission responded by sending a memorandum to China, which included a draft for a possible bilateral trade agreement. But it was not until the EU formally recognized the People's Republic as the only government of China, in 1975, that diplomatic relations were firmly established. In the decades that followed, the EU and China have been engaged in numerous trade disputes and this chapter provides a historical overview of these disputes, the nature and outcomes of which have drastically changed over time.

The chapter is organized as follows. First, it will look at the early years of EU–China trade relations and disputes, focusing both on diplomatic and legal aspects, from the first trade agreement signed in 1978 until the diplomatic tensions surrounding the Tiananmen Square massacre in June 1989. It will then look at the 1990s, during which relations were increasingly driven by China's economic lure but the EU also still had plenty of leeway to adopt protectionist measures on Chinese imports: it could threaten to withdraw its support for China's accession to the World Trade Organization (WTO) and, in addition, could quite easily impose all kinds of trade restrictions that are prohibited under WTO law. The final section will look at the period after China joined the WTO in 2002 and shows how, since then, trade disputes between the two trading blocs have become increasingly politicized, both between the EU and China but also within the EU itself. The concluding section will highlight some avenues for further research.

The early years of EU–China trade relations

The first time the EU and China seriously discussed their trade relations was when the two sides opened negotiations for a formal EU–China trade agreement, which was eventually signed in 1978. The agreement was hailed as a triumph on both sides (Algieri 2002). Roger Strange (1998, p. 61) explains why it was such a significant agreement for both trading blocs: it was important for the EU, "as it was the first trading agreement to be concluded by the Community with a state-trading country while, for China, it formalized relations with an increasingly important trading partner."

In that same year, 1978, the so-called EU–China Joint Committee for trade was set up. This body, which was comprised of representatives from both sides and started to meet regularly, became the central forum for the development of economic relations between the two parties. At the first meeting of this Joint Committee, China's inclusion in the Generalized System of Preferences (GSP) was negotiated, and in 1980 China was indeed included in the GSP albeit for a relatively limited number of products (Algieri 2002). The GSP, which was part of the General Agreements on Tariffs and Trade (GATT) and later the WTO, is a system that was established in the 1970s granting preferential access to certain products from low- income countries without reciprocal liberalization from developed countries (for a detailed account of the GSP history, see dos Santos et al. 2005).

In the course of the 1980s, it became clear that the 1978 Trade Agreement was no longer adequate for the increasing complexity of EU–China economic relations. In response, the two sides negotiated a new agreement, which was completed in 1985: the Trade and Economic Cooperation Agreement. This agreement extended the relations from trade matters to wider economic co-operation in areas such as industry, mining, agriculture, science and technology, energy, transport and communication, protection of the environment and co-operation with third countries (Colin 2010). Despite the signing of this agreement, as well as a series of high-level diplomatic meetings, and a sharp increase in trade and foreign direct investment (FDI) flows from the EU to China, bilateral economic diplomacy was overall quite tense from the mid-1980s onwards.

The main reason for these tensions was the fact that the EU resorted to many measures to try to stem the increasing inflow of Chinese imports. For instance, Chinese imports in textile and clothing products became subject to very restrictive EU quotas under the Multi Fibre Arrangement (MFA) (Eckhardt 2010; Underhill 1998), while the EU also imposed non-tariff barriers (NTBs) on a host of other Chinese products. By the end of the 1980s, quantitative restrictions and quotas covered more than 30 per cent of all EU imports from China; if only manufactured goods are considered, the share rises to almost 50 per cent (Bridges 1999). What is more, the EU also started to make intensive use of its trade defence instruments (TDI) from 1987 onwards. The most heavily used TDIs by the EU were anti-dumping (AD) measures and quite a few of these AD investigations were aimed at Chinese imports, with 23 cases launched between 1987 and 1992 (see Figure 3.1).

Around the end of the 1980s and beginning of the 1990s, a very large percentage of Chinese trade to the EU was subject to tariffs and NTBs and there was not much China could do about it. China was not a member of the GATT/WTO at this time, so it could not use the WTO/GATT dispute settlement mechanism (DSM) to bring a complaint against the EU, nor had put in place its own trade defence laws and regulations. The latter were, as discussed below, only developed in the second half of the 1990s (Young 1998; Soliman 2013). In other words,

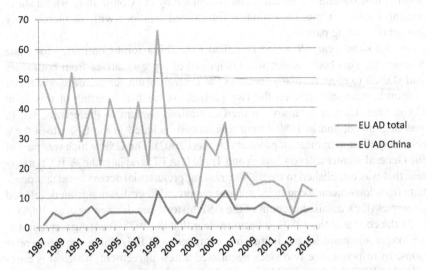

Figure 3.1 EU anti-dumping cases (all investigations, 1987–2015). Source: Author calculations are based on data from Bown (2012).

China neither had any legalized dispute settlement venue nor formal domestic
procedures to retaliate and, therefore, could only rely on the Joint Committee,
with its low level of legalization, or use the diplomatic route more in general to
try and solve its trade disputes with the EU. As a sign of the latter, China brought
up the issue of EU protectionism during sparse high-level summits and the two
sides negotiated several agreements within the framework of the MFA in the
course of the 1980s. This resulted in an increase in quotas on a limited number
of Chinese textile and clothing imports (Strange 1998) and some careful political
conciliation.

However, this pattern of slowly intensifying diplomatic exchange did not stop
the EU from imposing further measures to protect the EU market from Chinese
competition. What is more, diplomatic relations suffered a significant blow
as a result of the Tiananmen Square massacre in June 1989, to which the EU
responded immediately by instituting sanctions against China: high-level ministerial visits were stopped, just as arms sales and soft loans were suspended
(Bridges 1999). Although some of the sanctions were relaxed quite soon, the
political rehabilitation of China was about to take a while and this had a severe
impact on EU–China diplomatic and economic relations until well into the 1990s.

A "deeper" diplomatic relationship amid continued
EU protectionism

As European member states halfway through the 1990s grappled with the process of relaxing their individual sanctions, instituted after the Tiananmen Square
massacre in 1989, while maintaining some pressure on China over human rights,

the European Commission (EC) itself started to think about ways to deepen the relationship with China. In July 1995, the EC published a document entitled *A Long-Term Policy for China-Europe Relations* (European Commission 1995). The document belonged to a wider EU Asian strategy, which emphasized the need for the EU to take a more pro-active approach towards the countries in Asia so as to protect its economic interests against competition from the US, Japan and other global economic rivals (European Commission 1994). What is clear from those documents is that Europe's relation with China was seen by the Commission as one of the most important cornerstones of the EU's external (political and economic) relations, both with Asia and globally. The importance of China, in the eyes of the European Commission, found further expression in the EC communications of 1998 and 2001 (European Commission 1998, 2001).

The main aspects of the European approach towards China, as expressed in the above-mentioned communications, were to strengthen the economic co-operation, to bring China into the international trade framework, to support the development of a civil society, to help China fight poverty and to assist China in environmental matters. In order to do all this, it was very important, according to the EC, to invest in diplomatic relations with China and, in turn, in a political friendship (Algieri 2002). To this end, an ambitious new framework for bilateral political dialogue was set up, under which EU officials would hold regular ministerial meetings with China, supplemented by *ad hoc* meetings between the Chinese foreign minister and his EU counterparts or EU ambassadors. The final step in upgrading the political dialogue was the introduction of an EU–China summit, the first one of which took place in the margins of the Asia-Europe Meeting (ASEM) in London in April 1998. Although, this first official summit was a bit short on substance, it was nonetheless an important occasion for both sides (Bridges 1999). From that moment on, EU–China summits were held annually and became bigger, longer and better attended by high officials. All of this was highly symbolic for the huge increase in the European Union's economic relations with China during this period (Mergenthaler 2015).

The main rationale for the EU to develop relations with China had become China's commercial lure and, as a result, human rights issues and the weapons embargo were increasingly given second (or third) place to trade diplomacy, from the mid-1990s onwards. To be sure, biannual EU–China meetings specifically devoted to human rights issues were launched in 1995. However, these were suspended, at Beijing's initiative, already in the spring of 1996 and only resumed in November 1997. This suspension had everything to do with the fact that China was irritated by the fact that its new "best friend" Europe tried to encourage the international community to retain an interest in Chinese human rights issues not only by dialogue but also by sponsoring critical resolutions in the United Nations Human Rights Council (UNHRC) even after the beginning of dedicated bilateral meetings (Wan 2001; Wiessala 2005).

The EU drew satisfaction from the level of international support for a 1995 resolution, which stated that repeated instances of violations of human rights by China showed that China still had room for improvement, even though China lobbied hard enough for support to ensure that the resolution did not pass (Möller 2002; Wan 2001). The same happened with the 1996 resolution, although this time it almost passed. China feared that the next resolution might be accepted by a majority due to heavy lobbying by the EU and the United States, and thus it decided to pressure the EU by suspending their human rights dialogue. This appeared to be a smart diplomatic move, as soon cracks in the European unity were beginning to appear and some EU member states openly started to question the effectiveness of the UNHRC resolutions. France was becoming increasingly impatient to adopt a different approach to the human rights issue. The following year, 1997, France withdrew its support for the resolution and Germany, Italy, Spain and Greece followed suit (Möller 2002; Wan 2001).

The timing of this change of heart was a result of Chinese economic diplomatic craftsmanship. Around that time, French president Jacques Chirac "had instructed his government to fight unemployment with more China trade and to deny the US leadership in the Chinese market" (Möller 2002, p. 24). Chirac himself visited Beijing in May 1997 and was rewarded with some lucrative contracts for French businesses. Similar tactics were used to sway other EU member states: Beijing first postponed official planned visits from and to the Netherlands, Denmark and the UK, which all had supported the critical resolution, and once these countries dropped their support they were praised by the Chinese for their "discerning" and "just" move and received lucrative business contracts as well (Bridges 1999). One year later, the European unity was recovered: it was decided by the EU member countries that support of a critical resolution could no longer be maintained. So from that moment on, not one of the EU member states supported the UNHCR resolutions. Instead, they pushed for greater Chinese respect for human rights through silent diplomacy (King 1999).

The case of the UNHRC resolutions showed China's increasing diplomatic assertiveness. It proved that it was able to successfully use the carrot of commercial orders combined with the stick of economic weapons as a reprisal for what it saw as unfriendly actions by some European countries. However, China was not able to pursue the same divide-and-rule strategy when it came to its trade disputes with the EU. Given the nature of the EU's trade policymaking process, with its high level of political autonomy for the European Commission (see e.g. Dür and Zimmermann 2007; Gstöhl and De Bièvre 2018) and direct access for private actors to initiate trade defence procedures, Beijing was not able to stop EU protectionist measures vis-à-vis China. What is more, the EU was able to use China's WTO accession negotiations to keep forcing China to "voluntarily" restrict exports to the EU by threatening to drop its support for WTO membership (for a detailed account on EU's role in China WTO accession, see e.g. Eglin 1997; Zimmermann 2007). As a result, China's trade to the EU in key sectors such as textile, clothing and footwear remained subject to restrictive NTBs, while the EU also continued to impose TDI measures. As Figure 3.1 illustrates, the EU launched 43 new AD investigations against China between 1993 and 2000, with a peak of 12 new cases in 1999 alone.

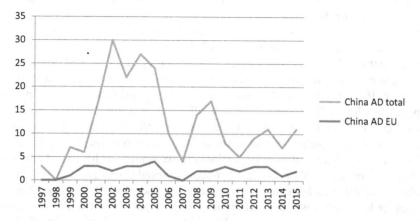

Figure 3.2 Chinca's AD cases (1997–2015). Source: Author calculations are based on data from Bown (2012).

China did not just lack the diplomatic tools to counter these EU protectionist tendencies; it also still lacked access to any legal mechanisms that would have allowed it to do so. As it was not yet a WTO member (although negotiations were far advanced at this stage), China still had to wait before it could bring any cases against the EU to the WTO DSM. Beijing had adopted, as part of its WTO accession process, its own TDI laws in 1997 – the so-called Anti-Dumping and Anti-Subsidy Regulations of the PRC (Potter 2005; Soliman 2013) – yet the new regulation was not used very frequently by China during the first years after it was enacted. However, as shown in Figure 3.2, these numbers went up gradually with 7, 6 and 17 AD cases launched in 1999, 2000 and 2001 respectively. Seven of these cases were brought against the EU.

From a "honeymoon period" to a (continuing) three-year itch

In the course of the 1990s China had already managed to become one of the most powerful forces in the global economy, and its impressive economic growth accelerated further after its WTO membership in 2001. It had become one of the world's largest traders and a key centre of world manufacturing, and in 2002, China overtook the United States as the largest recipient of FDI. China's gross domestic product (GDP) has grown on average with almost 10 per cent annually between 1989 and 2018[1] and, in 2013, China became the world's largest economy measured by GDP on purchasing power parity (PPP) basis.[2] Since the 2008 financial crisis, China's GDP growth has been slightly lower but still well above the world's average, and the country's economy has been solely responsible for 45 per cent of the gain in world GDP since 2008 (*The Economist* 2018).

In light of China's economic growth, and soon after its WTO accession, the European Commission published *A Maturing Partnership – Shared Interests and*

Challenges in EU – China Relations. Although some challenges were indeed identified in the document, the emphasis was very much on the fact that trade relations between the EU and China "have developed in step with the latter's emergence on the global economic scene," that "China in 2002 overtook Japan to become the EU's second largest trading partner outside Europe" and that this has brought economic fortunes for many sectors in the EU (European Commission 2003, p. 16). When in 2003 the Chinese government published its first ever policy paper on China–EU relations, it became officially clear that the "love" between the EU and China was not one-sided but mutual.[3] Not much later the two sides announced the establishment of a comprehensive strategic partnership, which in turn led to an intensification of diplomatic exchanges and high-level political visits. According to Men (2012), EU officials visited China 206 times in 2004 alone, which comes down to on average four visits per week, while then Chinese Premier Wen Jiabao was the first foreign leader to pay an official EU visit after the EU's eastward enlargement in 2004. That same year Romano Prodi, then president of the European Commission, stated at an EU–China business forum about EU–China relations that "if it is not a marriage, it is at least a very serious engagement" (Men 2012, pp. 34–35). This period around and after China's WTO accession is therefore often referred to as the EU–China "honeymoon period" (Berkofsky 2010).

However, this honeymoon period did not last very long and soon turned into a "three-year itch." That is, the EU and China, from approximately 2005 onward, became involved in numerous diplomatic and legal fights over, as the *Financial Times* (Spiegel et al. 2013) put it, "whether China is systematically using its tools of state power to break into the European market illegally." But tensions also grew over issues such as China's market access obstacles, intellectual property rights (IPR) protection and trademark rights in China. Many of these battles escalated and led to the imposition by the EU of tariffs or other trade-restrictive measures on Chinese products. In fact, China has in the last 15 years become by far the EU's most important target of TDI proceedings. If we just look at EU AD proceedings (see Figure 3.1), the overall numbers have decreased considerably in recent years while the number of cases against China has gone up. Between 2004 and 2016, the EU has brought 70 AD cases against China and in some years (e.g. 2013) all of the EU's AD cases where aimed at China.

The most obvious reason for the fact that China is on top of the EU's TDI target list is that China has become the EU's single most important source of imports and, therefore, poses the biggest threat to EU producers competing with foreign imports. However, this is not the only reason for the fact that China faces the bulk of EU TDI cases. A second and interrelated reason is that the EU does not have many tools other than TDIs at its disposal to protect its domestic producers when they feel threatened by (what they regard as) unfair trade with China. That is, ever since China joined the WTO, the EU and its import-competing firms have, more or less, one unilateral option if they want to shield their markets from the influx of (too many cheap) Chinese products: impose TDI measures. Naturally, in case of activities by the Chinese state that do not conform to WTO law, there is also the WTO DSM. But here the EU bears the burden of proof and it is likely to take years before policies are changed, making this is a far less attractive option.

The EU could of course also try to restrict Chinese imports through bilateral negotiations or the signing of bilateral trade agreements. However, recent trade talks have not led to many concrete results in this regard. Examples of such formal dialogues include the annual EU–China High-Level Economic and Trade Dialogue, which was launched in 2008. The high-level dialogue deals "with issues of strategic importance to EU-China trade and economic relations and provides impetus to progress concretely in sectoral dialogues. This dialogue provides a tool to address issues of mutual concern in the areas of investment, market access and intellectual property rights protection, as well as other issues related to trade."[4] Another example of a recent EU–China (trade) dialogue are the negotiations on a Partnership and Cooperation Agreement (PCA), which were launched in 2007, in order to "[...] provide the opportunity to further improve the framework for bilateral trade and investment relations and also include the upgrading of the 1985 EC-China Trade and Economic Cooperation Agreement"[5] (for a more in-depth discussion see Men and Balducci 2010). Not much progress has been made with the PCA negotiations since then, in part because of China's refusal to discuss non-trade issues such as human rights and labour conditions (Hu and Pelkmans 2017).

In other words, it is not that surprising that the EU at times protects those import-competing firms in the EU that are hurt by freer trade with China through the imposition of TDI measures. However, what is striking about these cases is the high level of politicization and escalation. That is, a series of recent EU–China trade disputes have led to intense lobbying in the EU from economic interests in favour and against the imposition of protectionist measures, which in turn has resulted in strong disagreements among EU member states on the imposition of such measures. Key examples of such highly politicized cases include the decision by the EU to (re)impose quotas on textile and clothing products in 2005 (Eckhardt 2015; Heron 2007), the adoption of AD duties on China's footwear imports in 2006 and an extension of those duties in 2009 (Eckhardt 2011; Curran and Eckhardt 2018a). What was striking about the latter case was that the duties got support from a very small majority of EU member states, while historically the Commission can count on the backing of a firm majority in such cases; duties were very low in comparison to typical EU AD cases and only imposed for two years (and a 15 months' extension), while five years is the usual length for initial AD duties as well as for extensions; and sport shoes were exempted from duties, despite sharply increasing levels of imports from China.

A more recent example of such a contentious EU–China TDI case was the decision by the EU to put in place (punitive) AD duties on Chinese solar panels in the course of 2013 (Dunford et al. 2013; Curran 2015; Kolk and Curran 2017; Voituriez and Wang 2015), which are about to expire now that the European Commission has recently decided to eliminate the duties (*Euractive* 2018). In addition, there have been cases where the EU threatened to impose AD measures but decided to drop the case such as the 2010–2014 dispute on Chinese imports of telecom products (Pepermans 2016), as well as (failed) attempts by the EU to radically reform its TDI policies in light of China's rise (De Bièvre and Eckhardt 2011; Tsakalidou 2017; Vermulst and Sud 2013).

The way these EU–China TDI/AD cases have unfolded is very different from the way that the EU dealt with AD and other TDI cases in the past. That is, until relatively recently, as Evenett and Vermulst put it, "a spirit of 'live and let live' co-operation prevailed...member states tended to support the European Commission's proposals to impose definitive anti-dumping duties" (Evenett and Vermulst 2005, p. 704). Typically, when the European Commission opens an AD investigation, it is very likely that this will lead to the imposition of AD duties. Marc Wellhausen (2001, pp. 1040–1041) puts it as follows: "[...] if the Member States have been consulted properly at all important stages of the investigation, the imposition of definitive [anti-dumping] measures and the collection of provisional duties is a mere formality." This is not to say that EU member states have no important say in AD cases: although it is the Commission that introduces provisional defence measures or negotiates price undertakings with exporters, member states are always consulted, and in the adoption of definitive measures they can stop the Commission with a simple majority against its proposal in the Trade Policy Committee. Council voting rules on AD cases have changed several times over the past decades and each change has eased the adoption of AD measures by the Council, and thus, increased the probability of protectionist outcomes. Voting rules were changed in 1995 from requiring a qualified majority vote to a simple majority vote in favour, which clearly lowered the hurdle for adopting duties. In 2004 this hurdle was lowered even further when the "abstention rule" was introduced (Evenett and Vermulst 2005; Vermulst and Waer 1996). Ever since then an abstention is considered as a vote in favour of an AD duty, which makes it relatively easy to get a majority behind the imposition of such duties. The current system goes back to the new AD Regulation of 2016,[6] which was, together with a more general modernization of EU's TDI policy, formally adopted in 2018 (for a more in-depth discussion, see Curran and Eckhardt 2020).

The recent EU–China AD (and other TDI) cases, described above, show that these dynamics are changing and that there is increasing disagreement between EU member states and between the Commission and the Council when it comes to the adoption of AD cases. How can this be explained? In the remainder of this section, two explanations are presented: China's increased legal capacity and changing patterns of investment and production between the EU and China.

China's increased trade law capacity

China had already put serious efforts in building its trade law capacity during its long road to WTO membership (Halverson 2004). After joining the WTO in 2002, Beijing stepped up these efforts by further investing heavily in its legal capacity, both as a way to reform its domestic regulatory state and economy (Eckhardt and Wang 2019) but also to be able to defend itself in the international economic and legal arena (Shaffer and Gao 2018). Shaffer and Gao argue that as

Table 3.1 WTO dispute settlement cases involving China (2002–2018) and the EU (1995–2018)

	As complainant	As respondent	As third party
China	22	43	152
EU	99	85	179

Source: WTO dispute settlement database, available at https://www.wto.org/english/tratop_e/dispu_e/dispu_status_e.htm

a result of these efforts, in combination with its increased market power, China has become "a serious rival to the United States and Europe in the development and enforcement of international trade law" (Shaffer and Gao 2018, p. 115).

This has resulted in a very active participation of China in WTO dispute settlement procedures, as Table 3.1 confirms. Particularly noteworthy is the fact that China has been a third party in an impressive 152 cases, which has helped the country massively in learning about the WTO dispute settlement system. The first DSM complaint it brought itself was against US safeguard measures on steel in 2003[7] and since then it has filed a total of 22 cases as a complainant, while it has been a respondent in 43 cases. This is still lower than the number of cases the EU (see Table 3.1) and the United States are involved in, as complainant and defendant, but China has gradually "become one of the most frequent users of WTO dispute settlement mechanism" (Chi 2012, p. 29). Most of China's 22 complaints where aimed at the United States (15 cases) and the other 7 against the EU.

Table 3.2 provides a detailed overview of China's complaints against the EU, and what this shows is that it took quite a few years (2009) until China brought its first case against the EU and that most of its complaints are about the EU's use of AD duties, one of which was the heavily politicized EU AD case against Chinese footwear, as described above. It is plausible that China's use of WTO disputes against EU AD measures is one of the reasons why certain EU member states have become more reluctant to support AD duties, which in turn, can be the reason for the increase in political conflicts among EU member states on the imposition of AD measures. Further research is needed to test this proposition but it would be in line with the deterrence effect of WTO dispute settlement cases, as observed by Davis (2016). On the other hand, we also see that the EU has brought nine WTO DSM cases against China (see Table 3.2) and that several of these are in fact aimed at China's own AD measures against the EU, which could be interpreted as retaliatory action on the part of the EU.

The politics of global value chains

A second factor that could help us to understand the politicization of recent EU–China trade disputes is the changing nature of production, trade and investment patterns between the two trading blocs and the resulting changes in trade

Table 3.2 EU–China WTO dispute settlement cases (2002–2018)

	DS number	Date of complaint	Issue
China's complaints against EU	DS397	31 July 2009	AD measures on iron/steel fasteners
	DS405	4 February 2010	AD measures on footwear
	DS452 (3 cases: EU, France, Greece)	5 November 2012	Measures affecting renewable energy generation sector (feed in tariffs)
	DS492	8 April 2015	Measures affecting tariff concessions on poultry/meat products
	DS516	12 December 2016	AD regulation related to "non-market economy" countries
EU's complaints against China	DS339	30 March 2006	Measures affecting imports of automobile parts
	DS372	3 March 2008	Measures affecting financial information services/suppliers
	DS395	23 June 2009	Measures related to exportation of raw materials
	DS407	7 May 2010	AD duties on iron/steel fasteners
	DS425	25 July 2011	AD duties on X-ray security inspection equipment
	DS432	13 March 2012	Measures related to the exportation of rare Earths, Tungsten, and Molybdenum
	DS460	13 June 2013	AD duties on high-performance stainless steel seamless tubes
	DS509	19 July 2016	Duties/measures concerning exportation of certain raw materials
	DS549	1 June 2018	Certain measures on the transfer of technology

Source: WTO dispute settlement database, available at https://www.wto.org/english/tratop_e/dispu_e/dispu_status_e.htm

policy preferences among societal interests in the EU. To understand this shift, it is useful to draw on the literature on global value chains (GVCs). The scholarship on GVCs has developed around the work of Gary Gereffi (1994, 1999) and Gereffi and colleagues (e.g. Gereffi et al. 2005). It falls outside the scope of this chapter to discuss this literature in much detail (for recent reviews of the state of the art of GVC research, see e.g. Eckhardt and Poletti 2018; Campling and Selwyn 2018), but several key elements in the GVC literature are worth highlighting here to better understand recent EU–China trade disputes.

GVCs can be defined as "sector-based structures of international trade, arising from the twin phenomena of dispersal of production (through outsourcing) and market integration (through trade liberalization)" (Gibbon 2003, p. 616; see also Bair 2005). In the past, production in most EU sectors would take place domestically. However, in order to improve competitiveness, cut costs and streamline production, many EU producers have over time redefined their core competencies and, in this context, shifted their attention to the "innovation and product strategy, marketing, and the highest value-added segments of manufacturing and services." At the same time, they reduced "their direct ownership over 'non-core' functions such as generic services and volume production" through outsourcing labour-intensive, less value-added operations to [suppliers in] countries with lower labour costs (Gereffi et al. 2005, p. 79). Many retailers in the EU have gone through a similar process: they used to buy the bulk of their products from EU suppliers but because of changing consumer preferences (better value for money) and the need to cut costs, they increasingly turned to imports by setting up decentralized production networks in a range of low-cost exporting countries. The production is commonly carried out by tiered networks of contractors in these low-cost countries that make (semi-)finished goods to the specifications of foreign buyers who, in turn, import these goods. By doing so, retailers were not only able to ask a lower price for their products and hence increase their sales, but they also saw their profits increase as a result of the elimination of some of the (expensive) middlemen in the value chain (Burch and Lawrence 2005; Eckhardt 2015; Gereffi 1999).

Many of these manufacturers and retailers in the EU have outsourced (part of their) production to or have started to source from China. In other words, China has become a key player in the GVCs of these EU firms, and this in turn means that they rely heavily on frictionless trade with China. So when the EU puts in place trade-restrictive measures like AD duties or other TDIs to protect import-competing firms in the EU, it hurts those firms in the EU that depend on imports from China. This group of "import-dependent firms" is growing in economic and political importance and, as such, is increasingly able to wield influence on EU trade policy (Eckhardt 2013; Eckhardt and Poletti 2016). That is, importers have increased their market power in key EU industries and at the same time witnessed a decrease of their collective action problems due to, among other things, a move towards concentrated interests. In certain industries, such as the food industry and apparel, this has even led to an oligopoly or a near oligopoly in some EU countries (Fuchs et al. 2011; Eckhardt 2015). As a result of these developments, import-dependent firms have managed to establish their first own interest groups and now play a much more significant role in EU trade politics, which is an important reason behind the increased politicization of EU–China trade disputes.

Conclusion

Since China has joined the WTO, EU–China trade relations have become increasingly complicated, as the EU has to play a difficult balancing act when it comes to its trade relations with China. On the one hand, the EU has basically promised to accept tough Chinese competition, as it does not want to jeopardize its carefully built-up relationship with the Chinese – which is worth hundreds of billions of euros – and because it is bound by WTO rules. On the other hand, the EU wants to match its liberalization efforts with measures for compensating, or at least cushioning, those in the EU adversely affected by increased Chinese imports, which it is doing by imposing AD duties and other trade defence measures against China. This in turn has led to rising political tensions between the EU and China as well as within the EU itself.

There is also ample scope for further research on EU–China trade relations in general and EU–China trade disputes in particular. There is very little research that has looked at the causes and consequences of EU–China trade dispute escalation and retaliation in a systematic way. There is huge variation in the unfolding and outcome of EU–China trade TDI disputes: some disputes are settled in an amicable way, while others escalate. Escalation can take the form of, first, the imposition of trade defence measures by one of the two sides and, ultimately, of WTO litigation. In the course of disputes, retaliation may play an important role as well. Retaliatory action can be either *de jure* – through the WTO dispute settlement "permissible retaliation" mechanism – or *de facto* (i.e. not officially sanctioned) in nature. Questions that future research could focus on are: can we observe changes over time when it comes to escalation and retaliation? What are the conditions under which disputes escalate or not? Moreover, it would be interesting to assess whether disputes between the EU and China are more prone to escalate than with other (Asian) countries and whether there is variation between China and other Asian countries in terms of retaliatory behaviour vis-à-vis the EU.

Future research could also focus on (ongoing) bilateral trade and investment negotiations as a way to manage EU–China trade disputes relations. Such bilateral trade negotiations have so far proven to be difficult, and it is clear that a free trade agreement (FTA) between the EU and China will not see the light of day any time soon. Yet, there was the same kind of scepticism about negotiations between China and some other major economies (in particular Australia, South Korea and Japan) and still China eventually took the step to officially launch FTA talks with these countries. That China is serious about a possible FTA with the EU, despite the political and economic tensions, became clear again in the course of 2013. Premier Li Keqiang announced in June 2013 that China would "welcome" the creation of an FTA with the EU, while earlier that year Wu Hailong, China's ambassador to the EU, held a speech in the aftermath of the 16th China–EU Summit in which he indicated that the two sides should "explore the path toward a free trade agreement, so that our economic ties will be driven by both trade and investment" (Wu 2013, p. 2). Moreover, the fact that China and the EU have started official talks over a bilateral investment treaty in 2013 is also regarded as an important step towards a possible Sino–EU FTA in the future (Meunier 2014; Shan and Wang 2015). Another interesting development is that China has signed FTAs with EFTA members in the hope that this will pave the way for a China–EU FTA in the future. In his study on the China-Iceland FTA, Lanteigne showed that when it became clear that a short-term launch of an FTA between China and the EU was not feasible (as a result of a series of political-economic disputes), China turned to Iceland in 2006 "to increase its visibility in the European economy […] through a 'side-door'" (Lanteigne 2010, p. 364).

Notes

1 "China GDP Annual Growth Rate," available at https://tradingeconomics.com/china/gdp-growth-annual.
2 PPP adjusts currencies so that a basket of goods/services has equal value in different countries.
3 An official English version of *China's EU policy Paper* is available at http://www.china.org.cn/english/international/77157.htm.
4 "Countries and Regions," available at http://ec.europa.eu/trade/creating-opportunities/bilateral-relations/countries/china/.
5 *Ibid.*
6 Regulation (EU) 2016/1036 of the European Parliament and of the Council of 8 June 2016 on protection against dumped imports from countries not members of the European Union, OJ 176/21, 30 June 2016.
7 Appellate Body Report on *US – Definitive Safeguard Measures on Imports of Certain Steel Products*, WT/DS252/R of 10 December 2003.

Bibliography

Algieri, F. (2002) 'EU economic relations with China: an institutionalist perspective', *The China Quarterly*, 169, pp. 64–77.

Bair, J. (2005) 'Global Capitalism and Commodity Chains: Looking Back, Going Forward', *Competition & Change*, 9(2), pp. 153–180.

Berkofsky, A. (2010) 'The EU-China Honeymoon is over for good: EU-China Relations and China as Actor in International Politics, Economics and Security-A European Perspective', *ISPI Commentary*, available at https://www.ispionline.it/sites/default/files/pubblicazioni/commentary_berkofsky_3.11.2010_0.pdf

Bell, J., McNaughton, R. and Young, S. (2001) '"Born-again global" Firms: An Extension to the "born global" Phenomenon', *Journal of International Management*, 7(3), pp. 173–189.

Bridges, B. (1999) *Europe and the Challenge of the Asia Pacific – Change, Continuity and Crisis*, Northampton: Edward Elgar Publishing.

Bown, C.P. (2012) 'Temporary Trade Barriers Database Including the Global Antidumping Database', *World Bank*, available at https://datacatalog.worldbank.org/dataset/temporary-trade-barriers-database-including-global-antidumping-database

Burch, D. and Lawrence, G.A. (2005) 'Supermarket own brands, supply chains and the transformation of the agri-food system', *International Journal of Sociology of Agriculture and Food*, 13(1), pp. 1–18.

Campling, L. and Selwyn, B. (2018) 'Value chains and the world economy: Genealogies and reformulations', in A. Nölke and C. May (eds.), *Handbook of the International Political Economy of the Corporation*, Cheltenham, UK: Edward Elgar Publishing, pp. 416–434.

Chi, M. (2012) 'China's participation in WTO dispute settlement over the past decade: Experiences and impacts', *Journal of International Economic Law*, 15(1), pp. 29–49.

Colin, B. (2010) 'Obstacles in upgrading the 1985 trade and economic cooperation agreement between the EU and China', *EU–China Observer*, 3, pp. 9–13.

Curran, L. (2015) 'The impact of trade policy on global production networks: The solar panel case', *Review of International Political Economy*, 22(5), pp. 1025–1054.

Curran, L. and Eckhardt, J. (2018a) 'Influencing trade policy in a multi-level system – Understanding corporate political activity in the context of global value chains and regime complexity', *Business and Politics*, 20(1), pp. 132–164.

Curran, L. and Eckhardt, J. (2020), "EU trade policy in a trade-skeptic context," *European Yearbook of International Economic Law.*

Davis, C.L. (2016) 'Deterring Disputes: WTO Dispute Settlement as a Tool for Conflict Management', *Manuscript*, available at https://scholar.harvard.edu/files/cldavis/files/davis2016.pdf

De Bièvre, D. and Eckhardt, J. (2011) 'Interest groups and EU anti-dumping policy', *Journal of European Public Policy*, 18(3), pp. 339–360.

dos Santos, N.B., Farias, R. and Cunha, R. (2005) 'Generalized System of Preferences in General Agreement on Tariffs and Trade/World Trade Organization: History and Current Issues', *Journal of World Trade*, 39(4), pp. 637–670.

Dunford, M., Lee, K.H., Liu, W. and Yeung, G. (2013) 'Geographical Interdependence, International Trade and Economic Dynamics: The Chinese and German Solar Energy Industries', *European Urban and Regional Studies*, 20(1), pp. 14–36.

Dür, A. and Zimmermann, H. (2007) 'Introduction: The EU in International Trade Negotiations', *Journal of Common Market Studies*, 45(4), pp. 771–787.

Eckhardt, J. (2010) 'The Evolution of EU Trade Policy towards China: The Case of Textiles and Clothing', in J. Men and G. Balducci (eds.), *Prospects and Challenges for EU-China Relations in the 21st Century: The Partnership and Cooperation Agreement*, Brussels: Peter Lang, pp. 151–172.

Eckhardt, J. (2011) 'Firm Lobbying and EU Trade Policymaking: Reflections on the Anti-dumping Case Against Chinese and Vietnamese Shoes (2005–2011)', *Journal of World Trade*, 45, pp. 965–991.

Eckhardt, J. (2013) 'EU Unilateral Trade Policy-Making: What Role for Import-Dependent Firms?' *Journal of Common Market Studies*, 51(6), pp. 989–1005.

Eckhardt, J. (2015) *Business Lobbying and Trade Governance: The Case of EU-China Relations*, London/Basingstoke: Palgrave Macmillan.

Eckhardt, J. and Poletti, A. (2016) 'The Politics of Global Value Chains: Import-Dependent Firms and EU–Asia Trade Agreements', *Journal of European Public Policy*, 23(10), pp. 1543–1562.

Eckhardt, J. and Poletti, A. (2018) 'Introduction: Bringing Institutions Back in the Study of Global Value Chains', *Global Policy*, 9(S2), pp. 5–11.

Eckhardt, J. and Wang, H. (2019) 'China's New Generation Trade Agreements: Importing Rules to Lock-in Domestic Reform?' *Regulation & Governance*. doi:10.1111/REGO.12258

Eglin, M. (1997) 'China's Entry into the WTO with a Little Help from the EU', *International Affairs*, 73(3), pp. 489–508.

European Commission (1994) 'Towards a New Asia Strategy', COM (1994) 314 final, Brussels, 13 July 1994.

European Commission (1995) 'A Long-Term Policy for China-Europe Relations', COM (1995) 279 final, Brussels, July 1995.

European Commission (1998) 'Building a Comprehensive Partnership with China', COM (1998) 181 final, Brussels, 25 March 1998.

European Commission (2001) 'EU Strategy towards China. Implementation of the 1998 Communication and Future Steps for a more effective EU Policy', COM (2001) 265 final, Brussels, 15 May 2001.

European Commission (2003) 'A Maturing Partnership – Shared Interests and Challenges in EU – China Relations', COM (2003) 533 final, Brussels, 10 September 2003.

Evenett, S.J. and Vermulst, E. (2005) 'The Politicisation of EC Anti-Dumping Policy: Member States, Their Votes and the European Commission', *The World Economy*, 28(5), pp. 701–717.

Fuchs, D., Kalfagianni, A. and Havinga, T. (2011) 'Actors in Private Food Governance: The Legitimacy of Retail Standards and Multistakeholder Initiatives with Civil Society Participation', *Agriculture and Human Values*, 28(3), pp. 353–367.

Gereffi, G. (1994) 'The Organization of Buyer-driven Global Commodity Chains: How US Retailers Shape Overseas Production Networks', in G. Gereffi and M. Korzeniewicz (eds.), *Commodity Chains and Global Capitalism*, Westport, CT: Praeger, pp. 95–122.

Gereffi, G. (1999) 'International Trade and Industrial Upgrading in the Apparel Commodity Chain', *Journal of International Economics*, 48(1), pp. 37–70.

Gereffi, G., Humphrey, J. and Sturgeon, T. (2005) 'The Governance of Global Value Chains', *Review of International Political Economy*, 12(1), pp. 78–104.

Gibbon, P. (2003) 'Value-chain governance, public regulation and entry barriers in the global fresh fruit and vegetable chain into the EU', *Development Policy Review*, 21(5–6): pp. 615–625.

Gstöhl, S. and De Bièvre, D. (2018) *The Trade Policy of the European Union*, London: Palgrave Macmillan.

Halverson, K. (2004) 'China's WTO Accession: Economic, Legal, and Political Implications', *Boston College International and Comparative Law Review*, 27(2), pp. 319–370.

Heron, T. (2007) 'European Trade Diplomacy and the Politics of Global Development: Reflections on the EU–China "Bra Wars" Dispute', *Government and Opposition*, 42(2), pp. 190–214.

Hu, W. and Pelkmans, J. (2017) 'China-EU Leadership in Globalisation: Ambition and capacity', *Centre for European Policy Studies (CEPS)*, available at https://www.ceps.eu/system/files/PI2017-18_WHandJP_China-EULeadership.pdf

King, T. (1999) 'Human Rights in European Foreign Policy: Success or Failure for Post-Modern Diplomacy?' *European Journal of International Law*, 10(2), pp. 313–337.

Kolk, A. and Curran, L. (2017) 'Contesting a Place in the Sun: On Ideologies in Foreign Markets and Liabilities of Origin', *Journal of Business Ethics*, 142(4), pp. 697–717.

Lanteigne, M. (2010) 'Northern Exposure: Cross-Regionalism and the China–Iceland Preferential Trade Negotiations', *The China Quarterly*, 202, pp. 362–380.

Men, J. (2012) 'The EU and China: Mismatched Partners?' *Journal of Contemporary China*, 21(74), pp. 333–349.

Men, J. and Balducci, G. (eds.) (2010) *Prospects and Challenges for EU-China Relations in the 21st Century: The Partnership and Cooperation Agreement*, Brussels: Peter Lang.

Mergenthaler, S. (2015) *Managing Global Challenges: The European Union, China and EU Network Diplomacy*, Springer VS.

Meunier, S. (2014) 'Divide and Conquer? China and the Cacophony of Foreign Investment Rules in the EU', *Journal of European Public Policy*, 21(7), pp. 996–1016.

Messerlin, P.A. (2004) 'China in the World Trade Organization: Antidumping and Safeguards', *The World Bank Economic Review*, 18(1), pp. 105–130.

Möller, K. (2002) 'Diplomatic Relations and Mutual Strategic Perceptions: China and the European Union', *The China Quarterly*, 169 (SP), pp. 10–32.

Pepermans, A. (2016) 'The Huawei Case and What It Reveals About Europe's Trade Policy', *European Foreign Affairs Review*, 21(4), pp. 539–557.

Potter, P.B. (2005) *The Chinese Legal System: Globalization and Local Legal Culture*, London: Routledge.

Shaffer, G. and Gao, H. (2018) 'China's Rise: How It Took on the US at the WTO', *The University of Illinois Law Review*, (1), pp. 115–184.

Shan, W. and Wang, L. (2015) 'The China–EU BIT and the Emerging "Global BIT 2.0"', *ICSID Review-Foreign Investment Law Journal*, 30(1), pp. 260–267.

Soliman, A. (2013) 'China's Anti-Dumping Regime and Compliance with Anti-Dumping Principles: An Analysis Using Agricultural Dumping Case Studies', *University of Miami International and Comparative Law Review*, 21(2), pp. 241–263.

Spiegel, P., Barker, A. and Hook, L. (2013) 'Brussels Offers Beijing Reprieve in Solar Panel Dispute', *Financial Times*, available at https://www.ft.com/content/1038136e-cd02-11e2-90e8-00144feab7de

Strange, R. (1998) 'EU Trade Policy towards China', in R. Strange, J. Slater and L. Wang (eds.), *Trade and Investment in China: The European Experience*, London and New York: Routledge, pp. 59–80.

The Economist (2018) 'The Chinese Century–Well Under Way', available at https://www.economist.com/graphic-detail/2018/10/27/the-chinese-century-is-well-under-way

Tsakalidou, M. (2017) 'EU's New Anti-Dumping Rules Threaten Trade Relations with China', *The Diplomat*, available at https://thediplomat.com/2017/12/eus-new-anti-dumping-rules-threaten-trade relations-with-china/

Underhill, G. (1998) *Industrial Crisis and the Open Economy: Politics, Global Trade and the Textile Industry in the Advanced Economies*, Basingstoke and London: Palgrave Macmillan.

Valero, J. (2018) 'Commission Scraps Tariffs on Chinese Solar Panels', *Euractive*, available at https://www.euractiv.com/section/economy-jobs/news/commission-scraps-tariffs-on-chinese-solar-panels/

Vermulst, E. and P. Waer (1996) *EC Anti-Dumping Law and Practice*, London: Sweet and Maxwell.

Vermulst, E. and Sud, J. (2013) 'Modernization of the EU's Trade Defense Instruments and the Law of Unintended Consequences', *Global Trade and Customs Journal*, 8(7), pp. 202–208.

Voituriez, T. and Wang, X. (2015) 'Real Challenges Behind the EU–China PV Trade Dispute Settlement', *Climate Policy*, 15(5), pp. 670–677.

Wan, M. (2001) *Human Rights in Chinese Foreign Relations: Defining and Defending National Interests*, Philadelphia: University of Pennsylvania Press.

Wellhausen, M. (2001) 'The Community Interest Test in Antidumping Proceedings of the European Union', *American University International Law Review*, 16(4), pp. 1027–1081.

Wiessala, E.G. (2005) *The Politics of Re-Orientation and Responsibility: European Union Foreign Policy and Human Rights Promotion in Asian Countries*, Doctoral dissertation, University of Central Lancashire.

Wu, H. (2013) 'Opening a New Chapter in China-EU Comprehensive Strategic Partnership', *EU-China Observer*, 6.

Young, L.W. (1998) 'China's Anti-Dumping Regulations', *The Law Offices of Wang & Wang*, available at https://www.wangandwang.com/news-articles/articles/china-anti-dumping/

Zimmermann, H. (2007) 'Realist Power Europe? The EU in the Negotiations about China's and Russia's WTO Accession', *JCMS: Journal of Common Market Studies*, 45(4), pp. 813–832.

4 EU–Asia investor–state disputes

Assertive legalism for economic and political autonomy

*Leïla Choukroune**

Beyond trade, the WTO and China, Asia's rapport with international investment dispute is equally most critical. After an obvious phase of rapprochement, starting in the mid-1990s, a certain distance has again developed, especially over dispute settlement for countries like Indonesia or India. Initially less integrated in the legal governance of international investment than in that of world trade, Asian states have above all sought to preserve their regulatory autonomy and thus their own development model. The progressive internationalization of Asian firms has, however, changed the *done* as emerging countries' foreign directive investment (FDI) now represents a large amount of the global volume. It remains to be seen whether capital exporter Asia will seek to renew investment law in taking into account societal issues at its centre through the integration of norms such as human rights and the environment. But Asia is participating to investor-state dispute settlement (ISDS) and so changing it. While Asian dispute stories largely vary with, for example, India at the centre of the investment dispute field, a silent revolution is taking place, so much so that some have argued in favour of an aggressive legalism supposedly best describing the new Asian dispute settlement activism.

In putting Asia's role in international investment dispute settlement into a legal and political perspective (section two), this chapter analyzes a number of recent landmark disputes (section three) and concludes with a critical account of the aggressive legalism thesis in favour of a more balanced approach of a truly universal international law (section four).

Asia and international investment law and disputes settlement

International investment law: a progressive and contrasted adhesion

It is an impossible task to render an accurate picture of such a diverse continent as Asia in the limited space of a book chapter. Foreign investment and investment law (domestic and international) have naturally different functions and

* I would like to thank the organizers of the Taiwan Conference on which this chapter is based, Chien-Huei Wu and Frank Gaenssmantel, for their invitation to contribute to a challenging and stimulating approach to EU–Asia Trade.

objectives. However, and in trying to avoid misleading simplifications, a few trends are interesting to highlight.

While Pakistan was the first ever country to sign a bilateral investment treaty (BIT) with Germany in 1959, a country like Japan, which has been a dynamic investor all over the world and remains the fourth capital exporter globally after the US, China and the Netherlands (WIR 2017), has been a late comer on the investment treaty scene. Before the early 2000s, indeed, Japan had only ratified a handful of BITs.[1] It is now a party to 28 BITs (against 127 for China) and 20 treaties with investment provisions (TIPs) (against 22 for China), most of them having been signed from the late 2000s and a large number very recently. However, Japan has been very active in the latest treaty negotiations, from the 2018 EU–Japan Economic Partnership Agreement to the 2018 Comprehensive and Progressive Agreement for Trans-Pacific Partnership (CPTPP), the new TPP.[2] The recent negotiation has been fascinating in that Japan seems to have literally replaced the failing United States in the hope of furthering its economic interest in Asia Pacific against the backdrop of a more and more powerful China. Japan indeed managed to revive the 2016 treaty text and convinced the 11 remaining members of the original TPP to follow its leadership. While two-thirds of the initial text has not been modified, the rest of it has been improved and can generally be considered as a carefully drafted legal piece showing a number of interesting advances in terms, for example, of protection of health and the environment in relation to (indirect) expropriation or the clarification of certain standards of treatment such as the fair and equitable treatment (FET) as well as dispute settlement.[3] A sound supporter of multilateralism, Japan, as we will see below with dispute settlement, remains discrete but certainly not passive.

Member countries of the Association of Southeast Asian Nations (ASEAN) offer a contrasted approach to investment with a country like Singapore having signed 46 BITs and 33 TIPs, while Lao has a much smaller presence on the global investment map and network (24 BITs and 16 TIPs) and Indonesia has recently terminated most of its BITs.[4] The case of Indonesia is particularly interesting since it decided to terminate its BIT with the Netherlands in March 2014 and a number of additional countries (67) in the following months. What appeared at that time as a radical decision is not quite surprising if a reaction to the landmark cases *Churchill Mining plc v Indonesia* and *Planet Mining Pty Ltd v Indonesia*, brought under the UK-Indonesia and Australia-Indonesia BITs, respectively and relating to expropriation claims arising from a coal project in East Kalimantan (Borneo). While eventually decided in favour of the State after a long, rocambolesque and costly procedure involving fraud and forgery, which annulment is now pending, this real saga has deeply impacted the country's trust in ISDS and its investment regime indeed (see our analysis below).[5] However, Indonesia is a member of ASEAN and signatory to the ASEAN Comprehensive Investment Agreement (ACIA), which provides protection to foreign investors who are from other ASEAN countries while the ASEAN has built a network of TIPs with a large number of Asian countries including New Zealand and Australia and the ASEAN-Australia-New-Zealand Foreign Trade Agreement (AANZFTA).[6]

In the same critical move towards ISDS, in July 2016, India sent a notice to 58 countries announcing its intention to terminate various BITs. Although a number of them are still in force for a period of 10–15 years on the basis of the sunset clauses they integrated, this decision was the direct result of its recent – and first – condemnation by an arbitral tribunal in the *White Industries case*. While based on the India-Australia BIT, the large interpretation of the most-favoured-nation (MFN) standard by the investment tribunal resulted in finding that standard of *"effective means of asserting claims and enforcing rights"* could be found in India-Kuwait BIT through the MFN indeed...[7]. It then concluded that: *"The Republic of India has breached its obligation to provide effective means of asserting and enforcing rights"* with respect to the White Industries Australia Limited's investment pursuant to the art. 4(2) of the BIT incorporating the article 4(5) of the India Kuwait BIT."[8] For these reasons, and because many other relatively similar (tax-related) cases are underway (see below), the Indian government has decided to review its BIT policy including its BIT model, the latest draft having no mention of the MFN standard, which may prove problematic for Indian investors going global (Ranjan 2015, 2019). Interestingly, India took an opposite stance to China as far as national treatment (NT) and MFN are concerned. While it generally granted the two standards of treatment (as well as FET) in most of its 1990s and 2000s treaties, its recent attempt shows a real suspicion against the MFN and so its absence in the new model BIT. Although a relatively latecomer on the BIT scene with a first treaty signed with the UK in 1994, India has progressively developed a very large number of treaties with developed and developing countries all over the world. While it restricted itself to BIT until 2004, it then accepted to enter into regional negotiations and FTA with countries such as Japan, Korea and Malaysia. The Regional Comprehensive Economic Partnership (RCEP) negotiations are to observe in this regard for they gather the 10 members of the ASEAN together with Japan, China, South Korea, India, Australia and New Zealand and indeed India. Once concluded, most probably in 2019, RCEP will cater to half of the world's gross domestic product (GDP) and half of the world's population.[9]

A similar independent path was somehow taken by Beijing. As far as China is concerned, one generally identifies three moments if not three generations of international investment agreements (IIAs). The initial phase started with China's first BIT with Sweden in 1982 and lasted until the late 1990s.[10] It was largely characterized by a prudent if not reluctant approach to normative internationalization with NT seldom granted and international dispute settlement limited to the determination of the amount of compensation for expropriation. From 1998 onwards, with the China-Barbados BIT of July 1998 that offered, for the first time, foreign investors unrestricted access to international arbitration, China entered into a new phase of BIT drafting inspired by EU model treaties and framing NT in a less restrictive and somehow personalized manner depending on whether the country was a developed or developing nation. The last phase, starting from 2007 and the China-Korea BIT, is generally described as a more liberal one partly inspired by the North American Free Trade Agreement

(NAFTA) in the sense that Chinese treaties granted FET in *de facto* accepting certain customary international law features, but also the NT and MFN often defined in using the now generalized yet difficult to interpret "in like circumstances" terminology (Hadley 2013; Berger 2013). To these three generations, one could add a fourth one corresponding to today's mega-regional trade and investment negotiations and China's expansion as a global investor. This fourth generation may well be characterized – and this is not China specific – by a certain distantiation from the late 1990s NAFTA model in relation to today's new investment issues. In addition, it integrates the lessons learned from China's accession and participation to the WTO. Lastly, the recent wave of foreign trade agreements (FTAs) drafting does not seem to add much to China's general BIT approach on the contrary to some thesis often put forward and according to which a regional negotiation's aim is to further liberalize trade in introducing greater protection and flexibilities.

It is now fascinating to observe how Asia has integrated the ISDS field. As progressive as its treaty adhesion, this evolution is now quite noticeable and corresponds, for most Asian states, to a phase of liberalization and greater integration, which started in the 1990s with investor-friendly treaties now used as a basis for a variety of claims. As visible from Table 4.1, Asia is now very much present in ISDS. It is mostly a host state with notably 24 cases (all quite recent) for a country like India, and to a lesser extent, yet fast-changing fashion, a home state with five

Table 4.1 Dispute settlement: Asia a new and fast-changing actor

Country	ISDS cases as host state	ISDS cases as home state
Bangladesh	1	0
Bhutan	0	0
Cambodia	0	0
China (PRC)	3	5
India	24	5
Indonesia	7	0
Japan	0	3
Korea	3	4
Laos	4	0
Malaysia	3	3
Mauritius	2	8
Myanmar	1	0
Mongolia	4	0
Nepal	0	0
Pakistan	9	0
Philippines	5	0
Singapore	0	3
Sri Lanka	4	0
Thailand	2	0
Vietnam	5	0

Source: Compiled by the author on the basis of UNCTAD, Investment Policy Hub, available at http://investmentpolicyhub.unctad.org/ISDS

cases, respectively for China and India, four for Japan or even eight for the tiny Mauritius, the latest cases having been initiated by multinational companies welcomed by Mauritius and so using its BIT as legal basis for international claims. Among these cases, a few have made the headlines and, in particular for India, the now infamous 2003 *Bechtel v. India* related to shareholding in local corporations established to operate the Dabhol power project in the state of Maharashtra, the 2010 *White Industries* case alluded to above, the 2015 *Cairn UK Holding* brought against India on the basis of yet another tax issue and the *Vodafone* saga[11] (discussed below).

As far is China is concerned, it is most probably the *Ping An v. Belgium* case that has produced the largest number of reactions, for it came as a surprise to European countries not prepared to see their interests challenged by a Chinese claimant (see Table 4.2).

As we can observe from Table 4.2, a large number of these ISDS cases have been brought by European firms or against European states. Here again, India provides the largest contingent of claims as a host state, primarily with UK companies responsible for the greatest number of claims, but also as a home state with the hardly studied, yet important *Flemingo Duty Free V. Poland* decided in favour of the Indian investor (see below).

Lastly, it is important to put this recent integration of Asian states in the ISDS field in perspective and against the backdrop of intra-Asian ISDS. Asian companies are indeed claiming against Asian states with, for example, six cases against India introduced by investors from Mauritius (five) and Japan (one) and one by India against Indonesia.[12] Chinese investors are also claiming against Asian states with the 2010 *Beijing Shougang and others v. Mongolia* decided in favour of the state and the 2017 *Sanum Investments v. Laos* II (pending).[13]

Table 4.2 EU–Asia-related ISDS

Country	ISDS as host state	ISDS as home state
Bangladesh	1	0
China	1	1
India	16	4
Indonesia	3	0
Japan		2
Korea	2	
Laos	2	
Malaysia	3	
Mauritius	2	0
Mongolia	2	0
Pakistan	4	0
Philippines	5	
Sri Lanka	3	0
Thailand	1	
Vietnam	4	

Source: Compiled by the author on the basis of UNCTAD, Investment Policy Hub, available at http://investmentpolicyhub.unctad.org/ISDS

Table 4.3 Intra-Asian ISDS

Country	ISDS as host state	ISDS as home state
China	0	2
Korea	1	0
India	6	1
Indonesia	3	
Japan	0	1
Laos	2	
Malaysia	0	1
Mauritius	6	
Mongolia	1	0
Myanmar	1	0
Pakistan	1	0
Singapore	0	3

Source: Compiled by the author on the basis of UNCTAD, Investment Policy Hub, available at http://investmentpolicyhub.unctad.org/ISDS

This burgeoning trend is likely to grow in relation to the greater integration of Asian firms globally as well as ambitious regional deals (RCEP) and other routes like the Chinese-led Belt and Road Initiative (BRI) for which Beijing has dedicated two branches of China International Commercial Court (CICC), one in Shenzhen to tackle the Maritime Road disputes and one in Xi'an to settle overland Belt issues (Table 4.3).

Responding and claiming: key disputes in perspectives

Let us now take a closer look at a number of chosen disputes, for they are revealing of the trends described above and show indeed an assertive Asia responding to European claims but also claiming against European states. This impressionistic account is naturally limited to the dedicated space of our demonstration but highlights important trends and a certain mastery of legal techniques, as well as a form of creativity in countering arguments, although these moves are not necessarily rule-based nor testify of the greatest legal rigour and consistency.

Vodafone v. India

In what is now a real legal saga, New Delhi recently managed to – momentarily – twist some legal arguments in its favour hence creating a stimulating debate on the limitations of international arbitration and the role domestic courts could play in framing disputes.

The first episode started in 2006 when Vodafone BV International (a Dutch company) bought Hutchison Telecommunications International Ltd (a Cayman Islands company), which it acquired 67 per cent shares in, and Indian Company Hutchison Essar Ltd (HEL) for the amount of US$ 11 billion. In reaction to this transaction,

Indian tax authorities imposed a tax of US\$ 2.2 billion on Vodafone. But the company contended that the transaction did not involve assets based in India and so was not taxable in India. In 2010, the Bombay High Court decided in favour of the state.[14] This decision was then challenged by the company in the Indian Supreme Court, which reversed the Bombay ruling for this was an offshore transaction on which India had no territorial tax jurisdiction.[15] But the saga did not stop there. In an unpredictable move, the Indian government amended its tax law and tried to impose its new rules retroactively to Vodafone. This naturally did not give the image of a stable and rule of law-based country but, on the contrary, is likely to have triggered a series of new tax-related investment disputes. As a logical consequence, Vodafone decided to challenge the Indian government in bringing an arbitration claim under the India-Netherlands BIT.[16] In addition, and while the first case is still pending, Vodafone served a new notice of arbitration in January 2017 under, this time, the India-UK BIT, challenging the same tax imposition.[17] Here comes a new domestic episode. The Indian government decided to play the "abuse of process" card to counter the second arbitration deemed superfluous. The Delhi High Court took the case and rendered a controversial decision concluding to an abuse of process indeed, as the two companies were *de facto* owned by the same shareholders.[18] The Delhi High Court then passed an *ex-parte* interim order in August 2017, restraining Vodafone from pursuing the second arbitration. While the issue of abuse of process in arbitration is fascinating and still very much debated (Gaillard 2017), the real question remains on whether an Indian court has any legal ground to issue a sort of anti-arbitration pronouncement (Ranjan 2019). One has then to look into domestic arbitration legislation to see if it can apply to BITs but also the very BITs for the dispute in question, as the countries (India and the Netherlands and the UK) gave explicit consent to arbitration. A more logical path would have been to push in favour of a joint arbitration of the different disputes. In any case, international tribunals do not seem particularly impressed by domestic courts' anti-arbitration injunctions as illustrated by the *SGS v. Pakistan* case in which the Supreme Court of Pakistan failed to stop the arbitration in issuing an order.[19] The arbitration process initiated by a Swiss company went on but was eventually discontinued. The very last episode of the Vodafone saga, however, took place in May 2018, at the very same Delhi High Court. In a new well-argued and lengthy decision addressing the questions of the applicability of the Indian Arbitration and Conciliation Act of 1996 (amended in 2015) to BITs, as well as Indian international obligations, the Court reversed its previous judgment.[20] According to the Court:

> 104. (…) there is no unqualified or indefeasible right to arbitrate. The National Courts in India do have and retain the jurisdiction to restrain international treaty arbitrations which are oppressive, vexatious, inequitable or constitute an abuse of the legal process.
> (…) But
> 120. There is no presumption or assumption that filing of multiple claims by entities in the same vertical corporate chain with regard to the same measure is per se vexatious.

(...) And

123. Since it is the case of the Plaintiff-Union of India that the claim under the Netherlands-India BIPA is without jurisdiction, invocation of another treaty by the parent company cannot be regarded as an abuse per se.

(...) Therefore

The Tribunal while deciding the said issue will take into account the Defendants' undertaking to this Court that if the Plaintiff-Union of India gives its consent, it would agree to consolidation of the two BIPA arbitration proceedings before the India-United Kingdom BIPA Tribunal. Accordingly, the ex parte interim order dated 22nd August, 2017 stands vacated. No order as to costs.[21]

The Court hence concluded in favour of the consolidation of the two arbitrations (if agreed by the parties) and in any event vacates its 2017 order. Indeed, as elaborated above, the Court concluded that there was no "vexatious" aspect in this very procedure and there was no abuse of procedure *per se*. Hence the Court recommended the consolidation of the two arbitrations but did not want to interfere further in trying to stop the procedure. What does this case say about India in ISDS? India *is* and *is not* a rule-based country at the same time, and it is certainly in search for a consistent strategy. There is both a sense of confusion created by contradictory legislative and judicial decisions and the idea that argumentative India is easily able to claim and counterclaim as demonstrated below by the *Flemingo* case.

Ping An v. Belgium

Also trying to gain confidence on the arbitration scene, China surprised many when one of its companies, *Ping An*, now the most powerful insurance company in the world, brought a case against Belgium.[22] Two BITs constituted the legal ground of the dispute: the 1986 and 2009 BITs between China and the Belgium-Luxembourg Economic Union (BLEU). The case took place against the backdrop of the global financial crisis of the late 2000s and the "rescue plan" of the company *Fortis* by Belgium. Between October 2007 and July 2008, *Ping An* acquired shares in *Fortis* in the open market for an aggregate sum of more than € 2 billion and hence became Fortis' single largest shareholder. On September 15, 2008, *Lehman Brothers* collapsed and a massive global financial crisis erupted. To save *Fortis* from complete failure, in September 2008, Belgium agreed with the Netherlands and Luxembourg to carry out a rescue plan agreed upon by *Fortis*. A second plan was later carried out in October. The claimant, *Ping An*, submitted that its interest was violated by these plans for the following reasons:

(a) Belgium failed to afford the Claimants' investments the required standard of protection, with respect to the Claimants' legitimate expectations as to the stability, transparency and predictability of Belgium's legal and business environment (including in particular, Belgium's banking sector)

(b) Belgium failed to adopt more reasonable and/or effective alternatives to the Interventions (which were extremely harmful to the Claimants), and instead coerced Fortis into accepting Belgium's expropriation of a substantial and significant part of the Claimants' investment;

(c) Belgium failed fairly and fully to compensate the Claimants in connection with the Interventions, and unjustly enriched itself in the process; and

(d) Belgium failed to afford the Claimants and their investments due process in its administrative decision-making, and arbitrarily and unreasonably discriminated against the Claimants and their investments by failing to provide the same assistance it provided to one of Fortis' competitors, and to the Claimants' expropriated investment itself, but only once it had been nationalized.[23]

Four arguments are put forward by the company indeed: failure by Belgium to fulfil the standard of protection with respect to the company's legitimate expectations, failure to adopt more reasonable and/or effective alternative, failure to fairly and fully compensate, failure to afford due process of law which resulted in arbitrarily and unreasonable discrimination against the Chinese investor. However, Belgium raised five objections to the jurisdiction of the arbitral Tribunal: objections *ratione temporis, ratione materiae, ratione voluntatis*, absence of *prima facie* case and involvement of a third party, the Netherlands, for which the arbitration was not able to address claims. Of these objections, the Tribunal retained and developed only one, the most important in its view: the objection *ratione temporis*. Indeed, in a quite questionable legal approach, the investor, *Ping An*, had brought a claim on the basis of the 2009 BIT provisions, which planned for greater access to dispute resolution but were obviously not available retroactively to preexisting disputes. It was then easy for the Tribunal to demonstrate the inadequacy of the legal approach of the Claimant in these terms:

The essential difference between the 1986 BIT and the 2009 BIT for present purposes is that:

(1) the combined effect of the 1986 BIT, Article 10, and the Protocol, Article 6, is that by way of exception to the jurisdiction of national courts, disputes "relating to the amount of compensation payable in case of expropriation, nationalization or any other measure similarly affecting investments" may (at the option of the investor) be submitted to the national courts of the place of the investment or be submitted directly to international arbitration under (at the option of the investor) Stockholm Chamber of Commerce Rules or ICSID Rules, whereas all other disputes may not be so submitted; and

(2) the effect of the 2009 BIT, Article 8, is that a much wider range of disputes (not limited to the amount of compensation for expropriation and analogous measures) may be submitted to ICSID arbitration.

As indicated above, it is common ground that the dispute arose before the 2009 BIT came into force. The Request for Arbitration treats the dispute as having arisen at the latest by October 14, 2009, and Belgium also relies on the fact that the dispute arose before the 2009 BIT came into force. It is also clear that the 2009 BIT does not expressly deal with the fate of disputes arising before December 1, 2009 which had been notified under the 1986 BIT but were not then the subject of judicial or arbitral process (in the sense of such proceedings having been formally initiated).

For all these reasons, in the view of the Tribunal there is nothing in the wording of the 2009 BIT to justify on the basis of its express language, or on the basis of an implication or inferences, that the more extensive remedies under the 2009 BIT would be available to pre-existing disputes that had been notified under the 1986 BIT but not yet subject to arbitral or judicial process.

It would, of course, be regrettable, if the Claimants had valid claims (on which there is a sharp difference of view between the parties) for which they had no effective remedy. But the Tribunal has, for the reasons given, come to the conclusion that there is no legitimate method of interpretation, having regard to the requirements and the Vienna Convention and the rules reflected therein, which gives the Claimants the remedy which they seek in this arbitration under the 2009 BIT. It should be emphasized, however, that the Tribunal takes no position on whether remedies may remain available to the Claimants either under the 1986 BIT or through Belgium's domestic courts.

Belgium's objection to the jurisdiction *ratione temporis* therefore prevails, and there is accordingly no reason for the Tribunal to address the other objections.[24]

What is there to understand from this lengthy yet precise reasoning? Two quite simple things: while the 2009 BIT offered a much wider range of possibilities for disputes to be submitted to ICSID arbitration, it came into force after the very case in question. Hence only the 1986 BIT can apply to this dispute no matter the possible valid claims argued by the Claimants for which they may have no effective remedy on this treaty basis. Regretting that the merits of the claims could not be addressed, the Tribunal so dismissed the dispute on the basis of the objection *ratione temporis* and the inadequate recourse to the 2009 BIT by the Claimant.

Although unsuccessful for the Chinese party, this case remains a landmark in that it shows a truly combative if not aggressive Chinese company battling for its interests against a European state. What was a quite unique situation at the time might now occur more frequently in the context of the massive Chinese investment encouraged by Beijing all over Europe within or without the Belt and Road Initiative.

Flemingo v. Poland

In *Flemingo v. Poland*, an Indian investor won, for the first time, against a European state.[25] Administered by the Permanent Court of Arbitration (PCA) on the basis of the United Nations Commission on International Trade Law (UNCITRAL) arbitration rules, this dispute arose out of the Polish Airports State

Enterprise's termination of a lease contract for retail stores at the Warsaw airport entered into with BH Travel, a duty-free operator in which Flemingo held indirect interests. Interestingly, the Claimant, headquartered in Dubai, chose to pursue the claim under the India-Poland BIT in place of the UAE-Poland BIT, which according to the Tribunal, did not amount to illegal treaty shopping. The Tribunal indeed decided in favour of the Indian investor in awarding EUR 20 million in compensation for the suspension of leases and key contracts by a Polish state-owned entity that amounted to a violation of the FET and expropriation provisions under the India-Poland BIT. In its reasoning, the Tribunal contributed directly to the issue of the definition of investor and investment and the clarification of what is often denounced as treaty shopping. It stated in particular:

> The Tribunal does not consider that Claimant has engaged in forum shopping by instigating the present claim.
>
> (...) In *Saluka*, to which Respondent refers to exclude Claimant from Treaty protection, the tribunal in fact confirmed that it is not necessary for the claimant to actively operate the investment and that a subsequent acquisition of shares does not preclude the claimant from having recourse to arbitration under the applicable treaty – as long as the acquisition was not made after the breach of the investment treaty has occurred. In this case, Claimant's acquisition of its indirect shareholding in Baltona took place on 31 March 2011 (when Claimant became the sole owner of Flemingo International), which is well before the dispute between BH Travel and PPL arose.
>
> Likewise, the fact that the termination of the Lease Agreements was – and is – the subject-matter of many proceedings before the Polish domestic courts is also not an obstacle for the Tribunal to exercise its jurisdiction, as defined by the India-Poland Treaty, which does not restrict tribunals' jurisdiction in cases where proceedings are underway before domestic courts. Besides, it appears from the record of evidence in this case that much of the litigation before Polish courts has been initiated by PPL.
>
> It is also not an impediment for the Tribunal to exercise jurisdiction if Claimant, an Indian company, allegedly does not deploy commercial activities in India and is not involved in the Polish operations of the Flemingo Group. The Treaty does not impose any of these requirements upon Claimant and it is not for the Tribunal to add such restrictions to the definition and scope of the Treaty.[26]

In a quite liberal approach indeed, the Tribunal concludes that there was no "forum shopping" in this case no matter the absence of commercial activity of this Indian company in India and its lack of involvement in the Polish operations of the group (Flemingo). This case is, in this regard and on the basis of the Tribunal reasoning on the question of expropriation, absolutely fascinating. For the first time, an Asian and India company used the very same legal tools and techniques resorted to by its Western counterparts against developing states, against a European country, Poland. Here again, with the internationalization of

Indian firms, but also in reaction to the large number of cases brought against India, it is likely that new cases are brought by Indian investors against a number of European states where they operate.

Churchill Mining Plc and Planet Mining Pty Ltd v. Indonesia

Churchill Mining Plc and Planet Mining Pty Ltd v. Indonesia provides yet another fascinating illustration of recent and unexpected developments in EU–Asia investment dispute litigation. Here is a real arbitral saga full of rocambolesque developments involving fraud and forgery, state's decentralization, local powers and nothing less than 20 procedural orders issued by the ICSID arbitral tribunal as well as an application for annulment of which the result is yet to be seen.[27] The facts and the procedure revealed are complex. But to simplify without hopefully altering the essence of the problems, the situation could be summarized as follow: the case was brought under the UK-Indonesia and Australia-Indonesia BITs, respectively and related to expropriation claims arising from a coal project in East Kalimantan (Borneo). Churchill is indeed a British company listed in the Alternative Investment Market (AIM) of the London Stock Exchange while Planet is an Australian subsidiary of Churchill. The two original cases brought by Churchill and Planet were joined, for they addressed similar factual issues. At the time of the investment, in 2005, Indonesia mining law regime was decentralized with the head of each "Bupati" (a regency and form of administrative unit) given the power to licence and regulate foreign investment for, as in this case, the exploration and mining of coal. Indonesia is indeed an extremely diverse and resources rich country with a territory spread out on about 18,000 islands. It is then understandable that decentralization could be seen as a good governance mechanism although, as we will see, a challenging one. Three main types of licences could be granted: general survey, exploration and exploitation. These three licences were consecutively granted to the investors. However, without prior notice, the Regent later issued decrees revoking the licences. Following several domestic procedures, the Claimants attempted to ascertain the status of their investment and engage with the government of Indonesia. The case eventually went to the Indonesian Supreme Court without success. Hence, in May 2012, Churchill filed a request for arbitration with ICSID alleging that its investments had been unlawfully expropriated and treated in a manner that violated the Fair and Equitable Treatment (FET) standard of the BIT (revocation of the licenses). In November 2012, Planet filled a similar request for arbitration under the Australia-Indonesia BIT this time. The two arbitrations were later consolidated while the Claimants were asking for over USD 1.3 billion in damages for Indonesia's treaty violations. This came naturally as a massive shock to Indonesia and its public opinion, which soon started questioning the value of ISDS and BITs.

Indonesia's defence was based on the claim of fraud. The Claimants were said to have forged licenses. Giving a sort of hint to the Claimants about its future decision, a few months prior to it, in September 2016, the Tribunal pointed out to the *Minnotte v. Poland* decision in which the following three important questions were addressed[28]:

1. The admissibility in international law of claims tainted by fraud or forgery where the alleged perpetrator is a third party;
2. The lack of due care or negligence of the investor to investigate the factual circumstances surrounding the making of an investment; and
3. The deliberate "closing of eyes" to indications of serious misconduct or crime, or an unreasonable failure to perceive such indications (the *Minnotte* direction).[29]

As a logical consequence, in December 2016, the Tribunal rendered its award finding that as the documents on which the case was based were not authentic and authorized, and the perpetrator of the fraud was most likely the Claimants' local partner including maybe the Regent himself, it decided to dismiss the claims:

> The Tribunal agrees with the Respondent that claims arising from rights based on fraud or forgery which a claimant deliberately or unreasonably ignored are inadmissible as a matter of international public policy.
>
> (...)
>
> The facts established above reveal the existence of a large scale fraudulent scheme implemented to obtain four coal mining concession areas in the EKCP. The forgeries are directly linked to the claims raised by the Claimants which all relate to the EKCP. The record contains 34 forged documents including ten mining licenses and four decrees purporting to re-enact the revoked Exploitation Licenses. With the exception of four of these forged documents, of them were filed by the Claimants in support of their case.
>
> The Tribunal has no hesitation in finding that the scheme was put in place intentionally. The record shows repeated acts of forgery, starting with the fabrication of the Survey and Exploration Licenses to gain access to the coal reserves. The record also shows that Ridlatama sent copies of these licenses to "affected governmental departments" so as to "ensure that our licenses were officially recognized at all government levels." By doing so, a façade was built that would provide legitimacy to an illegal enterprise.
>
> (...)
>
> The inadmissibility applies to all the claims raised in this arbitration, because the entire EKCP project is an illegal enterprise affected by multiple forgeries and all claims relate to the EKCP. This is further supported by the Claimants' lack of diligence in carrying out their investment.[30]

As demonstrated above indeed, the facts revealed a large "fraudulent scheme" to obtain mining concession. The whole project was so an "illegal enterprise." However, this decision is not without raising the question of State's responsibility as pointed out by the Claimants who have later requested for annulment on the basis that the Tribunal had:

- Seriously departed from several fundamental rules of procedure (warranting annulment under Art. 52(1)(d) of the ICSID Convention);
- Manifestly exceeded its powers (warranting annulment under Art. 52(1)(b) of the ICSID Convention).
- Failed to State the reasons on which the Award was based, including by giving reasons that were contradictory (warranting annulment under Art. 52(1)(e) of the ICSID Convention).[31]

The above-mentioned grounds for annulment are indeed in line with Art. 52 (annulment) of the ICSID Convention. Seen as a post-award remedy, annulment is quite rare but has been recently tried as a form of alternative to the absence of an appeal mechanism. A party may apply for full or partial annulment of an award on the basis of one or more of the following five grounds: (1) the Tribunal was not properly constituted; (2) the Tribunal has manifestly exceeded its powers; (3) there was corruption on the part of a member of the Tribunal; (4) there has been a serious departure from a fundamental rule of procedure; or (5) the award has failed to state the reasons on which it is based. While decided in favour of the state after a long, rocambolesque and costly procedure involving fraud and forgery, which annulment is now pending, this case remains fascinating as it basically addresses all contemporary issues in investment arbitration from due diligence in complex resources-led investment to decentralization of powers to possibly corrupted local authorities, procedural complexities and the question of annulment of arbitral awards. It led Indonesia to terminate its BITs and question the delegation of certain strategic powers to local government in a country where governance remains a complicated problem.[32]

Conclusion: Assertive Asia

What is "aggressive legalism" – where does it find its roots and is it revealing of developing Asia–EU trade and dispute settlement realities? A simple answer comes to mind: the concept originated in EU and US trade negotiations in reference to Japan's uses in the 1990s of the WTO dispute settlement system and has been constantly referred to as qualifying other Asian countries' strategies. As such, in 2001, Saadia M. Pekkanen argued that aggressive legalism was "a conscious strategy where a substantive set of international legal rules can be made to serve as both 'shield' and 'sword' in trade disputes among sovereign states." Already in the late 1990s China too had made use of its legal weapons and so been equally described as legally "aggressive." The dispute between China and Japan between December 2000 and December 2001 over three agricultural products gave an early indication of Beijing's determination to put its new legal arsenal to good use. In December 2000, Japan had undertaken a survey on taking provisional safeguards on several agricultural products, including shitake mushrooms and a variety of Asian leeks imported from China. On April 10, 2001, Tokyo announced it would take a provisional safeguard measure for 200 days (the very first since its entry into the GATT in 1955). In reaction to what it considered discriminatory treatment, Beijing decided to impose a special customs tax on 100 per cent of certain Japanese imports. The dispute was finally resolved in December 2001 through negotiations between the Chinese and Japanese economy ministers. While China was not yet a member of the WTO, both parties very frequently referred to the WTO agreements in their legal arguments. But it was the provisional safeguard measures China adopted with respect to certain American steel products that grabbed specialists' attention. The measures took effect on May 24, 2002, less than six months after China adopted legislation on safeguards, causing some specialists to qualify Beijing's attitude as "aggressive legalism." China also joined a group of seven complainants (the European Union, South Korea, Japan, Norway, Switzerland, New Zealand and Brazil) who took action before the WTO against President Bush's March 5, 2002, decision to impose safeguard measures on steel imports. In its final report of July 11, 2003, the WTO concluded these measures were illegal. Conversely, the United States introduced its first procedure requesting consultations before the DSB against China on March 18, 2004, with respect to the Chinese value-added tax on integrated circuits. The European Union, Japan, Mexico and Taiwan wanted to participate in these consultations, but the American Trade representative, Robert B. Zoellick, announced on July 8, 2004, in a press conference that the dispute had been resolved at the end of the consultation phase. The WTO was notified of this agreement eight days later. Such "aggressiveness" had pushed China to use its new legal weapons in the same way that the most hardened WTO members do, even though it has numerous problems implementing its commitments domestically. While this story indicates a certain taste for quasi-judicial risk, it above all illustrates China's desire to reach beyond the domestic law to confront international norms, perhaps to better assimilate them (Nakagawa 2002, pp. 1019–1036).[33]

Aggressive legalism then appears as a rather paradoxical concept to describe developing Asian states' recourse to trade and investment disputes. A silent revolution is indeed taking place, but one which could be characterized differently that is in a more subtle manner by *other* actors of trade and investment, and the EU in particular, which has constantly used the same tools but argued in favour of the benefits of a "multilateral rule of law," as exemplified by the WTO's compulsory jurisdiction and its ambition to "provide security and predictability to the multilateral trading system," as stated in the Dispute Settlement Understanding (DSU) Art. 3.2, while preserving "the rights and obligations of Members under the covered agreements, and to clarify the existing provisions of those agreements in accordance with customary rules of interpretation of public international law" without diminishing "the rights and obligations provided in the covered agreements." In the dispute settlement domain, more precisely, we have seen an upcoming Asia mastering certain legal techniques and voluntarily choosing a more assertive path to better protect its own strategic interest and heterodox choices. Sometimes deprived of coherence or consistence in their strategies (India, Indonesia), Asian states are nevertheless changing the ISDS scene. While the first step of investor–state dispute resolution often takes the form of a negotiation and so implies a form of hybrid diplomatic engagement, Asia has shown that it is not dispute adverse and will not resort more systematically to the available legal mechanism nationally and internationally. There is no general conclusion to be drawn here. Recent BITs denunciations by Indonesia or India do not mean that they are necessarily adverse to ISDS. They are certainly not keen to favour state-to-state dispute resolution mechanisms, for these are rather artificial, and diplomatic means are not suitable as they may be in trade. But it shows they are inclined to revalue their own domestic juridical system they are ready to reform for more investment protection and certainty. China or Japan would not disagree, as they feel their systems are certainly good to tackle disputes. However, as major investors abroad, they tend to support ISDS. Japan, for example, has recently introduced three energy-related cases against Spain on the basis of the Energy Charter Treaty.[34] While these cases are still pending, it is likely more will come against European countries. It remains to be seen if the lessons learnt in the ISDS context will now impact on treaty drafting (RCEP, BITs in the Chinese-led BRI), but Asia is to be counted in the new making of a genuine international law.

Notes

1 UNCTAD Investment Policy Hub, available at http://investmentpolicyhub.unctad. org/IIA.
2 The EU- and Japan-related negotiation pages, available at http://ec.europa.eu/trade/ policy/in-focus/eu-japan-economic-partnership-agreement/ and https://www.jetro. go.jp/en/eu-japan.html.
3 'Comprehensive and Progressive Agreement for Trans-Pacific Partnership Preamble' http://investmentpolicyhub.unctad.org/Download/TreatyFile/5672.
4 'International Investment Agreements Navigator: IIAs by Economy', available at http://investmentpolicyhub.unctad.org/IIA/IiasByCountry#iiaInnerMenu.
5 ICSID Case No. ARB/12/14 and 12/40 *Churchill Mining PLC and Planet Mining Pty Ltd v. Republic of Indonesia* [2017] (hereinafter *Churchill Mining PLC and Planet Mining Pty Ltd v. Republic of Indonesia*).
6 The ACIA, available at https://asean.org/?static_post=asean-comprehensive-investment-agreement and the AANZFTA at https://aanzfta.asean.org
7 Art. 4(5) of the India-Kuwait BIT provided that: "Each party shall ... provide effective means of asserting claims and enforcing rights with regard to investments...". Each Contracting State shall maintain a favourable environment for investments in its territory by investors of the other Contracting State. Each Contracting State shall in accordance with its applicable laws and regulations provide effective means of MFN.
8 The White Industries Final Award at 16.1.1., available at https://www.italaw.com/ cases/documents/1170.
9 'RCEP negotiations explained from Australia's perspective', available at https:// dfat.gov.au/trade/agreements/negotiations/rcep/Pages/regional-comprehensive-economic-partnership.aspx.
10 Agreement between the Government of the People's Republic of China and the Government of the Kingdom of Sweden on the Mutual Protection of Investments, 29 March 1982.
11 *Bechtel Enterprises Holdings, Inc. and GE Structured Finance (GESF) v. The Government of India* [2003] (hereinafter *Bechtel v. India*); PCA Case No. 2016-7 *Cairn Energy PLC and Cairn UK Holdings Limited v. The Republic of India*.

12 See *Bechtel v. India*; PCA Case No. 2013-09 *Devas (Mauritius) Ltd., Devas Employees Mauritius Private Limited, and Telcom Devas Mauritius Limited v. Republic of India* [2012]; *Khaitan Holdings Mauritius Limited v. India* [2013]; *Astro All Asia Networks and South Asia Entertainment Holdings Limited v. India* [2016]; PCA Case No. 2017-37 *Nissan Motor Co., Ltd. v. Republic of India* [2017] and *Carissa Investments LLC v. India* [2017].

13 PCA Case No. 2010-20 *Beijing Shougang Mining Investment Company Ltd., China Heilongjiang International Economic & Technical Cooperative Corp., and Qinhuangdaoshi Qinlong International Industrial Co. Ltd. v. Mongolia* [2010] and ICSID Case No. ADHOC/17/1 *Sanum Investments Limited v. Lao People's Democratic Republic (II)* [2017].

14 Civil Appellate Jurisdiction on *Vodafone International Holdings B.V. v. Union of India* [2012].

15 *Ibid.*

16 *Ibid.*

17 *Vodafone Group Plc and Vodafone Consolidated Holdings Limited v. India (II)* [2017].

18 Judgment Report on *Union of India v. Vodafone Group Plc United Kingdom*, CS (OS) 383/2017, adopted 22 August 2017.

19 ICSID Case No. ARB/01/13 *SGS Société de Surveillance SA v. Islamic Republic of Pakistan* [2004].

20 *Union of India vs Vodafone Group Plc United Kingdom*, CS(OS) 383/2017 & I. A. No. 9460/2017, adopted 7 May 2018.

21 *Ibid.*

22 ICSID Case No.ARB/12/29 *Ping An Life Insurance Company Limited and Ping An Insurance Group Limited v. the Government of Belgium* [2015].

23 *Ibid.*, para. 66.

24 *Ibid.*, Section F (overall conclusion).

25 *Flemingo DutyFree Shop Private Limited v. Republic of Poland* [2014].

26 *Ibid.*, paras. 337–342.

27 See *Churchill Mining Plc and Planet Mining Pty Ltd v. Indonesia*.

28 ICSID Case No. ARB (AF)/10/1 *David Minnotte & Robert Lewis v. Republic of Poland* [2014].

29 See *Churchill Mining Plc and Planet Mining Pty Ltd v. Indonesia*, para. 39.

30 *Ibid.*, paras. 508, 510–511 and 529.

31 *Ibid.*, para. 79.

32 'For Instance, Local News Reactions', available at https://www.thejakartapost.com/ news/2014/02/28/indonesia-should-learn-churchill-case-analysts.html.

33 Panel Report on *U.S.—Definitive Safeguard Measures on Imports of Certain Steel Products*, WT/DS252 of 7 November 2003; with respect to the United States request for consultations, see *China—Value-Added Tax on Integrated Circuits*, WT/DS309/6 and WT/DS309/1 of 18 March 2004. More generally, see the WTO site's rubric on China, available at http://www.wto.org/english/thewto_e/countries_e/china_e.htm.

34 'Investment Dispute Settlement Navigator: Japan – as home State', available at https:// investmentpolicyhub.unctad.org/ISDS/CountryCases/105?partyRole=1.

Bibliography

Berger, A. (2013) 'Investment Rules in Chinese Preferential Trade and Investment Agreements: Is China following the global trend towards comprehensive agreements?', *Discussion Paper*, paper 7/2013, Deutsches Institut für Entwicklungspolitik, pp. 1–30.

Choukroune, L. (2011) 'China's accession and participation to the WTO', in M. Delmas-Marty and W. Pierre-Etienne (eds.), *China, Democracy and the Law*, Leiden, the Netherlands: Boston by Brill, pp. 649–704.

Choukroune, L. (2014) 'Les BRICS et le droit international du commerce et de l'investissement, entre autonomie et intégration', in H. Gherari (ed.), *Les dérèglements économiques internationaux: Crise du droit ou droit des crises*, Paris, France: Pédone, pp. 203–205.

Choukroune, L. (2016) 'Human rights in international investment disputes: Global litigation as international Law Re-Unifier', in L. Choukroune (ed.), *Judging the State in International Trade and Investment Law*, Singapore: Springer, pp. 179–215.

Choukroune, L. (2016) *Emerging Countries and International Trade and Investment Law*, Paris, France: Pédone.

Choukroune, L. (2018) 'CSR and Indian Investment Law', *Transnational Dispute Management, Special India*. Investment Treaty Arbitration and Commercial Arbitration in and with India.

Choukroune, L. (2018) 'EU and developing Asia trade dispute settlement: Assertive legalism for political autonomy', in S. Khorana (ed.), *Handbook on EU Law Trade Policy*, Cheltenham, UK: Edward Elgar, pp. 333–351.

Gaillard, E. (2017) 'Abuse of Process in International Arbitration', *ICSID Review-Foreign Investment Law Journal*, 32(1), pp. 17–37.

Hadley, K. (2013) 'Do China's BITs Matter? Assessing the effect of China's investment agreements on foreign investment flows, investor's rights and the rule of law', *Georgetown Journal of International Law*, 45(1), pp. 255–321.

Nakagawa, J. (2002) 'Lessons from the Japan-China "Welsh Onion War"', *Journal of World Trade*, 36(6), pp. 1019–1036.

Pekkanen, S. (2008) *Japan's Aggressive Legalism: Law and Foreign Trade Politics Beyond the WTO*, Stanford, CA: Stanford University Press.

Ranjan, P. (2015) 'Most favoured nation provisions in India BIT, a case for reform', *Indian Journal of International Law*, 55(1), pp.39–64.

Ranjan, P. (2019) *India and Bilateral Investment Treaties: Refusal, Acceptance and Backlash*, Oxford, UK: Oxford University Press.

Takahashi, H. (2014) *Towards an Understanding of the Japanese Way of Dispute Resolution: How is it Different from the West?* in D. Vanoverbeke, J. Maesschalck, D. Nelken and S. Parmentier (eds.), *The Changing Role of Law in Japan: Empirical Studies in Culture, Society and Policy Making*, Cheltenham, UK: Edward Elgar, pp. 95–108.

Part II

Law and diplomacy in the management of disputes and disagreements

5 Embedding diplomacy in formal procedures

How the European commission navigated the solar panel dispute with China

Frank Gaenssmantel

In the years 2012 and 2013, China and the European Union (EU) went through a tense commercial dispute, triggered by trade defence procedures that the European Commission (EC) launched (upon the request of a European industry alliance) against imports of solar panels and related products originating from China. Such procedures are common in China–EU economic relations and so are complaints about them, countermeasures and episodes of tension. But this case stood out in terms of the sheer volume of trade concerned, which at roughly 21 billion Euro was not only greater than any other case before but also represented 65 per cent of China's total exports in this sector (Vaudin d'Imécourt 2012a). Beijing's answer was correspondingly harsh. In reaction to the various steps taken by the EC, the EU's lead actor in trade defence cases, its Chinese counterparts deployed threatening rhetoric and a series of barely veiled retaliatory measures. Observers quickly started to talk about a looming "trade war" (see e.g. EUobserver 2012; Vaudin d'Imécourt 2012c; Bao 2013). However, as the case unfolded, the EC came under pressure not only from China, but also from member states, some of which were adamantly opposed to the investigations and any defensive duties. In the end, the dispute was resolved through an agreement with Chinese exporters on a minimum import price (MIP), which also passed the scrutiny of EU member states in the Council of the EU.

The solar panel trade dispute between China and the EU has received considerable attention in academic literature, with special focus on the origins of the dispute as well as the interactive dynamics between the EU and China and their outcomes. With regard to the former, there is broad agreement that developments in China played a crucial role, most importantly the build-up of excessive production capacity, stimulated by policy measures to promote renewable energy sources. In combination with weak domestic demand, it pushed Chinese solar panel producers into dependence on massive exports, thus flooding world markets with cheap solar cells (Godement and Laurent 2013, p. 1; Chen 2015, p. 101). At the same time, researchers have also pointed to the context of economic crisis in the EU, which has had the effect of reducing subsidies on the demand side, thus exacerbating competition amongst suppliers and effectively pushing more and more European solar panel producers out of the market (Li 2018, p. 218; Curran, Lü and Spigarelli 2017, p. 475).

With regard to China–EU interaction in the solar panel dispute, scholars agree about the difficult position of the EU in this case as a result of internal divisions and the advantages this implied for the Chinese side (Chen 2015, pp. 6–7; Plasschaert 2016, p. 6; Bollen, de Ville and Orbie 2016, pp. 285–286; Pepermans 2017, pp. 1402–1403). In contrast to this, there are divergences on how to judge the final agreement. According to Plasschaert (2016), it "looks balanced" (p. 6), but others see a "victory for China" (Bollen, de Ville and Orbie 2016, p. 286). Pepermans (2017) argues that China used a "well-targeted carrot and stick approach to persuade the member states to vote against protective trade measures," thus limiting the options for the EC and forcing it towards the price agreement (p. 1406).

There are indeed signs that the outcome was favourable for China rather than the EU. One of them is the enormous dissatisfaction of the industry association that had filed the original complaint, visible in various (unsuccessful) attempts at having the MIP agreement cancelled by the Court of Justice of the EU (Goron 2018, pp. 108–109). Similarly, the shift in the EC's rhetoric and attitude, from strong language on defending European producers against unfair practices of Chinese exporters to negotiating a compromise, can be read as "caving in" (Bollen, de Ville and Orbie 2016, p. 286). At the same time, though, the very fact that the EU has been internally divided makes it extremely difficult to pinpoint winners and losers with any precision, in this case just as in many others. Did the EC yield to Chinese pressure or to that of EU member states opposed to this trade defence action against China? And were these member states victims of Chinese coercion or simply expressing their own particular economic interests? Obviously, China tried to put pressure on them, but this does not necessarily mean that their positions were determined by China and that no other factors played a role. Chapter 6 in this volume proposes an interesting explanation of member state positions beyond Chinese carrots and sticks that focuses on relevant interests and values. Even the quality of the Chinese "victory" can be questioned: while the final compromise may have been relatively favourable for Chinese exporters, it only came after more than a year of Chinese attempts to stop EU trade defence procedures and settle the issues diplomatically, all frustrated by the EC.

If it is difficult to identify winners and losers in an environment of multi-level and multi-actor governance, as described in Chapter 1, then it may be more rewarding to investigate how specific actors navigate governance structures to achieve certain outcomes. This chapter proposes to do precisely that, by tracing which strategies the EC chose in the solar panel case, in the diplomatic realm and amongst legally defined formal procedures, and how they were implemented and adjusted over time in light of specific constraints the EC had to face. The argument is that a purely diplomatic approach was not an option, while an approach based exclusively on formal tools, i.e. trade defence mechanisms, appeared promising at the outset but became untenable given the political context of the EU.

As a result, the EC risked a highly unfavourable outcome and was forced to adjust its strategy. In this context it managed to make creative use of the EU's anti-dumping rules to combine negotiations towards an MIP undertaking with the threat of temporarily increased duties on Chinese imports.

Even though the results of this instance of what can be termed "legally embedded diplomacy" may look modest to some, they were clearly the best the EC could achieve under the given circumstances. The chapter will proceed in three steps. A first section will reconstruct the development of the solar panel case, with particular emphasis on the actions of the EC and the various reactions to them. Secondly, I will discuss the diplomatic options available, before turning, in a third step, to the role of legally defined formal mechanisms and how they shaped activities of the EC. The second and third sections will make extensive reference to the conceptual discussion presented in Chapter 1 of this volume.

The China–EU solar panel dispute – an overview

At the end of July 2012, the European solar industry association EU ProSun filed a complaint against dumping of solar panels by Chinese producers on the European market. This triggered an almost immediate Chinese response. Four major solar panel producers issued a joint statement denying the accusations and calling on the Chinese government to help them defend their interests, while high officials in the government mentioned that China would most likely launch anti-dumping and anti-subsidy investigations into imports of polysilicon, a core component of solar photovoltaic cells that China imports in considerable quantities from the EU (Xinhua 2012; EUobserver.com 2012). About one month later, during a visit to Beijing, German Chancellor Angela Merkel expressed her opposition to an anti-dumping investigation against Chinese solar panels and called on the EC to find a negotiated solution with China (Falletti and Vaudin d'Imécourt 2012).

Thus it was soon clear that, if the EC decided to initiate anti-dumping investigations in this case, it would find itself confronted not only with an antagonistic China, but also with strong criticism from within the EU. Nevertheless, this is precisely what it did at the beginning of September, stating that it had found "sufficient prima facie evidence to warrant the opening of an investigation" and emphasizing that it is "*legally obliged* to open an anti-dumping investigation" in such cases (European Commission 2012; emphasis in original). Just a few weeks after that, the same industry association submitted a request for anti-subsidy investigations, which the EC launched in November (Vaudin d'Imécourt 2012c; Stern 2012). China reacted by engaging with and putting pressure on the EC. In mid-September, a few days before the China–EU summit meeting, a delegation of Chinese trade officials was dispatched to Brussels to persuade the EC to refrain from duties and to engage in bilateral talks instead (Falletti 2012). Already in August the Ministry of Commerce (MOFCOM) had received an industry complaint calling for anti-dumping and anti-subsidy action against polysilicon imports from the EU, and it launched investigations in November (China Energy Weekly 2012; Li and Du 2012). The same month, a complaint

98   *Frank Gaenssmantel*

against discriminatory practices in Greek and Italian solar energy subsidies was submitted to the Dispute Settlement Body of the World Trade Organization (WTO) (Zheng and Du 2012; Associated Press 2012).

The situation further precipitated in the first months of 2013. In early February, EU ProSun Glass, an association of solar glass producers, filed an anti-dumping complaint against imports of solar glass from China, and by the end of the month the EC launched investigations (Vaudin d'Imécourt 2013; Agence France Presse 2013a). As had happened for solar panels, the same association followed suit with an anti-subsidy complaint in March, and in April the EC, again, found *prima facie* evidence of hurtful subsidies and started investigations (European Commission 2013a; Buckens 2013). The following month it became known that the EC intended to impose provisional anti-dumping duties within weeks or the time needed for (nonbinding) consultations with member states (Kurop and Vaudin d'Imécourt 2013). At the beginning of June it eventually imposed provisional duties, initially at a fairly low 11.8 per cent, which would jump to 47.6 per cent after two months, however, unless a negotiated solution with China could be found (European Commission 2013c).

From the moment the EC's intention to impose duties became known, China stepped up its efforts at dialogue with the EC, though mostly with scarce results and thus creating considerable frustration amongst the involved government officials and industry representatives (United Press International 2013; Shenzhen Daily 2013). Once the EC had imposed provisional duties, Beijing almost immediately reacted by starting anti-dumping and anti-subsidy investigations against imports of wines from the EU, on the basis of an industry complaint from September 2013, thus increasing the pressure on EU members, especially France, the biggest EU wine exporter to China and previously an outspoken supporter of trade defence on solar panels (Vaudin d'Imécourt 2012b; Thompson 2013; Traynor 2013). China also raised the spectre of investigations against imports of luxury cars and this further strengthened Germany's opposition to the solar panel duties (Fletcher 2013). From mid-June, negotiation efforts intensified (Agence France Presse 2013b; China Daily 2013). Finally at the end of July, the two sides settled on a price undertaking that combined an MIP with quantitative restrictions (European Commission 2013d; Chaffin 2013). This meant that Chinese solar panels could be imported into the EU without anti-dumping duties if sold above the MIP and up to a certain total import volume.

The MIP undertaking of July 2013 allowed the two sides to ease most of the specific disputes that had built up around the solar panel case. Although negotiated in the context of the anti-dumping investigation, the EC applied the agreement to the parallel anti-subsidy procedure as well, which then went on without any provisional duties (European Commission 2013e). On the part of China, investigations against polysilicon and wine originating from the EU went on, but the MOFCOM re-emphasized its preference for dialogue and indeed in both instances mutual agreement could be reached (Li 2013). In the polysilicon case, China negotiated a price undertaking with the main European exporter, German Wacker Chemie AG (European Commission 2014a). For wine, EU and Chinese producers agreed on a memorandum of understanding, by which Chinese companies withdrew their anti-dumping and anti-subsidy complaints in exchange for technical assistance from their European counterparts (European Commission 2014b). The complaint China had lodged with the WTO's Dispute Settlement Body was not pursued.[1]

Within the EU, the soothing of tensions became obvious when the Council of the EU unanimously backed the package of anti-dumping and anti-subsidy measures of the EC in combination with the MIP undertaking (European Commission 2013f; interview with EC official, May 2016). This is noteworthy, considering that at the height of tensions some 15 to 18 member states were opposed to the EC action on this matter (European Council on Foreign Relations 2014; Pepermans 2017, p. 1403). Interestingly, the measures were imposed for two years rather than the usual five. After an extension (and an anti-circumvention investigation against Chinese solar panels imported from Taiwan and Malaysia) both measures expired in September 2018. The only investigation in the context of this dispute that proceeded in line with usual practice was that on solar glass, no doubt due to the much smaller trade volume concerned (Buckens 2013).

The context for commission diplomacy in the solar panel case

If after more than one year a negotiated settlement helped to diffuse much of the tension that had built up, both between China and the EU and within the latter, one might wonder whether it would not have been possible to achieve a similar (or possibly even better) outcome through consultations already at an earlier stage. In order to assess whether there were any realistic prospects for this, this section will examine the EC's situation in the context of the solar panel dispute with reference to the various factors that promote diplomatic approaches in economic relations as discussed in Chapter 1.

A first option for the EC might have presented itself in the context of the regular diplomatic contacts between the two sides or, put differently, on the basis of diplomacy as a "state of affairs." The assumption here is that the many informal diplomatic consultations between the two sides should be a convenient venue for approaching particular issues that are creating tensions or risk to do so in the future. Due to their confidential nature and low visibility, such contacts are very difficult to trace for the researcher. But they can be identified through interviews with policymakers or at times also in some of their public comments.

In the solar panel case, one should expect such informal consultations to have taken place already before the trade defence complaint was filed, in an effort of what might be termed preemptive diplomacy. In fact, the dispute did not come unexpectedly. Observers of the industry had long been aware of the Chinese competition for European producers and its growing market share (Richardson 2012). Also, the United States had launched anti-dumping and anti-subsidy investigations against Chinese solar panels in 2011 and imposed duties in spring 2012 (Crooks 2012). The industry request in the United States had been led by the US subsidiary of a German solar panel producer, SolarWorld, and the inclination of the German head offices towards bringing parallel complaints to the EC had been known for some time (Richardson 2012).

And yet it appears that no such informal consultations actually happened before the trade defence complaint was submitted to the EC. From public statements of the months and years before the solar panel dispute, no hint to any discussion on the issue emerges. In interviews, EC officials very explicitly rejected this hypothesis, expressing a strong sense that this would be against the trade defence rules, according to which the EC's work starts with the industry complaint and not before. More broadly, they pointed out that the EC is generally not very proactive in diplomacy due to a constant fear of going beyond the formal competences, which implies high political risks. The interviewees would not exclude that the issue might have been brought up by China on the side-lines of one or several of the many international meetings in which both sides participate, but even in such a case, the culture, norms and practice of the EC would push officials to close such discussions as quickly as possible with reference to EU rules (interviews with EC officials, May 2016 and October 2017).

Once launched by industry associations, trade defence tools constitute a straightjacket that the EC cannot simply disregard, and as a legally defined formal procedure they will receive more attention in the following section. But in principle it should still be possible to engage in a diplomatic dialogue that runs parallel to the formal procedures, in order to avoid escalation of tensions and to facilitate a mutually agreeable outcome through a price undertaking at a later stage. Parallel contacts did occur indeed, but rather than diplomatic efforts in their own right, for the EC they were simply the usual "pre-consultations" that are enacted with the concerned counterpart after receiving the industry complaint (interview EC official, October 2017). Instead of helping to avoid or ease tensions, in some instances these contacts may actually have increased them. While the Chinese side seemed to expect negotiations on the substance of the issue at hand, the EC emphasized that these contacts were parts of the regular procedures, or simply "preparatory talks," thus creating irritation amongst its counterparts in Beijing (Falletti 2012; Shenzhen Daily 2013).

Next to informal consultations in the context of regular diplomatic contacts, a second option for the EC would have been, at least in theory, to ask member states for a negotiation mandate and engage in a formal negotiation to solve the issue. However, this was never an option in practice, and neither in the interviews with EC officials nor in media coverage are there any signs of efforts in this direction. As also stated in Chapter 1 the length and political complexities of this procedure make it an unfitting tool for solving urgent commercial disputes like the solar panel case.

Aside from the fact that the rules of EU trade policy did not facilitate diplomatic efforts, the conditions that promote diplomatic success, as discussed in Chapter 1 were also not given in the solar panel case. On the one hand, the Commission should find it easier to reach agreement with its counterparts if there is a wide intra-EU agreement on a range of acceptable outcomes and therefore a large win-set. This was clearly not the case in the solar panel dispute, due to the divisions amongst member states. On the other hand, a small win-set may strengthen the diplomats' position through the "tied hands" argument but only under the condition that member states are not actively engaging in parallel diplomacy that would weaken this argument. In the solar panel case, by contrast, member states were actively engaging with the Chinese side on this topic, most vocally Germany, one of the leading opponents of trade defence measures in this case. So the solar panel case confirms the expectation that large win-sets and disciplined member states are rare in EU trade diplomacy.

Another set of factors presented in Chapter 1 that can enhance the chances of a successful diplomatic approach belong to the psychological and ideational realm. Naturally, the psychological compatibility of diplomats and its impact on the outcomes from diplomacy is very difficult to assess. In interviews, EC officials generally confirmed the importance of personal "chemistry" in diplomatic contacts but denied that they have much impact in relations with China. They linked this in particular to the hierarchical nature of China's foreign policy process, which leaves hardly any margin for the diplomats at a working level and thus constrains any positive dynamics that might otherwise emerge from personal interaction (interviews with EC officials, May 2016 and October 2017). The role of diplomats' worldviews is similarly challenging to analyze, especially in an opaque decision-making environment as in China. MOFCOM officials are reputed to hold comparatively liberal world views and support the WTO's rules-based trading regime (Gaenssmantel 2015, p. 402). However, according to one of the interviewees, this only has a very limited effect, as interaction remains difficult, though possibly a little less than in case of other ministerial bodies (interview with EC official October 2017).

In terms of perceptions of the issue at stake, the second ideational factor developed in Chapter 1, there is an obvious mismatch between the EU and China, rendering communication more complex. The EC adopted a very technical-legal language (European Commission 2012), in combination with hints that unfair trading practices on the part of China were a reality, like for example when Trade Commissioner De Gucht complained that China subsidized "nearly everything" (Blenkinsop and Emmott 2012). One of the interviewees at the EC emphasized that more than the specific interests of the complainants, what was at stake was the rules-based global trading system, which the EC was defending against abuses by China, in this and many other cases (interview with EC official May 2016). So, to some extent EC officials held the belief that what they did was simply "the right thing to do."

MOFCOM officials in China saw the dispute from a different perspective, as emerges from two interviews with policy consultants in Beijing (November 2014). On the one hand, they were keenly aware that the accusations were at least partially correct. For almost a decade local government had been promoting and investing in the solar industry, and this had resulted in distorted incentives and overproduction. Some officials even considered the external shocks of US and EU trade defence measures as welcome pressure to reform the sector in China. At the same time, however, they also felt unfairly treated. Solar energy was a pillar industry in China's development plan for renewable energy, but in contrast to what had been hoped for, it had not triggered much domestic innovation. Instead, production remained largely limited to processing semi-finished products, most of which had been previously imported, also from the EU among others.[2] With the EU itself an important link in the value chain (Curran 2015), and as a major economic partner, the expectation was that it would take Chinese concerns into account and jointly search for a compromise rather than apply trade defence measures unilaterally. This perception turned the solar panel case into a highly political issue and with substantial Chinese interests at stake. Accordingly, instead of following the EU's legal rhetoric, China explicitly called for "consultation and cooperation" and made it clear that it considered any duties unfair protectionism (Vaudin d'Imécourt 2012a; Xinhua 2012).

Overall, the rules and practice of EU trade policy left hardly any space for informal diplomatic consultations, and the constellation of member state interests (which were vocally expressed *vis-à-vis* China) created neither bargaining space nor bargaining power. Also, psychological or ideational factors did not facilitate interaction with Chinese counterparts. This implies that for the EC, formal procedures in which it has incontestable authority represented the only option for decisive action on the matter at hand.

Formal rules and procedures and how they were used by the commission

What were the legally defined formal mechanisms and procedures available to the EC in the solar panel case? In case of trade distortions through massive subsidies, one option is always to take the case to the WTO's dispute settlement mechanism. However, even though the issue was known in advance, no "preemptive legal action," as this might be called, was initiated. On the one hand, WTO dispute cases typically emerge from complaints under the EU's Trade Barriers Regulation (TBR), and such a complaint was not received. Unless there is a sudden shift in trade policy by the concerned counterpart (like for instance a new tariff that is considered nonconform with WTO rules), the EC depends on detailed information from industry groups, and this is usually provided through TBR complaints. On the other hand, the option of starting a WTO dispute had a number of disadvantages in comparison with trade defence procedures. Firstly, the trajectory from initiating a case to the moment distortions are redressed is likely to be considerably longer. Secondly, the entire process depends on the responding party, in particular whether it appeals and whether it is willing and able to implement measures necessary in light of the Panel or Appellate Body reports. In the case of a complex system of supportive legal and regulatory measures, in combination with financial stimulus, involving both central and local government, as was the case for China's renewable energy sector (Shi 2010, pp. 208–210), doubts on effective implementation may be legitimate. Thirdly, the target necessarily has to be a WTO member, that is a state, and that restrains the options, as a business practice like dumping cannot be addressed. However, dumping by Chinese competitors appeared to be the prime concern of the European industries that filed the complaint. Lastly, at the dispute settlement mechanism the burden of proof would be with the EU as complainant.

This means that there were few incentives for the EC to proactively take the issue of Chinese subsidies in the renewables sectors to the WTO. Another treaty-based venue for addressing divisive issues, which could have been an alternative, at least in principle, is the Joint Committee established by the China–EU Agreement on Trade and Economic Cooperation of 1985. In practice, however, this body has always functioned as a forum for diplomatic exchange, and despite the legal roots in the bilateral agreement it displays hardly any signs of legalization, which corresponds to the general characteristics of this sort of institution as pointed out in Chapter 1. This means that in line with the many factors that hindered or complicated diplomatic solutions in this case, one should not expect the Joint Committee to have been a prime locus for consultations on the solar panel issue. And indeed, there is no trace of any related discussions in this body.

Another alternative for formal action were naturally trade defence procedures. They had a number of clear advantages: they could be unilaterally launched and they would be following EU regulations, with the EC in charge of implementation; corrective duties could be imposed directly upon completion of the investigation, including the possibility of opting for provisional duties already at an earlier stage; both anti-dumping and anti-subsidy investigations could be started, also in parallel; and finally, the burden of proof would be on the Chinese side, as Chinese businesses or officials would have to demonstrate the *absence* of unfair trading practices. The fact that the EC would have to wait to receive a complaint was not a particular disadvantage in this case. The dissatisfaction in certain industry quarters had been such that there could be no doubt that a complaint would be arriving sooner or later.

So amongst formal mechanisms available in the context of this case, trade defence tools were particularly attractive in that they put the EC in a comparatively strong position *vis-à-vis* China, and this was despite constraining features like the dependence on private actors in order to take action and the obligation to follow a very specific procedure. In fact, precisely because such constraints are in place, the rules of the EU's trade defence system can be seen as having an enabling effect for the EC. They positively establish EC authority and discretion within a circumscribed subfield of trade policy, and this has a far greater weight than the related procedural limitations. In addition to this, on a political level, by following EU regulations to the letter, the EC defuses member state suspicions and criticisms about an independent political or diplomatic agenda. So the very reason for which the EC shies away from diplomatic initiatives should make trade defence procedures highly attractive. This effect is not limited to the application of EU rules alone. As claimed by German diplomats, the EC's role as "guardian of the treaties" is not necessarily limited to EU treaties alone but also confers it a special responsibility in maintaining the rules of the WTO system. This means that member states tend to tolerate EC activity as long as it is in conformity with and in pursuit of WTO law (interview, October 2017).

In the solar panel case, the EC was indeed intent on demonstrating both conformity of its actions with EU rules and their legitimacy and necessity in the context of the global trading system. This was visible, for example, in the following statement by De Gucht shortly after the imposition of provisional anti-dumping duties:

> Last summer, the Commission received a formal and valid complaint from a grouping of European solar panel manufactures – which obliged us to launch an investigation as required by EU law. [...] The truth is that our action is about *ensuring fair competition and the respect of international trade rules* to which both Europe and China have signed up to [sic] in the WTO. (European Commission 2013c; emphasis in original).

The insistence of the EC that meetings with Chinese counterparts were simply particular aspects of the trade defence procedure rather than negotiations in their own right, as mentioned above, can also be read as an effort of containing any suspicions amongst member states and other stakeholders in the EU that the EC might be trespassing the boundaries of its authority. At the same time, this may also have been a way for EC officials to strengthen their hand *vis-à-vis* China. In fact, the constant reference to formal constraints "back home" enabled the EC to define the terms of interaction in a logic akin to the tied-hands argument.

Aside from the advantages related to trade defence tools as such and the enabling effect of formally established rules and competence, the EC also made use of the flexibility available within the relevant procedures. This concerns first and foremost the possibility, provided by the EU's trade defence rules, to negotiate an MIP undertaking with the concerned third-country producers. From summer 2012 to spring 2013 the EC did not react to any of the calls for a negotiated settlement, neither those from China nor those from within the EU. However, when the EC decided to impose provisional anti-dumping duties in early June 2013, it suddenly sounded very much in favour of negotiating with China, and it was quite open in presenting the steep increase in duties after two months as a threat scenario. In Trade Commissioner De Gucht's words,

> it is a one-time offer to the Chinese side, providing a very clear incentive to negotiate. It provides a clear window of opportunity for negotiations, but the ball is now in China's court. It is clear that if China does not provide a solution by August, then the higher tariffs will apply (European Commission 2013c).

How to explain this shift from a simple insistence on trade defence procedures *tout court*, towards negotiations in combination with the open threat of increasing duties? A core reason lies in the intra-EU political context, that is in the consolidating resistance of member states against the solar panel investigations. By spring 2013, it had become sufficiently clear to the EC that while provisional anti-dumping duties would pass member state scrutiny, as blocking them would require a qualified majority against that was not materializing, this would not be the case for definitive duties, for which a simple majority of member states would be sufficient to stop the EC proposal.[3]

This meant that the EC found itself at an impasse. Continuing its previous approach would have led almost certainly to no measure at all, a very humiliating perspective after the strong rhetoric on the need to address and redress China's unfair trading practices. At the same time, simply giving in to Chinese and member state calls for negotiations after months of resistance would put the EC in a disastrous negotiating position.

The EC found a face-saving way out via an unusual, but entirely correct, use of the rules in the EU's anti-dumping regulation. By allowing for the negotiation of MIP undertakings,[4] the regulation introduces the option of shifting away from the legally defined formal procedure towards a diplomatic mode of interaction, an exercise that could be called "legally embedded diplomacy." The regulation also does not impose any limits on how provisional duties are structured,[5] meaning that there is no reason not to include a steep increase after two months. This creative setup of provisional duties meant that the compulsory character of the formal anti-dumping procedure produced an effective threat scenario in the context of the negotiations for a price undertaking.

Of course, there may be different views on these developments. In the same speech in which he called the two-step provisional duties an "incentive to negotiate," De Gucht also mentioned that his "sincere aim since the outset has been an amicable solution" (European Commission 2013c). It is true that formally an MIP undertaking only becomes an option after "provisional affirmative determination of dumping and injury has been made,"[6] so the fact that the possibility of negotiating an undertaking was only mentioned after provisional measures had been imposed does not necessarily have to indicate a change of mind. But one may wonder why the EC did not mention earlier in the process, or state more openly, that it was ready to negotiate an undertaking in case dumping was confirmed, especially as this might have helped to mitigate tensions with China and within the EU. Two other interpretations of the increasing provisional duties were presented by the EC: first, as an "offer," or kind gesture towards China, as regular practice would have been to implement the higher duties from the start; and second, as a measure to avoid shocks and allow markets to adapt smoothly (European Commission 2013c, interview with EC official May 2016). Naturally both sound plausible, but they are not fully convincing. The negotiation of undertakings cannot be called standard practice in trade defence procedures, but it is fairly common. However, provisional duties that rise significantly after a short period of time are not, and it would seem strange that kindness and market adaptation only matter in this instance of relations with China.

Despite these efforts, the EC remained in a difficult position. The prospect of definitive duties can be considered a serious threat, as it basically represents an altered status quo for exporters for many years. But the risk for China in this case was very limited in comparison. No success in the negotiations and no undertaking would simply have meant high anti-dumping duties for three months until the Council of the EU was expected to vote down the Commission's proposal for permanent duties. This explains, at least in part, why the EC was unable to achieve an undertaking that satisfied the expectations of the industries that had filed the complaint, while the outcome was generally considered to be favourable to the Chinese side. Nevertheless, through a creative use of the EU's anti-dumping rules, the EC had managed to make the situation a little more favourable for itself than had been the case before.

So amongst legally defined formal procedures, trade defence tools were clearly the most promising for the EC in the solar panel case. On the one hand they put it in a stronger position *vis-à-vis* China than the dispute settlement mechanism of the WTO. On the other hand, the constraints of formal procedure, including its reactive nature that presupposes private sector initiative, create an enabling effect within the EU. They unambiguously establish EC authority in a specific field and sticking to them helps the EC to mitigate member state suspicion about a runaway bureaucracy. Nevertheless, trade defence procedures in the solar panel case got derailed by lacking member state support, leaving the EC in an extremely difficult position. By initiating legally embedded negotiations towards a price undertaking in combination with a procedurally rooted threat scenario through the provisional duties, the EC managed to improve its situation to some extent, but it was not sufficient to allow for a negotiation outcome that would have satisfied the complainant industry in the EU.

Conclusion

This chapter has analyzed the respective role of diplomatic approaches and legally defined formal procedures in the EC's management of the solar panel dispute with China. It started from an overview of the dispute that lasted roughly from mid-2012 to mid-/late 2013. In the next step the discussion turned to the diplomatic options available and to what extent factors that facilitate diplomatic solutions were present. The finding was that EU rules and practice leave little room for diplomatic initiatives on the part of the EC. At the same time, none of the factors that could facilitate diplomatic solutions were in place. The last section then looked at available formal mechanisms, and whether and how they were used in the solar panel case. While trade defence procedures appeared as the most advantageous approach, their full implementation was hampered by lacking member state support. In this situation the EC had to deviate from standard practice, shift towards negotiations on a price undertaking with China and set up a threat scenario via the two levels of provisional duties. This approach allowed it to strengthen its bargaining position but only to a limited extent.

This research leads to several conclusions that are relevant in the context of the volume as a whole. Firstly, the character of the EU polity disincentivizes the EC from diplomatic approaches in the management of international economic relations, even in the trade policy field, where generally speaking it has the most authority and impact. The constant fear among member states that the EC might be overstepping the boundaries of its competence, and the related fear within the EC of the political difficulties it faces whenever under concrete suspicion of having done this, creates a climate in which the EC cannot but refrain as much as possible from diplomatic initiatives of virtually all sorts. Even the low visibility of diplomacy as "state of affairs," as discussed in Chapter 1, is apparently not sufficient to create room for diplomatic manoeuvre by the EC. The only context in which the EC can actively engage in diplomacy is under a formal Council mandate, which is not an option for managing economic relations on a daily basis, in particular disputes.

Secondly, even within the realm of legal and formal procedures, options are limited. The WTO's dispute settlement mechanism is always demanding for a complainant. For the EC, a proactive complaint may also expose it to criticism back home, unless it is a reaction to explicit policy shifts by a trade partner that imply clear disadvantages for EU exporters. More generally one might say that reacting rather than acting is a safe strategy for the EC, and this makes TBR complaints and especially trade defence procedures attractive, of course the latter also due to their unilateral nature.

These points suggest that in the EU, a highly legalized and regulated community, the logic of choice may be in the process of being crowded out by an ever more forceful and omnipresent logic of constraints. Rather than a choice between diplomacy and law, as discussed in Chapter 1, officials then end up having to choose between several legally defined formal options, such as between taking a case to the WTO's dispute settlement mechanism, despite all the challenges, and waiting for a complaint under the trade defence procedures. Diplomacy is then confined to diplomatic aspects of formal procedures, like the consultations before a panel is established in the WTO's dispute settlement mechanism, or negotiations towards a price undertaking, as in the solar panel case.

Interestingly, at about the same time as the invitation to negotiate a price undertaking for solar panels combined with the threat of higher duties, Trade Commissioner De Gucht proposed a similar though far less sophisticated approach towards mobile telecommunications networks imported from China. Here, an *ex officio* anti-dumping investigation, that is without industry complaint, was decided by the EC but immediately suspended "to allow for negotiations towards an amicable solution with the Chinese authorities" (European Commission 2013b). The attempt failed and the investigation was abandoned after a year without any results, but it is another illustration of the need for the EC to find a procedural "home" for any diplomatic efforts it intends to undertake. Legally embedded diplomacy is the only diplomatic choice the EC seems to have. Paradoxically, it can gain diplomatic space only through the constraints of legally defined formal procedures.

Notes

1 This is visible in the dispute summary provided on the website of the WTO; see https://www.wto.org/english/tratop_e/dispu_e/cases_e/ds452_e.htm.
2 Since the final products were mostly destined for export, the situation has been termed *liang tou zai wai* or "both ends out" (Chen 2015, p. 98).
3 Regulation (EC) 1225/2009 of 30 November 2009 on protection against dumped imports from countries not members of the European Community, OJ L 343/51, 22 December 2009 (hereinafter Regulation 1225/2009), Art. 7(6), 9(4).
4 Regulation 1225/2009, Art. 8.
5 Regulation 1225/2009, Art. 7.
6 Regulation 1225/2009, Art. 8(1).

References

Agence France Presse (2013a) 'EU launches solar glass probe against China', *Agence France Presse*, 28 February.

Agence France Presse (2013b) 'EU trade chief sees speedy end to China solar row', *Agence France Press*, 21 June.

Associated Press (2012) 'China launches WTO case against EU solar subsidies', *Associated Press Online*, 6 November.

Bao, C. (2013) 'EU official: Cool heads will prevail over trade war', *China Daily European Edition*, 17 January.

Blenkinsop, P. and Emmott, R. (2012) 'EU steps up solar panels trade battle with China', *Climate Spectator*, 8 November.

Bollen, Y., De Ville, F. and Orbie, J. (2016) 'EU trade policy: Persistent liberalisation, contentious protectionism', *Journal of European Integration*, 21(3), pp. 279–294.

Buckens, M.-M. (2013) 'EU/China: Anti-subsidy probe into Chinese solar glass', *Europolitics*, 30 April.

Chaffin, J. (2013) 'EU and China settle trade fight over solar panels', *Financial Times*, 27 July.

Chen, G. (2015) 'From mercantile strategy to domestic demand stimulation: Changes in China's solar PV subsidies', *Asia Pacific Business Review*, 21(3), pp. 96–112.

Chen, Y. (2015). *EU-China Solar Panels Trade Dispute: Settlement and Challenges to the EU*, Paper series EU-Asia at a Glance, European Institute for Asian Studies, June 2015.

China Daily. (2013) 'A growing rift', *China Daily European Edition*, 24 June.

China Energy Weekly. (2012) 'Policies & Regulations', *China Energy Weekly*, 24 August.

Crooks, E. (2012) 'Trade war fears over US solar duties', *Financial Times*, 18 May.

Curran, L. (2015) 'The impact of trade policy on global production networks: The solar panel case', *Review of International Political Economy*, 22(5), pp. 1025–1054.

Curran, L., Lü, P. and Spigarelli, F. (2017) 'More heat than light? Renewable energy policy and EU-China solar energy relations', *International Journal of Ambient Energy*, 38(5), pp. 471–480.

EUobserver.com. (2012) 'China-EU trade war looms over solar energy industry', *EUobserver.com*, 28 July.

European Commission. (2012) EU initiates anti-dumping investigation on solar panel imports from China, *Memo*, 6 September.

European Commission. (2013a) EU launches anti-subsidy investigation on solar glass from China, *Memo*, 27 April.

European Commission. (2013b) Statement by EU Trade Commissioner Karel De Gucht on mobile telecommunications networks from China, *Memo*, 15 May.

European Commission. (2013c) Remarks by EU Trade Commissioner Karel De Gucht on the decision to impose provisional anti-dumping measures on imports of solar panels from China, *Memo*, 4 June.

European Commission. (2013d) Commissioner De Gucht: "We found an amicable solution in the EU-China solar panels case that will lead to a new market equilibrium at sustainable prices," *Memo*, 27 July.

European Commission. (2013e) European Commission continues anti-subsidy investigation on solar panels from China without duties, *Press Release*, 7 August.

European Commission. (2013f) EU imposes definitive measures on Chinese solar panels, confirms undertaking with Chinese solar panel exporters, *Press Release*, 2 December.

European Commission. (2014a) Trade Defence Instruments: European Commission welcomes EU industry's agreement with China in the polysilicon anti-dumping and anti-subsidy cases, *Press Release*, 18 March.

European Commission. (2014b) European Commission welcomes agreement reached between European and Chinese wine industries which will put an end to China's anti-dumping and anti-subsidy cases, *Press Release*, 21 March.

European Council on Foreign Relations. (2014) 'EU-China Solar Panel Case', *European Foreign Policy Scorecard 2014*; available at http://www.ecfr.eu/scorecard/2014/china/4.

Falletti, S. (2012) 'EU/China: Beijing ups pressure on Commission in solar panel dispute', *Europolitics Energy*, 26 September.

Falletti, S. and Vaudin d'Imécourt, L. (2012) 'EU/China: Fresh trade frictions ahead of summit', *Europolitics*, 4 September.

Fletcher, I. (2013) 'EU monitors possible luxury car trade spat with China', *IHS Global Insight*, 10 June.

Gaenssmantel, F. (2015) 'Interpreting change: International challenges and variations in foreign policy beliefs as explanations for shifts in China's policy towards the European Union', *International Relations*, 29 (3), pp. 395–409.

Godement, F. and Laurent, E. (2013) 'Solar panels: A crisis "Made in China"', *China Analysis*, (SP), European Council on Foreign Relations and China Centre.

Goron, C. (2018) 'Fighting against climate change and for fair trade: Finding the EU's interest in the solar panels dispute with China', *China-EU Law Journal*, 6, pp. 103-125.

Kurop, N. and Vaudin d'Imécourt, L. (2013) EU/China: De Gucht to proposal punitive duties on Chinese solar panels, 8 May.

Li, J. (2013) 'China continues polysilicon, wine trade probes', *China Daily*, 8 August.

Li, J. and Du, J. (2012) 'Probe launched into polysilicon imports', *China Daily European Edition*, 27 November.

Li, X. (2018) 'Cooperation or conflicts: The development of the photovoltaic fields in China and the EU member states', *African and Asian Studies*, 17, pp. 115–144.

Pepermans, A. (2017) 'The Sino-European solar panel dispute: China's successful carrot and stick approach towards Europe', *Journal of Contemporary European Research*, 13(4), pp. 1394–1411.

Plasschaert, S. (2016) Assessing the solar energy dispute between the European Union and the People's Republic of China, *ECIPE Working Paper*, 01/2016.

Richardson, M. (2012) 'Serious trade war is on the cards', *Canberra Times*, 8 June.

Shenzhen Daily. (2013) 'EU denies breakdown in solar panel talks', *Shenzhen Daily*, 27 May.

Shi, D. (2010) 'China's renewable energy development targets and implementation effect analysis', in Amineh, M.P. and Guang, Y. (eds.) *The Globalization of Energy, the European Union and China*. Leiden, Boston: Brill Academic Publishers, pp. 201–225.

Stern, D. (2012) 'EU/China: EU launches anti-subsidy probe on Chinese solar panels', *Europolitics*, 9 November.

Thompson, M. (2013) 'China hits back at Europe with wine probe', *CNNMoney.com*, 5 June.

Traynor, I. (2013) 'China launches inquiry into European wine exports as trade war fears grow', *Guardian*, 5 June.

United Press International (UPI). (2013) 'China, EU talk over trade disputes', *United Press International (UPI)*, 27 May.

Vaudin d'Imécourt, L. (2012a) 'EU/China: EU Probes Chinese solar panel imports', *Europolitics*, 7 September.

Vaudin d'Imécourt, L. (2012b) 'EU/China: Trade spat escalates on eve of summit', *Europolitics*, 20 September.

Vaudin d'Imécourt, L. (2012c) 'EU/China: Solar war continues: First dumping, now subsidies', *Europolitics*, 26 September.

Vaudin d'Imécourt, L. (2013) 'EU/China: Solar industry files new dumping complaint against China', *Europolitics*, 6 February.

Xinhua. (2012) 'China Focus: Solar product tariffs may hurt EU industry: China', *Xinhua General News Service*, 27 July.

Zheng, Y. and Du, J. (2012) 'China takes EU solar dispute to WTO', *China Daily European Edition*, 6 November.

6 The China–EU solar panel trade dispute

Explaining different responses of the member states

Shaofeng Chen

Over the past decade, promoting the development of electricity generation through the use of renewable energy technology – wind and solar energy systems *in primis* – has not only been considered an important step towards containing the devastating effects of climate change worldwide but has also been regarded as an essential move for fostering a sector often regarded as "strategic," as it holds the potential of setting other industries in motion. Today, given the relative lack of on-grid competitiveness of electricity generated from renewable energy sources, the governmental practice of providing financial support – in the forms of feed-in tariffs (FiTs) and subsidies granted either to the supply or demand side of the renewable energy sector – has been implemented in almost every world region.[1] Over time, high levels of government support have led investors to rush into the renewable energy technology sector both at home and abroad. As a result, renewable energy investments have favoured the sudden growth of the sector (particularly solar photovoltaic energy), both in terms of installation and manufacturing.

This specific trend, however, reached unprecedented levels of growth in China, where manufacturers dealing with a relatively stagnant domestic demand started seeking to expand their share within North American and European markets. This soon caused the European Union (EU) and China to be embroiled in a highly politicized trade dispute, as part of a global trend of growing clean energy trade frictions (European Commission 2013).[2] The definitive duties, and the related price undertaking, were extended in March 2017 for 18 months and expired in September 2018.

The expansion of Chinese firms' market shares compelled European solar panel firms (manufacturers in particular) to file a complaint to the European Commission (EC), requesting the opening of investigations against the alleged dumping and subsidizing of photovoltaic (PV) systems originating from the People's Republic of China (PRC). On June 4, 2013, the EC imposed provisional import duties of 11.8 per cent on the majority of solar panel modules made by Chinese companies, which would be raised to 47.6 per cent if no agreement on a minimum import price (MIP) could be clinched by August 6 (European Commission 2013). Upon having introduced retaliatory measures against the EC's initial deliberations, China accepted an MIP undertaking after negotiating with the EC.

EU member states showed mixed reactions to the decisions taken by the European Commission as the solar panel case unfolded. This is noteworthy for two reasons. Firstly, the promotion of renewable energy is a core goal of the EU's climate change policy as set out in the Renewable Energy Directive, which requires the EU to satisfy at least 20 per cent of its total energy needs with renewables by 2020 and to have at least 27 per cent renewables in the final energy consumption in the EU by 2030 (Directive 2009/28/EC of the European Parliament and of the Council of 23 April 2009[3]). The "2020 climate and energy package" and the "2030 climate and energy framework" adopted by EU leaders also aspire to have a 20 per cent and 40 per cent cut in greenhouse gas emissions by 2020 and 2030, respectively (European Commission 2019). Therefore, one should expect that a growing offer of solar panels and decreasing prices are generally welcome. Also, there are various cases in which Chinese investments have saved EU solar panel producers.[4]

Secondly, even if we accept that some members nevertheless tend to protect their domestic industries, their respective positions in the solar panel case did not always correspond to expectations. Calls for the prompt imposition of anti-dumping (AD) duties on the part of countries such as France, Italy, Spain and Portugal are in line with a track record of more protectionist preferences. However, the PV production in these countries is smaller than in other EU member states, such as Germany, the UK, Sweden and the Netherlands, which opposed the provisional trade measures implemented by the EC against Chinese firms, and ultimately praised the Commission for having solved the dispute diplomatically by accepting the MIP proposed by Chinese solar manufacturers (on the protectionist dynamics in the renewable energy field, see Carbaugh and St. Brown 2012, Lewis 2014). At the same time, some EU member states behaved as "swing voters," proving hesitant (if not indifferent altogether) towards taking a definite stance on the issue.

The rules of the Common Commercial Policy (CCP) of the EU put the EC in a very central role in trade policy in general and in AD investigations in particular. The choices of this institutional body in the context of the solar panel dispute with China are explored in Chapter 5 of this volume. As outlined in Chapter 1, the EU's management of trade disputes, and in particular the choice between diplomatic and legal strategies, is the result of policymakers' choices under a complex set of constraints, particularly those deriving from private interest groups and member states. In this chapter, we focus on the latter, by looking at how to explain the different positions of member states and the constraints they represented for the EC.

This chapter thus seeks to address the following questions: (1) Why did EU member states hold different attitudes towards the European Commission's decision to initiate AD and anti-subsidy (AS) investigations against Chinese solar manufacturers, given that the EU is supposed to speak with one voice on trade policy? (2) What were the underlying reasons leading some EU member states to hold attitudes on this issue that were not in line with the EU's policies on renewable energy and with their own industries' interests?

It is the hope of the author that research on this topic will shed light not merely on the complexity of the China–EU trade and clean energy relations and their approach to managing disputes but also on the dynamicity of the economic and political ties existing among EU member states, alongside these actors' relations with EU institutions, and with domestic businesses. Measured by its trading volume, the China–EU solar panel wrangle was the biggest trade dispute between these two economies, covering a trade value estimated at 21 billion euros in 2011, or roughly 4.8 per cent of Chinese exports to the EU (Goron 2018), thus providing interesting insights in how divided European countries can be and what influenced their positions.

Literature review

The case presented by the 2012 China–EU solar panel trade dispute sparked one of the most heavily politicized[5] reactions against China within the European Union, and over the past few years it has drawn wide scholarly attention. Previous academic work has already sought to examine this case from three different angles. Authors belonging to a first strand of research either explored the dispute from the EU's viewpoint or from China's. For example, while François Godement (2013) of the European Council on Foreign Relations (ECFR) identifies the origins of the trade controversy in China's top-down subsidization policies alone – which allegedly created production gluts, spilling over into Europe – Yu Chen (2015) solely focuses on addressing the challenges that the EU faced in the attempt to avoid entering into a "trade war" with China. The latter author also claims that, in the future, it will be necessary for the EU to act in a more cohesive, coherent, and coordinated manner, provided it wants to act more effectively for the resolution of trade disputes with China (Chen 2015).

Belonging to this same strand of research, Sylvain Plasschaert (2016) assesses the roles of governments and firms, the conflict of interest between producers and importers in the light of a changing world economy, the current AD framework of the European Union and the economic impact of AD duties on different stakeholders. Although covering a wide range of topics, authors in this first group approach the solar panel case in a largely descriptive manner without any particular conceptual or analytical framework. By contrast, the present chapter follows the conceptual framework presented in Chapter 1 and proposes additional conceptual considerations in the following section that will guide the analysis.

A second strand of research has sought to study the solar panels case, taking into account both China and the EU, by either looking at China–EU bilateral ties or through comparative studies of the political processes and policies in China and the EU. For instance, Coraline Goron (2013) attempts to examine whether placing emphasis on the realization of low-carbon development strategies in China and the EU could lead to the realization of "win-win" projects on climate change.

She argues that both sides have not yet been able to solve the tensions stemming from their desire to achieve environmentally sustainable growth objectives, while at the same time maintaining their economic competitiveness (Goron 2013).

Ans Kolk and Louise Curran (2015) explore the role of ideology in China–EU market interactions, assessing the way in which they influence public policy and business representations in the solar panel anti-dumping dispute. By reference to the term "liability of origin," they note that Chinese firms are indeed more liable than other foreign firms to encounter discrimination hazards, including negative stereotyping, when entering the EU. Yet, the authors also explore ways in which Chinese solar panel firms have been able to react, to struggle more or less directly against these liabilities and to grow more embedded in the developed-country context of the European Union (Kolk and Curran 2015).

A third strand of research seeks to examine the China–EU solar panel trade dispute against the background of the broader international context in which it occurs. Using four large-scale AD investigations initiated by the EU, India and the United States against China, Daniel Peat and Christine Barthelemy (2015) examine whether claims that Chinese PV producers have "dumped" their products on export markets below their production cost are true. Llewelyn Hughes and Jonas Meckling (2015), answering the question as to why EU and US executives supported the rhetoric of "renewables protectionism" in the PV sector specifically, seek to shed light on two main factors at play: namely, issue salience among the general EU public and the interests of policymakers themselves. Last but not least, drawing on the PV products trade disputes between the EU, the United States and China, Kailan Tian and Cuihong Yang (2014) analyze the effect of AD on China's domestic value added generated by exports. They find that anti-dumping would decrease China's PV export by 30–40 per cent and China's value added by 20 per cent, which in turn would reduce China's demand for intermediate goods from both the United States and the EU.

The authors belonging to the strands of literature identified above have all contributed to providing a better understanding of the China–EU solar panel trade dispute, albeit having started from different intellectual premises. In particular, some significant variables highlighted by preceding works, such as ideology, as in the case of Kolk and Curran (2015), and issue salience, as in the case of Hughes and Meckling (2015), help to shed light on why countries with ambitious low-carbon targets would still resort to proposing the introduction of trade defence measures against third parties. Nevertheless, no scholarly work has yet explored why EU member states defended highly divergent, and in some cases counterintuitive, policy positions when it came to initiating AD and AS investigations against Chinese solar panel manufacturers.

What decides EU member states' preferences?

Several important actors are involved in deciding the use of trade defence instruments in the EU. The role played by EU institutions is undeniably important in determining how the international trade interests of member states are defended. Member states have delegated the policymaking authority in external trade to the EU. The EC is endowed with the power to negotiate trade agreements with third parties, and to launch investigations upon receiving sector-specific complaints from industry lobby organizations representing 25 per cent of their industry within the EU. After an EC investigation has determined that certain imports are being dumped and have caused injury, it has the power to introduce provisional AD measures but also the duty to consult member states.[6] At the time of the solar panels dispute with China, member states could still stop the EC from imposing provisional anti-dumping duties by a qualified majority in the Council.[7]

The EC can also impose definitive AD duties unless a simple majority of member states express opposition to them.[8] This means concretely that fewer than 15 of currently 28 members (or fewer than 14 of the 27 members after the exit of the United Kingdom) should actively oppose the measures, or, put differently, 15 or more (14 or more after the Brexit) either support them or remain neutral on the issue (i.e. abstain in case of a vote). In combination with the need for the EC to build trust among the member states and, to the extent possible, foster agreement among all main actors, as pointed out in Chapter 1, this means that EU members retain considerable formal and informal influence despite delegation.

Evenett and Vermulst (2005) have examined the role of member states and their internal divisions in influencing the outcome of the European Commission's anti-dumping proceedings. They argue that the EC's anti-dumping practice has been politicized and that the role of member states in the EU's AD system has become significant, especially since 1997. Despite the requirement to speak with one voice, member states of the EU may have concerns differing from the EC, which may result in divisions among themselves. Evenett and Vermulst (2005) find that divisions between member states and between the EC and the member states seem to have occurred more frequently since 1995.

Bollen (2016) also underscores that it matters to pay attention to member states, in that it helps to shed light on the nexus between various policy domains, such as foreign policy, industrial policy, trade policy, competition policy and so on. In addition, it helps to understand whether member states have aptly and fully aggregated different competing interests so that an EU-level trade policy is justifiable and "democratic" enough to ensure it can gain wide support.

This leads to another question: what determines EU member states' policy preferences? Public choice theory underscores that government decision makers would adopt a trade policy favourable to most voters so as to maximize their chances of being re-elected. Some scholars highlight the role of interest groups, arguing that a country's foreign trade policy is formulated through the interactions of different societal groups or a battle between import-competing and export-oriented producers (Hiscox 2001; Pahre 2008). As a country's foreign trade policy has income distribution effects, firms fare differently in international trade. Those who think they are losers are more liable to be mobilized to lobby for their preferred government policies. Milner (1989) argues that firms with greater international connections would be less protectionist than more domestically oriented firms.

In this chapter we focus on EU member states. Nevertheless, we do not overlook the importance of European businesses (and industry lobby organizations) throughout the dispute. Basic international trade theories show that interstate free trade helps to promote overall economic benefits. Then why do some business groups lobby their governments to seek trade restrictions? This is largely because of redistributive effects of trade restrictions such as import tariffs and the hope that they will change their disadvantageous position (Krueger 1974; Grossman and Helpman 1994). Eckhardt (2015) contends that the trade policy of EU member states is a result of the interplay between import-dependent firms, which favour open markets, and import-competitors, which prefer measures that protect them from foreign competition. The expected benefit of collective political action and the capacity to act collectively determine whether they choose political mobilization or adjustment as their preferred strategy. Arguably, it is companies in industries that directly feel threatened by sudden market changes that will promote import restrictions. Hence, companies strive hard to influence the policymaking process carried out by the European Commission.

Yet, it also needs to be noted that, as the 2012 China–EU solar panel trade dispute unfolded, even companies operating within the same industry had difficulties agreeing on which stance to take on the issue. As an example, the two main industry lobby organizations seeking to shape the outcome of the dispute were EU ProSun, the "defender" of 40 EU solar PV manufacturers and 4,000 certified installers that filed the complaint to the European Commission requesting the opening of investigations against Chinese solar PV companies, and the Alliance for Affordable Solar Energy (AFASE), representing 400 importers and large distributors interested in continuing to have access to cheap PV imports from China.

Such divisions within a given sector tend to strengthen the hand of policymakers in governments or European institutions and weaken the influence of business lobbies. As Hughes and Meckling (2015) argue, "indeed, to the extent that changes in patterns of production are leading to increasingly heterogeneous business interests, this suggests that the structural power of policymakers, not business, may be increasing by changes in the structure of production globally." Furthermore, whether businesses can obtain their preferred policy outcome is not only determined by the resources they can mobilize but also contingent on the independent preferences expressed by policymakers (Woll 2007). Hence, it is important to learn how businesses respond to the growing trade imprint of China in the EU solar energy sector. Yet, one cannot draw a conclusion independent from the underlying motives driving policymaking within single EU member states.

In this research, we seek to highlight two independent variables that are traditionally considered as conditioning a state's behaviour: interests and values. Yet, we also argue that we cannot explain the policy objectives of states by only looking at either interests or values. In fact, a combination of both interest-driven and value-driven considerations is always at play – and this is especially true when the actors examined are the member states of a highly value-driven political project: the European Union.

For our purposes, interests relate to the immediate or expected impact of the China–EU solar panel dispute on the general economic situation of the concerned EU member state. The impact may depend on economic ties with China in general, possible benefits and losses of free trade with China in solar PV products, possible benefits and costs to domestic industries and the public resulting from the European Commission's punitive measures and so on. Concretely, the "**variable of interests**" can be assessed empirically by looking at (1) the possible gains and losses of the domestic solar PV industry of the EU member state examined, related to the dispute, (2) its effects on a given EU country's exports to China and (3) China's total foreign direct investment (FDI) in the country in question. Depending on the balance between these three factors, the variable of interests can take two values, namely either **enhancing** or **harming** unrestrained trade in solar PV products between China and the EU.

On the other hand, the "**variable of values**" includes the two competing notions of **protectionism** and **open trade**, to which EU member states allegedly subscribe when deciding whether or not to side with trade policy decisions taken by the EC. The relevant constellation of values is assessed with reference to two policy papers published by the ECFR (Fox and Godement 2009, as well as Godement and Parello-Plesner 2011). On the basis of a "power audit" of each member state's policies towards China, Fox and Godement (2009) divide member states of the EU into four categories in light of two independent variables, namely economic and political attitudes. Godement and Parello-Plesner (2011) further assess how preferences of member states shifted with the global financial crisis. Figure 6.1 below is a graphic rendition of the research framework introduced here.

At the intersection of these sets of values and interests, individual EU member states are likely to fall under specific categories. This, in turn, will condition their behaviour towards China's attempts at expanding its trade and investment

		Interests	
		Enhancing interests	Harming interests
Values	Protective	Struggling state	Support trade defence
	Open market	Oppose trade defence	Struggling state

Figure 6.1 Combining the variables.

imprint on European markets in general, and more specifically in the context of the solar PV dispute. The possible combinations of variables and their values lead to the following hypotheses:

Hypothesis 1: EU member states that generally favour open market arrangements and project that keeping European solar PV markets open to Chinese
products is in their overall economic interest are the ones that oppose the
European Commission's introduction of trade defence measures.

Hypothesis 2: EU member states that favour the protection of national economies and project their overall economic interests would be jeopardized by
continued open access for Chinese PV products are the ones that tend to support the European Commission's implementation of trade defence measures.

Hypothesis 3: EU member states that either favour open market arrangements
but believe that their economic interests would be jeopardized by continuing openness for Chinese solar PV products, or prefer trade protection but
believe their economic interests can be further enhanced by keeping open
to China in this case, can be considered "struggling states," in that they find
it difficult to define their position. They have a mixed impact on the policy
process due to their mixed policy preferences.

Explaining member state preferences

This section seeks to test the validity of the hypotheses presented above. It will do so with reference to three EU member states and respective constellations of interests and values in the context of the EC's decision to initiate one AD and one AS investi-
gation against Chinese solar PV manufacturers. The EU countries examined include Germany, Italy and Poland. The three countries have been selected on the following grounds. First, they responded differently to the decision. Having a strong record of supporting AD actions, Italy and other four EU countries (France, Spain, Portugal and Greece) supported it, while Germany, Poland and other 16 member states were against the Commission's action (Carnegy and Fontanella-Khan 2013). Second, the three countries are considered to hold different attitudes towards China (see Godement and Parello-Plesner 2011, p. 23), and hence it is interesting to know whether their divergent views will affect their decisions. Third, the three countries are major benefi-
ciaries of the EU's trade protection measures in general. Despite having held starkly different political positions as the dispute between China and the European Union over solar panels unfolded between 2012 and 2013, what these three countries have in common is that significant numbers of jobs are related to products for which the EC has imposed AD measures on imports from China (European Commission 2016). It is thus intriguing to see why they responded differently nevertheless.

Case 1 – Germany

We will now focus on analyzing Germany and the position it defended as the China–EU solar panel trade dispute unfolded between 2012 and 2013. Germany represents the first case study of this research project given the country's high level of trade interdependence with China (variable of interests) and its commitment to the promotion of increasingly open trade with external partners (variable of values). Therefore, Germany's policy on the dispute should follow hypothesis 1 as described above, i.e. we would expect it to be in opposition to the AD and AS procedures of the EC and even more so to any duties against Chinese imports in general.

Germany – Variable of interest

When assessing the German government's long-term interests towards strengthening its economic ties with a partner as preponderant as China, it becomes clear that among the EU member states examined here, Germany has the highest stake in ensuring that its relations with Beijing continue along a smooth path of sustained growth. This emerges from a close look at the three indicators of interests identified in the previous section.

These data confirm trends identified by the Federal Ministry for Economic Affairs and Energy in a report on Germany's foreign trade (BMWi 2017). The People's Republic of China is still the world's fifth largest recipient of German exported goods, while also being Germany's largest source of imports. In terms of investment, Germany ranks as the world's largest recipient of new Chinese FDI projects in 2015 (Germany Trade & Invest 2019).

The level of FDI inflows from China to Germany increased throughout the mid-2000s. Initially, these had mostly taken the form of smaller-sized greenfield projects (Hanemann and Huotari 2015). Chinese FDI flows into Germany started soaring in 2011, when greenfield projects paved the way for the establishment of larger acquisitions. This trend became evident in a variety of sectors, from industrial machinery to the automotive and information technology sectors, as well as renewable energy technology.

These statistics are indicative of the current status of Germany's "special relationship" with Asia's largest economic powerhouse (Peel and Hille 2012). It is also worth noting at this stage that over the past few years Germany made itself more relevant to China as the first EU member state to engage actively in the realization of Beijing's goals regarding Eurasian connectivity through the Belt and Road (B&R) initiative. By linking Duisburg, one of its major transport and commercial hubs, directly to Chongqing, a critical juncture along China's Silk Road Economic Belt, Germany has in fact opened "a new channel for the transfer of goods to and from China's central and western regions to compete with the traditional maritime route from the east coast" (Xinhua News Agency 2016), while at the same time creating a possibility for itself to be able to re-equilibrate the trade deficits it records with China since the early 2000s.

With regard to the German government's specific interests in the solar PV energy industry, it needs to be noted that Germany was selected in 2012 by China's major state-owned enterprises (SOEs) in the solar sector, like Trina Solar, Yingli Solar and CSI, as testing ground for the establishment of AFASE, a lobby organization that sought to contrast the actions taken by EU ProSun.

Through its lobbying activities, AFASE called on the European Commission to evaluate a number of unintended consequences that would stem from the imposition of AD and AS duties against Chinese solar exporters, including the potential stalemate that could be inflicted to the EU's green energy transition. As noted by Kolk and Curran (2015) in their study on China's "reactions" to the European Union's politicization of China's trade imprint, the establishment of AFASE by Chinese SOEs is indicative of the level of familiarity China's major solar firms had acquired with the political and economic ecology in Germany.

It is also important to note that when the European Commission opted for the introduction of preliminary anti-dumping duties against the imports of PRC solar PV components into the EU, Beijing too opened AD and AS probes into goods imported from the European Union, hoping to deter the EC from implementing stricter tariffs on the imports of products from PRC solar manufacturers. On this occasion, Germany was faced with the tangible threat of having its trade and investment interests potentially harmed by decisions that had been taken in Brussels. The Chinese Minister of Commerce also threatened to conduct AD and AS investigations rounds not only against exports of wine from Italy and France but also on luxury cars specifically originating from Germany (Chen 2015). At the time, the element of novelty in China's common practice of introducing retaliatory measures to protect its trade interest came from the fact that China had targeted the leading industry of its longest-standing supporter, Germany, for the first time since the opening of the EC's investigations. In so doing, the PRC's Ministry of Commerce confirmed it would not remain on the sidelines of a dispute that it perceived as discriminatory to China's commercial interests, even at the expense of harming its own economic ties with its greatest trading partner within the EU. By this time, the dispute increasingly looked like it could have developed into a "trade war" between both partners, calling on both sides to find a prompt solution to the matter at hand.

Bearing the mercantile interests of the German government in mind, it is here argued that Germany falls in the category of EU member states which, in terms of mere interests, can be considered as willing to further enhance its trade ties with China.

Germany – Predominant values in international trade

Fox and Godement (2009) portray Germany as an economically liberal country but categorize it as an "Assertive Industrialist," which "will present China with specific demands for a given sector and support anti-dumping actions or other trade measures when they see them as justified." In their update about the changing Europe-China relations and member state attitudes towards China, Godement, Parello-Plesner and Richard (2011) find that Germany, despite its "salesman instincts," has laid more emphasis on reciprocity, pressing for more market access from China. In the 2014 joint declaration between Germany and China published by the German Press and Information Office of the Federal

Government (The Press and Information Office of the Federal Government 2014), both parties voiced their clear commitment to market-oriented goals:

> Germany and China are committed to an open global economy, worldwide trade liberalisation and mutual openness to investment. Both sides are opposed to trade and investment protectionism. [...] Both sides recognise that equal market access and intellectual property protection are important for healthy and sustainable growth as well as for thriving companies. Both sides aim to resolve trade conflicts, such as anti-dumping and anti-subsidy disputes, by means of dialogue.

As the largest European economic powerhouse, Germany has acted as the economic engine and backbone of the eurozone and even the whole European Union. Meanwhile, it has been heavily relying on foreign markets as well. Being economically liberal and stressing reciprocity is not merely for the sake of its own national interest but also a policy choice after drawing lessons from history where protectionism eventually triggered interstate conflict.

Germany – Shaping outcomes

On the basis of the evidence on German interests and values, hypothesis 1 would thus suggest that Germany should have been in opposition to EU trade defence on Chinese solar PV imports. It can indeed be noted that Berlin was particularly vocal throughout the dispute in its criticisms against investigations taking place in Brussels. Chancellor Merkel's most pressing concerns at the time, however, were not about the high prices the average German consumer would have had to pay for the installation of non-Chinese solar panels. Rather, it had mostly to deal with Germany's trade and investment interests, as the German executive was certainly aware that a deterioration in Sino-German commercial ties might ultimately lead China to take retaliatory measures against German exporters in the mechanic, electronic and automotive industries.

In August 2012, two months after the European Commission's imposition of preliminary AD duties on the imports of solar cells and panels from the PRC, Chancellor Merkel was welcomed in China to meet with President Hu Jintao and Prime Minister Wen Jiabao, also bringing along 7 German ministers to meet with 13 Chinese counterparts. The visit, which marked an important phase in the development of Sino-German ties, was used by Chancellor Merkel as an opportunity to voice her concerns over the EC's opening of trade defence investigations. Merkel confirmed her hopes for the European Commission to reach a negotiated settlement with Chinese solar PV manufacturers, calling on the former not to "always resort to the same weapons for legal disputes" (Beetz and Enkhardt 2012).

This idea was further reinforced throughout Chancellor Merkel's official high-level meeting with Premier Li Keqiang in May 2013, during which Merkel told reporters: "Germany will do what it can so that there are no permanent import duties, and we'll try to clear things up as quickly as possible" (Erik 2013). Other voices, such as Ralf Lüdemann of German-based equipment manufacturer

Schmid, confirmed in an interview with sector-specific publication *PV Magazine*: "If there is a political decision for duties, then it's better that they are moderate and with the option for further negotiations than to set them so high that they completely block the Chinese from the European market." He also added that what would be necessary to really support the European PV industry is the establishment of an appropriate political framework for the PV industry, rather than punitive duty measures against non-EU manufacturers (Meza, Ali-Oettinger and Neidlein 2013).

By looking at Berlin's values and interests in working with China, it becomes more apparent that the country falls into the category our research framework suggests: that of the country heavily opposed to the introduction of AD and AS duties against its long-standing commercial partners.

Case 2 – Italy

The discussion will now turn to the position Italy held throughout the China–EU solar panel trade dispute. Given the country's relatively asymmetric, yet ever-growing commercial relations with China (variable of interests) alongside its commitment to the protection of a newly formed class of green-collar workers (variable of values), one should expect Italy to take an attitude in the solar panel dispute that conforms to hypothesis 2 presented in the previous section.

Italy – Variable of interest

In a compelling research project from 2008, Valter Coralluzzo (2008) describes Sino-Italian bilateral relations as characterized by an "erratic and troubled history," reinforcing the idea by which Italy and China have been engaging with one another only sporadically – from an economic, political and diplomatic perspective – over the past 30 years.

Most recent data on the development of both countries' economic relations seem to suggest that the dawn of the twenty-first century has ushered in a period of more mature interactions for China and Italy. As shown in Table 6.1, before the global financial crisis in 2008, the amount of Chinese FDI inflows to Italy was very small, but since 2008 they increased dramatically. During 2001–2015, Italian exports to China also kept surging, and in 2014 for the first time, it has surpassed 10 billion Euro (see Figure 6.2). In 2015, China was confirmed in the rankings as the eighth largest destination for Italian exports, totalling imports worth 10.4 billion euro (Trade Map 2019). On its part, Italy was only the 22nd largest importer of Chinese goods, and the Italian government was consistently making great strides toward re-equilibrating a trade balance that still favours China, currently set at 14.6 billion euro in overall value. The bilateral trade outlook described above has led researchers from the Torino World Affairs Institute (T.wai) in Italy to argue that China, although an important market for the Italian economy, is not yet considered of strategic importance (author's interview 2016).

Table 6.1 Chinese FDI flows into Germany, Italy and Poland (in millions of Euros)

	Germany	*Italy*	*Poland*
2000	78.0	1.0	5.1
2001	218.0	2.0	1.7
2002	−156.0	0	−1.4
2003	308.0	5.0	9.9
2004	111.0	−2.0	1.8
2005	168.0	8.0	35.6
2006	330.0	3.0	20.5
2007	27.0	−6.0	68.3
2008	−51.0	16.9	95.4
2009	112.0	181.0	−137.8
2010	330.0	−19.8	0.3
2011	360.0	142.2	72.8
2012	697.0	147.4	−115.5

Sources: Eurostat, 2011; OECD Stat, 2016; Italian Ministry of Foreign Affairs, 'info Mercati Esteri: CINA', available at http://www.infomercatiesteri.it/public/schedesintesi/s_122_cina.pdf, 2017.

Note: Data reported in US dollars (for Poland) were converted to euros according to yearly exchange rate averages provided by US Forex.

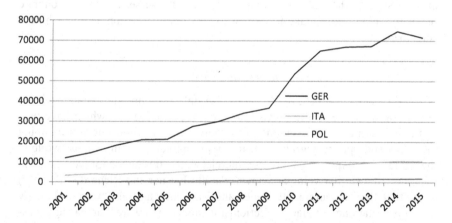

Figure 6.2 Export volumes from Germany, Italy and Poland to China (in millions of Euro). Source: From Eurostat, "EU trade since 1988," by SITC [DS-018995], Last update: October 16, 2019, https://appsso.eurostat.ec.europa.eu/nui/submitViewTableAction.do.

Bilateral relations offer a more positive outlook when looking at investment, however. According to recently published data by Baker and McKenzie, in 2015 Italy surpassed France and the United Kingdom as the EU's largest destination for Chinese FDI, especially in the form of mergers and acquisitions (M&A), the largest one of which involved ChemChina's taking of a majority stake in Pirelli.

Other attractive sectors for China are the ones belonging to the five "packages" of Sino-Italian economic cooperation – aerospace, agriculture, health, environment and renewable energy, and urbanization. It is among the priorities of the current government to continue fostering investment relations that can take the above-mentioned sectors into account.

For what concerns the solar PV sector, under Prime Minister Mario Monti (2011–2013), the Italian executive had set ambitious targets for the installation of solar PV systems throughout the peninsula, defending the argument by which 35 per cent of the country's total electricity output would need to be generated through renewable energy technologies by 2030. By 2015, Italy had become the only EU country to produce 8 per cent of its electricity output through solar energy. Italy's ambitious plan pushed up demand for solar panels. Domestic producers, in the face of much cheaper Chinese products, lost their market shares in both solar panels and installation. The solar PV companies that declared themselves to be insolvent or bankrupt prior to the eruption of the 2012 China–EU solar panel trade dispute were two: Solar Day and X Group S.p. A. This may have had a considerable impact on the further development of the industry in Italy.

Hence, the increasing presence of Chinese solar PV products in Europe would harm Rome's interests. Its need to develop large-scale solar power, along with fostering development of local solar PV companies, called for the Italian government to support the EC's anti-dumping action. Of course, its closer economic ties with China might make it hesitant to take punitive action against Chinese solar firms.

Italy – Predominant values in international trade

Fox and Godement (2009, p. 26) categorize Italy as a more protectionist economy as well as one of the "accommodating mercantilists" – which have protectionist instincts – as exemplified by their active lobbying for anti-dumping measures and opposing granting China with market economy status, while at the same time expecting more commercial gains through improved political relations. In a similar vein, Godement, Parello-Plesner and Richard (2011, p. 7) argue that the "accommodating mercantilists" such as Italy "were politically non-confrontational but had protectionist instincts" and were "increasingly desperate for Chinese investment." Other researchers arrive at similar conclusions: "Southern European states such as Italy, Spain and Portugal, whose economies are not as competitive as those of their northern neighbors, tend to have a favourable view of protectionist measures" (Stratfor 2017, p. 5).

In an official statement of the Italian government released by the European Commission's DG Trade, one of the key components of Italy's position was represented by the need to ensure that the country's international competitors "comply with the rules" (Neslen 2012). Yet, more attention was given to the previously mentioned issue of asymmetry and lack of reciprocity in Italy's relationship with many of its extra-EU partners, including China, rather than to issues pertaining to the imposition of AD and AS duties to target certain imports. The statement also called on the European Commission to consider the requests of small and medium-sized enterprises (SMEs) when drafting economic and trade policy, highlighting the central positions these play in EU member states along the Mediterranean (Neslen 2012).

Positions like this indicate an underlying level of suspicion of the Italian executive as it engages in trade relations with its non-EU commercial partners. A strong commitment to the openness of trade – to the point that the establishment of further bilateral trade agreements with third parties was encouraged – was part of the EU's experience, and it was also characteristic of Italy's general approach to commercial and trade issues. Yet, the issue that was deemed as being the most compelling of those continued in the government's official statement was the need for third parties to "comply to international trade law" – the same complaint China would move in 2012 against Italian wine exporters and solar manufacturers. Hence, Italy tended to resort to protectionism when it perceived that its economic ties with other countries were not on a reciprocal basis.

Italy – Shaping outcomes

The findings on Italy thus lead us to expect Italy to support the EC's trade defence investigations against Chinese solar PV imports, as suggested by hypothesis 2. In the specific context offered by the China–EU solar panel trade dispute, Italy played the role of the EU member state that values the protection of labour rights – especially in sectors considered "strategic" – over the fostering of greater trade openness with non-EU partners. In so doing, however, the Italian government recurrently ran the risk of harming its economic relations with Beijing – a threat that became especially tangible with China's initiation of AD and AS investigations against imports of Italian wine, alongside the filing of a complaint to the WTO against Italy's subsidization practices to the consumer side of the solar PV sector.

In October 2012, following a cabinet meeting of the ministers, Prime Minister Monti confirmed the introduction of new measures for the Italian government's greater financial support of solar PV products manufactured in Italy, rather than imported from abroad. No third countries were specifically mentioned throughout the press conference, but the initiative was considered as an assertive policy move against the growing market shares of Chinese solar PV companies expanding their "shallow" presence within the EU.

The general assumption is that Italy, an economy structured around the central role played by SMEs, is inherently in favour of the introduction of protectionist measures against external trade and investment actors that could undermine the overall stability of national industry sectors. Yet, what is interesting to note is that once the Chinese government announced the possibility for it to open AD and AS investigations against Chinese imports of Italian wine, the tone held by the Italian government immediately softened. In June 2013, Prime Minister Enrico Letta reaffirmed his commitment to the drafting of a peaceful resolution of the trade dispute in which China and the

European Union had got embroiled (Dell'Orefice 2013). Giorgio Squinzi, then president of the General Confederation of Italian Industry (Confindustria), had also supported a similar political stance, arguing Italy would have needed to react against a problem that was perceived as particularly cumbersome – yet, the negotiating parties would need to agree "to the same rules and regulations in the name of sustainable development," once again hinting at the fact that the EU's external trade partners do not generally "comply" to international trade norms (Pagni 2013).

The undertaking reached between the European Commission and Chinese solar manufacturers in August 2013 was thus welcomed by the Italian government; yet, it could be argued that the Italian executive was mostly satisfied with the agreement because it had put an end to China's retaliation measures against Italian wine (Pagni 2013) – the issue that had become the most pressing for Italy, as it represented the potential start of a formal trade war.

By looking at Italy's values and interests in working with China, it can be found that the country falls into the category our research framework suggests: that of a country that preferred the introduction of AD and AS duties against China, thanks to its protective instinct and local interests being harmed by the large-scale imports of Chinese solar PV products.

Case 3 – Poland

The third and last case study hereby presented is that of Poland, an EU member state chosen for its distinct interests surrounding the solar PV dispute and the values it embraces. By and large, like Italy, Poland tends to be an economic protectionist. Unlike Italy – which has a large solar PV sector undergoing fierce competition with Chinese firms and cherishes ambitious goals of promoting the use of solar energy – Poland was in a detached position, as it had insignificant interests in this dispute. Meanwhile, Poland has its own concerns when developing relations with China.

Poland – Variable of interest

Poland has played an interesting role in the drafting of trade policy outcomes at the EC level. This country has developed increased scepticism against the EU itself, particularly its renewable energy policies. The following factors best explain this situation: (1) Poland's reaction to the 2008 global financial crisis pressured Warsaw into convincing Brussels that EU green energy transition projects needed to be kept cheap across the value chain. This implies that the realization of ambitious green transition projects is highly discouraged in Poland and that the country has to import an exceeding number of clean energy products originating from third countries. (2) Poland is still overly reliant on coal for electricity generation, as this is used to generate about 90 per cent of the country's total electricity output.[9] (3) Poland has been a core opponent of the growing ambition of EU climate policies in the 2010–2020 time frame, and vocally against having Brussels setting green transition targets anywhere beyond 2020 for all EU member states, regardless of the energy priorities individually expressed.

Hence, compared with many other EU member states, Poland is lagging behind in the use of renewable energy. However, growing energy demands and serious environmental pollution in Poland have forced Warsaw to pay more attention to developing renewable energy. Moreover, despite its reservations, Poland has to make more efforts to meet the EU's mandatory goal of renewable energy use. For both purposes, Poland has to step up efforts to promote the use of renewable energy such as solar power. That end, however, calls for necessary investments and cheap solar products, both of which can be offered by China. Chinese companies, such as Industrial and Commercial Bank of China, have already invested heavily in Polish renewable energy and in the energy sector in general (Zacks Equity Research 2017). Thus, it would be unwise for Poland to support the EC's imposing AD measures against China.

At the same time, the growing trade imbalances between Poland and China have gradually raised concerns. China has replaced Russia to become Poland's second most important import partner in 2014, but its exports to China remain minuscule, less than 2 per cent of its total exports. However, the demand for Polish goods has been growing very rapidly in China. Poland's exports to China increased by 257 per cent in the 2000s, and it is projected to grow continuously, in the order of 11 per cent annually in the coming five years (Kania 2015). If the EC's AD decision had garnered enough support from the member states and come into force, a trade war with China would have been inevitable. That would have dampened the heartening trend in Poland's China trade. Therefore, the EC's AD measures against China would do more harm, rather than enhance Poland's interests.

Poland – Predominant values in international trade

It is said that Poland has not developed "a consistently implemented long-term and accurate strategy" in its overall foreign policy and its economic policy towards China specifically (Sarek 2018). By and large, like Germany, Poland has been identified as an "Assertive Industrialist" by Fox and Godement, meaning that it is ready to defend industrial interests or protect jobs at home from Chinese competition. Unlike Germany, they describe Poland as more protectionist in terms of economic attitude (Fox and Godement 2009).

However, when it comes to Sino-Polish relations, Poland's attitude towards China seems erratic. The signing of a strategic partnership agreement with China in 2011 marked Poland's revival of cooperation with China, a policy shift from the previous emphasis on human rights, and the debut of the CEE-China cooperation (so called 16 + 1 format) in 2012 has turned a new leaf in bilateral relations. With political rapprochement with China, Warsaw became less assertive on economic issues as it wanted to attract more Chinese investments (Godement, Parello-Plesner, Richard 2011, p. 7), and expand its exports to the Chinese market (Sarek 2018). To that end, the Polish coalition government even launched a Go-China programme in 2012. But with time passing by, Poland eventually felt disappointed as its pro-China policy had not brought about tangible economic gains from China (Sarek 2018). Poland has become more sceptical of the 16 + 1 structure, and in December 2014 Polish Prime Minister Ewa Kopacz even did not attend the 16 + 1 Summit in Belgrade (Tuszyński 2015). However, at the time when the EC threatened to impose AD duties on Chinese solar PV products, Poland was more on the side of open trade.

Poland – Shaping outcomes

Throughout the China–EU solar panel trade dispute, the preferences of the Polish government reflected the position of the UK-based Solar Trade Association (STA, formed by the EU national solar industry associations of the UK, Italy, Romania, Poland, Hungary, Sweden and Slovakia), which was central in opposing the introduction of AD and AS tariffs against Chinese solar manufacturers, as these argued that "duties at any level" were "having a significant impact (on the EU industry), dwarfing any possible benefit for European solar producers, and setting back the objective for grid parity for years" (Montgomery 2013). As a reaction to the EC's investigations, Polish solar firms expressed "deep concern" and an "overwhelming opposition" to the introduction of trade defence measures at the expenses of Chinese solar manufacturers and their growing market share in the EU's solar sector (Montgomery 2013).

Poland thus could be described, in accordance with our research framework, as a "struggling state." In light of its protectionist values, Poland should have sided with the EC to impose AD duties against Chinese products, and Poland itself is a state that very well recognized the importance of having EU states agreeing on commonly framed policies, especially when it comes to foreign policy and energy issues. Moreover, by doing so, it would help redress the bilateral trade imbalance. Yet, Poland did not tilt towards the EC; its desire for Chinese investment has overridden its trade imbalance concern and eventually led it to favour the continuous imports of Chinese solar PV products.

Comparing the case studies

The three countries studied in this chapter have responded in different ways to the EC proposal of punishing Chinese solar PV producers with AD measures. This was a result of their differing interests and values with regard to this case. Germany, having a high stake in the Chinese market and a growing bilateral economic linkage, was more willing to follow what its liberal economic values dictated. Consistent belief in free trade and interests in further developing bilateral economic ties have turned Germany into a spearhead to oppose the EC's decision of imposing AD duties against Chinese solar PV producers.

In the case of Italy, although it had growing economic ties with Beijing, its protectionist propensity in economic values and concerns over the increasing market shares of Chinese solar firms establishing their presence in Europe – and over labour rights for local employees – later compelled the Italian government to side with Commissioner De Gucht on the AD and AS investigations against Chinese solar manufacturers. Under such circumstances, a consistent belief in trade protection and expectations that its economic interests would be further harmed have led Italy to support the EC's protective action.

Unlike both Germany and Italy, Poland had to struggle with its conflicting interests as well as the contradiction between the choice it made and its economic values embracing trade protection. Despite concerns over the growing trade imbalance, the need for cheaper products from China and Chinese investments seemed to override its protectionist inclinations, eventually driving the Polish government to oppose the EC's trade defence initiatives against China. With such a choice, Poland had to deal with domestic criticism for making concessions to the authoritarian state.

The divisions among EU member states have thus undermined the unity of the EU's foreign trade policy. Despite the above divisions, to this day, it remains very difficult to determine their exact effect. Concretely this means that we cannot say for sure whether the minimum import price undertaking settlement, and Brussels' decision to accept it, were policy outcomes (1) profoundly influenced by the actions of Germany within the European Union, or (2) indicative of a certain level of autonomy recognized by the European Commission.

Conclusion

From the case studies above, it seems that the larger the stakes of relying on the Chinese market and FDI, and the firmer the belief in economic liberalism, the more likely a country is to oppose trade protection measures and *vice versa*. In a more complicated situation, when a country's economic values and interests are at odds, and its differing interests are counteracting, it tends to struggle when choosing its policy, as any option risks to create both winners and losers within the country.

In the immediate aftermath of the 2008 global financial crisis, numerous acquisitions by Chinese firms revived European companies entering a post-recovery phase with necessary restructuring and cash flows. Sustained imports of Chinese solar PV energy systems also contributed to the expansion of the EU's solar installation capacity – bringing European executives a step closer to fully achieving their green transition goals. Over the past few years, however, China's investment and trade imprint on the EU's solar energy industry have gradually prompted the rise of "renewables protectionism" across the EU (Hughes and Meckling, 2015). EU member states have been reacting to the same phenomenon in various ways, and the purpose of this research project was to identify and explain these differences. This chapter intends to employ a research framework built around their economic *interests* and *values* (in the sense of predominant preferences in international trade) defended by the involved officials.

This study has verified three hypotheses. Firstly, countries preferring free trade tend to oppose the EC's protective AD and AS measures when they perceive that continuing engagement with China would enhance their economic interests. Secondly, countries that generally tend to opt for trade protection and also perceive engagement with China to be harmful to their economic interests should be expected to strongly support the EC's protective measures against foreign imports into the European markets. Lastly, the countries whose perceptions of the impact on their economic interests conflict with their value-based preferences struggle in making their decision.

As pointed out in Chapter 1 of this volume, member states play an important role in EU trade policy despite the high level of integration. This can have a strong impact on the EU's management of trade disputes and on the use of diplomatic or legal strategies. Although only covering three member states, the case studies have shown that different economic interests *vis-à-vis* China, and diverging ideational orientations concerning international trade, have led member states to adopt very different attitudes towards the Commission's decision to start AD and AS investigations. As suggested in Chapter 1, strong divisions among member states make it more difficult, if not impossible, for the Commission to attempt to solve disputes through informal diplomatic consultations, as the potential win-set is minuscule. At the same time, if member states publicly expose their preferences to international counterparts, as in the case of Germany's Chancellor Merkel or Italian Premier Letta, it becomes virtually impossible to turn a small win-set into a bargaining advantage through the famous tied-hands argument. This would suggest that in the case of the China–EU solar panels dispute the conflicting interests among EU member states did not leave any space for the European Commission to envisage a negotiated solution and virtually pushed it to follow the formal logic of AD and AS procedures (see Chapter 5 for a discussion of the EC's role in the solar panel case).

It should be noted that the work presented here also shows some directions for the further development of research on the subject. Future projects, for instance, could focus on the reactions that the growing trade imprint of other developing economies in the renewable energy sector (such as India and Vietnam) have sparked within the EU. The author hopes that this study – and the research framework it introduces to fill an existing gap in the literature – could prove useful for the further theorization of issues pertaining to the dynamic trade interactions of developing economies, the EU and its member states.

Notes

1 As of 2013, 138 countries around the world had reportedly implemented renewable energy support schemes (Renewable Energy Policy Network for the 21st Century 2012).
2 As noted by Van de Graaf (2013), the 2012 China–EU solar panel trade dispute should be read in a global context.
3 Directive (EC) 2009/28 of the European Parliament and of the Council of 23 April 2009 on the promotion of the use of energy from renewable sources and amending and subsequently repealing Directives 2001/77/EC and 2003/30/EC (Text with EEA relevance), OJ L 140/16, 5 June 2009.
4 European businesses acquired by Chinese solar PV companies between 2012 and 2015 (including Hanergy, LDK, Shunfeng Photovoltaic and Chint Solar) have recurrently stated the positive effects derived from having established closer ties with China.

European companies such as Astronergy, Solibro GbmH and S.A.G. Solarstrom were able to withdraw their declarations of insolvency and undergo restructuring thanks to China's growing investment presence in the Union's solar sector.

5 "Politicization" here refers to the situation where EU member states' attitudes towards an EC proposal of imposing AD duties to a foreign product are mainly decided by their domestic politics or foreign policy interests.

6 Regulation (EU) 2016/1036 of the European Parliament and of the Council of 8 June 2016 on protection against dumped imports from countries not members of the European Union (codification), OJ L 176/21, 30 June 2016 (hereinafter Regulation 2016/1036), Art. 7(4) & 15(4).

7 Regulation (EC) 1225/2009 of 30 November 2009 on protection against dumped imports from countries not members of the European Community, OJ L 343/51, 22 December 2009 (hereinafter Regulation 1225/2009), Art. 7(6).

8 Regulation 1225/2009, Art. 9(4); Regulation 2016/1036, Art. 9(4) & 15(3).

9 The World Bank sets the share at 85 per cent, the International Energy Agency at 92 per cent.

References

Barthelemy, C. and Peat, D. (2015) 'Trade remedies in the renewable energy sector: Normal value and double remedies', *Journal of World Investment and Trade*, 16(3), pp. 436–466.

Beetz, B. and Enkhardt, S. (2012) 'Germany wants to avoid EU-Sino trade war', *PV Magazine*, 30 August 2012.

Bollen, Y. (2016) 'Unpacking member state preferences in trade policy: A research agenda', Presented at the EU Trade Policy at the Crossroads, available at https://biblio.ugent.be/publication/7104967 (accessed 19 October, 2019).

Carbaugh, B. and St. Brown, M. (2012) 'Industrial policy and renewable energy: Trade conflicts', *Journal of International and Global Economic Studies*, 5(1), pp. 1–16.

Carnegy, H. and Fontanella-Khan, J. (2013) 'China clash on solar panels exposes trade splits within Europe', *Financial Times*, available at https://www.ft.com/content/008cfcd2-cf72-11e2-be7b-00144feab7de (accessed 19 October, 2019).

Chen Y. (2015) 'EU-China solar panels trade dispute: Settlement and challenges to the EU', *European Institute for Asian Studies*, available at http://www.eias.org/wp-content/uploads/2016/02/EU-Asia-at-a-glance-EU-China-Solar-Panels-Dispute-Yu-Chen.pdf (accessed 19 October, 2019).

Coralluzzo, V. (2008) 'Italy's foreign policy toward China: Missed opportunities and new chances', *Journal of Modern Italian Studies*, 13(1), pp. 6–24.

Dell'Orefice, di G. (2013) 'Dazi cinesi sul vino: In campo Letta e Squinzi', *Il Sole 24 ORE*, available at https://www.ilsole24ore.com/art/impresa-e-territori/2013-06-06/dazi-cinesi-vino-campo-144856.shtml?uuid=AbyeBi2H (accessed 19 October, 2019).

Eckhardt, J. (2015) *Business Lobbying and EU Trade Governance in a World of Global Value Chains*, London: Palgrave Macmillan UK.

European Commission. (2013) 'Remarks by EU trade commissioner Karel De Gucht on the decision to impose provisional anti-dumping measures on imports of solar panels from China', Memo/13/499, 4 June 2013.

European Commission. (2016) 'Change in the methodology for anti-dumping investigations concerning China', available at http://trade.ec.europa.eu/doclib/docs/2016/february/tradoc_154241.pdf (accessed 19 October, 2019).

European Commission. (2019) 'Climate strategies & targets', available at https://ec.europa.eu/clima/policies/strategies_en (accessed 19 October, 2019).

Eurostat, "EU trade since 1988," by SITC [DS-018995], Last update: October 16, 2019, https://appsso.eurostat.ec.europa.eu/nui/submitViewTableAction.do (accessed October 23, 2019).

Evenett, S.J. and Vermulst, E. (2005) 'The politicisation of EC anti-dumping policy: Member states, their votes and the European commission', *The World Economy*, 28(5), pp. 701–717.

Federal Ministry for Economic Affairs and Energy (BMWi). (2017), "Facts about German foreign trade Berlin," August, https://www.bmwi.de/Redaktion/EN/Publikationen/facts-about-german-foreign-trade.pdf?__blob=publicationFile&v=7 (accessed 19 October, 2019).

Fox, J. and Godement, F. (2009) *A Power Audit of EU-China Relations*, ECFR, available at http://www.ecfr.eu/page/-/ECFR12_-_A_POWER_AUDIT_OF_EU-CHINA_RELATIONS.pdf (accessed 19 October, 2019).

Germany Trade & Invest. (2019) 'European Stocks at the Top', available at https://www.gtai.de/GTAI/Navigation/EN/Invest/Business-location-germany/FDI/fdi-data.html (accessed 19 October, 2019).

Godement, F. (2013) 'Solar panels: A crisis "Made in China"', *China Analysis of ECFR*, (SP), available at https://www.ecfr.eu/page/-/China_Analysis_Special_Issue_June2013.pdf (accessed 19 October, 2019).

Godement, F., Parello-Plesner, J. and Richard, A. (2011), 'The scramble for Europe', *ECFR*, available at http://www.ecfr.eu/page/-/ECFR37_Scramble_For_Europe_AW_v4.pdf (accessed 19 October, 2019).

Goron, C. (2013) 'Low carbon policies and the management of EU-China trade relations', Paper submitted for the Second Workshop on EU-China Relations in Global Politics, "Strategic Partnership, EU-China Relations under the New Leadership", 3–4 March, Renmin University, Beijing, P.R. China.

Goron, C. (2018) 'Fighting against climate change and for fair trade: Finding the EU's interest in the solar panels dispute with China', *China-EU Law Journal*, 6, pp. 103–125.

Grossman, G.M. and Helpman, E. (1994) 'Protection for sale', *The American Economic Review*, 84(4), pp. 833–850.

Hanemann, T. and Huotari, M. (2015) 'Chinese FDI in Europe and Germany: Preparing for a New Era of Chinese capital, a report by the Institute for China Studies and Rhodium Group', *Mercator Institute for China Studies*, 52(2), pp. 1–56.

Hiscox, M.J. (2001) 'Class versus industry cleavages: Inter-industry factor mobility and the politics of trade', *International Organization*, 55(1), pp. 1–46.

Hughes, L. and Meckling, J. (2015) 'Salient green: Business power and trade policy responses to Chinese solar imports', BRIE Working Paper 2015–2016, Berkeley University.

Kania, J. (2015) 'China: One of Poland's fastest growing export markets', *Ministry of Poland Treasury*, available at http://www.msp.gov.pl/en/polish-economy/economic-news/6640,China-One-of-Poland039s-fastest-growing-export-markets.html. (accessed 20 October, 2019).

Kirschbaum, E. (2013) 'Merkel, Li call for end to EU-China solar trade row', *Reuters*, available at www.reuters.com/article/us-china-eu-trade-merkel-idUSBRE94P0CD20130526. (accessed 19 October, 2019).

Kolk, A. and Curran, L. (2015) 'Contesting a place in the sun: On ideologies in foreign markets and liabilities of origin', *Journal of Business Ethics*, 142(4), pp. 697–717.

Krueger, A.O. (1974) 'The political economy of the rent-seeking society', *The American Economic Review*, 64(3), pp. 291–303.

Lewis, J.I. (2014) 'The rise of renewable energy protectionism: Emerging trade conflicts and implications for low carbon development', *Global Environmental Politics*, 14(4), pp. 10–35.

Meza, E., Ali-Oettinger, S. and Neidlein, H.-C. (2013) 'TOP NEWS: EC imposes 11.8% anti-dumping duties on Chinese PV imports', *PV Magazine*, available at https://www.pv-magazine.com/2013/06/04/top-news-ec-imposes-11-8-anti-dumping-duties-on-chinese-pv-imports_100011582/ (accessed 19 October, 2019).

Milner, H.V. (1989) *Resisting Protectionism: Global Industries and the Politics of International Trade*, Princeton University Press.

Montgomery, J. (2013) 'UPDATE: EU-China Solar Trade War Entering Endgame?', *Renewable Energy World*, available at https://www.renewableenergyworld.com/articles/2013/05/eu-china-solar-trade-war-entering-endgame.html (accessed 19 October, 2019).

Neslen, A. (2012) 'Solar industry pushing for anti-dumping case against China', *EURACTIV*, available at https://www.euractiv.com/section/climate-environment/news/solar-industry-pushing-for-anti-dumping-case-against-china/ (accessed 9 May, 2019).

OECD Statistics. (2019) 'Balanced International Merchandise Trade Statistics', available at https://stats.oecd.org/.

Tuszyński, R. (2015) 'Polish perspective on CEE-China 16+1 cooperation: The unexpected Ukranian factor', *Europolity: Continuity and Change in European Governance*, 9(1), pp. 189–220.

Pagni, di L. (2013) 'L'Europa impone i dazi ai pannelli solari: Scoppia la pace commerciale con la Cina', *La Repubblica*, available at https://www.repubblica.it/economia/finanza/2013/12/02/news/l_europa_impone_i_dazi_ai_pannelli_solari_scoppia_la_pace_commerciale_con_la_cina-72495011/ (accessed 20 August, 2019).

Pahre, R. (2008) *Politics and Trade Cooperation in the Nineteenth Century: The "Agreeable Customs" of 1815–1914*, Cambridge University Press.

Peel, Q. and Hille, K. (2012) 'Merkel to court Chinese investors: German chancellor flies to China to explain EU crisis management' *Financial Times*, available at https://next.ft.com/content/5086d228-4c27-11e1-bd09-00144feabdc0 (accessed 19 October, 2019).

Plasschaert, S. (2016) 'Assessing the Solar Energy Dispute between the European Union and the People's Republic of China (2016)', ECIPE (European Center for International Political Economy) Working Paper, 01/2016.

Renewable Energy Policy Network for the 21st Century (REN21). (2012) Renewables 2012 Global Status Report: Key Findings, available at http://ren21.net/Portals/0/documents/activities/gsr/REN21_GSR2012_Key%20Findings.pdf (accessed 19 October, 2019).

Sarek, Ł. (2018) 'Poland and the EU: Seeking a two-way street with China', *The Warsaw Institute Review*, available at https://warsawinstitute.org/poland-eu-seeking-two-way-street-china/ (accessed 19 October, 2019).

Stratfor. (2017) "In Europe, France Leads the Protectionist Charge," available at https://worldview.stratfor.com/article/europe-france-leads-protectionist-charge (accessed 19 October, 2019).

The Press and Information Office of the Federal Government. (2014) 'Joint Declaration between Germany and China', available at https://archiv.bundesregierung.de/archiv-de/meta/startseite/joint-declaration-between-germany-and-china-460244.

Tian, K. and Yang C. (2014) "The impact of antidumping on value-added generated by trade: A case study on the PV products trade dispute between the EU and China," *Conference Paper, 22nd International Input-Output Conference & 4th Edition of the International School of I-O Analysis*, 14–18 July, Lisbon, Portugal.

Van de Graaf, T. (2013) 'Fragmentation in global energy governance: Explaining the creation of IRENA', *Global Environmental Politics*, 13(3), pp. 14–33.

Woll, C. (2007) 'Leading the dance? Power and political resources of business lobbyists', *Journal of Public Policy*, 27(1), pp. 57–78.

Xinhua News Agency. (2016) 'Xinhua Insight: China-Europe freight rail route boosts Silk Road trade', *Xinhua News*, available at http://www.china.org.cn/china/Off_the_Wire/2016-06/18/content_38694380.htm (accessed 19 October, 2019).

Zacks Equity Research. (2017) 'ReneSola Wins Bid for 13 MW of Solar Projects in Poland', *Zacks*, available at https://www.zacks.com/stock/news/244745/renesola-wins-bid-for-13-mw-of-solar-projects-in-poland (accessed 19 October, 2019).

7 Disciplining export restrictions through negotiation and litigation

Chien-Huei Wu

With the completion of China's accession process, the focus of existent trade powers shifted to securing, through legal and diplomatic approaches, China's compliance with its WTO obligations and accession commitments. The EU, in conjunction with other WTO members, and with a view to enforcing commitments to which China agreed, filed two WTO complaints: *China – Raw Materials* and *China – Rare Earths*. With the lessons learnt during China's accession negotiations and the litigation process, the EU aims to globalize the disciplines on export restrictions to all WTO members through negotiation in the Doha negotiation process and, before it is done, through bilateral negotiations or dialogues with particular third countries.

This chapter aims to examine the EU's trade dispute management strategy with regards to disciplines on export restrictions by looking at the negotiation/litigation interaction. To this end, this chapter will firstly explore the role of export restrictions in the GATT/WTO regime. Special attention will be paid to the spillover effects of voluntary export restrictions and the great bargain in the Uruguay Rounds. Secondly, this chapter will examine the effects of negotiation in disciplining export restrictions during China's accession processes, followed by an exploration of how the EU secured enforcement of such obligations and commitments through WTO litigation. Chapter further reflects how the EU might react if China decides to comply with Panel/Appellate Body decisions by switching from export taxes to production quotas. In the absence of clear rules on production quotas, will diplomatic tools be the best instruments for the EU to resolve its differences with China? Finally, this chapter examines how the EU tries to globalize these China-specific disciplines to all WTO members, or at least to the new acceding WTO members and its counterparts in free trade agreements (FTA) negotiations. A conclusion summarizing the findings and main arguments is also provided.

The rise of Japan and the spillover of voluntary export restraints

The first instance of export restrictions in international relations is also related to the emergence of a new trading power, Japan, in the 1970s and 1980s. However, at that time, export restrictions took the form of voluntary export restraints (VERs), known as grey-area measures, and focused on the protection of domestic industry against trade diversion effects arising from enforcement of such VERs. To be more specific, what then plagued the EU (then the European Economic Community, the EEC) were a series of measures imposed by Japan with a view to enforcing confidential agreements between the United States and Japan regarding the exportation of various products, such as automobiles and semiconductors, to the United States. Pursuant to this agreement, Japan was obliged to monitor and control its exports to the United States in exchange for the latter's concession not to impose trade defence measures, notably, anti-dumping measures. These VERs nonetheless had trade diversion effects on third countries and posed a threat to the domestic industries thereof. In response to a VER concluded by the United States and Japan, the EU filed a complaint against Japan, *Japan – Semiconductors*,[1] under Art. XXIII of the GATT, arguing that the export restrictive measures imposed by Japan were incompatible with Art. XI of the GATT.

In *Japan – Semiconductors*, the Panel was faced with Japan's reliance on administrative guidance in achieving policy goals and the complexity arising therefrom. This dispute related mainly to the enforcement of an arrangement on voluntary export restraints between Japan and the United States, one central element of which was to monitor costs and export price to third countries with a view to avoid dumping. Japan argued that there were no legally binding rules involved in these monitoring processes and thus no governmental measures falling within the scope of Art. XI:1 of the GATT 1947, and that as the limitation on exports was initiated by private parties in their own interests to prevent dumping the issue was thus not subject to dispute settlement proceedings. This argument did not persuade the Panel, which firstly noted that Art. XI:1, unlike other provisions of the GATT (1947), did not refer to laws and regulations but used a broader catch-all term, "other measures." "This wording indicated clearly that any measure instituted or maintained by a contracting party which restricted the exportation or sale for export of products was covered by this provision, irrespective of the legal status of the measure."[2] In recognition of the differing degrees of intensity of government involvement in private actions, the task of the Panel was to carefully assess whether the measures in question fell under the purview of Art. XI:1, bearing in mind that "government-industry relations varied from country to country, from industry to industry, and from case to case."[3]

With this variance taken into consideration, the Panel put forward two criteria to determine whether a measure falls within the scope of Art. XI of the GATT 1947.

> First, there were reasonable grounds to believe that sufficient incentives or disincentives existed for non-mandatory measures to take effect. Second the operation of the measures to restrict export of semi-conductors at prices below company-specific costs was essentially dependent on Government action or intervention.[4]

The Panel concluded that the difference between a legally binding measure and an administrative guidance in this present complaint is only "a difference in form rather than substance because the measures were operated in a manner equivalent to mandatory requirements."[5] "[T]he complex of measures constituted a coherent system restricting the sale for export of monitored semi-conductors at prices below company-specific costs to markets other than the United States, inconsistent with Art. XI.1."[6]

The great bargain of the Uruguay round: Agreement on safeguards

The heavy reliance of the United States and Japan on VERs to resolve trade frictions, which adversely impacted the EU, brought VERs to the table during the great bargain of the Uruguay Round negotiations. Trade ministers exchanged market access commitments and legislated new trade rules, which yielded fruit in the Final Act Embodying the Results of the Uruguay Round of Multilateral Trade Negotiations. Among these Uruguay Round agreements, Agreement on Safeguards (ASG), in Art. 11, obliges WTO members to eliminate these measures and to refrain from imposing new ones (Sykes 2006, pp. 25–26).

The ASG does not employ the term of "grey-area measures"; rather, it employs the general term "certain measures." Art. 11 of the ASG regulates these certain (grey-area) measures in three ways. Firstly, it clarifies the scope of these "certain measures" to be prohibited or eliminated. Secondly, it sets out a schedule for WTO members to phase out existing grey-area measures. Thirdly, it addresses the role of the government of a member in encouraging or supporting the adoption or maintenance of grey-area measures by nongovernmental entities. From the outset, the ASG in Art. 11(1)(a) prohibits a WTO member from taking or seeking any emergency action under Art. XIX of the GATT 1994 unless the action complies with the requirement of that provision and is applied in accordance with the ASG. The objective of this provision is to reiterate the determination of the negotiators to discipline all emergency actions and bring them under scrutiny of Art. XIX of the GATT 1994 and the ASG. The ASG in Art. 11(1)(b) then dictates that a WTO member not to "seek, take or maintain any voluntary export restraints, orderly marketing arrangements or any other similar measures on the export or the import side." Three elements are put forward in this provision: the VERs, orderly marketing arrangements and any other similar measures. The focus of the Uruguay Round negotiations and its subsequent rule on VERs still relate to the trade adverse effects to third countries with the imposition of such grey-area measures. When a country, namely Japan, monitors and controls its exports to the United States, its products may spill over to the market of third countries and thus threaten the domestic industries thereof. At that stage, trading countries are concerned with how to defend their own domestic markets against the penetration of foreign (Japanese) products. This singular focus has changed in the processes of China's accession negotiations, as will be demonstrated below, *EEC – Semiconductors* concerns downstream products whereas *China – Raw Materials* and *China – Rare Earths* relate to upstream products with the focus being shifted to access to raw materials or natural resources.[7]

The return of China to international economic relations: offense and defence and the quest for raw materials

Since the introduction of its "reform and open" policy in 1978, the return of China to the international economic scene has presented great challenges to the GATT/WTO system. Given its legal, symbolic and economic importance, John Jackson regards the integration of China into the WTO as both the most important event in the WTO's first decade and as the event that made the WTO a truly "world" trade organization (Jackson 2003, pp. 18–19). There are some reasons for this. Firstly, China is a huge economy characterized by a socialist market economy capable of overwhelming competitors. Existent WTO members were concerned with the trade disruption that would follow on China's entry into the WTO and the potential threat posed to domestic industries. In response, existent WTO members designated special trade defence rules against Chinese products, notably methods to determine price comparability that differ from WTO rules. The label of non-market economy thus constituted the price China had to pay for its accession, but it is a label China is keen to get rid of. Secondly, China is a huge market that promises plenty of opportunities, leading existent WTO members to explore market access and expand their market share in China. In exchange for admission, China agreed on a wide range of market access commitments. Therefore, these WTO-plus obligations and market access commitments are the fruit that existent WTO members aim to reap, through legal and diplomatic approaches, during and after the accession negotiations.

In addition to protecting their domestic industries and accessing the Chinese market, during the negotiation process existent WTO members were concerned with China's manipulation of its rich reserve of strategically or technologically important natural resources for economic and political purposes.[8] In order to prevent such manipulative exploitation of its resources, existent WTO members successfully included a provision in China's Accession Protocol to regulate export duties. According to this provision, "China shall eliminate all taxes and charges applied to exports unless specifically provided for in Annex 6 of this Protocol or applied in conformity with the provisions of Article VIII of the GATT 1994."[9] This provision turns out to have provided the legal basis for the EU to challenge China export restrictions in *China – Raw Materials* and *China – Rare Earths*.[10]

The quest for natural resources: domestic policies and global context

The importance of rules on export restrictions should be appreciated from two perspectives. Globally, the formation of global supply chains transforms the production process of multinational enterprises, which are vulnerable to the disruption of supply in raw materials and critical components. Domestically, the EU relies heavily on the importation of natural resources which are sometimes reserved in some countries not operating in line with the rationale of market economy. These two combining factors motivate the EU's quest for national resources.

The formation of the global supply chain

Economic globalization driven by multinational enterprises has resulted in ever-faster trade and investment flows, dispersion of international production networks, international division of labour through specialization, fragmentation of production and ownership, international outsourcing and growing intra-firm trade and almost simultaneous transition of information (Snyder 1999, pp. 335–336). Moreover, the advances of two connective technologies of transportation and transmission that drive economic globalization and contribute to the formation of a global supply chain, help us to shift the focus from sectors to stages of production (Baldwin 2013, pp. 26–27).

Supply chains are as old as industry and are nothing new: automobiles need tyres that require rubber; steel requires iron that necessitates iron ore. The supply chain is understood as the sequence of plants that provide these inputs. Already in 1997, scholars have pointed to the difficulties in locating the exact origin of Swiss drugs, Japanese televisions and French videos and proposed the concept of "made in the world" (Ferdows 1997, pp. 102–109). Writing in 2002, Snyder used the example of a Barbie doll to illustrate the complexity of components originating from different parts of the world and being assembled in China with the logo of "Made in China" (Snyder 1999, pp. 336–337). Today, the best example today may be Apple's iPhone with the charm of "Designed in US" in the place of "Made in China."

The formation of a global supply chain can be best observed by the two phenomena of fractionalization and dispersion. Fractionalization refers to the unbundling of supply chains into finer stages of production; dispersion relates to geographic unbundling of stages. With fractionalization, finer division of labour is possible that brings about specialization and in turn boosts productivity. With geographic dispersion, firms and enterprises may exploit wage differences, capital cost and subsidies with careful management of transportation and transmission cost as well as time and risk during this management process (Baldwin 2013, pp. 27–34). Having understood contemporary production processes in the light of the global supply chain, it is thus not difficult to understand how export restrictions, regardless of being against strategic materials or key components, would impede international production network and subsequently international commerce.

The surge of commodity price and raw materials initiative

The scarcity of natural resources is well known. However, the EU suffered most during the recent commodity price spike preceding the beginning of the global financial crisis. In that era, the price of petroleum per barrel reached around 150 USD and gold topped 1,900 USD per oz in 2011. As Figures 7.1 and 7.2 show, an unprecedented surge of commodity price took place in the early twenty-first century, reaching its peak in 2008.

The threat and challenge posed by the surge in commodity prices, the global food crisis, European economic developments, social instability and energy insecurity aroused deep concerns among European policymakers. In order to overcome these challenges, a number of initiatives were proposed, including the Raw Material

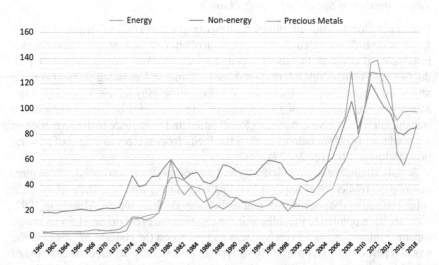

Figure 7.1 Commodity price indices – Nominal (1960–2018). Source: Compiled by the author based on World Bank data, http://www.worldbank.org/en/research/commodity-markets.

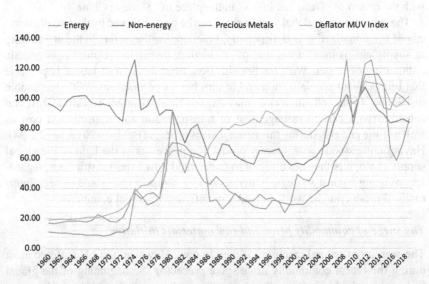

Figure 7.2 Commodity Price Indices – Real (1960–2018). Source: Compiled by the author based on World Bank data, http://www.worldbank.org/en/research/commodity-markets.

Initiative, with a view to meeting the EU's need for growth and jobs (European Commission 2008). With the Raw Material Initiative, the European Commission firstly underlined the importance of ensuring reliable and undistorted access to raw materials to safeguard the EU's competitiveness and consequently the success of the Lisbon partnership for growth and jobs (European Commission 2008, p. 1).

The European Commission noted that the EU is highly dependent on imports of metals such as cobalt, platinum, rare earths and titanium, which are essential to the development of technologically sophisticated products (European Commission 2008, p. 2). Three reasons help to explain the importance of such metals as platinum and indium to the EU: their significant economic importance in key sectors; high-risk supplies associated with very high import dependence and high concentrations in particular countries; and a current lack of substitutes. The European Commission then identified China, Africa, South America, Russia and Australia as Europe's leading suppliers of such technologically important raw materials. Significantly, the Commission noted: "[t] he fact that some important raw materials sources are located in parts of the world that do not have a market-based system, and/or are politically and/or economically unstable poses particular risks" (European Commission 2008, p. 3).

With a view to securing access to critical raw materials, the European Commission proposed an integrated strategy comprised of three pillars: access to raw material in the international market; framework conditions to foster sustainable supplies of raw materials from European sources; and reduce the EU's consumption by boosting efficiency and recycling (European Commission 2008, p. 6). Of greater relevance to this chapter is the access to raw materials in the international markets pillar. With this aim, the EU should pursue raw material diplomacy with better and more effective coordination and coherence among EU external policies, better coordination in the management of EU strategic partnerships, and policy dialogues with third partner countries and emerging economies (European Commission 2008, p. 6). Access to raw materials should also be prioritized in the EU's trade and regulatory policies. On the rule-making side, the EU should promote new rules and agreements on sustainable access to raw materials multilaterally and bilaterally; on the rule-enforcement side, the EU should take vigorous action to eliminate distorting measures taken by third countries; on the offensive front, the EU should also ensure that the functioning of the Market Access Partnership is conducive to raw material markets; on the defensive front, the EU should ensure that the distortion of costs arising from dual-pricing or similar practices is offset by anti-dumping investigations. Moreover, development and competition instruments may be relevant to the EU's efforts in securing access to raw materials (European Commission 2008, p. 7). In view of the objective spelled out in the Raw Material Initiative, the EU's proposal in the Doha Negotiation on a WTO Agreement on Export Taxes[11] can be seen as a prelude to this initiative while the pursuit of WTO complaints against China in *China – Raw Materials* and *China – Rare Earths* can be seen as an immediate policy response.

Enforcing the rules: China – raw materials and China – rare Earths

Since China's entry into the WTO, a number of trade disputes have arisen between the EU and China, most focusing on trade defence measures. In addition to these trade defence measures, the EU, in conjunction with other members, filed two similarly motivated complaints against China to secure access to certain raw materials. These two disputes relate to the legal status of "WTO-plus" obligations under WTO law (Qin 2003, pp. 483–522; 2004, pp. 863–919) and concern the applicability of Art. XX of the GATT 1994 (general exception) to provisions in China's Accession Protocol (Guo 2010, pp. 68–74; Gu 2012, pp. 1007–1031; Baroncini 2013, pp. 1–34). Further, these disputes addressed the less explored aspect of the international economic relations: the export dimension of WTO law. To be more specific, the original objective of the GATT/WTO regime was to permit access to foreign markets through the liberalization of domestic markets and elimination of trade barriers of trade nations. However, international economic activities have evolved so quickly and become so closely interconnected that supply shortages involving particular raw materials will interrupt global supply chains and undermine international economic relations. Therefore, the EU's focus has moved beyond safeguarding its domestic industries and accessing the Chinese market to secure raw materials from China, which gave rise to *China – Raw Materials* and *China – Rare Earths*.

China – raw materials

In June 2009, the EU requested consultations with China on a series of export restrictive measures adopted and maintained by China on such raw materials, ranging from export quotas to export duties and export licensing. Examples of such export restrictive measures include export quotas on certain forms of bauxite, coke, fluorspar, silicon carbide and zinc; and export duties on certain forms of bauxite, coke, fluorspar, magnesium, manganese, silicon metal and zinc. According to the EU, such measures are inconsistent with obligations and commitments China undertook when it acceded to the WTO. As the consultations failed to yield a mutually satisfactory result, the EU requested a panel to be established to examine the dispute: *China – Raw Materials*. Among the contentious issues raised before the Panel and Appellate Body, two are relevant to this chapter: the exception provided in Art. XI:2(a) and the applicability of Art. XX of the GATT 1994 (General Exception) to Paragraph 11.3 of China's Accession Protocol that obliges China to eliminate export duties.

Art. XI:2(a) of the GATT 1994 provides that the general obligation to eliminate quantitative restrictions, as dictated in Art. XI:1 thereof, shall not extend to "[e]xport prohibitions or restrictions temporarily applied to prevent or relieve critical shortages of foodstuffs or other products essential to the exporting contracting party." China resorted to Art. XI:2(a) with a view to justifying its export quota on refractory-grade bauxite. The Panel and Appellate Body ruled against China, as China had demonstrated neither that there was a "critical shortage" of refractory-grade bauxite nor that the export quota was "temporarily applied."

According to the Appellate Body, a measure temporarily applied is "a measure applied for a limited time, a measure taken to bridge a 'passing need.'"[12] "'[C]ritical shortage' thus refers to critical deficiencies in quantity that constitute a situation of decisive importance, or that reach a vitally important or decisive stage, or a turning point."[13] Moreover, different concepts embedded in Art. XI:2(a) may inform one another. As the Appellate Body held, whether a shortage is "critical" may be informed by how "essential" a particular product is. In addition, the characteristics of the product as well as factors pertaining to a critical situation, may inform the duration for which a measure can be maintained in order to bridge a passing need in conformity with Art. XI:2(a). Inherent in the notion of criticality is the expectation of reaching a point in time at which conditions are no longer "critical," such that measures will no longer fulfil the requirement of addressing a critical shortage.[14]

In applying this standard and taking different elements of Art. XI:2(a) of the GATT 1994 into consideration, the Appellate Body, in upholding the Panel's decision, ruled that China failed to demonstrate that there was a critical shortage of refractory-grade bauxite, nor did China demonstrate that the export quota was temporality applied.

With regards to the export taxes on other raw materials, the Panel and the Appellate Body ruled in favour of the EU and concluded that Art. XX of the GATT 1994 (general exception) is not applicable to Paragraph 11.3 of China's Accession Protocol. In reaching their conclusion, the Panel and Appellate Body relied heavily on textual interpretation and their previous jurisprudence laid down in *China – Publications and Audiovisual Products* (WTO 2009).[15] Indeed, the divergent decisions reached by the Appellate Body in *China – Publications and Audiovisual Products* and *China – Raw Materials* derived mainly from the different textual wording between Paragraphs 5.1 and 11.3 of China's Accession Protocol.

In *China – Publications and Audiovisual Products*, the Appellate Body clarified the legal value of the introductory clause of "without prejudice to China's right to regulate trade in a manner consistent with the WTO Agreement" in Paragraph 5.1 of China's Accession Protocol. According to the Appellate Body, the term "right" is twice referred to: the first time related to China's right to regulate trade in a manner consistent with the WTO Agreement, and the second reference relates to progressive liberalization of the right to trade, granted to all enterprises.[16] Given that the right to trade was "without prejudice to" China's right to regulate trade, it was to be granted to all enterprises but qualified by China's right to regulate trade on the condition that China do so in a manner consistent with the WTO Agreement.[17] "[I]n a manner consistent with the WTO Agreement" imposes two obligations. The first relates to the reliance of various WTO provisions to take regulatory measures in line with relevant disciplines or criteria; the second relates to the possibility of taking actions derogating from obligations from the WTO Agreement, that is, exceptions. Therefore, this introductory clause in Paragraph 5.1 of China's Accession Protocol, in recognizing China's rights to regulate trade in a manner consistent with the WTO Agreement, avails China of these two types of WTO consistency, including general exception as contained in Art. XX of the GATT 1994.[18]

This textual-oriented analysis led to a legally sound decision in view of the fact that the pertinent right in question, the right to trade, is defined as the right to import and export, and thus concerns trade in goods. However, this textual approach introduced an obstacle to interpreting China's obligation to eliminate export duties, which also relates to trade in goods. If a general exception, as set out for in Art. XX of the GATT 1994, constitutes a genuine "general" exception, it should be applicable to all types of activities concerning the trade in goods. In *China – Raw Materials,* the Appellate Body, following the approach of the Panel, relied heavily on the wording of the legal text of Paragraph 11.3 of China's Accession Protocol and ruled that in the absence of the same introductory clause as Art. 5.1 thereof, China's obligation to eliminate export duties is not subject to general exception of Art. XX of the GATT 1994.

As the Appellate Body further elaborated, Paragraph 11.3 of China's Accession Protocol reads as follows: "China shall eliminate all taxes and charges applied to exports unless specifically provided for in Annex 6 of this Protocol or applied in conformity with the provisions of Article VIII of the GATT 1994." Two avenues of exceptions are provided in this provision: those 84 products identified in Annex 6 or those fees or charges applied in conformity with Art. VIII of the GATT 1994. Annex 6 provides China with some flexibility, namely in exceptional circumstances, China, after consulting affected members, may increase its binding tariffs on those 84 products; nonetheless, those challenged products, excepting yellow phosphorus, are not among these 84 products. Therefore, China cannot adopt, nor maintain, export duties on those products listed in Annex 6. Secondly, Art. VIII of the GATT 1994 does not touch upon export duties. Consequently, the disputed series of export duties cannot be justified as applied in conformity of Art. VIII of the GATT 1994. Moreover, since Paragraph 11.3 of China's Accession Protocol explicitly refers only to Art. VIII without mentioning Art. XX of the GATT 1994, this suggests that the negotiators did not intend to include Art. XX as a way to exempt China's obligation to eliminate export duties.[19]

China – rare earths

In March 2012, the EU requested consultations with China under the WTO DSU concerning China's export quotas, including the allocation thereof by export licensing, and export duties on various forms of rare earths, tungsten and molybdenum. With the failure of the consultations, the EU, in conjunction with the United States and Japan (Inoue 2010), requested that a panel be established to examine the dispute. The Panel and Appellate Body heard the case and ruled that China's export restrictions, in the form of export duties and export quota, are inconsistent with China's obligations under its Accession Protocol and WTO agreements. In this case, the applicability of general exception of the GATT 1994 to China's obligation to eliminate export duties as put forward in Paragraph 11.3 of China's Accession Protocol was raised again. At the same time, China's export quota on rare earths, tungsten and molybdenum breaches its obligation under Art. XI:(1) and cannot be justified by Art. XX:(g) of the GATT 1994. I will discuss these two issues in great detail below.

China advanced three "new arguments that have not been asserted previously, or arguments which were neither argued nor addressed fully by the panel and Appellate Body in *China – Raw Materials*,"[20] and requested the Panel to re-examine the applicability of Art. XX to China's obligation to eliminate export duties arising from Paragraph 11.3 of its Accession Protocol. These three arguments were debated seriously and resulted in a division between the majority decision and a separate opinion of a Panel member. These three arguments are:

1. Paragraph 11.3 of China's Accession Protocol has to be treated as an integral part of the GATT 1994
2. The terms "nothing in this Agreement" in the chapeau of Article XX of the GATT 1994 do not exclude the availability of Article XX to defend a violation of Paragraph 11.3 of China's Accession Protocol; and
3. An appropriate holistic interpretation, taking due account of the object and purpose of the WTO Agreement, confirms that China may justify export duties through recourse to Article XX of the GATT 1994.[21]

The Panel first noted that it was fully aware of the distinct role played by the Panel and the Appellate Body in ensuring the "security and predictability" in the dispute settlement mechanism, and then recalled the holding of the Appellate Body that in the absence of "cogent reasons," a Panel shall not deviate from the settled jurisprudence of the Appellate Body in the absence of "cogent reasons." In recognition of the fact that the legal issue is "a central aspect of this dispute that is of fundamental systemic importance,"[22] the Panel decided to examine this issue and ascertain whether there is cogent reason for the Panel to deviate from past case law of the Appellate Body. In the end, the Panel found no cogent reason for doing so.

Regarding the first argument that Paragraph 11.3 should be treated as an integral part of the GATT 1994, China firstly argued that:

> [t]he legal effect of Paragraph 1.2 of China's Accession Protocol and Art. XII:1 of the Marrakesh Agreement is to make China's Accession Protocol an integral part of the Marrakesh Agreement, and *also to make each of the Accession Protocol-specific provisions an integral part of one of the Multilateral Trade Agreements (e.g. GATT 1994) annexed to the Marrakesh Agreement.*[23]

Based on this argument, China maintained that in order to determine which multilateral trade agreements referenced in specific provisions of China's Accession Protocol were integral parts thereof, the Panel had to ascertain to which agreements such provisions are intrinsically related. However, these two arguments failed to impress the Panel.

The Panel firstly looked at the legal text of China's Accession Protocol, which in Paragraph 1.2 provides that "[t]his Protocol, which shall include the commitments referred to in paragraph 342 of the Working Party Report, shall be an integral part of the WTO Agreement."[24] The Panel then pointed to the Preamble of China's Accession Protocol where the term "WTO Agreement" is used as an abbreviation for the Marrakesh Agreement Establishing the World Trade Organization.[25] The Panel opined that according to the ordinary meanings of the words used in Paragraph 1.2 of China's Accession Protocol, it is the Accession Protocol, in its entirety rather than individual provisions, that constitutes an integral part of the Marrakesh Agreement. Individual provisions can and have been made to integral parts of specific multilateral trade agreements; in fact, the drafters of the Accession Protocol, in Paragraph of Part II, annexed the schedules to the Accession Protocol, making them "the Schedule of Concessions and Commitments annexed to the GATT 1994 and the Schedule of Specific Commitments annexed to the GATS relating to China."[26] Moreover, whereas China argued that export duties are intrinsically related to Art. II and XI of the GATT 1994, the argument finds no solid basis in the legal text. Had the negotiators been aware of this intrinsic relationship, and had they intended to make export duties an integral part of the subject matter falling into the purview of Art. II of the GATT 1994, the drafters could have incorporated export duties into the Schedule of Concessions and Commitments. But this is not what the drafters chose to do.[27]

In response to China's argument that "there is an intrinsic link between the provisions contained in post-1994 Accession Protocols on the one side and those enshrined in the WTO Agreement and the Multilateral Trade Agreements annexed thereto on the other,"[28] the Panel held that Art. XII:1 of the Marrakesh Agreement does not entail such interpretation of an intrinsic relationship. Besides, while China contended that "its Accession Protocol merely serves to specify, including by means of 'WTO-plus' commitments, China's obligations under the WTO Agreement and the multilateral trade agreements annexed thereto,"[29] it is difficult to accept that a "WTO-plus" obligation, which by definition goes beyond the obligations contained in the multilateral trade agreements, merely serves to specify a member's obligations under the multilateral trade agreements.[30] Moreover, as the Panel noted, Art. XI of the GATT 1994 relates to export restrictions other than duties, taxes or charges, which cannot be said to intrinsically relate to export duties as regulated by Paragraph 11.3 of China's Accession Protocol.[31]

Regarding the second argument on relating to "nothing in this Agreement" in the chapeau of Art. XX of the GATT 1994, the Panel referred to the ruling of the Appellate Body in *China – Raw Materials*, and reinstated the position that "this Agreement" refers to GATT 1994 and not the Marrakesh Agreement or other multilateral trade agreements. The Panel quickly rejected China's argument in that China's second argument was based on its first argument of intrinsic relationship. Since the Panel found no such intrinsic relationship between Paragraph 11.3 of China's Accession Protocol, the second argument could not be sustained either.[32]

Finally, regarding the third argument based on the object and purpose of the WTO Agreement, China referred to the passage on sustainable development and argued that if a general exception is not available to China, that would lead to the conclusion that a member is forced to promote trade liberalization at whatever cost, including environmental degradation and the exhaustion of scare natural resources.[33] Nonetheless, as the Panel clarified, export duties are not the only instrument available to China for the perseveration of natural resources. Therefore, this argument also failed.

With regards to the WTO consistency of the export quotas on rare earths, tungsten and molybdenum, the Panel was asked to examine whether such measures were justified by Art. XX:(g) of the GATT 1994. The Panel opined that Art. XX:(g) puts forward two criteria for justifying a WTO-inconsistent measure: it has to be "relating to" the conservation of exhaustible natural resources and to be "made effective in conjunction with restrictions on domestic production or consumption." In addition, in order to be justified by a general exception, a WTO-inconsistent measure has to pass the threshold set out by the chapeau of Art. XX, which dictates that the measure in question does not "constitute a means of arbitrary or unjustifiable discrimination" or "a disguised restriction on international trade." The Panel concluded that the export quota did not fulfil the two criteria of Art. XX:(g) and cannot pass the scrutiny of the chapeau. The criterion put forward in the Art. XX:(g) of the GATT 1994 is of greater relevance to this chapter.

China argued that its export quota was situated in a comprehensive conservation policy, including extraction and production quota, which complement one another to achieve China's goals of sustainable use and natural resource management. The Panel first cautioned that whereas the preservation of exhaustible natural resource is not limited to the maintenance of the current status of natural resource, it extends to its sustainable use and management; nonetheless, such preservation measures cannot be used as an instrument for industry policy.[34]

Regarding whether the export quota is "relating to" preservation of an exhaustible natural resource, China argued that the export quota, *inter alia*, contributes to monitoring illegal export activities of rare earths, tungsten and molybdenum and helps to signal to foreign consumers that a sufficient supply will be guaranteed and there is thus no need for speculative buying. These arguments failed to persuade the Panel. The Panel held that monitoring and working to prevent exports of illegally extracted or produced products can be done without export quotas, but through enforcement measures. In fact, export quotas may increase rather than decrease smuggling. Moreover, whereas the export quota may send a signal to foreign consumers, it at the same time sends a reverse signal to domestic consumers and encourages domestic consumers to consume due to the price difference between domestic and foreign markets resulting from the segregation of the two markets by export quota. China has not put measures into place so as to counteract these reverse effects and thus did not meet the requirement of "even-handedness" since this price difference favours domestic downstream producers at the expense of foreign ones.[35]

Regarding the criterion of "made effective in conjunction with restrictions on domestic production or consumption," China argued that a number of measures were put into place to restrict domestic production or consumption, notably, extraction and production quotas. According to the Panel, whereas it is not necessary for China to set its extraction and production quotas at levels lower than the previous year, such extraction and production quotas must be lower than the expected demand so as to have "a limiting effect" and thus qualify as a "restriction" in terms of Art. XX:(g). Nonetheless, the extraction and production quotas China set were too high to have such limiting effect. Moreover, the Panel failed to see how production and extraction quotas operated with the export quota, and finally held that an export quota is not made effective in conjunction with restrictions on domestic production or consumption.[36]

Globalizing the rules: multilateral and bilateral negotiations

Backstopped by WTO-plus obligations, the EU successfully challenged the WTO compatibility of China's export restrictive measures on raw materials and rare earths. The battle was, nonetheless, only half won given that the objective of securing supplies of raw materials cannot be achieved if the obligation not to impose export restrictive measures is binding only on China. Therefore, the EU has to globalize the rule on export restrictions to all WTO members, which can be done only through multilateral negotiations in the Doha Negotiation agenda. Alternatively, such an objective could be partially realized through bilateral WTO accession negotiations with acceding countries or FTA talks with third countries.

In the context of the DDA negotiations, the EU proposed a WTO Agreement on Export Taxes. According to the EU, export taxes remain a policy instrument not subject to disciplines due to the GATT's traditional focus on import policies.[37] With a view to redressing their distortive effect on international trade, the EU thus proposed regulating export taxes having the following effects: transferring the gains of trade between WTO members; creating unfair advantages for domestic industries at the expense of the producers of other WTO members; and evading existent WTO rules on export restrictions by shifting to prohibitive export taxes on the exportation of goods.

Art. 1 of the proposed Agreement on Export Taxes regulates two kinds of levies imposed on the exportation of non-agricultural goods. The first relates to the duties, taxes or other charges collected upon, or in connection with, their exportation from the territory of one member to another. The second deals with internal taxes and other charges imposed on exporting products that are in excess of those imposed on like products for internal sale. The former is normally collected by customs agencies while the latter is generally imposed by other administrative agencies, such as the Ministry of Finance.

Art. 2 of the proposed Agreement on Export Taxes provides for special and differential treatment of developing country members and least developed country (LDC) members in particular. Art. 3 then prescribes two conditions for developing country members to maintain low-level export taxes on a limited number of products listed in their schedules. Firstly, the export taxes are necessary "to maintain financial stability to satisfy fiscal needs, or to facilitate economic diversification and avoid excessive dependence on the export of primary products."[38] In order to achieve these objectives, the developing country member concerned should adopt relevant domestic measures in conjunction with export taxes. Secondly, the maintenance of export taxes should not adversely affect international trade either by limiting the availability of the goods subject to export taxes to the WTO members or by raising the world price of such goods. The maintenance of export taxes should not seriously prejudice the interests of other developing country members.[39] When imposing export duties, the rules on customs valuation as set out in Art. VII of the GATT 1994 should be followed.[40]

Art. 3.2 of the proposed Agreement on Export Taxes then makes it clear that the obligation of most-favoured-nation treatment applies wherever export taxes are maintained by a developing country member. Besides, the proposed agreement also reaffirms members' rights to collect fees and charges in accordance with Art. VIII of the GATT 1994 and their right to impose export taxes based on general exception and security exception as set out in Art. XX and XXI thereof.[41] The rights of developing country members relating to balance of payments, exchange arrangements and governmental assistance to economic development remain unaffected.[42] Further, Art. XXII and XXIII of the GATT 1994, as elaborated in Dispute Settlement Understanding, should be applicable to this Agreement on Export Taxes.[43]

The proposed Agreement on Export Taxes reiterates members' obligations on transparency and notification, as set out in Art. X of the GATT 1994 and in the Ministerial Decision on Notification Procedures. A member imposing a new export tax or increasing existing export taxes is obliged to notify the WTO Secretariat 60 days before the entry into force of such measures. Upon request, the member concerned should provide relevant information and offer adequate and prompt opportunity for consultation.[44]

When law ends, diplomacy comes: transforming export taxes to production quotas

In *China – Rare Earths*, China referred to Art. XX:(g) of the GATT 1994 to justify its export quota, arguing that the export quota is related to the preservation of exhaustible natural resource and is made effective in conjunction with restrictions on domestic production or consumption, notably, extraction and production quota. Nonetheless, this argument was not accepted by the Panel in that export quotas are not relating to preservation of natural resources and China's extraction and production quotas do not have a limiting effect since they are not set at a level lower than expected demand. According the Panel, this permanent sovereignty over natural resources and the right of WTO members to adopt conservation programs pursuant to Art. XX(g) allows WTO members to develop and implement processes, means or tools that put into practice a conservation policy in a way that responds to a member's development and conservation concerns. It is not, however, a general right to regulate and control a natural resource market for any purpose ... natural resource products that will necessarily enter the market and are available for sale are subject to GATT disciplines in the same way as any other product. As such, no WTO member has, under WTO law, the right to dictate or control the allocation or distribution of rare earth resources to achieve an economic objective. WTO members' right to adopt conservation programs is not a right to control the international markets in which extracted products are bought and sold.[45]

Therefore, a trading nation is free to decide whether to extract the natural resource or not as the decision falls within its permanent sovereignty over natural resource. Therefore, if China develops its environmental/industrial policy through extraction and production quota, such a measure falls outside the purview of the WTO law. If China replaces its export quota with an extraction or production quota, the legal approach to resolving commercial differences will not work as China will not be violating any legal rules. In this context, the EU will have to rely upon a diplomatic approach to resolve this issue. However, the context in which this negotiation occurs differs significantly from the negotiations over China's accession. Two elements are pertinent here. Firstly, such negotiations would require a willingness not only from the EU and China but all other WTO members to reach an agreement and to bring extraction or production quotas under the control of the WTO. This would require a tremendous diplomatic effort. Secondly, China would not be in a position to favour the EU with a greater share of rare earth exports, as this would not be compatible with most-favoured-nation treatment. Therefore, whereas the EU may resort to the diplomatic approach to resolve its differences with China, its scope for manoeuvre is constrained by WTO law and contingent on its bargain power, which is rather weak in this case. The EU does not have the upper hand in blocking China's accession but at the same needs to have the agreement of all WTO members to make new law within the WTO.

Conclusion

This chapter investigates how the EU aims to discipline export restrictions through negotiation and litigation approaches. We can see a shift of focus on export restrictions from the adverse effects of VERs to access to raw material reserved in foreign countries. *Japan – Semiconductors* related to the adverse effects to EU producers arising from a confidential VER between Japan and the United States. By contrast, *China – Raw Materials* and *China – Rare Earths* concerned how the EU tried to secure the supply of technologically or strategically important raw materials reserved in China, where international commerce may be interrupted due to economic or political considerations. The case of export restrictions demonstrates the demand and supply of norms and the interaction between rule-making through negotiation and rule-enforcement through litigation. From the onset, the rule on export restrictions was limited; trading nations relied upon mainly Art. XI of the

GATT that prohibits quantitative restrictions on imports and exports to challenge export restrictions. The litigation before the GATT in *Japan – Semiconductors* illustrated the inadequacy of trade rules addressing the external dimension of international trade and called for supply of more rules through negotiations. In response to this case, the great bargain in the Uruguay Rounds confirmed the illegality of VERs and included a provision in ASG to address the grey-area measures.

Nonetheless, this conception of export restrictions focusing their adverse effects to domestic industries seems insufficient given fast-growing international economic interdependence and the formation of global supply chains. The spike in commodity prices in the first decade of the twenty-first century also heated up trading nations' quest for natural resources. This again led to a demand for rules addressing external dimension of international commerce. In this context, during negotiations over China's accession to the WTO, the existent WTO members, including the EU, successfully secured a WTO-plus commitment from China relating to export duties. With this obligation, the EU was able to challenge the WTO consistency of Chinese export restrictive measures on raw materials and rare earths. Success in WTO litigation, in fact, depends on clear WTO-plus rules as contained in China's Accession Protocol. In recognition of this limitation, the EU thus aims to globalize the disciplines on export restrictions through multilateral negotiations in the DDA or bilateral negotiations in the FTA negotiations or WTO accession negotiations. This again evidences how litigation relates to negotiations. Moreover, if China transforms its export quota into an extraction or production quota, the EU can rely only on the diplomatic approach to resolve its difference with China since there is no rule on extraction or production quota. Finally, we have seen a shift of economic gravity from Japan to China. In *Japan – Semiconductors*, Japan was the respondent member whose measures were challenged by the EU. However, in *China – Raw Materials* and *China – Rare Earths*, the EU in fact cooperated with Japan in challenging China's export trade restrictive measures. The once competitor becoming a partner illustrates the change in international economic relations.

Notes

1 Panel Report on *Japan – Trade in semi-conductors*, L/6309 – 35S/116 of 4 May 1988.
2 GATT Panel Report, *Japan – Trade in semi-conductors (Japan – Semi-Conductors)*, L/6309, adopted 4 May 1988, BISD 35S/116, para. 104.
3 GATT Panel Report, *Japan – Semi-Conductors*, para. 108.
4 GATT Panel Report, *Japan – Semi-Conductors*, para. 108.
5 GATT Panel Report, *Japan – Semi-Conductors*, para. 117.
6 GATT Panel Report, *Japan – Semi-Conductors*, para. 117.
7 The author owes this point to Dr. Han-Wei Liu.
8 Paragraphs 155 and 156 of the Working Party Report of China's Accession to the WTO recorded the concerns of these existent members: '[s]ome members of the Working Party raised concerns over taxes and charges applied exclusively to exports. In their view, such taxes and charges should be eliminated unless applied in conformity with GATT Article VIII or listed in Annex 6 to the Draft Protocol. The representative of China noted that the majority of products were free of export duty, although 84 items,

including tungsten ore, ferrosilicon and some aluminum products, were subject to export duties. He noted that the customs value of exported goods was the F.O.B. price of the goods'. Working Party Report of China's Accession to the WTO.

9 China's Accession Protocol, para. 11.3.
10 It should also be noted that before the EU's challenge against China's export restrictive measures, the EU, in the WTO era, challenged the WTO consistency of Argentinean export administration and export licensing regime and in *Argentina –Hides*. However, given the paucity of regulation of export restrictions under the WTO agreements, the EU relied mainly on Articles X and XI of the GATT 1994 to challenge the legality of the Argentinean export administration and export licensing regime and had not been successful in making a *prima facie* case.
11 Negotiating Proposal on Export Taxes, *Communication from the European Communities*, TN/MA/W/11/Add.6 (27 April 2006).
12 Appellate Body Reports, *China – Measures Related to the Exportation of Various Raw Materials (China - Raw Materials)*, WT/DS394/AB/R / WT/DS395/AB/R / WT/DS398/AB/R, adopted 22 February 2012, DSR 2012:VII, p. 3295, para. 323.
13 Appellate Body Report, *China – Raw Materials*, para. 324.
14 Appellate Body Report, *China – Raw Materials*, para. 328.
15 Appellate Body Report on *China – Measures Affecting Trading Rights and Distribution Services for Certain Publications and Audiovisual Entertainment Products*, WT/DS363/AB/R of 19 January 2010, DSR 2010: I, p. 3.
16 Appellate Body Report, *China – Measures Affecting Trading Rights and Distribution Services for Certain Publications and Audiovisual Entertainment Products (China – Publications and Audiovisual Products)*, WT/DS363/AB/R, adopted 19 January 2010, DSR 2010:I, p. 3.
17 Appellate Body report, *China – Publications and Audiovisual Products*, paras. 213–221.
18 Appellate Body report, *China – Publications and Audiovisual Products*, paras. 223.
19 Appellate Body Report, *China – Raw Materials*, paras. 282–291.
20 Panel Reports, *China – Measures Related to the Exportation of Rare Earths, Tungsten, and Molybdenum (China – Rare Earths)*, WT/DS431/R and Add.1 / WT/DS432/R and Add.1 / WT/DS433/R and Add.1, adopted 29 August 2014, upheld by Appellate Body Reports WT/DS431/AB/R / WT/DS432/AB/R / WT/DS433/AB/R, DSR 2014:IV, p. 1127, para. 7.54.
21 Panel Report, *China – Rare Earths*, para. 7.62.
22 Panel Report, *China – Rare Earths*, para. 7.59.
23 Panel Report, *China – Rare Earths*, para. 7.76.
24 Paragraph 1.2 of China's Accession Protocol.
25 Panel Report, *China – Rare Earths*, para. 7.79.
26 Paragraph 1, Part II of China's Accession Protocol.
27 Panel Report, *China – Rare Earths*, para. 7.84–88.
28 Panel Report, *China – Rare Earths*, para. 7.90.
29 Panel Report, *China – Rare Earths*, para. 7.90.
30 Panel Report, *China – Rare Earths*, paras. 7.84–88.
31 Panel Report, *China – Rare Earths*, para. 7.91.
32 Panel Report, *China – Rare Earths*, para. 7.103.
33 Panel Report, *China – Rare Earths*, para. 7.110.
34 Panel Report, *China – Rare Earths*, para. 7.460.
35 Panel Report, *China – Rare Earths*, paras. 7.378–448.
36 Panel Report, *China – Rare Earths*, paras. 7.378–448.
37 Non-Tariff Barriers, *Communication from European Communities*, TN/MA/W/11/Add.3 (1 April 2003), para. 13.
38 Proposed Agreement on Export Taxes, Art. 3.1(a).
39 Proposed Agreement on Export Taxes, Art. 3.1(b).

40 Proposed Agreement on Export Taxes, Art. 6.
41 Proposed Agreement on Export Taxes, Art. 5(a) and (b).
42 Proposed Agreement on Export Taxes, Art. 5(c).
43 Proposed Agreement on Export Taxes, Art. 8.
44 Proposed Agreement on Export Taxes, Art. 7.
45 Panel Report, *China – Rare Earths*, paras. 7.268.

Bibliography

Baldwin, R. (2013) 'Global supply chains: Why they emerged, why they matter, and where they are going', in D.K. Elms and P. Low (eds.), *Global Value Chains in Changing World*, Geneva, Switzerland: World Trade Organisation, pp. 13–59.

Baroncini, E. (2013) 'The applicability of GATT Article XX to China's WTO accession protocol in the appellate body report of the China—raw materials case: Suggestions for a different interpretative approach', *China-EU Law Journal*, 1(3–4), pp. 1–34.

European Commission (2008) 'The raw materials initiative: Meeting our critical needs for growth and jobs in Europe', *COM* (2008) 699 final, Brussels, 4 November 2008.

Ferdows, K. (1997) 'Made in the world: The global spread of production', *Production and Operation Management*, 6(2), pp. 102–109.

Gu, B. (2012) 'Applicability of GATT Article XX in China—raw materials: A clash within the WTO agreement', *Journal of International Economic Law*, 15(4), pp. 1007–1031.

Guo, W.L. (2010) 'On the application of Article 20 of GATT1994 to China's accession protocol', *International Economics and Trade Research*, 11, pp. 68–74.

Inoue, Y. (2010) 'China lifts rare earth export ban to Japan: Trader', *Reuters*, available at http://www.reuters.com/article/2010/09/29/us-japan-china-export-idUSTRE68S0BT20100929.

Jackson, J.H. (2003) 'The impacts of China's accession to the WTO', In D.Z. Cass, B. Williams and G.R. Barker (eds.), *China and the World Trading System: Entering the New Millennium*, Cambridge, MA and New York: Cambridge University Press, pp. 19–30.

Qin, J.Y. (2003) '"WTO-plus" obligations and their implications for the world trade organization legal system – An appraisal of the China accession protocol', *Journal of World Trade*, 37(3), pp. 483–522.

Qin, J.Y. (2004) 'WTO regulation of subsidies to state-owned enterprises (SOEs)–a critical appraisal of the China accession protocol', *Journal of International Economic Law*, 7(4), pp. 863–919.

Snyder, F. (1999) 'Governing economic globalisation: Global legal pluralism and European law', *European Law Journal*, 5(4), pp. 334–374.

Sykes, A. (2006) *The WTO Agreement on Safeguards: A Commentary*, Oxford, UK: Oxford University Press.

WTO (2003) 'Market access for non-agricultural products, communication from the European Communities', negotiating proposal on export taxes, TN/MA/W/11/Add.3, 1 April 2003.

WTO (2006) 'Negotiating proposal on export taxes, communication from the European Communities', TN/MA/W/11/Add.6, 27 April 2006.

8 The limits of a legal approach in resolving EU–China trade disputes on non-market economy status

Ching-Wen Hsueh

EU law, the non-market economy (NME) is not a clearly defined legal concept but rather it was a constructed idea reflecting the historical, political, economic and social circumstances. The special treatment for non-market economies had its root in the Cold War, where two blocs of courtiers had absolutely different political philosophies about government intervention on economies (Snyder 2001, pp. 374–375). The Soviet block of central and eastern European courtiers and China stand for the East, while the United States and eastern European countries stand for the West. The two blocs of countries; economic, social and legal systems are not compatible with each other. Measures should be taken to even the gap between the two systems; otherwise, the trade among those countries is hard to work, if not impossible. In terms of dumping, the "normal value" of a product in the NME cannot reflect the fair value as it would had been in a market economy because the NME could control the domestic prices and the costs of production. The trade rules specifically designed for the NME could avoid deliberate deviation from the trade obligations and encourage the market economies to accept the imports from the NME (Jackson 1989).

When the differences between the economic systems became smaller, there would be less ground for special trade rules for the NME. With the fall of the Soviet Union, NMEs started to or accelerate to transform their economic systems to market-oriented ones. When the transformation is completed, the concept of NME should be outdated. However, the evolution of NME treatment in law usually is a few steps behind the actual phase of transition of an economic system. The inconsistency between the law and the actual phase of transformation lead to trade disputes, because NMEs might disagree with the trade rules less favourable than necessary to adjust the differences in economic systems. Between 1995 and 2010, the share of anti-dumping investigations against NMEs steadily increased up to 60% in EU, and 77% of all NME cases involved Chinese firms (Dunoff and Moore 2014, p. 153). When the "2016 deadline" was approaching, the European Parliament had voted with overwhelming majority (European Parliament 2016) to refuse China's long-standing wish to be treated as a market economy in the investigations for trade remedies. Instead of trade retaliations or diplomatic negotiations, China filed a WTO case against the EU over the NME treatments, the result of which should be issued in the second half of 2018.[1] It seems both

EU and China prefer the legal approach, even though the NME issues in EU are governed not by law but mainly by political concerns. In this chapter, the author analyzes the China–EU trade disputes pertinent to the NME treatment to explain the limits of the legal approach to address such commercial tension. Section II will brief the NME treatments of China under the EU anti-dumping regime, which could provide the legal background for further discussion. The focuses are the developments of the NME treatment and the grounds for the legislations. In Section III, the cases concerning the Chinese NME treatments are examined to show the extent to which the China–EU disputes could be solved by the legal approach. In Section IV, the author concludes with her observations on the role the legal mechanism can play in these disputes.

The NME status of China in EU anti-dumping regulations and its grounds

China as an NME is subject to the special calculation methodology of the dumping margin. Back in the 1960s the European Economic Community (EEC) had treated NMEs differently. As NMEs transformed their economic systems, their treatment under EU law changed. Furthermore, the EU laws concerning NME treatments evolved to avoid explicit inconsistency with the WTO rulings. Regulation 2016/1036,[2] amended by Regulation 2017/2321[3] (hereinafter the Basic AD Regulation), is the latest version governing the anti-dumping investigations. In response to the "2016 deadline," when China was not presumably treated as an NME, the EU created the concept of "country of significant distortions" to cover the NMEs with WTO membership. Nonetheless, the treatments of the county of significant distortions and the NME treatments are basically similar in content but different by name. For the ease of discussion, the treatments of the county of significant distortions are referred to as "NME treatments in the broad sense."

The development of NME treatments of China in AD regulations

The development of the NME treatments in the EU anti-dumping regime could be divided in four phases. The previous three phases, which would be elaborated upon in Subsection a, established the founding principles that are still followed in the fourth phase, where the NME treatments were adjusted to the "significant market distortions." The anti-dumping regulations would adjust to the situations of the time; however, the main theme is always about defence against unfair trade.

Special rules for China as NME: deviation from strict comparison of domestic prices

The Regulation 459/68 was the EEC's first regulation on anti-dumping providing that strict comparison of the domestic price does not apply to the country, where government can strongly intervene on domestic price.[4] The methodology for determination of normal value could be deduced from Art. 3.2 of Council Regulation 459/68, which resembled Art. 2(d) of the Kennedy Code. However, the term "non-market economies" was not used in the Regulation. The concept of the NME and the specific methodology for the normal value of the NME was established until Regulation 1681/79. The EEC referred to the NME as the "state trading countries" and China.[5] The EEC provided market access to some non-market economies, termed as "state trading countries," from which imports were free from quantitative restrictions, provided the imports did not increase to great extent so as to cause injuries to the producers in the EEC.[6] China was included in the list of states in 1971[7] and had been removed from the list in 1978. However, the removal does not mean that the EEC will treat China substantially different from the state trading countries. China was subject to the same rules as the state trading countries, except the scope of products eligible for market access was slightly different.[8] The normal value of imports from NMEs, i.e. state trading countries and China, could be determined by any of the three criteria: price sold in an analogue market economy; the construed value in a market economy and price sold in EEC with due adjustments.[9] In addition, a single dumping margin was given to all the imports from NMEs, and as a result the dumping rate for imports from NMEs usually is nationwide.[10] The analogous country shall be selected in a "not unreasonable manner, and due account being taken of any reliable information made available at the time of selection."[11]

In the 1990s, when the Soviet Union had fallen and the economic reforms in China had progressed to great extent, the European Community (EC) started to provide different tracks for the imports from NMEs. The analogue country approach is the general principle for determination of normal value in NMEs. In the meantime, the EC separated some NMEs from the others and excluded them from subjecting to the analogue country method because the economic reforms in certain countries had allowed the firms to operate under market conditions.[12] The EC/EU divided NMEs in two groups. One is the NMEs in a narrow sense, which can only apply the analogue country method, and the other is the NMEs with the possibility to have market economy treatment (the MET) in a given anti-dumping investigation. The list of the NMEs in the narrow sense became shorter[13] and was cut down to 5 in 2009[14] but went back to 12 in 2016.[15] Furthermore, NMEs can obtain market economy statutes (MES) and therefore graduate from the NME treatments, when the EU finds the market conditions have been established. Russia obtained the MES in 2002,[16] while China has not passed the test.

Before 2002, all the producers subject to the NME treatment were usually given a nationwide anti-dumping tariff. In order to increase transparency and legal certainty, requirements were set for the producers entitled to individual duty rate, which is known as individual treatment (IT).[17] However, the IT was abolished in 2012 due to the inconsistency with the WTO rules.[18]

Special rules for country of significant distortions

At the end of 2017, the EU modified the multiple tracks for imports from NMEs. The rules for NMEs in a narrow sense, which is not a WTO member, remain unchanged, while NMEs eligible for MET are subject to the new rules designed for the market distortion circumstances. If the government intervention on the free market significantly distorts the domestic prices or costs, the Commission may use the prices and costs in an appropriate representative country, or undistorted international benchmark or undistorted domestic costs.[19] The Commission seems to have full discretion on the methodologies, given no further instructions were provided.

The "significant distortions" refers to the substantial government intervention that affects the prices and costs, including the costs of raw materials and energy. In assessing the significant distortions, the Commission could, but not have to, consider the following six elements: the extent of the market served by SOEs or enterprises under policy supervision or guidance of the authorities; state presence in firms allowing the state to interfere with respect to prices or costs; public policies or measures discriminating in favour of domestic suppliers or otherwise influencing free market forces; the lack of discriminatory application or inadequate enforcement of bankruptcy, corporate or property laws; wage costs being distorted; access to finance granted by institutions that implement public policy objectives or otherwise do not act independently of the state.[20] By definition, the significant distortions can cover the government interventions both in NMEs and market economies. The new rules nevertheless aid the NMEs with WTO membership, including *inter alia* China (European Commission 2016, p. 13). In addition, the Commission may issue a report on the significant distortions in a specific country or sector, which serves as factual basis for all the AD investigations related to that country or sector.[21] In 2017, the EU issued a report stating China as a "country of significant distortion" (European Commission 2017, p. 3).

Grounds for the NME status of China

The fair trade remedies as explicit grounds

The rationale for the NME treatment was never explicitly provided in the EU anti-dumping regulations. The closest statement was in the preamble of the Regulation 905/98 declaring that the process of reform in Russia and China had "fundamentally altered their economies and has led to the emergence of firms for which market economy conditions prevail"; as a result they had "moved away from the economic circumstances which inspired the use of the analogue country method." The criteria for the MET in Regulation 2016/1036 and the EU practices of the assessment on the MES provide further elaborations on what kind of "economic circumstances" would lead to the use of NME treatment. In terms of MET, the firms should be free from significant state interference on their decision-making and operations, and follow international accounting standards.[22] In term of MES, the focuses were the government laws and measures intervening allocation of resources, prices, taxes and financial sectors (European Commission 2015, pp. 39–40). These concerns are of economic nature about the creditability of the domestic prices of the NMEs. The domestic prices in the NMEs could not reflect the true value under market economies for their irrationally pricing structure, which does not react to the supply and demand in the market, but to government indications (Wang 1999). For instance, the price of energy or raw materials could be artificially low, or unrealistically low, because these goods are required to be available to the consumers at a certain price. In addition, an artificially low price usually comes hand in hand with government subsidized inputs. In other words, the firms in the NMEs undertook the responsibility to meet the policy need, and not necessarily profit oriented, which could lead to an artificially low price. The domestic price in NMEs might not be reliable so as to allow a fair resort to trade remedy.

The EU has criticized the creditability of the domestic price in China and therefore maintained its NME status. In 2004, China was acknowledged to have no "state-induced distortions in the operation of enterprises linked to privatization and the use of non-market trading or compensation system" (European Commission 2008, p. 12). Although the EU recognized China's progress in economic transition, the Chinese government was found to fail to keep "a low degree of government influence over the allocation of resources and decisions of enterprises, whether directly or indirectly." This is because China controlled the price setting in the energy sector, which has a widespread effect on the cost of production and the economy in general (European Commission 2008, p. 8). Also, the EU indicated the export restrictions on raw materials, probably the rare earth, as inconsistent with the criterion of low degree of government influences (European Commission 2008, p. 7). By the time of 2008, the EU was not convinced by the information at hand that China had implemented "a transparent and non-discriminatory company law which ensures adequate corporate governance" (European Commission 2008, p. 14). In addition, while the EU acknowledged the legal protection for private properties had been improved, most of the laws were enacted one or two years before 2008. The EU needed more time to assure the implementation (European Commission 2008, p. 15). Last but not least, the EU doubted the Chinese banking system operated by virtue of commercial rules or independently because the allocation of lending obviously was in favour of state-owned enterprise (European Commission 2008, p. 19).

The political leverage and economic losses as implicit grounds

In 2008, the EU did agree that China made progress in providing "a clear platform for fulfilling the criteria of market economy," although the implementation of the laws was not satisfying (European Commission 2008, p. 27). It seemed to be a matter of time for the EU to move China from the NME list if the fair trade remedies were the only concern. However, the Commission never finished a new assessment on China's application for MES (European Commission 2015, p. 39). On the contrary, the EU declared China as a "country of significant distortion" in 2017. During the review of China's status, the Commission itself acted inconsistently. In 2013, the Commission stated its willingness to grant China MES in 2016 (De Gucht 2013), while it hesitated to do so one year later (Dalton 2014). The grounds other than fair trade remedies came to surface during the discussion of China's MES.

First, the EU perceives the MES as the leverage for political negations. The EU is aware that countries granted MES to China, because they planned to sign the FTA with China, or to attract Chinese investments, loans (Puccio 2015). Furthermore, the EU granted MES to Russia and Ukraine out of political concerns, in particular in exchange for natural gas (Popescu 2010). Such a position was confirmed by the European Parliament's refusal to the unilateral granting of MES to China (European Parliament 2016). Second, the EU is aware of the trade diversion effect. The United States has found that China remains an NME, which implies a higher anti-dumping duty (Ringel 2017). If the EU applies the standard methodology for market economy, the trade volumes of China would excessively divert from the United States to the EU (European Commission 2016, p. 9). Third, the EU worries about the job losses in the strategic sectors and the chain effects coming afterwards. The EU acknowledges that dropping China out of the NME list would have little impact on the EU GDP; however, it considered the trade defence measures could be essential for the survival of a specific industry, at the present time for the steel industry. Fourth, the NME treatments can counter the subsidies that are not subject to the countervailing duties, either because the EU producers do not know the subsidies, or because the subsidies are general, systematic benefits as a result of state capitalism. The EU interests groups complained the subsidies in China not transparent and often not specific, which increases the burden for the EU industries to file the investigations on subsidies (European Commission 2016, p. 63). In addition, China skilfully controls its currency so as to subsidize the Chinese industry in general (Huang 2016). Last, the NME treatments in a broad sense are deemed as an overarching protection for the EU industries to offset any competitive advantages of Chinese imports. The EU found that the Chinese government still has decisive control over the market through the tight connections with enterprises (going far beyond the boundaries of SOEs). China has developed an extensive and sophisticated economic planning system that the policy goals are done by varies of tools, such as guiding catalogues, investment screening, financial incentives, etc (European Commission 2017, pp. 20–21). The EU sees the Chinese economy system so distinct from the market economy that any difference between them is presumed to be unfair advantages granted to Chinese producers (European Commission 2016, p. 28). In sum, the grounds for NME status of China go beyond the credibility of domestic price in the AD investigations, which is relatively technical. They are intertwined with political, economic and environmental issues.

The deficiency of legal approach to the China–EU disputes involving NME treatments

As elaborated in the previous section, the NME status of China concerns more about political and economic problems that cannot be fully covered by the EU anti-dumping laws. Although China has made progress on loosening the control over private sectors, the EU insisted on special treatments for China, either in the name of NME or "countries of significant distortions." The empirical study showed that the share of cases against NMEs in total anti-dumping cases sharply increased, and most of them involved Chinese firms. What raises more concerns is the anti-dumping rate of NMEs is significantly higher than the rate of the firms with MET status, and only one-fifth of applicants are eligible for the MET (Dunoff and Moore 2014). The disadvantages to Chinese firms motivate them and China to litigate at a regional level and a global level, respectively. However, as confirmed by the findings of the relevant cases, the courts refrain themselves from exercising the law-creating discretion that is an essential function of the judicial system to safeguard the certainty and determinacy of the laws (Hart 1994). The legal approach has some limits because of relatively broad discretion given to the politic departments and judicial passiveness.

Insufficient legal protection for the firms subject to NME regime under EU law

The Court of Justice of European Union (hereinafter the CJEU) took the WTO agreements as criteria for the lawfulness of act of EU, where the conditions provided in settled case law were met.[23] The application of WTO law at the EU level exposed the act of EU institutions to the norms generated outside the Union and thereby decreased the political influences within the Union over the pertinent issues. However, that is not the case for anti-dumping. The CJEU in *European Commission v. Rusal Armenal ZAO* found that the EU showed no intent in the Basic AD Regulation to implement the anti-dumping agreement, in particular the provisions regarding NME (see Chapter 2).[24]

Limited legal control over the designation of NME status and analogue countries

The first problem of the legal approach to the NMEs disputes is the designation of the NME and the analogue countries in a given ant-dumping investigation are subject to the discretion of the EU political branch. The EU anti-dumping regulations do not provide definition of the NME, neither do they describe, not even once, the features of the NME. The legal concept of NME was transformed from the political perceptions during the Cold War (Snyder, 2001), where there were a clear line between friends and foes in the name of freedom. The list of NMEs changed constantly, which narrowed down to five in 2009,[25] but went back to twelve in 2016.[26] The countries subject to the NME treatment could cover any of the former centrally planned economy countries, unless the EU agreed to exclude them. The missing indication on the NMEs in the Basic AD Regulation and its predecessors made it impossible for the judicial branch to review the appropriateness of the NME status. That is to say, the dispute over the NME status of China can never be solved through legal approach.

The legal approach is similarly dissatisfying for the Chinese firms in disputes about the designation of analogue country. The Basic AD Regulation entrusted the European Commission (hereinafter the Commission) with the selection of analogue countries under the conditions that they shall act "in a not unreasonable manner," taken into account the time limit, and that countries in the same investigation shall be chosen where "appropriate."[27] For the Chinese firms subject to investigation, the result of the selection seemed to come out of a mysterious black box because the United States, where the production cost could be higher than that in China, is the most used analogue country for China (Wang 1999, p. 131; Detlof and Fridh 2006, p. 27). The criteria of the selection raised concerns of the firms. The Commission focuses more on the competitive situations of the product than on the comparison of the economic situations of NMEs in general. The population and the stage of economic development of the analogue countries are usually irrelevant[28] (Wu 2015) although they could reflect what the NMEs could have been as a market economy. The Commission considers the wishes of the applicants to action, the availability of information in the investigation, similarity of the production process and technical standard or the amount of sale of the product (Wang 1999). These factors would vary in each case, and the firms under investigations can hardly predict the result, which makes them unable to know how to adjust pricing structure to avoid the charge as their competitors in market economies do (Denton 1987). However, the firms have no chance to change the situation because the CJEU has refused to review the choice of the criteria for the selection by stating it is "*a matter falling within the discretion enjoyed by the institutions in analyzing complex economic situations.*"[29]

If the criteria chosen by the Commission were not subjected to judicial review, the firms under investigation would argue whether the Commission had correctly applied the chosen criteria in the case at hand. In this regard, the CJEU will review the exercise of the discretion and verify "*whether the relevant procedural rules have been complied with, whether the facts on which the choice is based have been accurately stated and whether there has been a manifest error of appraisal or a misuse of powers.*"[30] In practice, the standard of review is relatively moderate. For instance, in the *Rotexchemie* case the European Court of Justice (ECJ), predecessor of the CJEU, recognized that the Commission does not have to carry out a detailed analysis on all potential analogue countries proposed by the parties under investigation, unless the parties can provide evidence sufficient to raise doubts of the Commission and the Council on their choice of selection.[31] Furthermore, the Advocate General in *Fliesen-Zentrum* suggested the CJEU tolerate that the Commission rely the choice of selection fully on the responses to the questionnaire, even if the number of responses is limited.[32] That is to say, the Commission is not required to investigate at all cost, but to endeavour to obtain

data available, most of which are the responses to the questionnaire. Such practices would cause two problems. The data obtained will be very limited, because
producers in the potential analogue countries usually do not have motive to cooperate, or the data came from the competing producers with higher production
cost (Dunoff and Moore 2014). Either way is unacceptable to the Chinese firms.
In addition, the firms would bear the risk of unsound analysis of the Commission
in the absence of easily available data, since the Commission would not be criticized for failing to find more access to the information.

Difficulties in challenging MET determination

The Chinese firms in cases concerning the MET status have difficulties similar
to those challenging the NME status and designation of analogue country. Three
reasons are particularly relevant. First of all, the CJEU and the General Court
have never reviewed the legality of the criteria listed in the Basic AD Regulation.
Second, the courts granted relatively broad discretion to the Commission on
determination of MET status. Third, the burden of proof for the MET status lies
on the applicant firms.

It is doubtful whether criteria for MET status are appropriate to identify the
firms operating in market economy conditions (Detlof and Fridh 2006). In practice, the legality of the criteria *per se* is not an issue for the CJEU and General
Court. In regards to the determination of the MET status, the involvement of
the courts is desirable because the application of the criteria is also problematic. For instance, the Commission used to presume a state-owned company
not to be entitled to the MET status, without analyzing the actual governmental
influence on its decision-making process. Also, the Commission did not reveal
the benchmarks to the evaluations of the assets from the non-market system
(Vermulst and Graafsma 2006, p. 126). However, the courts had refrained themselves from reviewing the substance of the Commission's determination until
Council v. Xinanchem[33] and *Zhejiang v. Council*.[34] Even when the CJEU finally
expanded the scope of judicial review to the substantial part of the Commission's
determination, the CJEU did not deny the broad discretion of the Commission.
The Commission found against the Xinanchem's application for MET, because
it is a state controlled company, and therefore rejected the applicant for MET.
The General Court reviewed the facts and reversed the Commission's interpretation that the state control over the company equals to the "significant state interference" in Art. 2(7)(c) (*Council v. Xinanchem* 2012, paras. 84–87). This ruling
could improve, to some extent, the situation of the applicant firms for MET in
challenging the Commission's determinations. Nevertheless, the Commission's
discretion is not explicitly denied. A similar approach was adopted in *Zhejiang
v. Council*, where the CJEU found against the Commission's sampling practices
on the applications for MET. The CJEU did not challenge the Commission's
discretion but criticized the methodology the Commission adopted. The CJEU
insisted the MET status should be reviewed on the merits of each applicant,
whether it was sampled or not.[35]

It should be noted that an active judicial intervention might backfire and motivate the political institutes to change the laws entirely. The *Zhejiang* case is also an example showing that the judicial review does not guarantee a lower obstacle to challenge the MET determination, when the political institutes insisted the opposite. Disagreeing with the finding of the CJEU, the Council issued Regulation 1168/2012 to substantially override the *Zhejiang v. Council.*[36]

The last difficulties for the applicant firms are that they bear the burden of proof on the MET status, according to Art. 2(7)(c) of the Basic AD Regulation, which requires the applicant firms to provide "sufficient evidence" of the fulfilment of the MET criteria. Again, the CJEU and General Court in *Xinanchem* stated the Commission enjoyed wide discretion in assessing the evidence submitted by the applicant firms, due to the complexity of economic, political and legal situations.[37] The Court would only review whether the Commission had made a manifest error in the assessment.[38] However, the CJEU emphasized that the exercise of discretion is not unlimited, and the guarantees conferred to individuals in administrative procedures is more important.[39] The Commission is required *"under the principle of sound administration, to examine with all due care and impartiality the evidence provided by the producer."*[40] As long as the applicant firms can provide evidence sufficient to rebut the *prima facie* assessment of the Commission, the Commission shall not disregard that evidence.[41] Although the Courts tide up the judicial control over the Commission's discretion on the assessment of evidence, the burden of proof on applicant firms is intact and the Commission has no obligation to prove that the applicant failed to meet the MET criteria. Furthermore, the Commission is entitled to presume the Chinese applicant is not eligible for MET, because it is subject to measures concerns with the five-year plan in China, which could be broadly interpreted to cover many sectors and signify the government's intervention in the market.[42] The burden of proof in fact might become even higher than expected.

Modification of "one country one duty" rule as a result
of the imperative outside the EU legal regime

The individual treatment (IT) is another issue that Chinese firms would like to but usually fail to challenge. Art. 9(5) of the Regulation 1225/2009 stipulated that the producers subject to NME status in general are given a single duty rate, which could *de facto* release the Commission from burdensome investigation on the dumping margin for each firm. According to this provision, the firms subject to NME status are presumed to be a single unit, in which each firm takes the consequences of the other's dumping, unless the firms could prove otherwise and therefore subject to IT. The presumption is sustainable, only if the firms did act jointly or consistently, such as the like products sold at same prices. In the economy in transition, the state's interference on economic system does imply a stronger consistency in pricing among the firms; however, it does not lead necessarily to a single price of all firms. Otherwise, those firms that failed the MET status by nature cannot meet the IT requirements because state interference in those situation are established. If that is the case, it seems redundant to create the IT. Furthermore, the criteria for IT do not all reflect the independence of firms in terms of their pricing activities. For instance, the freedom to repatriate capital and profits in item (a) of 9(5) reflects the protection for foreign investors. The connection between them is far distant. However, the CJEU and its predecessors did not criticize the "one country on duty rule" and the IT requirements, once again, due to the discretion given to the Commission and Council.

The passivism of the courts shows the limits of the legal approach under the EU law. The issue moved forward to the judicial forum at a global level and was found to be WTO inconsistent.[43] Later on, the IT was abolished by Regulation (EU) No 765/201, Preamble) According to the suggestions of the Appellate Body, the EU modified Art. 9(5) to apply single duty to firms that are legally distinct, but in a close relationship to be treated as a single entity. In determination of the single duty, the Commission should take into account factors such as "*the existence of structural or corporate links between the suppliers and the State or between suppliers*," "*control or material influence by the State in respect of pricing and output*," or "*the economic structure of the supplying country.*"[44] The Regulation does not explicitly repeal the "one country one duty" rule but confines its application to an extreme case, where all firms under investigation are in a relationship so close that all the firms in that country are considered a single entity. However, the single duty for firms in NMEs could survive, if the Commission heavily relied on the last factors of "*the economic structure of the supplying country.*"

Difficulty to avoid double remedies in concurrent imposition on anti-dumping duties and countervailing duties

Concurrent imposition of anti-dumping and countervailing duty is a relatively new problem for the Chinese firms. In principle, the EU did not impose countervailing duties to the NME, because there were be no reliable benchmarks for comparison in an economy, where the market forces do not play the role. Without a reliable benchmark, it would be extremely difficult, if not impossible, to calculate the subsidies and benefits conferred. However, the policy was changed in 2011, when the EU imposed concurrently anti-dumping duties and countervailing duties on the coated fine papers from China by two Regulations.[45] The concurrent impositions of two duties raise the concerns about double remedies that exceed the appropriate amount of anti-dumping duty or/and countervailing duty as provided in Art. 9(5) of the Basic AD Regulation and Art. 15(1) of Regulation 2016/1037.[46] In a market economy, the effect of domestic subsidy in theory cannot be offset by the anti-dumping duties because the normal value and the export price are both reduced by the same subsidy. In contrast, the normal value in NMEs is replaced by the higher normal value in an analogue country, where no domestic subsidy has taken place, and therefore it does not reflect the reduction by the subsidy. The dumping margin would inflate to offset the effect of the domestic subsidy (Antonini and Monard 2011). The most critical issue in concurrent imposition of the two duties is how to avoid the double counting on the effect of subsidies. There are three reasonable options: (a) granting the MET to all the applicants automatically, (b) adjusting the dumping calculation, either adjusting normal value or export price, and (c) deducting the subsidy margin from the dumping margin (Antonini and Monard 2011, pp. 93, 95). All of these can exclude the effect of subsides from the anti-dumping duty. However, the Commission and Council took different approaches in the investigations on Chinese coated fine papers.[47] The Council stated double remedies

> by definition, could only occur where there is a *cumulation* of the dumping margin and the amount of subsidy, i.e. where the combined level of two types of duty exceeds the higher of the dumping margin or the amount of subsidy.[48]

It was not necessary for the Council to further examine whether and to what degree the same subsidies were offset twice, due to the "lesser duty rule" applied in concurrent imposition of the two duties.[49] According to the lesser duty rule provided in Art. 9(4) of the Basic AD Regulation and Art. 15(1) of the Basic Anti-Subsidy Regulation, the level of the duties imposed cannot be higher than the injury margins if the latter is lower than the dumping margin. In the present case, the subsidy margin is lower than the injury margin, which is the same as the injury margin in anti-dumping, while the dumping margin is much higher than that.[50] In other words, the combined level of two duties would not exceed the dumping margin.

The lesser duty rule seems to work in the concurrent investigations on the Chinese coated fine papers. However, it doesn't work for all the cases. The EU might not be able to exclude the effect of subsidies, even when the less duty rule applies. In theory, the dumping margin of the NMEs captures both the specific subsidies, which fall within the scope of countervailing duty, and the nonspecific subsidies, which are by nature not qualified for anti-subsidy investigation (Cornelis and Graafsma 2012). In this vein, the double remedy would occur, unless the subsidy margin is fully deducted from the dumping margin. Applying the lesser duty rule on anti-dumping could not guarantee the fully exclusion of the subsidy margin, because the applied rate of countervailing duties cannot be higher than the subsidy margin. There should be the double remedy, if the difference between applied rate of anti-dumping and anti-dumping margin is not great enough to cover the subsidy margin that is not fully deduced from the applied rate of anti-dumping.

The Chinese firms in the investigations obviously did not agree with the concurrent imposition of two duties and brought the case to the General Court. In the *Chinese Coated Fine Paper* case, the parties did not argue whether the concurrent imposition of the duties actually cause double remedies.[51] Rather, the Chinese firms were concerned with whether the Council could impose both anti-dumping and countervailing measures, even if it did not cause double remedy, when the anti-dumping measure alone could offset the subsidy.[52] The General Court found the Council is not obliged to choose between the two measures, if the measures do not exceed the amount of dumping and subsidy, or injury margin.[53] The complainant lost the case, mainly because the anti-dumping rate is almost four times lower than the difference between the dumping margin and subsidy margin.[54] It is not clear yet whether or to what extent the CJEU and General Court would require the Council to put efforts on avoiding double remedy.

The solved and unsolved issues of NME treatments under WTO law

In light of the practice of the CJEU and General Court, the legal approach is not a good option for solving the NME issues. The EU courts in the NME cases were inclined not to override the legality of the Regulations. Furthermore, they favoured the broad discretion of the EU institutions, which would further increase the burden of proof on the complaining firms. If the disputes cannot be properly solved at the EU level, they will escalate to the global level. However, a legal approach at a global level sometimes made limited contribution to the dispute settlement as well. In this section, it will be elaborated through the Appellate Body reports on *EC-Fasteners* (WTO 2011a), *US-Antidumping and Countervailing Duties* (WTO 2011b) and Panel Report on *EU-Footwear* (WTO 2011c) that under what conditions a legal approach would work for disputes concerning NMEs.

IT treatment and double remedies

The IT treatment and the double remedies issues are the two among the four NME-related problems solved through the legal mechanism. China challenged the legality of IT in *EC-Fasteners* and *EU-Footwear*. The panel in *EU-Footwear* agreed with the finding and the reasoning in *EC-Fasteners*.[55] In *EC-Fasteners*, the EU argued that Art. 9(5) of the Basic Regulation should be allowed according to paragraph 15(a) of China's Accession Protocol,[56] which provided a flexible application of the AD rules to China.[57] After reviewing the Accession Protocol and second Ad Note to GATT Art. VI:1, the Appellate Body found the members are authorized to treat China differently only in the aspects of price comparability. The protocol does not "*contain an open-ended exception that allows WTO Members to treat China differently for other purposes.*"[58] In addition, the Appellate Body rejected the EU's contention that Art. 6.10 of the ADA showed only a preference for determining the individual dumping margin rule, by referring to the term "shall" and "as a rule" in the legal text. On the contrary, the EU is abided by the individual dumping rule and there is no exception to such rule other than sampling.[59] Also, a similar interpretation was given to Art. 9.2 of ADA.[60] In the light of the previous two findings, the only question left with IT is whether all the producers in NMEs could be deemed as a single unit, so that the IT could be consistent with ADA. The Appellate Body found that

> [T]he economic structure of a WTO Member may be used as evidence before an investigating authority to determine whether the State and a number of exporters or producers subject to an investigation are sufficiently related to

constitute a single entity such that a single margin should be calculated and a single duty be imposed on them. It cannot, however, be used to imply a legal presumption that has not been written into the covered agreements.[61]

Relatively clear legal texts of arts 6.10 and 9.2 of the ADA contribute, to great extent, to the effectiveness of legal approach, because they could provide the legitimacy for the Appellate Body's intervention and form the expectation of the WTO members. The same factor was found in the *US-Antidumping and Countervailing Duties*. In this case, the Appellate Body first recognized double remedy would occur not only in case of export subsidies, but also of domestic subsidies in NMEs.[62] Then, it relied on Art. 19.3, which requires the countervailing duties to be imposed in "appropriate amount," to establish a general prohibition on double remedies.[63] Such interpretation was read in conjunction with arts. 10, 19.1, 19.2, 21.1 and 32.1 of the SCM agreement.[64] Nonetheless, it is still unknown what the methodology should be taken to avoid double remedy and how detailed the analysis should be.

Definition of non-market economies, selection of analogue countries

China filed a WTO case against the EU over the NME treatments (*EU – Price Comparison Methodologies*), but at the time of the writing of this chapter the result is yet to come. The Appellate Body and the Panel should address four underlying questions to the NME treatments. First, what kind of members should subject to NME treatments? Second, do the WTO rules allow for the surrogate methodology? Third, if it is allowed, what are the requirements for the choice of analogue country? And fourth, is there any provision enabling the EU to adopt an alternative methodology? These issues did not emerge earlier, largely because China agreed not to challenge its NME status until 2016 as provided in paragraphs 15(a) and (d) of its Accession Protocol.[65]

When paragraph 15 (a)(ii) expire, the Appellate Body and the Panel might not be the best option for the parties in disputes. This is because neither the GATT nor the ADA provides clear definition of the NME (Zhou and Peng 2018, p. 531), or a sunset for the NME treatment. Although the second Ad Note to Art. VI: 1 allows the Members to consider the special difficulties arising from the economic system in determining the comparability of prices, its wording might not necessarily support the contention that the second Ad Note provides an exhaustive list for NMEs. Furthermore, Art. 2.2 of the ADA authorizes the members to made adjustment to the comparison because of the sales in a "particular market situation" not permit a proper comparison, which in theory could also include more forms of NMEs. In practice, the Appellate Body in *EU-Biodiesel* indicated that the government intervention might not in itself be sufficient basis for the exclusion of the data in exporting members.[66] Nevertheless, the Appellate Body remains silent on the coverage of the "particular market situation." In addition, many WTO members have applied the NME treatment for decades, which might be considered as subsequent practices in Art. 31 of VCLT. What is even worse is little discussion on the NME issue could be found in the negotiation history, which is commonly agreed among members. China has its perception about the negotiation history (Zhou and Peng, 2018 pp. 523–528), while the EU doubts that the treaty interpreter can re-live the circumstances during the negotiations.[67] In the absence of a clear legal instruction, the Appellate Body and the Panel would be cautious about making decisions to "add or diminish the rights and the obligations in the covered agreement."[68] That is to say, the teleological interpretation is usually not an option to the Appellate Body and the Panel.

The ruling of Panel in *EU footwear* is an example of how the judicial organ keeps distant from contentious issues for lacking of explicit legal text. China argued the "fair comparison" in Art. 2.4 of the ADA and the term "comparable price" should inform the boundaries of authorities' discretion in the choice of analogue country.[69] The Panel held Art. 2.1 is only a definitional provision and does not in itself impose independent obligation to be applied to the choice of analogue country.[70] The fair comparison requirement in Art. 2.4 was considered to provide guidance to the determination of the component elements of comparison to be made, i.e. normal value and export price.[71] The Panel disagreed that the establishment of the normal value is subject to a general obligation of fairness. The Panel's opinion seems to turn a blind eye on the WTO members' manoeuvre on the normal value, which is contrary to the purpose of the ADA.

Conclusion

The cases involving the NMEs show that the legal approach on EU–China trade disputes would work, if the laws applicable provide sufficient indications and competence for the courts to make the final decisions, which are closely related to political concerns. The grounds for the NME status/country of significant distortion involve political and economic concerns that go beyond the coverage of the AD regulations of EU or the ADA. In conclude, the NME issues could not efficiently solve through the legal approach neither at the EU level nor at the global level. However, there are different reasons for such phenomena at the EU level and at the global level. The CJEU and the General Courts seems to avoid intensive review on the issues concerning IT, MET and double remedies, even if the AD regulations may have provided them legal grounds to do so. The courts might have been aware that the political department would insist on issues of trade remedies as part of trade policies, so much as to adopt new regulation to override the court's ruling, such as *Zhejiang v. Council*. Accordingly, the EU courts tend to respect the relatively broad discretion given to the EU politic departments and to keep judicial passiveness. At a global level, the Appellate Body and the Panel keep their distance from the contentious issue in the absence of explicit legal instruction. In addition, many WTO members have applied the NME treatment for decades, which might be considered as subsequent practices in Art. 31 of VCLT. What is even worse is little discussion on the NME issue could be found in the negotiation history, which is commonly agreed among members. That is to say, there could be no strong judicial control over the powers of the EU institutions concerning the NME treatments. The EU could feel confident, or even comfortable, to resort to the legal mechanism, as they are the respondent who does not have to prove their innocence. In contrast, China would resort to political negotiation, once it realizes the judicial institutions might not declare the NME as an outdated concept as soon as expected.

Notes

1 Panel Report on *European Union – Measures Related to Price Comparison Methodologies* WT/DS516/R of 11 December 2017.
2 Regulation (EU) 2016/1036 of the European Parliament and of the Council of 8 June 2016 on protection against dumped imports from countries not members of the European Union, OJ L 176/21, 30 June 2016 (hereinafter Regulation 2016/1036).
3 Regulation (EU) 2017/2321 of the European Parliament and of the Council of 12 December 2017 amending Regulation (EU) 2016/1036 on protection against dumped imports from countries not members of the European Union and Regulation (EU) 2016/1037 on protection against subsidized imports from countries not members of the European Union, OJ L 338/1, 19 December 2017 (hereinafter Regulation 2017/2321).
4 Regulation (EEC) No 459/68, of the Council of 5 April 1968 on Protection against Dumping or the Granting of bounties or Subsidies by Countries Which Are Not Members of the European Economic Community, 1968 O.J. (L 93) 1,3.
5 Regulation (EEC) 1681/79 of 1 August 1979 amending Regulation (EEC) No 459/68 on protection against dumping or the granting of bounties or subsidies by countries which are not members of the European Economic Community, OJ L 196/1, 2 August 1979, (hereinafter Regulation 1681/79), Art. 3.2 (c).
6 Regulation (EEC) 109/70 of the Council of 19 December 1969 establishing common rules for imports from state-trading countries, OJ L 9/1, 26 January 1970, Art. 7.
7 Regulation (EEC) 2385/71 of the Council of 8 November 1971 extending to other imports the Annex to Regulation (EEC) No 109/70 establishing common rules for imports from state-trading countries, OJ L 249/3, 10 November 1971.
8 Regulation (EEC) 2532/78 of 16 October 1978 on common rules for imports from the People's Republic of China, OJ L 306/1, 31 October 1978.
9 See Regulation 1681/79.
10 Regulation (EC) 384/96 of 22 December 1995 on protection against dumped imports from countries not members of the European Community, OJ L 56/1, 6 March 1996, Art. 9(5).
11 See Regulation 2017/2321, Art. 2.7(a).
12 Regulation (EC) 905/98 of 27 April 1998 amending Regulation (EC) No 384/96 on protection against dumped imports from countries not members of the European Community, OJ L 128/18, 30 April 1998.
13 Regulation (EC) 2238/2000 of 9 October 2000 amending Regulation (EC) No 384/96 on protection against dumped imports from countries not members of the European Community, OJ L 257/2, 11 October 2000.
14 Regulation (EC) 1225/2009 of 30 November 2009 on protection against dumped imports from countries not members of the European Community, OJ L 343/51, 22 December 2009 (hereinafter Regulation 1225/2009).
15 See Regulation 2017/2321.
16 Regulation (EC) 1972/2002 of 5 November 2002 amending Regulation (EC) No 384/96 on the protection against dumped imports from countries not members of the European Community, OJ L 305/1, 7 November 2002, Recital 3.
17 *Ibid.*, Recital 7 and Art. 1.

18 Regulation (EU) 755/2012 of 16 August 2012 amending Implementing Regulation (EU) No 543/2011 as regards the eligibility of specific costs of environmental actions under operational programmes of producer organisations in the fruit and vegetables sector, OJ L 223/6, 21 August 2012, Art. 1.
19 See Regulation 2017/2321, Art. 2.6a.(a).
20 *Ibid.*, Art. 2.6a.(b).
21 *Ibid.*, Art. 2.6a.(c).
22 See Regulation 2017/2321, Art. 2.7(c).
23 Case C-69/89 *Nakajima v. Council* [1991] ECR I-2169; Case 70/87, *FEDIOL v. Commission* [1989] ECR 1825.
24 Case C-21/14 P *Commission v. Rusal Armenal* [2015] ECLI:EU:C:2015:494.
25 See Regulation 1225/2009.
26 See Regulation 2017/2321.
27 *Ibid.*
28 Case C-687/13, *Fliesen-Zentrum Deutschland GmbH v. Hauptzollamt Regensburg* [2015] ECLI:EU:C:2015:573 (hereinafter *Fliesen-Zentrum Deutschland GmbH v. Hauptzollamt Regensburg*).
29 Case C-16/90, *Detlef Nölle v. Hauptzollamt Bremen-Freihafen* [1991] ECR 1-5163 (hereinafter *Detlef Nölle v. Hauptzollamt Bremen-Freihafen*); Case C-26/96, *Rotexchemie International Handels GmbH & Co. v. Hauptzollamt Hamburg-Waltershof* [1997] ECR I-02817; Case C-338/10, *Grünwald Logistik Service GmbH (GLS) v. Hauptzollamt Hamburg-Stadt* [2012] ECR 00000.
30 See *Detlef Nölle v Hauptzollamt Bremen-Freihafen*.
31 Rotex Chemie case [1997], para. 22.
32 See *Fliesen-Zentrum Deutschland GmbH v. Hauptzollamt Regensburg*.
33 Case 337/09 P, *Council v. Zhejiang Xinan Chemical Industrial Group Co., Ltd*, [2012] ECLI:EU:C:2012:471 (hereinafter *Council v. Zhejiang Xinan Chemical Industrial Group Co., Ltd*).
34 Case T-407/06, *Zhejiang Aokang Shoes and Wenzhou Taima Shoes v. Council* and Case T-408/06, *Wenzhou Taima Shoes Co., Ltd v. Council* [2010] ECLI:EU:T:2010:68.
35 See *Council v. Zhejiang Xinan Chemical Industrial Group Co., Ltd*.
36 Regulation (EU) 1168/2012 of the European Parliament and of the Council of 12 December 2012 amending Council Regulation (EC) No 1225/2009 on protection against dumped imports from countries not members of the European Community, OJ L 344/1, 14 December 2012, Recitals 1–6.
37 See *Council v. Zhejiang Xinan Chemical Industrial Group Co., Ltd*.
38 Case C-249/10 P, *Brosmann Footwear (HK) and Others v. Council* [2012] ECLI:EU:C:2012:53.
39 See *Council v. Zhejiang Xinan Chemical Industrial Group Co., Ltd*, para. 107.
40 *Ibid.*, para. 104.
41 *Ibid.*, para. 102.
42 Case C-301/16, *Commission v. Xinyi PV Products (Anhui) Holdings Ltd.* [2018] ECLI: EU:C:2018:132.
43 Appellate Body Report on *European Communities—Definitive Anti-Dumping Measures on Certain Iron or Steel Fasteners from China* WT/DS397AB/R of 12 February 2016, para. 385.
44 Regulation (EU) 765/2012 of the European Parliament and of the Council of 13 June 2012 amending Council Regulation (EC) No 1225/2009 on protection against dumped imports from countries not members of the European Community, OJ L 237/1, 3 September 2012, Art. 1.
45 Regulation (EU) 452/2011 of 6 May 2011 imposing a definitive anti-subsidy duty on imports of coated fine paper originating in the People's Republic of China, OJ L 128/18, 14 May 2011 (hereinafter Regulation 452/2011).

46 Regulation (EU) 2016/1037 of the European Parliament and of the Council of 8 June 2016 on protection against subsidised imports from countries not members of the European Union, OJ L 176/55, 30 June 2016.

47 See Regulation 451/2011, para. 165.

48 See Regulation 452/2011, para. 272.

49 See Regulation 452/2011, para. 273.

50 See Regulation 451/2011, para. 165.

51 Case T-444/11, *Gold East Paper (Jiangsu) Co. Ltd and Gold Huasheng Paper (Suzhou Industrial Park) Co. Ltd v. Council* [2014] ECLI:EU:T:2014:773.

52 *Ibid.*

53 *Ibid.*

54 *Ibid.*

55 Panel Report on *European Communities – Definitive Anti-Dumping Measures on Certain Iron or Steel Fasteners from China*, WT/DS397/R and Corr.1 of 28 July 2011, as modified by Appellate Body Report WT/DS397/AB/R, DSR 2011: VIII, p. 4289 (hereinafter Panel Report on *EC – Fasteners (China)*), paras. 7.84–88.

56 Paragraph 15(a) provides: In determining price comparability under Article VI of the GATT 1994 and the Anti-Dumping Agreement, the importing WTO Member shall use either Chinese prices or costs for the industry under investigation or a methodology that is not based on a strict comparison with domestic prices or costs in China based on the following rules:

(i) If the producers under investigation can clearly show that market economy conditions prevail in the industry producing the like product with regard to the manufacture, production and sale of that product, the importing WTO Member shall use Chinese prices or costs for the industry under investigation in determining price comparability;

(ii) The importing WTO Member may use a methodology that is not based on a strict comparison with domestic prices or costs in China if the producers under investigation cannot clearly show that market economy conditions prevail in the industry producing the like product with regard to manufacture, production and sale of that product.

57 See Panel Report on *EC – Fasteners (China)*), paras. 283–342.

58 *Ibid.*

59 *Ibid.*

60 *Ibid.*

61 *Ibid.*

62 Appellate Body Report on *United States—Definitive Anti-Dumping and Counter-vailing Duties on Certain Products from China*, WT/DS379/AB/R of 31 August 2012, paras. 543–583.

63 *Ibid.*

64 *Ibid.*

65 See paragraph 15 of China accession protocol: (d) Once China has established, under the national law of the importing WTO Member, that it is a market economy, the provisions of subparagraph (a) shall be terminated provided that the importing Member's national law contains market economy criteria as of the date of accession. In any event, the provisions of subparagraph (a)(ii) shall expire 15 years after the date of accession. In addition, should China establish, pursuant to the national law of the importing WTO Member, that market economy conditions prevail in a particular industry or sector, the non-market economy provisions of subparagraph (a) shall no longer apply to that industry or sector.

66 Appellate Body Report on *European Union—Anti-Dumping Measures on Biodiesel from Argentina*, WT/DS473/AB/R of 26 October 2016, para. 5.56.

67 European Union 2017, *EU-Price Comparison Methodologies (DS 516), First Written Submission by the European Union*, view viewed 31 May 2018, http://trade.ec.europa.eu/doclib/docs/2017/november/tradoc_156401.pdf.

68 Appellate Body Report on *Understanding on Rules and Procedures Governing the Settlement of Disputes* (1995), Annex II to WTO Agreements, Art. 3.2.
69 Panel Report on European *Union—Anti-Dumping Measures on Certain Footwear from China*, WT/DS405/R of 17 December 2012, paras. 7.258–263.
70 *Ibid.*
71 *Ibid.*

Bibliography

Antonini, R. and Monard, E. (2011) 'The concurrent imposition of anti-dumping and countervailing measures on non-market economies: Time for a clean sheet of (Chinese) paper approach?', *International Trade Law and Regulation*, 17(3), pp. 87–96.

Cornelis, J. and Graafsma, F. (2012) 'The appellate body's findings on double remedies and EU practices: What if the lesser duty rule does not come to the rescue?', *International Trade Law and Regulation*, 18(1), pp. 20–27.

Dalton, M. (2014) 'Malmstrom: No automatic market economy status for China in 2016', *Wall Street Journal*, available at http://www.euroalliages.com/data/1418984848MES%20 Malmstrom%20Wall%20street%20journal%20December%2011.pdf.

de Gucht, K. (2013) Modernisation of trade defence – getting the job done, available at http://trade.ec.europa.eu/doclib/docs/2013/november/tradoc_151873.pdf.

Denton, R. (1987) 'The non-market economy rules of European Community's anti-dumping and countervailing duties legislation', *International & Comparative Quarterly*, 36(2), pp. 198–239.

Detlof, H. and Fridh, H. (2006) *The EU treatment of non-market economy countries in antidumping proceedings*, available at https://www.kommers.se/upload/Analysarkiv/Arbetsområden/Antidumpning/Antidumpning%20-%20huvudsida/The_EU_Treatment_of_Non-market_Economy_countries_in_antidumping-proceedings.pdf.

Dunoff, J.L. and Moore, M.O. (2014) 'Footloose and duty-free? reflections on European Union-anti-dumping measures on certain footwear from China', *World Trade Review*, 13(2), pp. 149–178.

European Commission (2008) 'Commission staff working document on progress by the People's Republic of China towards graduation to market economy status in trade defence investigations', *SEC* (2008) 2503 final, Brussels, 19 September 2008.

European Commission (2015) 'Commission staff working document accompanying the 33rd annual report from the Commission to the Council and the European Parliament on the EU's anti-dumping, anti-subsidy and safeguard activities', *SWD* (2015) 149 final, Brussels, 3 August 2015, pp. 39–40.

European Commission (2016) 'Commission staff working document impact assessment: Possible change in the calculation methodology of dumping regarding the People's Republic of China (and other non-market economies)', *SWD* (2016) 370 final, Brussels, 9 November 2016, p. 13.

European Commission (2017) 'Commission staff working document on significant distortions in the economy of the People's Republic of China for the purposes of trade defence investigations', SWD (2017) 483 final/2, Brussels, 20 December 2017, p. 3.

European Parliament (2016) 'European Parliament resolution of 12 May 2016 on China's market economy status', 2016/2667(RSP), final edition, 12 May 2016.

Hart, H.L.A. (1994) *The Concept of Law*, 2nd edn, Oxford, UK: Oxford University Press.

Huang, Y. (2016) 'State capitalism in China', in W.B. Palmer (ed.), *The Annual Proceedings of the Wealth and Well-Being of Nations VIII*, Beloit, WI: Beloit College Press, pp. 19–50.

Jackson, J.H. (1989) 'State trading and nonmarket economies', *International Lawyer*, 23(4), pp. 891–908.

Puccio, L. (2015) *Granting market status to China: An analysis of WTO law and of selected WTO members' policy*, European Parliamentary Research Service, European Union.

Popescu, L. (2010) 'The NME status of the Republic of Moldova and market economy status of Ukraine and Russia: Political decision of the European Union and its implications within the WTO legal framework', *Global Trade and Customs Journal*, 5(3), pp. 113–119.

Ringel, B. (2017) 'Commerce continues China's status as a non-market economy', *Kelley Drye*, available at https://www.ustrademonitor.com/2017/10/commerce-continues-chinas-status-as-a-non-market-economy/

Snyder, F. (2001) 'The origins of the 'Nonmarket Economy': Ideas, pluralism and power in EC anti-dumping law about China', *European Law Journal*, 7(4), pp. 369–434.

Vermulst, E. and Graafsma, F. (2006) 'Recent EC anti-dumping practice towards China and Vietnam: The great leap backward?', *International Trade Law and Regulation*, 12(5), pp. 124–129.

Wang, J. (1999) 'A critique of the application to China of the non-market economy rules of anti-dumping legislation and practice of European Union', *Journal of World Trade*, 33(3), pp. 117–145.

Wu, C.H. (2015) 'Key issues regarding the EU's concurrent imposition of anti-dumping and countervailing duties on Chinese Coated Fine Papers: Analogue country, market economy treatment, individual treatment, and double remedy', *Asian Journal of WTO & International Health Law and Policy*, 10, pp. 263–305.

Zhou, W. and Peng, D. (2018) 'EU-price comparison methodologies (DS 516): Challenging the non-market economy methodology in light of the negotiating history of article 15 of China's WTO accession protocol', *Journal of World Trade*, 52(3), pp. 505–534.

Part III

Diplomacy and the creation of law

9 Preventing divergences from becoming disputes

The elusive EU–China investment negotiations

Julien Chaisse, Qian Xu and Xueliang Ji*

The European public debate deals with the Transatlantic Trade and Investment Partnership (TTIP) and a series of other treaties. The most important treaty will be the EU-wide international investment agreement (IIA) with China. The aim of the treaty is to substitute the present legal assemblage, which consists of 26 different bilateral treaties, that the member states of the European Union (EU) agreed upon three decades ago with China. The two parties believe strongly that the treaty would affect international investment flow by supplying legal security for existing investment in addition to opening a new market for foreign investors.

China and the EU realized the need to formalize and control their economic relationship with a diverse legal framework to solve different matters ranging from economic, political and legal levels in recent time. The existing trade and political agreements between the EU and China contain the challenges and successful stories of both parties that are based on the political economy procedures initiated by both regions' government. The regulation of economic and political issues between China and the EU is a journey that started in the 1970s. The journey is still ongoing but with the objective of the negotiation for a Comprehensive Agreement on Investment (CAI).

The hope for an increased investment flow of an EU–China BIT may be a mirage because the problems Chinese investors encounter in Europe is not mainly based on lack of investment protection or unfair (legal) treatment. It should be noted that European investors are likely to benefit in China if there is an increased market access (Rohde 2018). Domestic reform existing in China is an outcome of the opening of the Chinese market for foreign companies, although the ultimate economic effect from an EU–China CAI will remain limited.

There has been criticism on the EU–China CAI due to the inclusion of controversial investor–state dispute settlement (ISDS) clauses that permit foreign

* This research was supported by the Asia-Europe Comparative Studies Research Project - Institute of European Studies of Macau Academic Research (AECSRP - IEEM AR) Grant 2017–2018. The authors would like to thank Yuwen Li, Pascal Kerneis, Manjiao Chi, Jiaxiang Hu, Sufian Jusoh and Jane Willems for comments on earlier drafts of this article. The views expressed herein by the authors are their own personal ones.

investors to institute an action against host states before international tribunals without having recourse to their national legal system. The principle of fair hearing and equitable treatment has been hidden by the ISDS clauses, which has led to its criticism in recent time, and this has resulted in the negative influence on host governments' ability to regulate in the public interest (Chaisse 2018).

Although the status quo is unsatisfactory, the EU–China CAI would not create new sets of investment rules in comparison with the TTIP. This is because most of the IIAs negotiations between China and practically all, except one EU member state, contain unrestrained ISDS provisions and far-reaching substantive provisions. As a result, Chinese investors already have recourse to international arbitration/mediation to enforce their rights against European governments. A typical example of this is a claim filed by the Chinese insurer Ping An against the Belgian government in the wake of the global financial crisis in 2012 (Rabinovitch and Fontanella-Khan 2012). As explained by Leïla Choukroune in Chapter 4, although the Chinese claimant has failed, this case illustrates that the Chinese company will fight for its interests against a European country. And this condition may happen more often due to the growing Chinese investment in the EU.

China has taken a step forward in its most recent IIAs negotiated with countries from the Americas and Asia, in a bid to recalibrate the existing set of investment rules in order to pursue a better balance between foreign investors' rights and the ability of host states to regulate foreign direct investments (FDIs) in the public interest, using the EU–China IIA as a perfect pivot. As a result, it has gained a lot of ground in the EU in light of its trade agreement finalized with Canada.

In addition, the EU–China CAI will help immensely in building a coherent global investment era, which will aid in improving the status of existing investment treaties on the grounds of an EU-wide IIA with China, by replacing the investment treaties already existing. If the investment treaties are not replaced, it would result in the complexity of the total system, which could affect foreign investors, and they may decide to sue based on the old treaties that are favourable to them. The termination approach becomes the alternative for the EU and China and other counties like South Africa or Indonesia who also terminated their IIA instead of renegotiating their terms of the agreement. A more coherent global investment governance will emerge if more countries adopt the EU's "replacement approach," which is geared towards regionalization of investment rule-making.

More so, in view of the above, China has also been negotiating with the United States with regard to an investment treaty with similar features to that of the European-Chinese agreement. Also, a comprehensive investment charter may be established in the TTIP between the United States and Europe. The legal framework being developed from this tripartite relationship will most likely be more stable compared to the treaty practiced in the past 50 years and is likely to provide a blueprint for IIAs to be emulated by other countries. The investment negotiations between the EU, the United States and China should include a process of global investment dialogue for it to be all-inclusive.

This chapter is segmented into five sections. Section two gives a vivid picture of the economic, political and social drivers between the EU and China, and it also analyzes the economic agreements and policy papers issued between 1973 and 2013. Section three concentrates on the EU–China relations in respect to regional economic governance and analyzes the general economic strategy carried out from the EU in Asia. Section four proposes to look closely at the behaviour between the EU and its member state on one part, and that of the EU and China on the other part right from the drafting and signing of their respective investment agreements, with the objective of highlighting the areas that modified their negotiating strategy in answer to different economic and political situations. Section five deals with the conclusion of the discussion. The thesis of this discussion is to provide helpful tools to academics, legal counsels and policymakers and to also contribute to the knowledge of some aspects of investment treaties and the view of the possible implication of the provisions contained therein.

International policy drivers towards an EU–China comprehensive agreement on investment

The need for the EU and China to seek an "ambitious and comprehensive" agreement on investment is based on a series of tactical considerations and motivations. There is the likelihood that an EU–China CAI will strengthen the EU–China comprehensive strategic partnership, better regulate Chinese investment flooding the EU, provide a level playing field for both investors, improve on the investment roles of the Asia continent and increase EU and China competitiveness in the global economy. The above reasons are unexhausted but vividly float on the negotiation table. The EU and China are expected to make frantic efforts to strike a deal that would reflect the relationship between the EU and China and pave the way for a high-level free trade agreement by meeting their domestic demands.

The EU–China CAI dynamics of negotiating is divided into four aspects, namely economic, political, legal and regional governance to enable the painting of the image on how both parties have come together. The successful story for leaders of both parties should be told.

The 26 BITs between 27 EU MS and China (except Ireland)

The legal instrument of EU–China relations is comprised of 26 BITs covering 27 EU member states, with the exception of Ireland, in addition to EU–China trade relations governed by the 1985 Trade and Economic Cooperation Agreement.

Unequal investment protection among the EU member states and China still constitutes a major setback spreading across the 26 BITs, as issues like environment and labour were not provided for. The fair and equitable treatment (FET) clause as contained in the agreement is not enforceable due to it not being linked to the minimum standard of treatment of foreigners under the customary international law (United Nations 2012).

Secondly, the use of vague languages in drafting BITs – together with the broad and innovative interpretation of such languages by arbitral tribunals – are features contained in the old generation of BITs, which were later incorporated in the signing of BITs, thereby inviting criticism and lawsuit among the parties and creating another major setback (Berger 2013).

The investment promotion and protection guaranteed under BITs between the EU members states and a third-party country is acknowledged by the EU but also identified the unequal level playing field for EU companies investing abroad (Bungenberg and Titi 2014). The desperate need for foreign investments by China to boost its economic development in the 1980s and 1990s when the 26 BITs were signed with the EU member states prompted China to accept rules and terms respecting European investors' interests (Xu 2013).

The launch of negotiations of partnership and cooperation agreement

The need for the EU and China to further strengthen their bilateral relations at the 9th EU–China Summit brought about the launching of the Partnership and Cooperation Agreement (PCA) by both parties, *to enable them to determine the full scope of today's comprehensive strategic partnership between themselves and also update the 1985 EEC-China Trade and Economic Co-operation Agreement* (Council of the European Union 2006, then the EC). The PCA *"will cover the full scope of their bilateral relations together with improve cooperation in political matters."* (EC 2006).

The objectives set down in the PCA were in consonance with the original use of the PCA, which was for the EU *"to strengthen democracies and develop economies through cooperation in a wide range of areas and through political dialogue"* (PCAs 2018). However, contracting a PCA is not a usual practice in China's foreign policy (Zhang 2011). The EU is expected to "guarantee sustainable and fair socio-economic development with third-party countries" (European Union 2010)[1] in respect to an area that deals with human rights and democratization and the European Parliament attaches "considerable importance" to. On this note, resistance from other parties is expected (Zeng 2009; Lang 2015). The EU and China were not on the same page on whether to incorporate the new PCA and updating the 1985 Agreement on a single document or made separately if concluded. This disagreement led to the omission of the PCA from the EU–China 2020 Strategic Agenda for Cooperation (Godement and Vasselier 2017).

The 2013 launch of negotiations of a comprehensive EU–China CAI

In 2010, China was seen as an important partner who would help the EU in its communication by ensuring the openness that already existed and the accessing of its investment market through the delivering of new liberalization in the Commission was heightened (European Commission 2013). The negotiation of an EU–China CAI witnessed its birth on the 16th EU–China Summit in 2013, which had its first negotiation in 2014 (European Commission 2014) and has had 20 different negotiations to date (European Commission 2019).

As outlined by the European Commission, the absence of a level playing field for prospective and European investors already in China and the absence of a framework that will help solve the shortcomings of the EU–China investment relationship are the two major problems affecting the accessing of the EU–China investment relation at the EU level (European Commission 2016). The EU, in order to solve the problem, decided to set the objectives of the CAI negotiation that will "help accelerate the increased freedom of investment and removing restriction that affect investors in each other's market" by making sure an easier and a secured legal framework is experienced by investors of both sides, a predictable long-term entrance to the EU and China market is secured and a secured protection is provided to investors and their investments (European Commission 2017). To China, a CAI with the EU is divided twofold, which is bringing together the 26 BITs to become one set of comprehensive rules and making sure there is an operative involvement in the global investment rule-making.

The EU member states do not share the same view with what the Commission envisages (Koeth 2016). This was firstly seen in the continuous criticism of international investment law, as it relates to ISDS in the TTIP and the Canada–EU Comprehensive Economic and Trade Agreement (CETA), which has led to a country like Germany to take an official stand to preserve its position on international investment law and investor–state arbitration generally (Schill 2015a). ISDS is not accepted well by the wider public of the EU (Koeth 2016). However, the EU wants to maintain its stand in defining international regulations and make the ISDS a de facto international standard with China (Koeth 2016). Also, differences between the objectives of the EU and those of its member state practices are contained in documents of the European Parliament on EU–China negotiation for a bilateral investment agreement, which stated that the EU–China treaty "should be based on the best practices derived from Member States experiences" and sets the standard that must be included in CAI (European Parliament 2019). It is worthy of note that "best practice" and "standards" differ with respect to the member states, leading to the obvious formulation of the FET standard (Titi 2015).

The EU and China agreed to strengthen their future investment deal in January 2016 by advocating that it "should improve market access opportunities for their investors by establishing a genuine right to invest and by guaranteeing that they will not discriminate against their respective companies" (European Commission 2016). This position had earlier been stated at the EU–China Summit in 2015 by both parties in "viewing the ongoing investment agreement negotiations as one of the most important issues in EU-China bilateral economic and trade relation" and "aiming the expeditious conclusion" (EC 2015). Some of the major challenges the EU–China investment deal might face include the difficulties in making progress in market access (Shan and Wang 2015) and free trade zones (Huang 2015, pp. 307–339) in the EU–China BIT. Because of the criticisms of the ISDS, the EU proposed an Investment Court System to replace the ISDS (Koeth 2016). However, this proposal received criticisms from some main stakeholders, such as Business Europe (Koeth 2016). It seems that China can accept ISDS with traditional protection areas (Bickenbach et al. 2015). And China supports improving ISDS but subject to an appellate body (Roberts 2018).

In conclusion, China categorically stated in its first paper on the EU in 2003 that "no fundamental conflict of interest" between both parties and set out its vision by emphasizing that "the common ground between China and the EU far outweighs their disagreements" (Scott 2014; Zhang 2009). This position will guide and develop EU–China relations "in greater pragmatically-driven economic, financial and environmental directions" (Scott 2014; Zhang 2009). And it has earlier been emphasized by Chinese President Xi Jinping's speech at the College of Europe when he said that China and Europe "need to build four bridges for peace, growth, reform, and progress of civilization, so that the China-EU comprehensive strategic partnership, will take on even greater global significance" (Mission of the People's Republic of China to the European Union 2014). For the interest of the EU, its member states and China, there is a need for both parties to continue to build on the success achieved previously to attain a long-term goal and avoid conflict and shared interests.

EU–China relations in the context of regional economic governance

Wen Jiabao, the premier of the State Council of the People's Republic of China, stated on May 6 2004, that

> Developing the comprehensive strategic partnership at the beginning of the 21st century not only serves the mutual interests of China and the European Union but also contribute to peace, stability, and development in our respective regions and the world at large. (Prodi 2004).

The competition existing between the EU, China and the transatlantic alliance is based on who should take lead worldwide on an economic agenda. The EU and China will set the pace in restructuring the economic framework in the Asia Pacific (USCC 2005). In order to carry out its strategic pivot to Asia, the EU, unlike the United States, had to rebrand its strategy by engaging in a "smart pivot" (Solana 2013), which is making sure that trade comes first in its engagement with Asian countries.

Accordingly, the Asia-Pacific countries and region negotiating an FTA with the EU are ASEAN, Japan, India, Malaysia, Thailand, Indonesia, Philippines and Myanmar (European Commission 2017). It must be noted that Vietnam and Singapore have reached a conclusion to negotiate an FTA with the EU but it has not yet been ratified (Hai 2017). In regard to the 10 FTA partners of the EU, China is likely to conclude a bilateral FTA with ASEAN and Singapore or engage in a tripartite trade deal (China-Korea FTA) and regional deal (RCEP). The strength in writing the rules for the twenty-first century trade for different intelligent shadow arguments in support for or against free trade agreements grabbed increasing support although it was frustrating.

The good news is that in the Asia-Pacific region, the international investment regime is working towards unity (Feldman et al. 2016). China as a country is the most important partner of the EU to attain CAI for the present and FTA for the future in respect to economic and geopolitical significance (China Institute for Reform and Development 2016). The end effects of an ambitious and comprehensive investment agreement among the largest economies of the world will pattern the future investment that was written with and among third countries in the Asia Pacific.

There is a need for both parties to ensure that the force gathered so far by them and their various political commitments is sustained for greater prosperity and common interest both domestically and globally in future. As far as both parties are ready to sort out their difference as highlighted in sections three and four, and also respond practically to the current trend of the world economy, the CAI will be a reality.

Issues of EU–China negotiations

The EU and China decided to negotiate a CAI as a result of their constantly evolving economic relationship (China Institute for Reform and Development 2016). After a critical discussion of the fundamental factors such as economic, political and legal drivers that motivated China and the EU to conclude an investment agreement, we shall now narrow our attention on specific issues as contained in the EU–China CAI negotiations. The enormous responsibility of providing protection for their respective national investors in the territory of the other contracting party, coupled with the protection of their internal market from the competition inherent in the goods and services provided by investors on their prospective partners' territory, lies squarely on the negotiators.

China's outward direct investment has increased drastically from USD 1.9 billion in 2004 to USD 80.4 billion in 2014 as contained in the official statistics issued by the State Administration of Foreign Exchange (SAFE), which is an administrative agency of the People's Republic of China (Freeman 2015, pp. 5–10).

The impact of these negotiations is largely dependent upon the positive outcome of the investment treaty, which may strengthen the path for a potential FTA between the EU and China. More so, the importance of the EU–China treaty may spread beyond the original regions that are signatory to it and enhance the liberalization of global economic relations with regard to future trade and investment agreements (Bickenbach et al. 2015). There is a need for both parties to strike a balance between protecting the rights of investors and the right of member states regulating in the interest of the public in considering the main issues under discussion (Koeth 2016). Frankly speaking, whereas investment agreements are targeted to attract foreign investment and also to ensure that in achieving such purpose, the power of the State to attain its objectives of public policy is not obstructed (Bickenbach et al. 2015). In view of the above, the EU and China are presently strategizing on the inclusion of specific provisions and clauses that will facilitate the reaching of the said equilibrium.

Specific clauses in IIAs concluded by the EU and its member states, on the one hand, and the EU and China, on the other hand, will be the focus of this section. The purport of this is to understand whether or not the prospective partners have reacted to the evolution of the economic and political situation with a parallel mode of drafting IIAs.

We shall commence with the details of the state of negotiations between China and the EU and then proceed to the research plan and the methodology applied, and then conclude by extracting a pattern in the behaviour of the global powers in the drafting of their international investment agreements.

The state of the negotiations

The wide range of issues open for negotiation in an IIA includes the definition of investment, the standard of treatment such as most-favoured nation, national treatment, full protection and security, fair and equitable treatment, direct and indirect expropriation, investor–state dispute settlement and state-to-state dispute settlement.

The EU and China in the course of their negotiations have settled considerable issues that will not give rise to further debate in their respective positions. Both parties are aimed at revitalizing their economies by boosting their still under-developed investment relations and have agreed on the need to replace the old legal framework; therefore, they have a common interest in stipulating certain provisions.

There are already disagreements on certain issues that will prompt the parties to reach an agreement during negotiations. This section will focus on three major provisions, namely transparency, fair and equitable treatment and taxation. Firstly, the reasons for choosing the aforementioned three provisions is that regulatory transparency is highly considered a qualified standard to measure a treatment that is fair and equitable (Malanczuk 2015, pp. 65–109); Research and some arbitrations awards have proved that the three concepts are interwoven. Secondly, they are the deciding factors of every treaty. Lastly, they form the contentious issues during and after the conclusion of every treaty.

The EU faces the challenges of reforming its FDI policy, both addressing the security concerns that have been raised for some types of FDI and at the same time ensuring greater openness, transparency and a level playing field for European FDI in China (Bickenbach and Liu 2018). The divide between law and policy has been blurred in China given under certain circumstances, government policies may also become guiding legal instruments, which causes the whole investment regime to be unpredictable and subject to arbitrariness (Pelkmans et al. 2018). China's new foreign investment law adopted a "negative list," which involves fundamental changes to raise the transparency and openness of the investment environment. However, the regulations are too general to tell how it will operate in practice.

As for Chinese investors, they frequently complain about the rising protectionism to restrict investments; among the EU member states, Greece and Poland have the highest threshold to set up business. In addition, the tax base and rates of corporate taxation are not uniform, which reflects the issue of fragmentation in the EU market (Pelkmans et al. 2018). The issues related to fair and equitable treatment still require further substantial follow-up, together with the discussions on "transfers and capital movement provisions, the latter still in an initial stage" (European Commission 2018). It is based on the above strength that we come to the conclusion that a cursory look at these concepts can provide an overview of the main issues discussed during the negotiations.

Behaviour in concluding international investment agreements

The major reasons for the EU–China treaty are centred on legal, political and economic benefits as enshrined in section one of the current article. It should be noted that if the negotiation gets to the thirteenth round (European Commission 2016) it would be needless to wait for the parties to deliver a result since more is needed to conclude an agreement.

The approach used for this work embraces a normative analysis of previous treaties in a comparative way and still being abreast of the ongoing negotiations. The EU–China CAI will consolidate on previous BITs and FTAs between both parties in the future. This work is carried out by focusing on the comparative analysis of completed, signed but not ratified and ongoing negotiation of international investment agreements.

So far, three aspects of the problems have been looked into, namely the EU's behaviour in the perfecting of its international investment agreements, the relationship previously established through international investment treaties between the member states of the EU and China and China's behaviour in perfecting its international investment agreement.

It is foreseeable that market access will be one of the biggest challenges between the parties, especially in the sectors of service and financial regulation in order to obtain national treatment in China. Moreover, the EU traditionally has high standards regarding human rights, labour rights and environment protection, which may also challenge the negotiation process (Wang 2018). The main reason for looking into the three aspects of the problems is to examine the constant behaviour and development trends in a manner that will predict the future result of the EU–China negotiations, which is aimed at perfecting an investment agreement.

The behaviour of China and the EU in perfecting an international agreement will determine the priorities of both parties in regard to the manner of their evolution in previous years, resulting in their respective positions in different treaties coupled with their areas of similarity and differences in their negotiations.

EU's approach to CAI

Previously signed bilateral agreements between the EU and other states such as EU–Vietnam (European Commission 2016), EU–Singapore (European Commission 2015), the FTA EU–South Korea and the CETA were critically analyzed with respect to the availability of text. In the following, the EU's possible approaches towards the CAI could be derived from a few FTAs that include investment.

Referring to the EU–Vietnam FTA, the scope of investment and measures on investment are regulated under Chapter 8. The agreement abolished the "performance requirements" in both trade in goods and services, which goes beyond the TRIMS. The agreement also took Vietnam's WTO commitments as a benchmark for the service commitments. In this case, Vietnam has offered the EU the best possible access to its market by making commitments deeper than those outlined in the WTO as well as opening additional sectors or subsectors for EU service providers (EU Commission 2018). However, compared to China, the scale of foreign investment in China is so much bigger and the country has a more matured foreign investment system, as China opened up its market decades earlier than Vietnam did (Pelkmans et al. 2018).

In terms of the EU–Singapore FTA, which shares the same depth and breadth with the EU–Vietnam FTA, the provisions on investment protection are elaborate. The agreement sets the standard of fair and equitable treatment (FET), which includes, for example, loans are supported by the government while insurance is not covered. The agreement also made efforts to strike a balance between the state's right to regulate and unreasonable expropriation. For instance, state's decisions on sovereign debt restructuring are outside the scope of investment arbitration. The agreement also emphasizes transparency during the disputes between investors and states, such as providing additional guarantee to the public regarding access to information, documents, hearings and third-party submissions (European Commission 2018).

The EU–Canada Trade Agreement provides another alternative modality as a reference for the CAI negotiations, as the CETA also takes a negative-list approach, which is applicable to all investors and investment in terms of establishment and operation. As mentioned by Yumiko Nakanishi in Chapter 12, CETA "preserves the right to regulate," which allows the EU to keep its right to stipulate environmental norms. CETA confirms a high level of protection for investors while fully preserving the right of governments to regulate and pursue legitimate public policy objectives, for example, the protection of health, safety and the environment. CEPA represents a significant break at two levels. On the one hand, it made explicit reference to the government's right to regulate in the public interest and more precise and clearer investment protection standards. On the other hand, it creates an independent court system, consisting of a permanent tribunal and an appeal tribunal (European Commission 2018).

The EU has also concluded an agreement with the Interim Economic Partnership Agreement with the East African Countries (EAC) (European

Commission 2015), the Economic Partnership Agreement with West Africa (European Commission 2015) and the Trade agreement with Ecuador (European Commission 2016) but which has yet to be applied.

Although one of the major purposes of both the Interim Economic Partnership Agreement with East African Countries and the Economic Partnership Agreement with West Africa is to promote investment, the agreements fail to name investment provisions in their content. Additionally, the trade agreement with Ecuador also falls short of the same standard, thereby restraining the analysis of these agreements for the purpose of this article.

Although we have analyzed the proposal made by the European Commission for the TTIP, it is still under negotiations (European Commission 2015). It is currently not absolutely safe to conclude with certainty that the TTIP will be signed and ratified. The numbers of inhabitants will be defined by the wording of the different treaty sections, what it stands for, in addition to CETA and the future China agreement.

So far, a comprehensive analysis of the BITs in force between China and each of the EU member states (in exception of Ireland) has been conducted, comparing the 26 BITs.[2] Also, Belgium and Luxembourg signed an agreement with China in 2005, BLEU (Belgium-Luxembourg Economic Union) – China BIT, which is equivalent to a bilateral investment treaty.

China's approach to CAI

On the other hand, attention was drawn to the BITs entered into by China and those still in the process with third parties, together with the Chinese model BITs, in order to understand China's stand.

It should be noted in this respect that China was majorly a capital importing state in the past, making all the agreements concluded in this era to reflect its intention to preserve the space to regulate (Zweig 2010, pp. 192–221). But in recent times, beginning from the 1990s, China engaged the going out policy by promoting foreign investment on behalf of state-owned enterprises (Du 2016). This was evident in international agreements entered into during that period. China then became both a capital importing country (as reflected in the investment on the Chinese territory) and a capital exporting country (as reflected in the investments realized abroad by Chinese enterprises) at the same time (Wang et al. 2015). Based on the above, China decided to strike a balance between its interests as a host nation and its desire to give fair legal protection to the interests of Chinese enterprises, whether privately or state-owned, thereby deviating from its previous idea of giving maximum liberty to the host state to regulate.

In the China-South Korea FTA, investment protections are regulated under Chapter 12. The protection of the investments only covers "management, conduct, operation, maintenance, use, enjoyment and sale or other disposition of investments," which preclude the pre-establishment stage (MOFCOM 2019). FET and full protection and security are subject to the minimum standard of treatment under customary international law (Art. 12.5).

Looking at the China-Australia FTA, which concluded in 2015, the "pre-establishment" phase of investment is not covered under the national treatment. The ISDS measures specified procedures and conduct of arbitrators and mediators, which are elaborated upon as those concluded between the EU and third countries (Pelkmans et al. 2018).

To recall, CETA is also the first agreement where the EU has agreed to a negative listing approach. This matters to CAI negotiations, as with the new Chinese foreign investment law, because the Chinese government may well be motived to adopt a negative listing in the future FTA negotiations, although remain at the central level.

One of the potential disagreements between the EU and China CAI is the post-establishment national and most-favoured-nation treatment, which is true for the existing BITs between China and EU member states. However, European companies in China still face different forms of unfair and discriminatory treatment, in particular related to subsidies, IPRs and public procurement (Bickenbach et al. 2015). It is envisaged that during the ongoing negotiations, the EU will require China to make concrete commitments in terms of introducing the post-establishment national treatment (Bickenbach and Liu 2018).

The treatment of SOEs can be controversial as well. The EU's aim is to limit various forms of preferential treatment of Chinese SOEs to encourage greater transparency in the agreement. Chinese SOEs are extremely important as a key instrument for the government to pursue its industrial policies including acquiring advanced technologies (Bickenbach and Liu 2018).

Another controversial issue lies in the ISDS; the main question is whether the parties will resolve the disputes through the traditional ISDS or by the permanent court system advocated by the EU. It is still highly unclear whether China will accept the proposal. On the one hand, China has intensified its engagement with ICSID; on the other hand, China has also established its own commercial arbitration institutions. In the end, it may be subject to the counterpart who has the right powerful leverage.

Conclusion

Although the treaty negotiated between the EU and China is centred on only BIT, it has a potential of creating an FTA. Also, its importance surpasses the economic and legal benefits achieved by both parties economically and otherwise in their "wider neighbourhood" and worldwide, which is in contrast to the interest of other world powers, thereby making the CAI a treaty as a stepping stone to a more intimate relationship between China and the EU, not just one of those bilateral and multilateral agreements establishing the "fragmented patchwork" of the international investment law (Schill 2015b, pp. 1886–1887).

The achievement of the CAI and its corresponding outcome will surpass the impact of an agreement that is narrowed down to bilateral cooperation. The future of the China–EU relation with regard to BIT will strengthen the countries' cooperation and improve their economic relationship, which is mutually profitable to them, or lead to a rivalry between them on who has the biggest portion of the global market, depending on other PTAs with a third-party state.

From the political point of view, the EU strategy in this negotiation is clearly economic, since it focuses on issues that are economic and leaves geopolitical matters that are essentially troubling. The future of such a union will importantly result in both regions becoming capital importing and exporting countries through economic conditions. At present, both the EU and China have enough reasons to negotiate and sign a CAI fostering investment between themselves. Although the negotiation of this agreement requires a lot of effort to satisfy the parties' interests, either as a home state or a host state, it will be accepted by both parties and their investors, and it can be treated as a precedent for the rest of the world (Bickenbach et al. 2015).

Notes

1 Council Decision (EU) 2011/265 of 16 September 2010 on the Signing, on behalf of the European Union, and Provisional Application of the Free Trade Agreement between the European Union and its Member States, of the one part, and the Republic of Korea, of the other part, OJ L 127/1, 14 May 2011.

2 China – Sweden supplementary agreement (signed 29.03.1982), China – Denmark (signed 29.04.1985), China – United Kingdom exchange of no (signed 15.05.1986), China – Austria (signed 12.09.1985), China – Italy (signed 28.01.1985), China – Poland (signed 07.06.1988), China – Slovakia (signed 04.12.1991), China – Greece (signed 25.06.1992), China – Hungary supplementary agreement (signed 29.05.1991), China – Bulgaria (signed 27.06.1989), China – Croatia (signed 07.06.1993), China – Estonia (signed 02.09.1993), China – Lithuania (signed 08.11.1993), China – Slovenia (signed 13.09.1993, China – Romania additional protocol 4 (signed 12.07.1994), China – Cyprus (signed 17.01.2001), China – Netherlands protocol (signed 26.11.2001), China – Germany protocol (signed 01.12.2003), China – Latvia protocol (signed 15.04.2004), China – Finland (signed 15.11.2004), China – Belgium/Luxemburg protocol (signed 06.06.2005), China – Czech republic (signed 08.12.2005), China – Spain protocol (signed 24.11.2005), China – Portugal protocol (signed 09.12.2005), China – Malta (signed 22.02.2009), China – France (signed 26.11.2007).

Bibliography

Berger, A. (2013) 'Investment Rules in Chinese Preferential Trade and Investment Agreements: Is China following the global trend towards comprehensive agreements?' *Discussion Paper*, paper 7/2013. Deutsches Institut für Entwicklungspolitik, pp. 1–30.

Bickenbach, F., Liu, W.H. and Li, G. (2015) 'The EU-China Bilateral Investment Agreement in Negotiation: Motivation, Conflicts and Perspectives', *Kiel Policy Brief*, 95(1), pp. 1–32.

Bickenbach, F. and Liu, W.H. (2018) 'Chinese Direct Investment in Europe–Challenges for EU FDI Policy', *CESifo Forum*, pp. 15–22.

Bungenberg, M. and Titi, C. (2014) 'The Evolution of EU Investment Law and the Future of EU-China Investment Relations', in W. Shan and J. Su (eds.), *China and International Investment Law: Twenty Years of ICSID Membership*, Brill – Nijhoff, pp. 297–371.

Chaisse, J. (ed.) (2018) *China-European Union Investment Relationship: Towards A New Leadership in Global Investment Governance?* Cheltenham, UK: Edward Elgar Publishing.

China Institute for Reform and Development (2016) 'China-EU FTA: A decisive option for deepening China-EU cooperation by 2020', available at http://www.chinareform.org/publications/reports/201607/W020160721637054536284.pdf

China Mission (2014) 'Speech by H.E. Xi Jinping President of the People's Republic of China at the College of Europe', available at http://www.chinamission.be/eng/jd/t1143591.htm

Colin, B. (2010) 'Obstacles in Upgrading the 1985 Trade and Economic Cooperation Agreement between the EU and China', *EU-China Observer*, pp. 9–13.

Council of the European Onion (2015) 'EU-China summit joint statement', available at https://www.consilium.europa.eu/media/23732/150629-eu-china-summit-joint-statement-final.pdf

Du, M. (2016) 'The Regulation of Chinese State-owned Enterprises in National Foreign Investment Laws: A Comparative Analysis', *Global Journal of Comparative Law*, 5(1), pp. 118–145.

European Commission (2001) 'The European Union's Role in Promoting Human Rights and Democratisation in Third Countries', COM (2001) 252 final, Brussels, 8 May 2001.

European Commission (2006) '9th EU-China Summit Joint Statement', 12642/06 (Presse 249), Brussels, 11 September 2006. Available at https://www.consilium.europa.eu/ueDocs/cms_Data/docs/pressData/en/er/90951.pdf

European Commission (2013) 'Commission Proposes to Open Negotiations for an Investment Agreement with China', available at http://trade.ec.europa.eu/doclib/press/index.cfm?id=900

European Commission (2013) 'Staff Working Paper, Impact Assessment Report on the EU-China Investment Relations', SWD (2013) 185 final, Brussels, 23 May 2013.

European Commission (2013) 'Trade Policy on China', available at http://ec.europa.eu/trade/policy/countries-and-regions/countries/china/

European Commission (2014) 'Comprehensive Economic and Trade Agreement (CETA) between Canada, of the one Part, and the European Union and its Member States', available at http://trade.ec.europa.eu/doclib/docs/2014/september/tradoc_152806.pdf

European Commission (2014) 'EU and China begin Investment Talks', Press Release, Brussels, 20 January 2014.

European Commission (2015) 'Commission Draft Text TTIP – Investment', available at http://trade.ec.europa.eu/doclib/docs/2015/september/tradoc_153807.pdf

European Commission (2015) 'Economic Partnership Agreement between the East African Community Partner States, of the one Part, and the European Union and its Member States of the other Part', COM (2016) 64 final, Brussels, 11 February 2016.

European Commission (2015) 'Economic Partnership Agreement between the West African States, the Economic Community of West African States (ECOWAS) and the West African Economic and Monetary Union (UEMOA), of the one Part, and the European Union and its Member States, of the other Part', available at http://trade.ec.europa.eu/doclib/docs/2015/october/tradoc_153867.pdf

European Commission (2015) 'EU-Singapore Free Trade Agreement', available at http://trade.ec.europa.eu/doclib/press/index.cfm?id=961

European Commission (2016) 'EU and China Agree on Scope of the Future Investment Deal', available at http://trade.ec.europa.eu/doclib/press/index.cfm?id=1435

European Commission (2016) 'EU-Ecuador Trade Negotiations', available at http://trade.ec.europa.eu/doclib/press/index.cfm?id=1261

European Commission (2016) 'European Commission Directorate-General for Trade, Directorate B – Services and Investment, Intellectual Property and Public Procurement Investment', Trade/B2/AK –, EU-China Investment Agreement: Report of the 12th Round of negotiations, Brussels, 26–30 September 2016.

European Commission (2016) 'Sustainability Impact Assessment (SIA) in support of an Investment Agreement between the European Union and the People's Republic of China', final inception report, available at http://www.trade-sia.com/china/wp-content/uploads/sites/9/2014/12/SIA-EU-China-Final-inception-report-17-June-2016.pdf

European Commission (2018) 'EU-Vietnam Free Trade Agreement', available at http://trade.ec.europa.eu/doclib/press/index.cfm?id=1437

European Commission (2019) 'Overview of FTA and other Trade Negotiations', available at http://trade.ec.europa.eu/doclib/docs/2006/december/tradoc_118238.pdf

European Parliament (2019) 'State of play of EU-China relations', Briefing Note, January 2019, available at http://www.europarl.europa.eu/RegData/etudes/BRIE/2019/633149/EPRS_BRI(2019)633149_EN.pdf

European Union (2010) 'Partnership and Cooperation Agreements (PCAs): Russia, Eastern Europe, the Southern Caucasus and Central Asia', available at https://eur-lex.europa.eu/legal-content/EN/TXT/?uri=LEGISSUM%3Ar17002

Feldman M., Monardes, R. and Rodriguez-Chiffelle, C. (2016) 'The Role of Pacific Rim FTAs in the Harmonisation of International Investment Law: Towards a Free Trade Area of the Asia-Pacific', *World Economic Forum*, available at http://e15initiative.org/publications/the-role-of-pacific-rim-ftas-in-the-harmonisation-of-international-investment-law-towards-a-free-trade-area-of-the-asia-pacific/

Freeman, D. (2015) 'China's Outward Direct Investment in the EU: Challenges of Rapid Change, In EU-China Observer', *Exchanging Ideas on EU-China Relations: An Interdisciplinary Approach*, 15(3), pp. 5–10.

Godement, F. and Vasselier, A. (2017) *China at the Gates: A New Power Audit of EU-China Relations,* European Council on Foreign Relations CFR.

Hai, H.H. (2017) 'The Social Dimension in EU Free Trade Agreements: ASEAN Perspectives', *European Review*, 25(4), pp. 532–549.

Huang, J. (2015) 'Challenges and Solutions for the China-US BIT Negotiations: Insights from the Recent Development of FTZs in China', *Journal of International Economic Law*, 18(2), pp. 307–339.

Koeth, W. (2016) 'Can the Investment Court System (ICS) save TTIP and CETA?' *EIPA Working Paper 2016/W/01*, pp. 1–14.

Lang, B. (2015) 'The Prospective EU-China Bilateral Investment Treaty: Wider Regional Implications in East and Southeast Asia', *EU-China Observer*, pp. 1–11.

Malanczuk, P. (2015) 'China and the Emerging Standard of Transparency in Investor-State Dispute Settlement (ISDS)', *Trade Development Through Harmonization of Commercial Law*, 19, pp. 65–109.

Men, J. and Balducci, G. (eds.) (2010) Prospects and Challenges for EU-China Relations in the 21st Century: The Partnership and Cooperation Agreement, P.I.E-Peter Lang S.A., Éditions Scientifiques Internationales.

MOFCOM (2019) 'Free Trade Agreement between the Government of the People's Republic of China and the Government of the Republic of Korea,' available at http://fta.mofcom.gov.cn/korea/annex/xdzw_en.pdf

Niblett, R. (2005) 'China, the EU, and the Transatlantic Alliance', available at https://csis-prod.s3.amazonaws.com/s3fspublic/legacy_files/files/attachments/ts050722niblett.pdf

Pelkmans, J. et al. (2018) 'Tomorrow's Silk Road-Assessing an EU-China Free Trade Agreement', *Centre for European Policy Studies (CEPS)*, pp. 5–333.

Prodi, R. (2004) 'Relations between the EU and China: More than Just Business', *EU-China Business Forum*, Brussels, 6 May 2004, available at http://www.europa.eu.int/comm/external_relations/news/prodi/sp04_227.htm

Rabinovitch, S. and Fontanella-Khan, J. (2012) 'Ping An in Arbitration Claim Over Fortis', *Financial Times*, available at https://www.ft.com/content/87437290-0620-11e2-bd29-00144feabdc0

Roberts, A. (2018) 'UNCITRAL and ISDS Reforms: Moving to Reform Options … the Politics', *Blog of the International Journal of International Law*, available at https://www.ejiltalk.org/uncitral-and-isds-reforms-moving-to-reform-options-the-politics/

Rohde, A. (2018) 'EU-China Investments: Europe's Strategic Interest', available at https://spectator.clingendael.org/en/publication/eu-china-investments-europes-strategic-interest#

Saarela, A. (2018) 'A new era in EU-China relations: more wide-ranging strategic cooperation?' European Parliament 2018, available at http://www.iberchina.org/files/2018-2/eu_china_relations_new_era_parlamento.pdf.

Schill, S.W. (2015a) 'Editorial: The German Debate on International Investment Law', *The Journal of World Investment & Trade*, 16(1), pp. 1–9.

Schill, S.W. (2015b) 'Multilateralization: An Ordering Paradigm for International Investment Law' in M. Bungenberg et al. (eds.), *International Investment Law*, München/Oxford/Baden-Baden: Nomos/Hart, pp. 1866–1887.

Scott, D. (2014) 'New Horizons in EU-China Relations?' *EU-China Observer*, pp. 2–7.

Shan, W. and Wang, L. (2015) 'The China–EU BIT and the Emerging "Global BIT 2.0"', *ICSID Review-Foreign Investment Law Journal*, 30(1), pp. 260–267.

Solana, J. (2013) 'Europe's Smart Asian Pivot', *Project Syndicate*, available at https://www.politico.eu/article/europes-smart-asian-pivot/

Tenuta, F. (2015) 'The Motivations behind the EU-China Bilateral Investment Treaty Negotiations', *EU-China Observer*, pp. 16–22.

Titi, C. (2015) 'International Investment Law and the European Union', *European Journal of International Law*, 26(3), pp. 639–661.

United Nations (2012) Fair and Equitable Treatment *UNCTAD Series on Issues in International Investment Agreements II*, United Nations Publication.

Wang, M.L., Zhen, Q. and Zhang, J.J. (2015) 'China Becomes a Capital Exporter' in L. Song et al. (eds.), *China's Domestic Transformation in a Global Context*, ANU Press, pp. 315–338.

Wenhua, S. and Wang, L. (2017) 'The China–EU BIT and the Emerging "Global BIT 2.0"', *ICSID Review-Foreign Investment Law Journal*, 30(1), pp. 260–267.

Xu, M. (2013) 'The launch of China-EU Negotiations on the Investment Agreement Came at a Right Time', *People's Daily*, available at http://world.people.com.cn/n/2013/1121/c157278-23609503.html

Yelery, A. (2015) 'China's 'Going Out' Policy: Sub-National Economic Trajectories', *Institute of Chinese Studies*, available at http://www.icsin.org/uploads/2015/04/12/e50f1e532774c4c354b24885fcb327c5.pdf

Zeng, L. (2009) 'A Preliminary Perspective of Negotiations of EU-China PCA: A New Bottle *Carrying Old Wine or New Wine or Both?'* European Law Journal*, 15(1), pp. 121–141.

Zhang, J. (2011) 'The EU-China Relationship Arriving at a Bottleneck-a Look at the Ongoing Negotiation of the PCA', *EU-China Observer*, (4), pp. 2–3.

Zhang, T. (2009) 'Sino-European Relations: From the Height to the Width', in J. Jokela (ed.), *The Role of the European Union in Asia: China and India as Strategic Partners*, Routledge, pp. 141–158.

Zweig, D. (2010) 'China's Political Economy', in W.A. Joseph (ed.), *Politics in China: An Introduction*, Oxford: Oxford University Press, pp. 192–221.

10 A legal approach for trade issues and a diplomatic approach for non-trade and sustainability issues? From the EUSFTA via the Singapore opinion of the court of justice of the EU to the JEFTA

Herman H. Voogsgeerd

International trade policy in general and free trade agreements (FTAs) more specifically are under increasing pressure in Western countries. Critical notes on free trade used during the current U.S. presidency and by some political parties in Europe are proof of this pressure. Many complain about the lack of democracy during the conclusion of trade agreements (Holmes 2006, p. 815; Ranald 2015, pp. 241–260). In terms of the two-level game approach, referred to in the conceptual framework presented by Gaenssmantel and Wu in Chapter 1 of this book, the win-sets of free trade seem to have shrunk somewhat, due to the perception by some domestic constituencies that they suffer because of free trade. Because of these pressures, the European Commission adapted its trade policy (European Commission 2015) and now includes issues such as human rights, labour and the environment in FTAs under the heading of "sustainability." The language used in these sustainability chapters is relatively vague and of a more promotional nature than the chapters on trade barriers (TBs) and traditional non-trade barriers (NTBs). The enforcement is also of a different nature. Civil society actors are involved in the treatment of these issues, while TBs and traditional NTBs are dealt with in a more legal approach through dispute settlement or tribunals. The first of such new-style agreements has been between the European Union (EU) and the Republic of Korea in 2011, and this FTA has a Chapter 13 on trade and sustainable development.

Do sustainability issues have more than a symbolic role? Is it only about creating focal points for future diplomatic consultations or is there really a legal approach possible for these issues as well? The negotiations between the EU and Japan towards the Japan–EU Free Trade Agreement (JEFTA), better known in Japan as Japan–European Union Economic Partnership Agreement (JEEPA), concluded in December 2017, will form the central case study of this chapter. In comparison with the earlier deal with Singapore, the EU–Singapore Free Trade Agreement (EUSFTA), considerable changes have been made in the JEFTA sustainability chapter. Both the EU and Japan are supporters of the multilateral trade system of the World Trade Organization

(WTO). Both also want to pay attention to certain regulatory issues on top of their obligations under the WTO; they want to build a normative partnership or a "civilian power relationship" (Bacon et al. 2016). Both parties face constraints at home.

When negotiating FTAs, the EU has the choice between an approach exclusively centred on the common commercial policy (CCP), where the EU is exclusively competent, and a broader one leading to so-called "mixed agreements," where both the EU and the member states are parties to the treaty. In the second case, the agreement will also have to pass the hurdle which require ratification by member states or even regional parliaments such as the Walloon parliament during the final stage of the Comprehensive Economic and Trade Agreement (CETA), the agreement between Canada and the EU. I will start with this "vertical" relationship between the EU and the member states and study competency issues concerning the CCP and sustainability issues with a particular focus on the Opinion of the Court of Justice of the EU (CJEU) on the EUSFTA. Afterwards, the "horizontal" relationship between the EU and Japan and their position concerning sustainability issues under the shadow of the WTO rules will be treated. Finally, labour-related issues during JEFTA negotiations will be studied in detail.

The scope of the EU's CCP after the treaty of Lisbon and competency issues between the EU and the member-states

The CCP after Lisbon (2009)

The EU, and not the member states, is competent concerning the CCP. Member states' diplomats do have large influence, though, in the special committee of national representatives, mentioned in Art. 207, 3 of the Treaty on the Functioning of the European Union (TFEU), paragraph 3 committee. The new legal situation after the Treaty of Lisbon (2009) has led to a more robust external trade policy of the EU. But is there, indeed, an increasing opportunity to protect Europe's internal values "beyond the single market"? (Eeckhout 2009). Legal issues concerning competencies are of the highest importance in the EU, as EU competences are based on the principle of conferral. The EU legal order is an autonomous one in which institutions have prerogatives that may be protected by the CJEU. General provisions with respect to all external action of the EU have been introduced in Art. 21 of the Treaty on European Union (TEU), creating a "mission statement" for EU external action. Exporting important values such as democracy, the rule of law, protection of human rights, promotion of international law and economic liberalism is now a major goal of the EU. That this has a consequence for the CCP becomes clear in Art. 205 TFEU, which refers to Art. 21 TEU. The EU is now able to embed its trade policy in a broader, "global" approach. On the other hand, these general objectives such as human rights and the rule of law still have to be qualified as "transversal objectives," general objectives that influence a number of individual policies.[1] These general objectives are not of a prescriptive but of a promotional character. They are more political in nature than legal obligations concerning TBs and traditional NTBs, and they are essentially characterized by political discretion of the competent bodies.

Another innovation in the Treaty of Lisbon is the strengthening of the role of the European Parliament (EP) in the CCP. The EP is no longer only involved in the ratification of trade agreements (from "assent" to "consent," Art. 218(6) TFEU) but now also in setting the framework for implementing the CCP. Powers of the EP and its International Trade Committee have been increased (Art. 207(2) TFEU). This new legal situation definitely is an improvement from the point of view of democratic legitimacy at the EU level. On the other hand, suspension of the application of an international agreement is possible under Art. 218(9) of the TFEU by the Council after a proposal from the Commission or the High Representative of the Union for Foreign Affairs and Security Policy. The European Parliament is not even mentioned in this provision. Such a suspension is deemed to be a "highly political act" (Kaddous and Piçarra 2018, pp. 89–90). This points again to transparency as a major issue, as critical voices on trade policy increasingly request more information on goals, achievements and compromises in trade negotiations.

The European Commission has two ways for dealing with this issue. First, it can separate the issues where the EU is exclusively competent from those where the EU and the member states are both competent. This approach has the advantage of clarity, also for the general public. The problem is that this does not address the widespread concerns about commercial liberalization and related fears, thus leading to agreements that lack a perception of legitimacy. Second, the European Commission may continue with its approach of having large, integrated FTAs as mixed agreements, which require ratification by member states or even regional provincial parliaments. In this situation it may be best to get these parliaments involved earlier on in the negotiating process. This may frustrate transparency, as many actors will be involved. As a reaction to the cumbersome CETA negotiations, the former Australian Minister for Trade, Steven Ciobo, submitted that Australia may prefer to have a more limited trade agreement in the future with the EU, focused especially on the trade in services. In that situation the member states of the EU would not need to ratify that agreement (Heck 2016, p. 6). This choice is therefore put under some constraints. Splitting FTAs in EU-exclusive and other issues may seem attractive for the sake of transparency. It might, however, not please some of the member states that insist on having an investment disputes system in the FTA. Investment disputes and the investor state dispute settlement are issues where the EU is not exclusively competent. Disagreements between the member states on having such a system might therefore spill over to the question of the acceptability of the FTA as a whole.

Whether or not member states have to ratify an agreement between the EU and a third state relates to the question of the proper legal base. The CJEU gave an interesting decision in 2013 on the scope of the CCP after Lisbon in *Daiichi Sankyo*, concerning trade-related intellectual property measures.[2] Going against the opinion of its Advocate-General, the CJEU reversed its earlier case law on the CCP in which the member states remained principally competent in issues concerning "trade-related" intellectual property issues. These issues were, however, explicitly included in the scope of the CCP in Art. 207(1) of the TFEU after Lisbon. The Court made two important distinctions. First, there was the one between the EU's internal market and the CCP. Before Lisbon, the Court was of the view that the CCP was introduced in the Treaty to buttress and facilitate the good operation of the internal market.[3] After Lisbon, the two will be treated separately. Second, there was the one between the exclusive competence of the EU and a "mixed" competence between the EU and its member states. If an issue is within the scope of the CCP, the EU is exclusively competent. The CJEU gives a broad definition in order to determine the scope of the CCP: an act concerning a patent is within that scope "if it relates specifically to international trade in that it is essentially intended to promote, facilitate or govern trade and has direct and immediate effects on trade." This new definition is interesting in that it seems to focus on the terms specific and essential a "specifically" and "essentially" criterion. When the relation with trade is minimal, the legal basis of the CCP may be out of reach. Ankersmit submits that a measure of external harmonization with a limited number of third countries of insignificant importance (in terms of trade) might not be possible on the legal base of Art. 207 TFEU (Ankersmit 2014, p. 208). This argument would introduce a *de minimis* test in the area of the CCP and is in my view highly inefficient, as it would lead to a difficult analysis of quantitative effects on trade.

In the earlier years of the European Community there was a struggle between the Council of Ministers (that is, the member states), who supported a "subjective" approach focused on the content and the aim of the measure in order to determine whether it is under the scope of the CCP, and the European Commission supporting an "objective," instrumental approach considering whether the measure "in fact" regulates trade relations in spite of the aim. The CJEU now combines both approaches. The scope rule in *Daiichi Sankyo* pays attention to the content, the aim and the effects of the measure, but it relates all three clearly to the topic of international trade. A concrete link with international trade will have to be provided.

More specifically, related to the subject matter in *Daiichi Sankyo*, the "trade-relatedness" in the decision concerned the trade-related intellectual property rights (TRIPs) agreement in general and the issue of patentability in Art. 27 thereof in particular. The Court focuses on the fact that the TRIPs agreement was concluded within the framework of the WTO and therefore in the context of international trade. These instruments are meant to standardize rules at the world level and to facilitate international trade. In *Commission v. Council*, both institutions disagreed on the correct legal base of a directive on the legal protection of services and the suppression of illicit activities.[4] The Commission pleaded for Art. 207 TFEU and the Court agreed; although the provisions of the directive were almost similar to an internal market directive, the directive on the legal protection of services was specifically meant to extend legal protection beyond the borders of the EU to other non-member countries in Europe in order to promote supply and therefore trade in these services. Moreover, a ban on the export of illicit services to the EU, with which the EU's global interests can be defended, is in its very nature within the scope of the CCP.

This development may lead to an inclination on the part of the EU institutions to bring as many issues as possible under the CCP in order to be exclusively competent and thereby circumvent ratification by all the individual member states. Sharpston and De Baere warn with reason against these inclinations (Sharpston and de Baere 2011, p. 149); one should not assimilate the whole field of external economic relations to the CCP, as this would be against the principle of conferral. This principle is also responsible for the hybrid approach by the CJEU in matters of CCP, focusing both on the content of the instrument and on aims pursued. That the exclusive competence is important also becomes clear from national constitutional courts. The German constitutional court, for example, decided in a summary proceeding that a provisional application of CETA between the EU and Canada by way of a Council decision is only possible when it concerns areas where the EU is exclusively competent.[5] Where there are mixed competencies between the EU and its member states, the principle of democracy needs to be safeguarded through a vote by national parliaments. The German court iterates that the EU is not competent in issues such as protection of investments, including investment court systems; portfolio investments; international sea traffic; mutual recognition of professional qualifications and protection of labour. With respect to these topics, CETA can therefore not be provisionally applied. The European Commission now chooses for a separate treaty on investment protection, apart from the FTA. An example is the Investment protection agreement between the EU and Singapore of February 2019, recently approved by the European Parliament. Negotiations with Japan concerning an investment protection agreement are not finished yet.

The Singapore opinion of the CJEU of May 2017

In order to clarify competency issues, the European Commission asked for a binding opinion from the CJEU under Art. 218(11) TFEU on EUSFTA, concluded in October 2014. Now that the Art. 207 includes "the progressive abolition of restrictions on international trade and on foreign direct investment," the Commission wanted to know whether the EU has exclusive competence to conclude FTAs concerning foreign direct investment (FDI) or only a shared one with the member states.

Sustainability issues were also raised. According to the criteria in *Daiichi Sankyo*, there has to be a "specific" connection between the non-trade issue and trade for the former to fall under the CCP. In the EUSFTA opinion proceedings, the Commission argued that there is a specific connection in that the purpose of the sustainability chapter is to make sure that conditions for trade are not hampered by different levels of protection of labour and the environment. By contrast, the Advocate-General Sharpston was of the opinion that in order to come within the scope of the CCP there is either a need for "a form of trade conditionality" or a need for a commercial policy instrument.[6] Trade conditionality implies the use of trade sanctions when the other party does not comply with environmental or labour standards in the FTA. The criterion of a typical commercial policy instrument is understandable; a form of conditionality is more difficult to assess *ex ante*, e.g. before a sanction is imposed.

The opinion of the CJEU from May 16, 2017, of binding character notwithstanding the word "opinion," is more in line with the Commission's approach.[7] Again, it reiterates the seminal change in character of the CCP pre- and post-Lisbon, as it did earlier in *Daiichi Sankyo*. It refers to Art. 3(5) TFEU in which the obligation to contribute to not only free but also fair trade is contained. "New aspects of contemporary international trade" could be read as simply including environmental and social concerns. Then, the CJEU studies the preamble and the text of Chapter 12 of the EUSFTA in order to satisfy the criteria given in *Daiichi Sankyo*. The CJEU seems to attach some importance to Art. 12.16 of the EUSFTA in which it is stated that the dispute settlement procedure of the agreement is *not* applicable to Chapter 12. This leads the Court to the conclusion that Chapter 12 neither concerns the powers of the member states, nor the scope of the other international agreements, such as the conventions of the International Labour Organization (ILO), to which the CJEU refers (paragraph 155). On the other hand, the chapter gives a "specific" link with trade between the EU and Singapore, and this fulfils (part of) the definition given in *Daiichi Sankyo*. This link is also specific because one of the parties to the EUSFTA may terminate or suspend the liberalization of trade between the partners according to the UN Convention of the Law of Treaties.

The needed direct and immediate effects on trade are derived from the commitment of the EU and Singapore in Art. 12.1(3) to not encourage trade by reducing levels of social and environmental protection, from the reduction of the risk of major disparities between the production costs in the EU and Singapore, and finally from the undertaking by the parties to implement or encourage verification schemes concerning illegally harvested timber or illegal fishing. After this step-by-step application of the *Daiichi Sankyo* definition to Chapter 12, the Court clearly makes a distinction between the CCP including requirements of sustainable development on the one hand, and the regulation of social and environmental protection in Singapore and in the member states of the EU. Art. 207(6) of the TFEU states that the exercise of the CCP cannot alter the division of competences between the Union and the member states. Art. 12.1(4) of the EUSFTA clearly states that the agreement between the EU and Singapore is not intended to harmonize the labour or environmental standards of the parties. Therefore, division of competences is not changed and all of the sustainability provisions fall under CCP, which places the agreement thus under exclusive competence of the EU. While the scope of trade-related issues has been broadened after Lisbon, FDI and the investment court system still belong to the competences of the member states. In principle, this should imply that mega-treaties such as CETA and the Japan–EU FTA still qualify as mixed agreements.

The CJEU with this opinion takes a very practical view and takes the seminal change since Lisbon to its logical conclusion. The CCP is different in nature to the internal market and social and environmental policies of the member states. Sustainability issues are just "new issues of contemporary international trade" (paragraph 141). The opinion is very relevant for the main questions this chapter is proposing to answer, especially concerning the distinction between a legal and a diplomatic approach. The CJEU treats problems in the implementation or enforcement of the sustainability chapter as a public international law problem between the two parties and not as an EU law issue. The remark in paragraph 156 is most striking: the bad application or enforcement of the chapter by the other party may lead to an "artificial or unjustified restriction of trade." This consists of legal language derived from the internal market law of the TFEU, but also from the provisions of the General Agreement on Tariffs and Trade (GATT), and this language may blur the distinction between a diplomatic and a more legal manner to address conflicts. Nevertheless, it is for the competent authorities of the EU (and the other party to the treaty) to make a decision in this respect and the diplomatic manner in my view still prevails.

Further legalization of sustainability issues is therefore possible, but it is doubtful whether political discretion is limited by the language used by the CJEU.[8] Complaints about an artificial or unjustified restriction of trade in relation with labour and the environment regularly arise as a last resort. A trade deal is not easily suspended. And restrictions of this nature must be large and serious before a real conflict between the trading parties will occur. And even in such a serious stage diplomatic options will be tried first. After commenting on the text of the JEFTA in section 4, I will come back to this important issue.

Implications of the Singapore opinion for the diplomacy versus law debate

Trade has high political relevance these days, not only for the interplay between EU institutions and member states, but more broadly in relation to the popular protests against FTAs. This political resistance has had a strong influence on EU decision makers, meaning that parameters of the logic of constraint have been shifting lately. Although trade Commissioner Malmström argued in July 2016, that, from a purely legal point of view, the EU could be seen as exclusively competent concerning CETA (European Commission 2016a), for political reasons and resistance from the member states the Commission proposed to treat CETA as mixed agreement.

If in the future the EU chooses from the outset pure CCP agreements over mixed ones, the CJEU rulings since Lisbon as discussed above seem to strengthen the choice available for the Commission, in that trade is not necessarily limited to TBs and NTBs, but it can choose to legalize non-trade issues in FTAs, as long as the matter is specifically related to trade. There is no automatic legalization as the language of the CJEU in the Singapore opinion might suggest, but it is subject to political discretion. Suspending the operation of an FTA under Art. 208(9) TFEU is a "highly political act" where the European Parliament is not even directly involved.

Negotiations on sustainability issues between Japan and the EU in the "Shadow of WTO obligations"[9]

Both the EU and Japan are now supporters of the WTO as well as the trend to bilateral and regional FTAs. This becomes clear from the texts of the EU–Japan summits, held annually since 1991 (Morii 2015, p. 422). Negotiations between Japan and the EU for an FTA officially started in March 2013. While Japan preferred to conclude an FTA only (Nakanishi 2014, p. 11), the EU wanted to embed this agreement in a strategic partnership agreement (SPA). Although the focus in the negotiations is clearly on trade issues such as traditional NTBs and public procurement, the EU proposed from the beginning to focus on sustainability issues. Because Japan is a developed country and a member of the OECD, not much friction in this respect was to be expected. In general, Japan is already fully supporting the EU in topics such as human rights, democracy and the rule of law (Hosoya 2012, p. 332). However, more specific regulatory issues are potentially contentious. Under the old EU–Japan Regulatory Reform Dialogue (RRD) of 1994, the Japanese side raised issues against the EU such as nationality requirements for tour and tourist guides in southern EU member states and rules on excessive sick leave in eastern EU member states, as well as complaints about extensive consumer protection rules, taxation, maritime and environmental policy of the EU (Rothacher 2013, pp. 172–173). JEFTA was concluded in December 2017. The SPA between Japan and the EU, with references to some of the fundamental values also mentioned in art. 21 TEU, was concluded in 2018. Talks about regulatory cooperation and negotiations on investment and an investment court system are ongoing (Hilpert 2017, p. 1).

Both the EU and Japan are members of the WTO and a potential free trade agreement may not violate the rules of this international organization. The primary purpose of this organization is trade. There is no consensus within the WTO on the role of non-trade issues such as labour and the environment. Developing countries have a negative opinion on the inclusion of these concerns in the jurisdiction of the Dispute Settlement Body (DSB) of the WTO (Arun 2016). These countries fear restrictions to trade from the developed countries. Still, some non-trade issues are dealt with in the WTO and others are not. Examples of the former are environmental protection and cultural issues (Art. XX(g) and (f) GATT) and also food security within the framework of agriculture.[10] For Japan, the domestic agricultural sector is of the utmost importance and food security is therefore a topic defended by Japan during negotiations with the EU.

Non-trade relations sit uneasily with the WTO rules. In 2003, Simpson and Schoenbaum made a proposal to incorporate non-trade concerns within the WTO. In order to forego criticism of protectionism, non-trade concerns (NTCs) should become better defined and be limited to a positive externality "that contributes to sustainable development" (Simpson and Schoenbaum 2003, p. 10). NTCs should also be quantified, and countries that want to subsidize their agriculture because of an NTC concern should show a causal link between the NTC and a domestic support program (Simpson and Schoenbaum 2003, p. 11). Since 2003 not much progress has been made concerning these issues, as WTO member states still disagree and the Doha Round is stalled. The approach of Simpson and Schoenbaum is interesting in that it explicitly focusses on the incorporation of non-trade concerns within a subfield of the WTO.

The EU and Japan are also users of the WTO dispute settlement procedure. While the EU and the United States have used the procedure extensively, Japan in the beginning lacked experience in handling this dispute settlement procedure. Some "institutional learning" from the side of the Japanese administration (especially by the Ministry of Economy, Trade and Industry, METI, and its predecessor, the Ministry of International Trade and Industry, MITI) has taken place (Yoshimatsu 2009, p. 296). In the use of the improved dispute settlement procedure under the WTO, the Japanese position has been named "aggressive legalism" (Pekkanen 2001), after the successful *Kodak v. Fuji* case between Japan and the United States.[11] Japan has hardly ever used this procedure against developing countries. The United States was a prime target. Japan followed closely the EU in its trade disputes with the United States, and the complaints of Japan against the United States were carefully selected cases "under a powerful cover of the EC [European Community]" (Araki 2006, p. 794). Moreover, Araki argues, Japan only started selective, highly targeted and winnable cases.

There has been only one complaint by Japan against the EU, namely *European Communities and its Member States – Tariff Treatment of Certain Information Technology Products* (DS376) from 2011. This is a very specific case where Japan protested against the treatment by the European Communities of information products under the Information Technology Agreement (ITA). It was joined by the United States and Taiwan ("Chinese Taipei") and the panel decided that the EU had to repeal two of its regulations. On the other hand, eight complaints have been started by Japan against the United States with a clear emphasis on anti-dumping duties levied by the United States. The EU has started six complaints against Japan under the WTO dispute settlement system. One of these, *Taxes on Alcoholic Beverages* (DS8), lasted about three years and was concluded only in 1997 with the publication of the report of the Appellate Body. After 1998 there have been no new complaints by the EU on Japan. That Japan will use the WTO procedure against the EU in non-trade concerns is highly unlikely.

Japan is, however, not always on the same side as the EU. In the *European Communities – Measures Prohibiting the Importation and Marketing of Seal Products* case (DS400 and 401), Japan acted as a third party. Canada and Norway complained that EC Regulation No. 1007/2009 banned the importation and sale of all seal products on the European market. The dispute settlement panel considered that the EU regulation could not be justified by the exception under Art. XX(b) because the EU did not clearly show that the ban was imposed due to the protection of animal life or health. The regime also did not meet the test of the "chapeau" of Art. XX, as there is arbitrary and unjustified discrimination between seal products from Canada and Norway on the one hand, and the same products from the Inuit in Greenland on the other hand, who profited from an exception in the regulation. The panel qualified the EU seal regime as a technical regulation and applied the Technical Barriers to Trade (TBT) Agreement. The EU did not violate Art. 2(2) of this agreement, as the regime is related to the objective of EU public moral concerns on seal welfare. Canada and Norway appealed this decision.

The Appellate Body (AB), by contrast, considered that the EU regulation did not qualify as a technical regulation because there is no prescription or imposition of any "characteristics" of seal products. The regulation only puts conditions on market access, related to the type and purpose of seal hunt. It found that the EU regulation was necessary to protect public morals within Art. XX(a). The rules, however, failed to satisfy the test of the "chapeau." In order to pass the test of Art. XX, the measures must not be applied in such a way that it leads to arbitrary or unjustifiable discrimination or leads to a disguised restriction on international trade. The EU regulation made exceptions for the prohibition for seal products from indigenous peoples from Greenland, the Inuit, and for products from hunts for reasons of marine resource management.

It is these exceptions that made that the ban was judged to be against the obligations of the WTO. If you give a special treatment to the Inuit of Greenland, this special treatment cannot be refused to inhabitants of small communities in coastal areas of Canada and Norway. The "chapeau" means, in the words of the AB, that an exception is invoked without abuse or misuse. The EU did not show that the situation in Greenland is different from the one of indigenous populations in Canada and Norway. The relation between the public morals exception in Art. XX GATT and the protection of the Inuit was also not sufficiently established by the EU. It was still possible for commercial hunts to enter the EU market under the exception regarding the protection of the indigenous peoples of Greenland, the Inuit. The applicable administrative provisions in the regulation, in order to benefit from the exception, were burdensome. In the application of the EU measure, therefore, there was an additional discrimination.

In general it is hard to pass this test of the "chapeau" (Desmedt 2001, pp. 473–475). This implies that trade concerns are more easily processed through the dispute settlement route, than non-trade, or more specifically sustainability issues. If a national measure is justified by a legitimate reason of public policy, then it still will not be allowed if there is "arbitrary discrimination" or a "disguised restriction." The positive point of the *Seal products* case is that public morals is a valid ground to limit importations. The negative point is that this additional guarantee in the chapeau in favour of nondiscriminatory international trade has the effect of a high hurdle concerning the effectuation of the non-trade concern. Note, however, that the terminology in the chapeau is the same as the one used in paragraph 156 of the EUFSTA opinion of the Court of Justice of the EU: arbitrary and unjustified discrimination. While the Court contemplates the idea that violation of environmental or labour issues could lead to such a discrimination, the DSB and the AB focus on the discriminatory treatment of one trade partner *vis-à-vis* another.

According to Boisson de Chazournes, non-trade issues should be analyzed by the DSB on their protection of these issues, not on their effects on trade (Boisson de Chazournes 2016, p. 280). This implies that the DSB should not only look at the effects on trade, but also on the effects on the non-trade issues themselves, and compare both before making a decision. For the moment, however, the realization of many non-trade concerns is contrary to the WTO rules, if there is arbitrary discrimination involved. Any form of conditionality and trade sanctions for not realizing non-trade concerns, targeted against trade partners that are also members of the WTO, may therefore be at variance with WTO rules. This is also an argument to treat some NTCs in a political manner in FTAs and not in a legal manner. Political consultations are not per se against the spirit of the WTO system. On the other hand, unilateral sanctions of one WTO member against the other could violate the WTO rules. This is an additional reason to treat these issues first and for all in a diplomatic manner.

Case study: EU–Japan negotiations, JEFTA and labour-related sustainability issues

Already in their 2000 summit the EU and Japan submitted that the Doha Round should strive both for trade policy and "sustainable development" (Wright 2013, p. 162). Peace, stability and prosperity are dealt with in a general sense, i.e. with no concrete commitments or proposals for legally binding rules (European Commission 2015). In the texts of the yearly Japan–EU Summits and in the speeches of former and current External Trade Commissioners Karel De Gucht and Cecilia Malmström at, respectively, the EU–Japan Business Summit in Tokyo, March 25, 2013, and the Keidanren in Tokyo, May 29, 2015, there is, however, a clear focus on the main topics: non-tariff barriers, public procurement and "deep" regulatory cooperation. Non-trade concerns are not mentioned in these texts and speeches. In the meeting with Keidanren in May 2015, Malmström defined regulatory cooperation as follows: "trying to remove unnecessary technical differences between our systems, on the basis of international standards, in order to boost growth, and to save time, money and energy" (Keidanren 2015). The most interesting words in this definition are "international standards" and "unnecessary." Who will decide when something is unnecessary? International standards are also often made on the basis of input by business actors. Increased involvement of other civil society actors is important in this respect. This increased involvement has to imply a qualitative step beyond the participation of the small circle of diplomats and bureaucrats that underpinned the annual summits held since 1991.

There is attention for sustainability issues in the JEFTA in a chapter called "Trade and Sustainable Development" (Chapter 16). The language on the commitments in this field is rather vague in comparison with the language in the chapters concerning trade issues. It mentions that the parties "strive" to ensure that their laws provide high levels of labour (and environmental) protection and to continue to improve these levels of protection (Art. 16.2(1)). Encouragement of trade or FDI will not be done by lowering these levels of protection (Art. 16.2(2)). Effective enforcement is also mentioned and the parties will "not use their laws as a means of arbitrary or unjustifiable discrimination against the other Party" (Art. 16.2(3)). The main mechanism concerning these topics is, however, "exchange of views and information" (Art. 16.3(1); Art. 16.3(3); Art. 16.5(e)) and "cooperation" (Art. 16.12). It is clearly stated that there is no intention to harmonize labour or environmental standards of the parties. Violation of the eight fundamental ILO conventions may not be done for reasons of comparative advantage, but these conventions may also not be used for protectionist purposes (Art. 16.3(6)).

There are provisions concerning the involvement of civil society organizations, also including trade unions. Cooperation with the ILO as an institution is a new element in JEFTA (see Art. 16.17(4)). The last provision concerns the panel of experts parties may refer a dispute to. This panel "should seek information and advice from relevant international organizations." This language looks promising, but its legal value remains to be seen (Vogt 2015, pp. 857–858).[12] It would really be a qualitative step forward if the reports of the ILO supervisory committees would be used in the evaluation of EU and Japanese labour-related policies. However, there is already an asymmetry here: Japan is a member state, while the ILO reports do not concern the EU as an international organization but only the member states of the ILO, including those of the EU.

Is it possible that the substance of this chapter will be tested in a court-like body or an EU court? Is it about politics or law, or is the sustainability chapter deliberately blurring the line between a legal and a diplomatic road to deal with disputes between the EU and Japan in that political discretion remains pivotal? From the text of the JEFTA it becomes clear that sustainable development is dealt with in a separate specialized committee, different from the committees that oversee the TBs and traditional NTBs. Dispute settlers in the trade chapters need "specialized knowledge or experience of law and international trade." By contrast, only if the specialized committee on sustainable development is not able to reach a mutually satisfactory outcome, one of the parties may ask for the matter to be dealt with in a panel of experts. This panel "shall interpret the relevant articles of this chapter in accordance with customary rules of interpretation of public international law." This is a huge step forward in relation to the EUSFTA chapter on sustainability. Law is explicitly mentioned here, but it is public international law and not EU trade law, giving more political discretion to the parties. The legal value of this remains to be seen. The commitments are therefore not only meant to have some kind of indirect legally binding character but most probably will become focal points for subsequent diplomatic consultations.

Although Japan is a developed country like South Korea and Singapore, we might find some specific problems in the sphere of labour-related sustainability issues. The first problem is related to the fact that only six out of eight ILO fundamental conventions have been ratified by Japan. Japan has not yet ratified convention no. 111 on non-discrimination in employment and convention no. 105 on the abolition of forced labour. Discrimination on the labour market is a sensitive topic in Japan and treated very differently in comparison with EU law. Non-discrimination practices on the basis of nationality, later on sex, and recently also on handicap are extremely important rules within the EU. In Japan there is less experience with concepts such as indirect discrimination (Hanami et al. 2015, p. 150). The CJEU developed rather radical concepts of indirect and substantive discrimination. In Japan there is also an issue with the important freedom of association convention, no. 87. The issue of the right to strike for public servants such as teachers and firefighters is still not completely solved, notwithstanding regular requests and observations of the ILO's Committee of Experts on the Application of Conventions and Recommendations (CEACR) and the Committee on Freedom of Association (CFA) of the ILO (Voogsgeerd 2015). These kinds of sensitivities may be difficult to solve under the heading of JEFTA, even by the panel of experts, as culturally specific issues are involved.

Another major topic is the lack of experience with civil society in Japan. Also, the experience with trade unions is mixed in Japan. There are strong company-based unions, but these depend often on the employer. The national umbrella of trade unions, JTUC-RENGO, is loud in its demands but hardly influential in the current Liberal Democratic Party (LDP) administration of Prime Minister Abe. It was much more linked to the major opposition party, the Democratic Party of Japan (DPJ), which was in government from 2009 until 2012. These stakeholders will be invited to the extensive discussions in the Committee on Trade and Sustainable Development.

In the *Final Report of the Trade Sustainability Impact Assessment of a Free Trade Agreement between the EU and Japan*, issued before the signature of JEFTA, it was recommended that the EU should ensure greater compliance, implementation and monitoring of ILO conventions by Japan (European Commission 2016c, pp. 211–212). Conventions no. 111 on non-discrimination in employment and occupation and no. 105 on specific issues concerning forced labour were specifically mentioned, as these two fundamental ILO Conventions have still not been ratified by Japan. Gender discrimination, another topic of high concern in Japan, was also extensively discussed in this report.

It is interesting to see that the European umbrella of trade unions and JTUC-Rengo made a statement together on the (future) trade deal between the EU and Japan. They requested the immediate ratification by Japan of ILO conventions no. 111 and no. 105. ILO issues such as tripartism and the role of the ILO supervisory bodies in the monitoring of a potential trade agreement feature high in the statement. There was a strong focus on monitoring and compliance of international labour standards. The social partners also wanted to be regularly involved in the trade talks. In the statement, they preferred mainstreaming of labour protection throughout the whole FTA and labour provisions not to be limited to the trade and sustainability chapter.[13] Socially sustainable public procurement and a ban on the privatization of public services were also asked for.

In its own updates on its website, JTUC-Rengo not only supported the inclusion of labour issues in the agreement but even showed open opposition to any NTB agreements in the FTA that would risk to affect in a negative way internal Japanese regulations, when these are "rational and necessary for the Japanese society."[14] This specifically refers to standards concerning vehicle safety, food safety, processed foods, medical equipment and pharmaceuticals. At the same time, JTUC-Rengo expressed the hope that the FTA would bring both employment creation and greater employment security. Quality of life for the working people in a "safe and reliable society" is one of the most important goals for the trade union umbrella organization, along with the issue of compliance with labour standards.

Labour issues are particularly sensitive. The EU is unlikely to relinquish on these issues, as they are an important part of the new EU trade agenda. Within Japan labour is relatively weak; it often needs the support of other labour organizations in the world and other trade unions to strengthen its position *vis-à-vis* the government. Still, the umbrella organization positioned itself very clearly against any concessions on regulations that might imply disadvantages for Japanese workers. In both the EU and Japan, free trade is critically watched by the general public, and safeguarding existing jobs and creating new jobs are extremely important in this context.

Labour-related sustainability issues have become more visible in the public debate. This means that free trade agreements will have to be handled in a more transparent manner. Even between two advanced democratic countries as the EU and Japan, there is no complete agreement on culture, norms and values, and this translates, for example, into diverging views on labour issues and on some of the ILO core conventions. Consensus will not always be easy to find under the JEFTA. If there is more normative agreement among the civil society organizations and movements on both sides, then more civil society involvement in the framework of the FTA negotiations might help in this respect. Because of the sensitivities it is likely that a legal approach in these labour issues will not be chosen, although there is a possibility to invoke a panel of experts using public international law. Involvement of the ILO supervisory committees is also possible, but this route is also often of a promotional and not a conditional character. After the conclusion of JEFTA a joint statement by ETUC and JTUC-Rengo on July 9, 2018, critically assessed the lack of "effective labour enforcement provisions" in the FTA.[15] There is also concern for rising protectionism, globally.

Conclusion

Free trade is recently under pressure, at least in the West. The (perceived) winsets are changing. There are choices to be made with regard to FTAs. First, a choice concerning the legal basis: exclusive EU competence on the basis of the CCP or a mixed competence between the EU and all its member states. The European Commission chose to treat CETA as a mixed agreement; involvement of the member states of the EU might be the better option for the sake of legitimacy. Some form of (re)politicization of trade policy is useful in the context of growing political/civil society constraints on the public authorities involved in trade negotiations. So in a complex polity as the EU, the choice that seems easy given the constraints may not be the best choice in the medium to long term. Avoiding the constraints does not address the concerns of the civil society groups behind them. But some of these groups have now a place in the architecture of the JEFTA. This could alleviate the logic of constraints a little.

Second, there is the role of labour-related sustainability issues in an FTA. Inclusion of these issues in the CCP seems to be possible after the opinion of the CJEU in the EUSFTA case of 2017. Some aspects of the opinion have found their way in the text of JEFTA, e.g. that domestic labour laws should not be used "as a means of arbitrary or unjustifiable discrimination" (Art. 16.2(3)) and that a panel of experts in case of a dispute submitted by one of the parties is able to contact the ILO in Geneva and is obliged to interpret the chapter "in accordance with custom-ary rules of interpretation of public international law, including those codified in the Vienna Convention on the Law of Treaties" (Art. 16.18(2,3)). It remains to be seen whether this increased legal character of the language and the reference to international customary law will lead to a form of trade conditionality in that rights under the JEFTA may become suspended. First, there will be discussions among diplomats and civil society actors in case of conflicts. Normative agree-ment among the civil society actors between the EU and Japan, in particular trade unions, may start processes of arguing that could lead to agreement on at least some of the contested labour-related issues. Put differently, if normative agree-ment cannot be brought about in a single round of negotiations, then joint cam-paigns by civil society groups might create arguments that are difficult to refute, especially if they are supported by international bodies like the ILO. In any case, a lot of arguing and institutional learning are needed in the near future. Some con-vergence on these issues is possible between the EU and Japan (see also Hilpert 2017, p. 3). That is why a diplomatic approach is still to be expected in the area of labour-related sustainability issues and not a legal approach, although the text of JEFTA is making this possible.

Notes

1 Case C-268/94 *Portugal v. Council*, [1996] ECLI:EU:C:1996:207, point 34. See for an interesting contribution on these objectives (Neframi, 2014, p. 94).
2 Case C-414/11, *Daiichi Sankyo Co. Ltd, Sanofi-Aventis Deutschland GmbH v. DEMO* [2013] ECLI:EU:C:2013:520.
3 "Opinion of the Court of 11 November 1975 given pursuant to Article 228 of the EEC Treaty. Avis 1/75," [1975] ECLI:EU:C:1975:145.
4 Case C-137/12, *Commission v. Council* [2013] ECLI:EU:C:2013:675.
5 BVerfG, Judgement of the Second Senate of 13 October 2016 – 2BvR 1368/16. http://www.bverfg.de/e/rs20161013_2bvr136816.en.html.
6 "Opinion Advocate-General," [2016] ECLI:EU:C:2016:992, point 491.
7 Opinion CJEU, A-2/15, 16 May 2017, [2017] ECLI:EU:C:2017:376.
8 Ankersmit defends this view in his blog entry *Opinion 2/15: Adding some spice to the trade & environment debate*, available at https://europeanlawblog.eu/2017/06/15.
9 The idea of bargaining under the "shadow" of obligations is borrowed from Shaffer (2006).

10 Art. 20 of the Uruguay Round Agreement explicitly states that non-trade concerns should be taken into account during the negotiations on agriculture.
11 Panel Report on *Japan – Measures affecting Consumer Photographic Film and Paper*, WT/DS44/R of 22 April 1998.
12 Vogt is critical on the GSP+ of the EU in that decisions made in this framework do not take into account the reports of the ILO supervisory bodies. In the JEFTA there is now at least the possibility for the panel of experts to take into account the views of the ILO committees concerning the sustainability.
13 "ETUC-Rengo Joint Statement on EU-Japan Free Trade Agreement negotiation," available at https://www.etuc.org/sites/default/files/press-release/files/etuc_rengo_joint_statement_as_of_20151217en.pdf.
14 "RENGO calls for job creation and better working conditions through Japan-EU EPA: RENGO & ETUC Joint Action," available at http://www.jtuc-rengo.org/updates/index.cgi?mode=view&no=362&dir=2015/05.
15 "ETUC - JTUC-RENGO Joint Statement on EU-Japan EPA negotiations," available at http://www.jtuc-rengo.org/updates/index.cgi?mode=view&no=384&dir=2018/07; see also "Statement on the Signing of the Japan-EU Economic Partnership Agreement (EPA)," available at http://www.jtuc-rengo.org/updates/index.cgi?mode=view&no=385&dir=2018/07.

References

Ankersmit, L. (2014) 'The scope of the common commercial policy after Lisbon: The Daiichi Sankyo and Conditional Access Services Grand Chamber Judgments', *Legal Issues of Economic Integration*, 41(2), pp. 193–209.

Araki, I. (2006) 'The evolution of Japan's aggressive legalism', *World Economy*, 29(6), pp. 783–803.

Arun, S. (2016) 'Non-trade issues at WTO, lack of legal experts worry India', *The Hindu*, available at https://www.thehindu.com/business/Economy/nontrade-issues-at-wto-lack-of-legal-experts-worry-india/article8548230.ece.

Bacon, P., Mayer, H. and Nakamura H. (eds.) (2016) *The European Union and Japan. A New Chapter in Civilian Power Cooperation?* Routledge.

Boisson de Chazournes, L. (2016) 'WTO and non-trade and non-trade issues: Inside/outside WTO', *Journal of International Economic Law*, 19(2), pp. 379–381.

Council of the European Union. (2015) 'Joint Press Statement: 23rd Japan-EU Summit, Tokyo, 29 May 2015', available at https://www.consilium.europa.eu/media/24517/joint-press-statement-eu-japan.pdf.

Desmedt, A. (2001) 'Proportionality in WTO Law', *Journal of International Economic Law*, 4(3), pp. 441–480.

Eeckhout, P. (2009) 'A normative basis for EU external relations? Protecting internal values beyond the Single Market', in K. Markus, van de G. Johan and N. Ulla (eds.), *The Changing Legal Framework for Services of General Interest in Europe: Between Competition and Solidarity*, Nijmegen: T.M.C. Asser press, pp. 219–232.

European Commission. (2015) *Trade for All: Towards a More Responsible Trade and Investment Policy*, European Publications Office, available at http://trade.ec.europa.eu/doclib/docs/2015/october/tradoc_153846.pdf.

European Commission. (2016a) 'European Commission proposes signature and conclusion of EU-Canada trade deal', available at http://europa.eu/rapid/press-release_IP-16-2371_en.htm.

European Commission. (2016b) *Final Report of the Trade Sustainability Impact Assessment of a Free Trade Agreement between the EU and Japan*, European Publications Office, available at www.trade.ec.europa.eu/doclib/html/154522.htm.

European Commission. (2016c) *Trade Sustainability Impact Assessment of the Free Trade Agreement between the European Union and Japan – Final Report*, Luxembourg: Publications Office of the European Union, available at http://trade.ec.europa.eu/doclib/docs/2016/may/tradoc_154522.pdf.

Hanami, T.A., Komya, F. and Yamakawa, R. (2015) *Labour Law in Japan*, 2nd edn., Wolters Kluwer.

Heck, W. (2016) 'We zijn geen bedreiging voor de EU', *NRC Handelsblad*, available at https://www.nrc.nl/nieuws/2016/10/25/wij-zijn-geen-bedreiging-voor-de-eu-4980215-a1528395.

Hilpert, H.G. (2017) 'The Japan-EU economic partnership agreement: Economic potentials and policy perspectives', *SWP Comments*, available at https://www.swp-berlin.org/fileadmin/contents/products/comments/2017C49_hlp.pdf.

Holmes, P. (2006) 'Trade and "domestic" policies: The European mix', *Journal of European Public Policy*, 13(6), pp. 815–831.

Hosoya, Y. (2012) 'The evolution of the EU-Japan relationship: A "normative partnership"?', *Japan Forum*, 24(3), pp. 317–337.

Kaddous, C. and Piçarra N. (2018) "General report," in Cruz, J. L. da, et al., *The External Dimension of the EU policies: Horizontal issues; trade and investment; immigration and asylum.* 2018 FIDE proceedings Vol. 3, pp. 63–153, Edições Almedina, Coimbra.

Keidanren. (2015) 'Renewed call for promoting Japan-EU regulatory cooperation', available at http://www.keidanren.or.jp/en/policy/2015/103.html.

Morii, A. (2015) 'Dialogue without cooperation? Diplomatic implications of EU-Japan summits', *Asia Europe Journal*, 13(4), pp. 413–424.

Nakanishi, Y. (2014) 'Political principles in art. 21 TEU and constitutionalism', *Hitotsubashi Journal of Law and Politics*, 42, pp. 3–21.

Neframi, E. (2014) 'Vertical division of competences and the objectives of the European Union's external action', in M. Cremona and A. Thies (eds.), *The European Court of Justice and External Relations Law. Constitutional Challenges*, Portland: Oxford.

Pekkanen, S.M. (2001) 'Aggressive legalism: The rules of the WTO and Japan's emerging trade strategy', *The World Economy*, 24(5), pp. 707–737.

Ranald, P. (2015) 'The trans-pacific partnership agreement: Reaching behind the border, challenging democracy', *The Economic and Labour Relations Review*, 26(2), pp. 241–260.

Rothacher, A. (2013) '2000–2010: Shaping a common future in the decade of Japan-Europe cooperation: Rhetoric and policies', in J. Keck, D. Vanoverbeke and F. Waldenberger (eds.), *EU-Japan Relations 1970–2012: From Confrontation to Partnership*, Routledge, pp. 170–183.

Shaffer, G. (2006) 'What's new in EU trade dispute settlement? Judicialization, Public-Private Networks and the WTO Legal Order', *Journal of European Public Policy*, 13(6), pp. 832–850.

Sharpston, E. and de Baere, G. (2011) 'The court of justice as a constitutional adjudicator', in A. Arnull, C. Barnard, M. Dougan and E. Spaventa (eds.), *A Constitutional Order of States? Essays in EU Law in Honour of Alan Dashwood*, Hart Publishing, pp. 123–150.

Simpson, J.R. and Schoenbaum, T.J. (2003) 'Non-trade concerns in WTO negotiations: Legal and legitimate reasons for revising the "Box" System?', *International Journal of Agricultural Resources, Governance and Ecology*, 2(3/4), pp. 399–410.

Vogt, J. (2015) 'A little less conversation: The EU and the (Non) application of labor conditionality in the general system of preferences', *The International Journal of Comparative Labor Law and Industrial Relations*, 31(1), pp. 285–304.

Voogsgeerd, H.H. (2015) 'Trade unions, civil society, democracy and authority in Japan', in C.K. Lamont, J. van der Harst and F. Gaenssmantel (eds.), *Non-Western Encounters with Democratization. Imagining Democracy after the Arab Spring*, Routledge, pp. 197–215.

Wright, R. (2013) '1996–2000: Consolidating a mature relationship', in J. Keck, D. Vanoverbeke and F. Waldenberger (eds.), *EU-Japan Relations 1970–2012: From Confrontation to Partnership*, Routledge, pp. 155–169.

Yoshimatsu, H. (2009) 'Japan's policy on steel trade-disputes with the United States: A comparative analysis', *The Pacific Review*, 20(3), pp. 273–300.

11 More than words?
Labour standards in the
future EU–India FTA

*Gerda van Roozendaal**

Since 2007, the European Union (EU) and India have been involved in negotiations over a free trade agreement. That these negotiations are long and difficult is not a surprise, considering the issues and interests at stake, although more than 10 years is unusual even for this kind of complex agreement. One of the challenging issues concerns the inclusion of labour standards provisions in the agreement. This chapter presents an analysis of how the issue of labour standards is tackled in the negotiations, what can be reasonably expected for the status of labour standards in the future agreement, and what this implies in terms of how disputes over trade-related labour issues will probably be handled in the future: through a diplomatic or a legal approach.

With the help of the two concepts explained in Gaenssmantel and Wu's Chapter 1 of this volume—the *logic of choice* and the *logic of constraints*—the likelihood of a prevalence of the diplomatic scenario will be explained. On the one hand, the logic of choice entails an analysis of the costs and benefits of a certain action. At the same time, choice can also be based on the logic of appropriateness, which means that an actor proceeds "[...] according to the institutionalized practices of a collectivity, based on mutual, and often tacit understandings of what is true, reasonable, natural, right, and good" (March and Olsen 2009, p. 2). This helps to understand collective action beyond calculation of the consequences of such action. Bilateral agreements such as free trade agreements (FTAs) are not only a good indicator of a shared sense of appropriateness amongst the members of the international community, but also of a careful calculation of costs and benefits of (not) joining. In addition, the logic of constraints determines whether the legal or diplomatic tool is opted for. In Chapter 1, Gaenssmantel and Wu describe this as the way through which preferences for either the diplomatic or the legal route are limited by "multilevel and multi-actor nature of contemporary governance." These forms of governance may result in all kinds of regulation, amongst which mandatory institutional procedures, for example, with regard to an FTA's obligations and dispute settlement procedures, which will be the focus of this chapter.

* I would like to thank Frank Gaenssmantel and Biswajit Dhar for their valuable comments on earlier drafts of this paper.

In short, understanding the way in which labour standards are integrated in the FTA under negotiation requires this chapter to make an analysis of both the logic of choice as well as of the logic of constraints. For example, if both parties desire the agreement but one or both do not appreciate the labour standards part equally, we cannot expect concrete binding obligations in this area. Instead, in such cases it is much more likely that if action in the area of labour standards is undertaken at all, a low level of legalization will characterize the agreement. Treaty provisions that de facto do not more but establish reference points for future diplomatic consultation seem both more appropriate and more of a rational choice for the two negotiating parties.

Appropriateness under the logic of choice: the development of a "globally" shared set of principles

The inclusion of labour standards in trade agreements has a long and contentious history. The issue has been brought up in different forums since the Second World War. This is no surprise, as the increasing economic interconnectedness of countries has raised questions about the fairness of the basis on which economic exchange takes place, both from a human rights point of view, as well as from the point of view of economic competition.

The question is whether those organizations and agreements promoting free trade should also demand the respect for certain labour standards in the countries involved. The proponents of such linkage between trade and labour standards argue that such demand is not only reasonable but also feasible, as international trade negotiations have already started to include issues that are not intrinsically trade-centred, but do have an impact on trade and investment, such as intellectual property rights. One of the most important debates on trade-related labour standards took place during the establishment of the World Trade Organization (WTO). In 1996, the Singapore Declaration, signed during the first WTO meeting of Ministers, expressed a commitment to internationally recognized core labour standards (CLS). However, it did so in an ambiguous way, by renewing the commitment of the WTO to core labour standards, while reaffirming the position of the International Labour Organization (ILO) as the main organization to deal with core labour standards. These CLS referred to a specific set of principles already discussed in 1994 during the World Summit for Social Development in Copenhagen. They were more specifically defined in 1998 by the ILO as those principles part of ILO conventions no. 87 (on the freedom of association and the right to organize), no. 98 (on the right to organize and bargain collectively), no. 111 (on the prohibition of employment and occupation-related discrimination), no. 138 (on a minimum age for employment), no. 29 (on the abolition of forced labour) and finally no. 182 (on the abolition of the worst forms of child labour). While the Singapore Declaration was rather vague in terms of what this WTO commitment really entailed, it did set the stage for an increased attention to the linkage between trade and labour standards (van Roozendaal 2002).

The identification of CLS has had a profound impact on trade and investment agreements worldwide. Since the mid-2000s, mainly stimulated by the lack of progress in the WTO, bilateral trade negotiations instead of multilateral trade negotiations in the WTO have been the focus of the attention of many countries. Such agreements have proven to be fertile ground for the inclusion of a "universal norm" of labour standards (for example, see the US FTAs as shown by Giumelli and van Roozendaal 2016). This means that bilateral and multilateral agreements tend to refer to a similar package of labour standards, even though this does not necessarily mean that the package referred to in all agreements is always exactly the same. In 2013, 58 bilateral trade agreements included some reference to labour standards, compared to 4 in 1995 (Campling et al. 2014, p. 5).

In this global environment, labour standards also found their way to the EU's external policy. Initially, labour standards were not mentioned separately but as part of human rights,[1] and were integrated into agreements that were unilaterally providing for preferential access to the European market (through the Generalized System of Preferences, GSP) and into more specific trade agreements. The 1989 Lomé Convention already mentioned respect for human rights as a goal of development cooperation, and the GSP of 1991 made preferential access conditional upon respect for human rights. In 2001, the GSP started to rely on the Copenhagen Social Summit's definition of labour rights and added the possibility of withdrawing the preferential access in case of violation of CLS (Beke et al. 2014, p. 32).

With respect to bilateral and plurilateral trade agreements,[2] it was the EU–Argentina agreement for trade and economic cooperation in 1990 that first formulated human rights as an essential element to the agreement (at that time without specifically calling it an "essential element"). Including human rights as an "essential element" meant that violation of the specified human rights could result in a suspension of treaty obligations or in other sanctions (Beke et al. 2014, pp. 60–61).[3]

Further progress was made at the end of the 1990s. Inspired by the Copenhagen Social Summit and the 1998 ILO Declaration, the EU started to emphasize the specific set of four labour standards as social human rights, which was expressed in the 1999 Trade, Development and Cooperation Agreement with South Africa. This was reaffirmed in 2000, with the adoption of the Charter of Fundamental Rights of the European Union, which included references to the content of CLS (van Roozendaal, 2012, pp. 67–68; Van den Putte and Orbie 2015, p. 268), in the 2006 Global Europe Strategy in which the Commission set the goal of promoting labour standards (Gupwell and Gupta 2009, p. 80) and in the Treaty of Lisbon of 2009, in which fair trade is mentioned as an objective (Campling et al. 2014, p. 7). In its trade and investment policy document of 2015, the Commission declared its commitment to promoting CLS and high standards of health and safety and decent work circumstances through FTAs (European Commission 2015, p. 24). The European Parliament has made it clear on different occasions that it would not accept agreements without reference to CLS (Gupwell and Gupta 2009, p. 93).[4] Van den Putte and Orbie (2015) show that the EU has slowly accepted CLS as "an unobjectionable norm," while simultaneously delinking them from human rights and instead reframing them in the context of sustainable development. They argue that this reframing has made CLS less threatening for opponents of the trade-labour linkage. Currently, EU trade agreements include a chapter on trade and sustainable development, which contains both labour and environmental provisions, thereby separating human and labour rights. This chapter has its own dispute settlement procedure and does not foresee any sanctions but instead relies on consultation and cooperation.

On the basis of the above, it can be concluded that the desire of the EU to include labour standards in its FTAs is indeed based on the logic of appropriateness, whereby normative change has stimulated a new course of action, which is seen as the legitimate way to go. This is, however, a one-sided commitment, as such inclusion is not necessarily seen as a similarly appropriate way by trading partners such as India. In fact, there has been much resistance against the inclusion of labour standards in FTAs since the start of the trade-labour standards debate in the context of the General Agreement on Tariffs and Trade (GATT) and then the WTO. During the Uruguay Round negotiations, the then Indian Minister of Commerce stated that "[...] while we are strongly committed to internationally recognized labour standards, we see no merit whatsoever in the attempt to force linkages where they do not exist," and in Seattle this sentiment was repeated (WTO 1994, 1999). India perceived the attempts to link trade and labour standards as a protectionist move by countries unable to compete through low wages, taking away India's comparative advantage on the world market. Moreover, India saw such possible linkage as an infringement on its sovereignty, this being reinforced by the fact that the trade-labour standards linkage debate in the GATT/WTO did not take place in isolation, but in the context of a debate on many non-trade issues that—to the dismay of India—threatened to become part of regular trade negotiations: intellectual property rights (IPR), services and trade-related investment measures (van Roozendaal 2002, pp. 126–128).

However, India's opposition to the linkage did not mean that human rights were not included in any EU–India agreements. On the contrary, human rights have been mentioned in the 1994 EU–India Cooperation Agreement and the EU–India Joint Action Plan of 2005 (Orbie and Khorana 2015, p. 260), with a specific reference in the latter to "[...] full respect for fundamental principles, fair wages and rights at work" (Council of the European Union 2005). In 2016, commitment to enhancing fair trade was part of the joint statement and the action plan of 2020, following the 13th EU–India Summit in 2016 (European Commission 2016a; Council of the European Union 2016). However, while in none of these documents CLS were specifically mentioned, the Commission has recommended to the Council to include sustainability issues (labour and environment) in the free trade negotiations with India (European Commission 2006, p. 3), and according to Gupwell and Gupta (2009, p. 84), the Commission's negotiating mandate for the agreement with India indeed requires "consultation and cooperation on trade-related labour and employment issues, [...] decent work and support for core labour standards and the up to date ILO Conventions."

The issue the EU addresses is a sensitive one. India has ratified six of the ILO's eight core conventions. Two of those eight, nos. 138 and 182 on minimum employment age and the abolition of the worst forms of child labour, were only recently ratified and are not yet in force. Thus far India has failed to ratify conventions nos. 87 and 98 (ILO 2018). The non-ratified conventions are related to the freedom of association and the right to organize, and on the right to organize and bargain collectively. In practice, India has been criticized for problems concerning compliance with both the ratified and the non-ratified conventions, and for the working conditions in general. Although it has a very comprehensive body of labour legislation, the vast majority of workers are in the informal sector and oftentimes do not benefit from the laws, and those who are self-employed are left without any protection (Lerche 2012, pp. 22–23). The International Trade Union Confederation (ITUC) reported in 2011 that there are limitations to the establishment of unions that are not in accordance with international standards. There have been reports that participating in strikes can lead to being fired, being arrested or being locked out, and state laws may weaken federal laws by, for example, making the establishment of trade unions in special economic zones impossible. Discrimination and the lack of equal remuneration are commonplace where, for example, female workers, Dalits (the caste of people at the lowest levels of the social order of the Indian society) and indigenous people, are concerned. Child labour, forced labour and bonded labour also occur on a large scale. ITUC rated the country in 2015 with a 5, the second worst category, meaning that there is no guarantee of rights (ITUC 2011, 2016a, 2016b). A similar picture emerges from the reports of the US Department of State and the Cingranelli-Richards (CIRI) database (Cingranelli, Richards and Clay 2014a). The human rights report of the US Department of State (2015) confirms strong limitations to freedom of association and collective bargaining in export processing zones and the nonexistence of these and the other rights in the large informal sector.[5] The CIRI database shows that between 2002 and 2011, India has only scored a 1 with respect to freedom of association and collective bargaining, which "[…] is given to governments that generally protect the rights to association and collective bargaining but there are occasional violations of these rights or there are other significant violations of worker rights" (Cingranelli, Richards and Clay 2014b, p. 65).

This evidence from India shows that addressing CLS in the negotiations of an EU–India FTA remains a sensitive issue. While for the EU it seems to be nonnegotiable, until today India is very consistent in its opposition to a CLS clause and is still viewing it as a breach of its sovereignty (Gupwell and Gupta 2009, p. 91; Wouters et al. 2013, p. 10; Orbie and Khorana 2015, pp. 260–261). India has not included CLS in any of its own FTAs (Mukherjee, Goyal and Giswami 2013, p. 38; Engen 2017, p. 38), and the country also opposes it in other trade negotiations (see e.g. Government of India, Ministry of Commerce & Industry, Department of Commerce/New Zealand Government, Ministry of Foreign Affairs and Trade 2009, pp. 64–66). According to Lerche (2012, p. 23), the Indian government seems to be of the opinion that labour standards will be respected after full employment is achieved.

In conclusion, while from the EU perspective including CLS in trade agreements is consistent with internationally agreed norms and practice, India considers this as inappropriate given its socioeconomic situation and in light of its sovereignty. Aside from this, the different preferences of the EU and India might also be seen as a result of conflicting economic interests, as the following section will discuss.

Costs versus benefits in the logic of choice

The costs and benefits of a possible agreement between the EU and India should be considered in two different ways. The first is from the perspective of what an agreement as such would bring the two parties. This will give us insight into the possible importance of such an agreement. Second, a prospective FTA should be viewed in light of what the inclusion of labour standards itself entails for both parties.

To start with the first, even though the current trade flows are – from the perspective of the EU – not as impressive as the other way around,[6] India has belonged since 2004 to a group of 10 countries that have been identified as "strategic partners" of the EU, which signals a more-than-average interest of the EU in this country. Grevi (2012) maintains that, while the meaning and function of "strategic partnership" is unclear, partnerships can serve multiple purposes, such as cooperation on economic and on broader security issues. According to Jain (2014, pp. 7–9), both India and the EU perceive trade relations to be the main interest of the strategic partnership. Through the liberalization of trade, investment and services, the Indian market would become easier to reach for European producers, while at the same time India would benefit from better access to its main export destination. The EU has the prospect of accessing the market of the "world's fastest-growing large economy" (European Commission 2019). In addition, characterized by economic growth and protective policies (both tariff and non-tariff barriers), India makes negotiations worthwhile (Wouters et al. 2013, pp. 2–5). The protection of the Indian market has always been high (Saha 2016, pp. 9–10), and according to a study of the European Commission, amongst 31 trading partners studied, India occupies a sixth place concerning the total of protectionist measures in place since 2008, and a fourth place with respect to new measures taken since mid-2014. Duties increased on steel, motors and information and communication technology (ICT) items, and India has, compared to other countries, relatively strong restrictions on sanitary and phytosanitary grounds, strong technical barriers to trade in certain areas (such as in cars, steel products and tires), provides for little effective patent protection and implements a restrictive investment policy (European Commission 2016b, pp. 5, 13–14). For India, the gains of an FTA are to be found in increased access to the EU markets for clothing, textile and services, as well as addressing tariff and non-tariff barriers in the agricultural EU market (Khorana and Perdikis 2010, pp. 185, 192, 195).

Despite these mutual interests, it has proven to be difficult to reach an agreement on trade and investment. Amongst the most challenging issues are European market access in India in sectors such as automobiles, alcoholic products and dairy products. For India, it is important to be identified as a "data secure nation" (The Economic Times 2018). Such identification depends on an adequacy decision by the EU, which makes the transfer of privacy-sensitive, personal information to businesses operating in non-EU countries much easier. While the EU regulations are not part of the negotiations with India, an adequacy decision will facilitate concluding a trade agreement (European Commission 2017, pp. 6, 9). Wouters et al. (2013) identified the following issues as amongst the most controversial in the EU–India negotiations: labour standards and services liberalization, IPR and the impact of EU subsidies. Khorana and Perdikis (2010) further show that there are different conclusions with respect to the possible benefits in trade and welfare that both countries might get from the FTA, and that India itself concluded in a 2007 study that it would not gain from the FTA as proposed.[7] In fact, in 2013 the negotiations discontinued due to irreconcilable differences, and since then meetings have taken place to find a common basis to resume the negotiations (European Commission 2018a, p. 4). In the meantime, controversy has emerged about India's plans to renegotiate the bilateral investment agreements it currently has with individual EU countries (Arun 2016). In sum, while there are obvious interests for both countries to cut a trade deal, doubts about the benefits that cripple the current negotiations remain profound.

While labour standards form a stumbling block in the negotiations from an ideational point of view, economic interests may also play a role. India and the EU both believe that such inclusion, or the lack of it, might hurt their respective interests. This is best illustrated by the debate on labour standards and service liberalization. Wouters et al. (2013, pp. 8–10) explain how India would like to see Indian nationals having access to the EU as posted workers,[8] and the main concern here is that these Indian nationals would be working under different labour conditions than their European counterparts. This is something that could be prevented by either providing similar working conditions for Indian nationals as for the European workers when moving temporarily to the EU, or by making sure that CLS are respected also in India. Allowing that people work under different conditions might put pressure on labour standards and job security, some argue (see e.g. Kaucher 2013). In addition, as Lerche (2015) argues, weakening India's labour legislation is at the core of Prime Minster Modi's strategy for economic growth.

Besides this, there is the issue of the general economic effects of differences in labour standards once an FTA is concluded. Some (see e.g. Jatkar 2012) suggest fears on the EU side about an unfair trade advantage for India and on the Indian side about EU protectionism are the main driving forces behind the debate on labour standards between the negotiators. The British Trade Union Congress (TUC), for example, argues in favour of respect for labour standards "[t]o ensure that our trading partners are not violating workers' rights to gain an unfair trade advantage" (TUC 2012, p. 1). The extent to which protectionism is (also) a characteristic of the EU approach is subject to debate (see for a discussion about this, Van den Putte and Orbie 2015). India itself is not clear about its motives to refuse the inclusion of labour standards in the negotiations (see e.g. Government of India, Ministry of Commerce & Industry, Department of Commerce/New Zealand Government, Ministry of Foreign Affairs and Trade 2009, p. 66).

In sum, cost-benefit calculations are likely also motivating the different positions on the inclusion of CLS in the agreement. Both positions, i.e. the fear for unfair trade advantages and protectionism respectively, are related to economic interest. From a rational choice perspective, either India or the EU need to be convinced that specific economic gains cannot be obtained without an FTA, and be willing to give in on the labour standards issue. While giving in may come at a reputational cost and may not be politically feasible, the economic costs of giving in for either the EU or India will likely be low, as the actual nature and legal constraining effects of a CLS clause will be weak at best. This is the issue we turn to in the next section.

The logic of constraints: the inclusion of labour standards and their implementation in the FTA

As explained earlier, CLS are increasingly included in FTAs between the EU and its trading partners. Over time, the *language* on labour standards of the EU FTAs has become more specific and more binding. As this section will show, while the *wording* is ambitious, and the *process* by which disputes are handled has become more elaborate over the years, the *options to enforce CLS* remain limited (Van den Putte et al. 2013, pp. 44–46; Van den Putte and Orbie 2015).

When the European Commission received its negotiating mandate for India, South Korea and ASEAN from the Council in April 2007, CLS and up-to-date ILO conventions were included in the mandate, as well as suggestions on the mechanisms to assure the implementation (Gupwell and Gupta 2009, pp. 79, 84). After the negotiations with ASEAN failed, bilateral FTAs were concluded with Vietnam and Singapore, and the inclusion of labour rights as part of bilateral negotiations was still on the agenda and very strongly supported by the European Parliament, thereby putting some constraint on excluding labour standards from the negotiations, whether in the FTA itself or in related agreements (Sicurelli 2015; European Parliament 2017, p. 4). For this reason, the FTAs with South Korea (already in effect) and with Singapore and Vietnam (concluded) may illustrate what the EU is aiming at in its negotiations with India.

In terms of *wording*, these three FTAs agree to national and international commitments. The international commitments make references to CLS and to the ratification and implementation of ILO conventions. In the FTAs, the signatories reaffirm that their ILO membership gives them certain obligations and that they should promote and implement *the fundamental principles and rights* contained in the CLS and implement the Conventions ratified. With respect to the ratification, it is stipulated that the signatories "[...] will make continued and sustained efforts towards ratifying the fundamental ILO Conventions [...]" (see e.g. the EU–Singapore FTA, European Commission 2018b). The EU–Korea FTA adds to make efforts to ratify other conventions that are "up-to-date," and the other two FTAs urge to "consider ratification" of other conventions. Implementation is defined as "[...] the commitment to effectively implementing the ILO Conventions that Korea and the Member States of the European Union have ratified respectively" (European Commission 2011).

The national commitments posit that parties have the right to regulate but that the regulation needs to be consistent with the principles of internationally recognized labour standards, and each party is expected to make sure that high levels of labour protection are stimulated. In addition, the FTAs include broad commitments not to weaken levels of protection, waive or derogate from legislation, or "fail to effectively enforce" labour laws, in order to encourage or otherwise affect trade and investment.

While the wording may sound ambitious, the specific *enforcement mechanisms* in all FTAs are weak and characterized by consultation. All three specify that the general dispute settlement provisions in the agreement do not apply to labour disputes and that special institutions and procedures are established for monitoring the implementation of the chapter and handling disputes. In the case of the FTA between the EU and South Korea, it involves compulsory creation of domestic advisory groups, to which civil stakeholders are invited. Once a year, representatives of these advisory groups will meet in a civil society forum. This forum can put its views forward to the signatory parties. However, there is no requirement for governments to respond to the views (or complaints) of the forum. In addition, the parties may request the Committee on Trade and Sustainable Development to further discuss specific matters. Membership to this committee is limited to government officials of both the parties. While civil society may provide advice to the committee on a specific matter directly, there is nothing in the agreement stipulating that the committee should respond to the civil society communications, while there is such requirement for communications delivered by the parties.

The EU–Singapore FTAs differs from the agreement with South Korea, as it lacks a provision that provides for the establishment of a civil society forum but instead provides for a public session of the committee (or Board as it is called in the Singapore FTA) with stakeholders. Furthermore, it lacks a provision that enables domestic advisory groups to submit a communication on a specific matter on its own initiative to the committee, once parties have requested the committee to consider such a specific matter. This latter provision is also absent from the EU–Vietnam FTA (European Commission 2018c), while it does provide for a joint civil society forum meeting.

If parties fail to solve an issue, they may refer it to a panel of independent experts, which has a task limited to giving advice and recommendations, of which the implementation is monitored by the committee.[9] Interestingly, the EU–Korea FTA does not provide specifically for the stakeholders or domestic advisory groups to submit observations about the implementation of the experts' opinion, while the other two do.

With a separate procedure to handle disputes about labour standards, there is no mechanism in the FTAs to evoke sanctions against a country not upholding the standards, as the dispute settlement mechanism is weaker compared to that of violations of other parts of the agreement (European Commission 2010; Campling et al. 2014, pp. 8–9).[10] However, it is interesting that with respect to the handling of disputes on CLS the EU–Singapore FTA includes that "[t]he Parties shall discuss appropriate measures to be implemented taking into account the report and the recommendations of the Panel of Experts" (Art. 12.17, EU–Singapore FTA). Similar wording is included in the EU–Vietnam FTA but not in the EU–Korea FTA. While it is unclear what such measures involve, it is safe to assume that it does not involve any sanctions.

In sum, while the specific wording may differ, and the procedure when a dispute arises too, the discussion of the three other agreements shows that CLS are part of the FTAs negotiated by the EU, with the possibility of submitting communications in case of violations. However, the three provide for separate mechanisms to handle resulting disputes, in a way that differs from the normal trade dispute mechanisms. As Bartels (2015, p. 90) posits, "[…] the EU's sustainable development obligations are not enforceable, except insofar as the parties agree to take into account the recommendations and advice of a panel of experts appointed to determine disputes under the relevant provisions." From that, it may be concluded that constraints on parties that result from CLS provisions are quite limited, with direct sanctions excluded as an appropriate measure. There is no reason to expect that this will be different in an FTA between the EU and India.

Despite the above, the agreements do not need to be without consequences in terms of sanctions. The panel of experts that looks into complaints filed under the agreements may influence a party's future benefits under an agreement. This can take the form of further refraining from trade concessions or from financial and technical assistance (Van den Putte and Orbie 2015, pp. 269–270).

Some argue that there might still be other options to enforce commitments on CLS through sanctions, in particular through the essential elements clause found in some FTAs and in some other agreements between the trading parties. Other agreements can be relevant for FTAs, as they provide the political framework in which human rights can be linked to the FTAs (Sicurelli 2015, p. 235).

Since 1995, all framework agreements that the EU concludes need to have an essential elements clause that includes human rights, as well as a non-execution clause (Bartels 2014, pp. 8–11, 2015, p. 83; Velluti 2016, p. 53). Such clause, "[…] on which the reciprocal obligations of the parties were premised" means "[…] that human rights violations of a certain scale by one of them could amount to a material breach of the treaty and justify suspension or other counter-measures" (Hachez 2015, p. 8). The possibility to evoke measures is described in the "non-execution clause" (Bartels 2015, p. 84). Such measures need to be appropriate, which means according to Bartels (2015, p. 85) that they should not conflict with international law, will try not to "disrupt the functioning of the agreement" and will only lead to suspension of the agreement if all other options are exhausted.

Essential element clauses and non-execution clauses can be part of an FTA itself but can also be included in another agreement to which the FTA is linked, so-called cross-referencing (Bartels 2015, p. 83).[11] An example is the EU–Vietnam FTA. Before embarking on the negotiations for an FTA, a partnership and cooperation agreement (PCA) was negotiated, which was signed in 2012. PCAs aim for increasing the cooperation in areas not covered by economic agreements and include references to international norms and rules. The EU–Vietnam PCA includes the promotion of respect for human rights as an essential element of the agreement in Art. 1 and also mentions the objective to ensure respect for CLS separately in Art. 50. The FTA between the EU and Vietnam refers to this PCA in a legally binding way. In the PCA it is stipulated that in case of a violation of basic human rights, appropriate measures may be taken. This is because a violation of human rights is considered a violation of an essential element of the agreement, and therefore to be a material breach, which can in turn lead to immediate measures (European Commission 2012, p. 157, 2016c, pp. 2–4). The EU–Vietnam FTA stipulates in Art. 17.18(2) that "[i]f a Party considers that the other Party has committed a material breach of the Partnership and Cooperation Agreement it may take appropriate measures with respect to this Agreement [...]." A Commission's staff document argues that "[...] a Party may unilaterally take appropriate measures with respect to the FTA when it considers that the other Party has committed a material breach of the PCA (such as violating the essential element constituted by the 'human rights clause'). Thus, the EU maintains its full discretion to take appropriate measures also concerning the FTA in case it considers that Vietnam violates its commitment to respect basic human rights obligations" (European Commission 2016c, p. 8).[12] However, the PCAs of both Vietnam and Singapore do not explicitly allow trade sanctions in case of human rights violations, while other PCAs do (Hoang and Sicurelli 2017, p. 379).

Even though FTAs may be linked to the essential elements and non-execution clauses in other agreements, and in this sense the case of Vietnam shows how this could potentially strengthen the enforcement of CLS, this does not necessarily mean that such a link will help to support commitment to CLS. One of the reasons for this is that there is some debate about whether the human rights mentioned as part of the essential element clause are also covering CLS, not in the last place because CLS are sometimes mentioned separately, as is the case with the EU–Vietnam FTA, Art. 50(3) (see also Hachez 2015, p. 16). While some argue that there is a consensus that human rights do include CLS (Hachez 2015, p. 16), others argue that over the years the EU's understanding of labour standards has shifted from a human rights issue to a sustainability issue, making the application of the essential elements clause to labour standards less likely (Van den Putte and Orbie 2015, pp. 269–282).[13]

In terms of logic of constraints, the negotiating mandate and the procedural role of the European Parliament make it difficult to accept an FTA that does not contain any reference to CLS. However, in terms of legal obligations or constraints that will arise from such inclusion, the examples of recent other FTAs suggest that only fairly limited effects should be expected, giving India much leeway. The above shows that there are several options available for the

EU–India FTA. Art. 1 of the 1994 Cooperation Agreement (CA) between the EU and India includes a similar essential elements clause and lacks an article specifically on labour standards. This lack would strengthen the case to see CLS as part of human rights. However, a non-execution clause is absent and it does not contain a provision that this agreement forms a framework in which future agreements are negotiated (European Commission 1994). Therefore, an EU–India FTA "[...] would [...] have to contain its own non-execution clause to ensure that the human rights clause can have full effect" (Bartels 2015, p. 85). Given the fact that the EU obliged itself to link trade to human rights (directly or indirectly by cross-referencing) and to a sustainability chapter referring to CLS too, it seems likely that India has to accept this as part of a future trade agreement.

Conclusion

The analysis shows that India and the EU have a clear difference of opinion concerning the need to include CLS in FTAs. The EU considers the inclusion of CLS to be an appropriate way of promoting fair trade in its external relations, whereas India does not support this, as it rather sees it as an inappropriate risk for its sovereignty. In addition, it is safe to assume that India fears the costs it expects to be associated with the inclusion of labour standards, as it will raise the prices of its export products. That being said, India might eventually choose to accept such inclusion, if this was supported by cost-benefit considerations, i.e. the knowledge that the material benefits of the FTA as a whole outweigh its economic loses.

When taking into consideration the agreements already concluded with other countries, one is led to think that including CLS in the agreement with the EU should not be so difficult to accept for India. The legal enforcement of CLS is rather weak, and it is unlikely that an essential elements clause will be evoked on the account of labour standards violations. Even if the clause were evoked, there is little chance that it would lead to sanctions or suspension. This means that in case of a dispute on issues related to the CLS clause, the diplomatic rather than the legal way will prevail when labour standards are concerned. The question is whether this will be enough to convince India to give up its opposition and enter into an agreement including labour standards.

Notes

1 The EU includes social human rights as a subcategory of human rights (Beke et al. 2014, pp. 14–16).
2 Such commercial agreements include "exclusive trade agreements," "trade and economic cooperation agreements," "association agreements" and "wide-ranging partnerships" (Beke et al. 2014, p. 57).
3 Currently, human rights are part and parcel of the EU's international agreements (sometimes through a link with a framework agreement) and include a non-execution

provision, allowing for measures to be taken in case of human rights violations (Beke et al. 2014, pp. 60–63).

4 In contrast to the European Parliament, the role of the Indian Parliament with respect to trade negotiations is very limited in the phase of drafting the negotiating mandate, during the negotiations as well as in the treaty approval phase, as the Indian Constitution gives these powers to the central government or gives the government leeway to circumvent approval by parliament (email correspondence with Professor Biswajit Dhar 13 June/19 June 2018; Daruwala and Nayak 2013). This is not the case in the EU, where the parliament, and with respect to mixed treaties also the members states individually, have a much stronger role in the process (Van den Putte, De Ville and Orbie 2014; see also Voogsgeerd in Chapter 10 of this volume).

5 The European Parliament has also demanded that European companies working in Indian export processing zones should adhere to the CLS, the four priority conventions and other conventions ratified by India (European Parliament 2011). These priority conventions were identified by the ILO in 2008 as conventions that help to govern labour relations. They include conventions no. 81 and 129 on labour inspection, no.122 on employment policy and no.144 tripartite labour consultation (ILO 2015).

6 While the EU is India's largest trading partner (in 2016 the main destination for exports and the second main origin of imports), India occupies the ninth position amongst the EU's trading partners (WTO 2016; European Commission 2019).

7 In fact, some of India's current FTAs have caused increased trade deficits with the respective countries, which makes India cautious about other agreements (Dhar 2018).

8 India also aims for the European market to open up for service suppliers such as call centers. The EU, on the other hand, wants to have access to India's service sector such as banking and insurance (Wouters et al. 2013, p. 8).

9 Or "Board" in case of Singapore.

10 This is different in the Generalized System of Preferences+ (GSP+). Under this mechanism, trade preferences can be cut in case of violations of labours standards. This has actually happened in the instances of Burma and Belarus (Van den Putte and Orbie 2015, p. 227).

11 Bartels (2015, p. 85) suggests that even without such explicit cross-referencing, a human rights clause combined with a non-execution clause in one agreement may have consequences for another agreement.

12 While the EU–Korea FTA itself does not make such a connection, the EU–Korea Framework Agreement makes its essential elements and non-execution clause consequential to the FTA between the two parties (Hachez 2015, p. 12).

13 There is some debate about whether stronger enforcement options would actually be helpful. A study by Zhou and Cuyvers (2011) on the EU GSP, where the EU actually can and has cut preferences in case of systematic violation of labour standards, has shown that the effects in cases of Burma and Belarus are limited, although it has been pointed out that the effects may depend on the strength of the trading relation and the availability of other trading partners to the sanctioned countries. Also, while some FTAs do allow for sanctions, such as some of the US ones, this instrument has never been used (see Giumelli and van Roozendaal 2016).

References

Arun, S. (2016) 'India, EU aims to break free trade agreement impasse', *The Hindu*, available at http://www.thehindu.com/business/Industry/india-eu-aim-to-break-free-trade-agreement-impasse/article8677993.ece.

Bartels, L. (2014) *The European Parliament's Role in Relation to Human Rights and Investment Agreements.* Brussels: Directorate-General for External Policies of the Union, available at https://www.europarl.europa.eu/cmsdata/86031/Study.pdf.

Bartels, L. (2015) 'The EU's approach to social standards and the TTIP', in S. Khorana, (ed.), *The Transatlantic Trade and Investment Partnership (TTIP) Negotiations Between the EU and the USA*, Barcelona: Centre for International Affairs, pp. 83–91.

Beke, L., D'Hollander, D., Hachez, N. and Pérez de las Heras, B. (2014) *The Integration of Human Rights in EU Development and Trade Policies*, Brussels: Frame, available at http://www.fp7-frame.eu/wp-content/uploads/2016/08/07-Deliverable-9.1.pdf.

Campling, L., Harrison, J., Richardson, B. and Smith, A. (2014) *Working Beyond the Border? A New Research Agenda for the Evaluation of Labour Standards in Trade Agreements*, Coventry: University of Warwick, School of Law, Legal Studies Research Paper 2014/2013.

Cingranelli, D., Richards, D. and Clay, C.K. (2014b) *The Cingranelli-Richards (CIRI) Human Rights Data Project Coding Manual*, version 75.20.14, available at https://drive.google.com/file/d/0BxDpF6GQ-6fbWkpxTDZCQ0IjYnc/edit.

Cingranelli, D., Richards, D., Clay, C.K. (2014a) *The CIRI Human Rights Dataset*, available at http://www.humanrightsdata.com/p/data-documentation.html.

Council of the European Union. (2005) 'EU-India Strategic Partnership Joint Action Plan', 11984/05 (presse 223), Brussels, 7 September 2005.

Council of the European Union. (2016) 'EU-India Agenda for Action – 2020', EU – India Summit, Brussels, 30 March 2016.

Daruwala, M. and Nayak, V. (2013) 'India's Engagement with Free Trade Agreements (FTAs): Challenges and Opportunities. Measures for Improving Transparency and Accountability in Relation to FTAs', (Draft), New Delhi: Commonwealth Human Rights Initiative (CHRI).

Dhar, B. (2018) 'India must focus on manufacturing turnaround at RCEP talks in Singapore. Successive governments have failed to make agriculture and manufacturing competitive', *LiveMint*, available at https://www.livemint.com/Home-Page/e3V9qp2YqSqjNYyxQHirQN/India-must-focus-on-manufacturing-turnaround-at-RCEP-talks-i.html.

Engen, L. (2017) *Labour Provisions in Asia-Pacific Free Trade Agreements*, United Nations ESCAP, Ninth Tranche of the Development Account Project Enhancing the Contribution of Preferential Trade Agreements to Inclusive and Equitable Trade, Background Paper 1/2017, available at https://www.unescap.org/sites/default/files/Background%20Material%20-%20Labour%20provisions%20in%20Asia-Pacific%20PTAs.pdf.

European Commission. (1994) 'Cooperation agreement between the European Community and the republic of India on partnership and development', OJ L 223/24, 27 August 1994.

European Commission. (2006) 'Recommendation from the commission to the council authoring the commission to negotiate a free trade agreement with India on behalf of the European community and its Member States', SEC (2006) 1558 final/2, Brussels, 6 December 2006.

European Commission. (2010) 'EU-South Korea quick reading guide', available at https://eeas.europa.eu/sites/eeas/files/tradoc_145203.pdf.

European Commission. (2011) 'International agreements: EU-Korea FTA', OJ L 127/54, 14 May 2011, pp. 6–1343.

European Commission. (2012) 'Framework agreement on comprehensive partnership and cooperation between the European Union and its member states, of the one part, and the Socialist Republic of Viet Nam, of the other part', available at https://eur-lex.europa.eu/legal-content/HR/ALL/?uri=uriserv:OJ.L_.2016.329.01.0008.01.ENG.

European Commission. (2015) Trade for All: Towards a More Responsible Trade and Investment Policy', Luxembourg: Publications Office of the European Union.

European Commission. (2016a) *'Joint Statement 13th EU-India Summit'*, Brussels: Press release, 30 March 2016.

European Commission. (2016b) 'Report from the Commission to the Council and the European Parliament on trade and investment barriers and protectionist trends', COM (2016) 406 final, Brussels, 20 June 2016.

European Commission. (2016c) 'Human rights and sustainable development in the EU-Vietnam relations with specific regard to the EU-Vietnam Free Trade Agreement', SWD (2016) 21 final, Brussels, 26 January 2016.

European Commission. (2017) 'Communication from the Commission to the European Parliament and the Council. Exchanging and protecting personal data in a globalised world', COM (2017) 7 final, Brussels, 10 January 2017.

European Commission. (2018a) 'Overview of FTA and other trade negotiations', Updated May 2018.

European Commission. (2018b) 'Annex to the Proposal for a Council Decision on the conclusion of the Free Trade Agreement between the European Union and the Republic of Singapore', COM (2018) 196 final, Brussels, 18 April 2018, Annex 1.

European Commission. (2018c) 'EU-Vietnam trade and investment agreements', 24 September 2018, available at http://trade.ec.europa.eu/doclib/press/index.cfm?id=1437.

European Commission. (2019) 'Countries and Regions: India', 17 March 2019, available at http://ec.europa.eu/trade/policy/countries-and-regions/countries/india/.

European Parliament. (2011) 'European Parliament resolution of 2 May 2011 of the state of play in the EU-India free trade agreement negotiations', available at https://www.europarl.europa.eu/sides/getDoc.do?pubRef=-//EP//TEXT+TA+P7-TA-2011-0224+0+DOC+XML+V0//EN.

European Parliament. (2017) *'EU-Singapore Free Trade Agreement Stimulus for Negotiations in the Region.* Briefing: International Agreements in Progress', June 2017, available at https://www.europarl.europa.eu/RegData/etudes/BRIE/2017/607255/EPRS_BRI(2017)607255_EN.pdf.

Giumelli, F. and van Roozendaal, G. (2016) 'Trade agreements and labour standards' clauses: Explaining labour standards developments through a qualitative comparative analysis of US free trade agreements', *Global Social Policy*, 17(1), pp. 38–61.

Government of India, Ministry of Commerce & Industry, Department of Commerce/New Zealand Government, Ministry of Foreign Affairs and Trade. (2009). 'India: New Zealand joint study for a free trade agreement/comprehensive economic cooperation agreement', available at https://www.mfat.govt.nz/assets/FTAs-in-negotiations/India/nz-india-joint-study-report.pdf.

Grevi, G. (2012) *'Why EU Strategic Partnerships Matter'*, Madrid: Fride, ESPO Working Paper 1, available at https://www.files.ethz.ch/isn/145464/WP_ESPO_1_Strategic_Partnerships.pdf.

Gupwell, D. and Gupta, N. (2009) 'EU FTA negotiations with India, ASEAN and Korea: The question of fair labour standards', *Asia Europe Journal*, 7(1), pp. 79–95.

Hachez, N. (2015) *'Essential Elements' Clauses in EU Trade Agreements: Making Trade Work in a Way that Helps Human Rights?'*, Leuven: KU Leuven Centre for Global Governance Studies, Working Paper 158, available at https://ghum.kuleuven.be/ggs/publications/working_papers/2015/158hachez.

Hoang, H. and Sicurelli, D. (2017) 'The EU's preferential trade agreements with Singapore and Vietnam: Market vs. normative imperatives', *Contemporary Politics*, 23(4), pp. 369–387.

ILO. (2015) 'Conventions and recommendations', available at https://www.ilo.org/global/standards/introduction-to-international-labour-standards/conventions-and-recommendations/lang--en/index.htm.

ILO. (2018) 'Ratifications of fundamental conventions and protocols by country', available at http://www.ilo.org/dyn/normlex/en/f?p=1000:10011:1854796394987018::::P10011_DISPLAY_BY:1.

ITUC. (2011) 'Internationally recognized core labour standards in India. *Report for the WTO General Council Review of the Trade Policies of India*', Geneva, 14 and 16 September 2011, available at https://www.ituc-csi.org/IMG/pdf/final_India_TPR_Report_3.pdf.

ITUC. (2016a) 'The 2016 ITUC global rights index. The world's worst countries for workers', available at https://www.ituc-csi.org/IMG/pdf/ituc-violationmap-2016-en_final.pdf.

ITUC. (2016b) 'Description of ratings', available at http://survey.ituc-csi.org/IMG/pdf/description_of_ratings.pdf.

Jain, R.K. (2014) 'India-EU Strategic Partnership: Perception and Perspectives', Berlin: Freie Universität, NFG Working Paper 10, available at http://www.asianperceptions.fu-berlin.de/system/files/private/wp1014-india-eu-strategic-partnership_0.pdf.

Jatkar, A. (2012) 'Human Rights in the EU-India FTA: Is it a valuable option?', Great Insights Magazine, 1(2), available at https://ecdpm.org/great-insights/trade-and-human-rights/human-rights-eu-india-fta-viable-option/.

Kaucher, L. (2013) 'What was the real purpose of David Cameron's visit to India?', *Open Democracy*, available at https://economictimes.indiatimes.com/news/economy/foreign-trade/india-eu-fta-negotiations-likely-to-resume-soon/articleshow/63467513.cms?from=mdr.

Khorana, S. and Perdikis, N. (2010) 'EU-India free trade agreement: Deal or no deal?', *South Asia Economic Journal*, 11(2), pp. 181–206.

Lerche, J. (2012) 'Labour regulations and labour standards in India: Decent work?', *Global Labour Journal*, 3(1), pp. 16–39.

Lerche, J. (2015) 'Making India? The labour law reforms of Narendra Modi's government', *South Asia Notes*, available at https://eprints.soas.ac.uk/23862/.

March, J.G. and Olsen, J.P. (2009) 'The logic of appropriateness', in R.E. Goodin, M. Moran and M. Rein (eds.), *The Oxford Handbook of Public Policy*, Oxford: Oxford University Press, pp. 1–22, available at doi:10.1093/oxfordhb/9780199548453.003.0034.

Mukherjee, A., Goyal, T.M. and Giswami, R. (2013) 'India as a trading partner: Issues in India-EU BTIA and way forward', The Long Road Towards an EU-India Free Trade Agreement, Brussels: Workshop October 2013, available at http://www.europarl.europa.eu/RegData/etudes/workshop/join/2013/433709/EXPO-INTA_AT(2013)433709_EN.pdf.

Orbie, J. and Khorana, S. (2015) 'Normative versus market power? The EU-India trade agreement', *Asia Europe Journal*, 13(3), pp. 253–264.

Saha, A. (2016) *Essays in India Trade Policy*, Brighton: University of Sussex, Phd Thesis.

Sicurelli, D. (2015) 'The EU as a promoter of human rights in bilateral trade agreements: The Case of the negotiations with Vietnam', *Journal of Contemporary European Research*, 11(2), pp. 230–245.

The Economic Times. (2018) 'India-EU FTA negotiations likely to resume soon', available at https://economictimes.indiatimes.com/news/economy/foreign-trade/india-eu-fta-negotiations-likely-to-resume-soon/articleshow/63467513.cms?utm_source=contentofinterest&utm_medium=text&utm campaign=cppst.

TUC. (2012) *'The EU-India Free Trade Agreement: TUC Briefing'*. London: Trades Union Congress, available at https://www.tuc.org.uk/research-analysis/reports/tuc-briefing-eu-india-free-trade-agreement.

US Department of State. (2015) 'India 2015 human rights report', Washington, D.C.

Van den Putte, L. and Orbie, J. (2015) 'EU bilateral agreements and the surprising rise of labour provisions', *The International Journal of Comparative Labour Law and Industrial Relations*, 31(3), pp. 263–284.

Van den Putte, L., de Ville, F. and Orbie, J. (2014), The European Parliament's new role in trade policy: Turning power into impact', *CEPS*, 89(SP), available at http://aei.pitt.edu/51025/1/CEPS_SR_89_EP_New_Role_in_EU_Trade_Policy.pdf.

Van den Putte, L., Orbie, J., Bossuyt, F. and de Ville, F. (2013) 'Social norms in EU bilateral trade agreements: A comparative overview', in T. Takacs, A. Ott and A. Dimopoulos (eds.), *Linking Trade and Non-commercial Interests: The EU as Global Role Model*, The Hague: CLEER. Working Paper 2013/4, pp. 35–48.

van Roozendaal, G. (2002) *Trade Unions and Global Governance: The Debate on a Social Clause*, London: Continuum.

van Roozendaal, G. (2012) 'Why international financial institutions adopt labour standards: The case of the European Investment Bank', *Studia Diplomatica*, LXV 2, pp. 59–77.

Velluti, S. (2016) The promotion and integration of human rights in EU external trade relations', *Utrecht Journal of International and European Law*, 32(83), pp. 41–68.

Wouters, J., Goddeeris, I. Natens, B. and Ciortuz, F. (2013). *Some Critical Issues in the EU-India Free Trade Agreement Negotiations*. Leuven: Leuven Centre for Global Governance Issues, available at https://limo.libis.be/primo-explore/fulldisplay?docid=LIRIAS492626&context=L&vid=Lirias&search_scope=Lirias&tab=default_tab&lang=en_US&fromSitemap=1.

WTO. (1994) 'Statement by Mr. Pranab Mukherjee Minister of Commerce, India', trade negotiations committee, MTN.TNC/MIN(94)/ST/38, 13 April 1994.

WTO. (1999) 'Statement by H.E. Mr. Murasoli Maran Minister of Commerce and Industry, India', WT/MIN(99)/ST/16, 30 November 1999.

WTO. (2016) 'International trade and market access data', 'India', available at http://webservices.wto.org/resources/profiles/TP/ZZ/2016/IN_e.pdf

Zhou, W. and Cuyvers, L. (2011) 'Linking international trade and labour standards: The effectiveness of sanctions under the European Union's GSP', *Journal of World Trade*, 45(1), pp. 63–85.

12 New trade rule-making regarding sustainable development in EU FTAs with Asian countries

Yumiko Nakanishi

The concept of sustainable development (SD) is important in the EU. It is laid down in the preamble of the TEU and Art. 3(3) TEU and Art. 11 TFEU after the Treaty of Lisbon (Durán and Morgera 2012, pp. 34–43). Further, the European Commission published a COM document "Mainstreaming sustainable development into EU policies" in 2009 (European Commission 2009). The concept of SD is a key concept for the Union. Bartels points out that the EU's practice of including chapter on sustainable development in its FTAs has more recent origins (Bartels 2015, p. 82). Cremona indicated that sustainable development is an important element in considering the significance of treaty-based CCP objectives (Cremona 2017, p. 15). The EU's FTAs emphasize the importance of the concept. Therefore, they have a chapter on trade and sustainable development (TSD). Barrel indicates that states are under an obligation to pursue sustainable development; they are bound by an obligation of means and by implementing countless treaties they contribute, day after day, to progressively making sustainable development requirements real (Barrel 2012, p. 398). The EU has contributed to make sustainable development requirements real by concluding FTAs with third countries (Cf. Nakanishi 2018, pp. 366–367).

This chapter aims to analyze environmental protection under Chapter Trade and Sustainable Development (TSD) in the FTAs, focusing on a specific dispute settlement mechanism (DSM) and the right to regulate environmental standards, which are considered as new trade rule-making. First, a specific DSM under Chapter TSD will be elaborated on in comparison with a general DSM under the chapter on dispute settlement. Second, the right to regulate environmental standards will be discussed.

The EU started negotiations with the Association of Southeast Asian Nations (ASEAN) as an entity; however, it changed its policy and instead negotiates with ASEAN countries individually. In this paper, the topic of discussion is the countries with which the EU completed negotiations. Specifically, those countries are South Korea, Singapore, Japan and Vietnam, and, where necessary, Canada will be used as comparison.

The special dispute settlement mechanism under chapter trade and sustainable development

Introduction

If a conflict between the EU member states occurs regarding the EU law, the CJEU has exclusive jurisdiction and solves it. However, how will a conflict between the EU and the third country be solved? In the case of bilateral agreements, the EU and the other party envisage provisions for dispute resolution. The UK government explains regarding dispute resolution mechanisms in the following way: Dispute resolution mechanisms ensure that all parties share a single understanding of an agreement, both in terms of interpretation and application (HM Government 2017, p. 14). International agreements include dispute settlement mechanisms (judicial procedures and/or non-judicial procedures), which are essential to ensure fair interpretation and application of those agreements (Cf. Tanaka 2018, pp. 21–23). In the case of the WTO, the Dispute Settlement Body (panels or Appellate Body) decides disputes and makes recommendations. On the one hand, a new generation of the EU's FTAs also lays down a general dispute settlement mechanism. On the other hand, the general mechanisms shall not be applied for Chapter TSD and instead the FTAs provide a special DSM as discussed below.

Korea–EU FTA (2011)

Background

In 2007, the EU and South Korea began to negotiate an FTA. Those negotiations finished and the FTA was initialled on October 15, 2009. The FTA entered into force in July 2011. The Korea–EU FTA is the first among a new generation of FTAs (European Union 2011). Chapter 13 is TSD (arts. 13.1–13.16).

The special dispute settlement mechanism

As for disputes arising under Chapter 13 TSD, the parties shall have recourse only to the procedures set forth under the chapter. This means that the parties cannot use the mechanism provided in Chapter 14: Dispute Settlement. Kim pointed out that the general DSM under Chapter 14 has a judicial nature; therefore, it would take a long time to resolve the issue because conclusions would be reached only after lengthy legal debates on the consistency of certain measures with the Korea–EU FTA (Kim 2010, p. 223). Further, Kim assumes that since sustainable development is newly introduced in the FTA, it would not yet be appropriate for a judicial decision (Kim 2010, p. 219). Frank Gaenssmantel and Chien-Huei Wu also indicate in this book that a dispute settlement mechanism demonstrates a certain degree of judicialization but has limited scope of jurisdiction, in particular when a dispute relates to certain sensitive service sectors. As a result, the EU and its trading partners might designate a special dispute settlement mechanism with less judicialized characteristics to resolve such a dispute. It means that for emergent issues, such as Chapter TSD, the negotiators may be tempted to design the DSM to be based on consultation in nature or consensus-based so that the states can control the result of the dispute.

Chapter 13 provides two methods: government consultations (Art. 13.14) and a panel of experts (Art. 13.15). According to Art. 13.14, a party may request consultations with the other party and consultations shall commence promptly. The parties shall make every attempt to arrive at a mutually satisfactory resolution of the matter, but if a party considers that the matter needs further discussion, that party may request that the Committee on TSD (hereinafter referred to as "the Committee") be convened to consider the matter. The Committee is a specialized committee which shall comprise senior officials from within the administrations of the parties (Art. 13.12(2)). The Committee's resolution will be published. If this procedure does not work satisfactorily, a party may request that a panel of experts be convened to examine the matter. The experts will be chosen among the list of at least 15 persons (nationals and at least 5 non-nationals) and shall be independent of either party or organizations represented in the domestic advisory groups (DAGs). The panel of experts presents a report to the parties. The report is not binding on the parties. It differs from the ruling of the arbitration panel under Chapter 14 dispute settlement, since the ruling of the arbitration panel is binding on the parties (Art. 14.17(2)). The parties must make efforts to accommodate the recommendations of the panel of experts, and the implementation of the recommendations will be monitored by the Committee.

Additionally, a DAG will be established by each party (Art. 13.12(4)). It comprises independent representative organizations of civil society in a balanced representation of environment, labour and business organisations as well as other relevant stakeholders (Art. 13.12(5)). Members of DAG will meet at a Civil Society Forum in order to conduct a dialogue encompassing sustainable development aspects of trade relations between the parties (Art. 13.13(1)). The parties can present an update on the implementation to the Civil Society Forum and the views, opinions or findings of the Civil Society Forum can be submitted to the parties (Art. 13.13(3)). During the government consultations procedure, the Committee and each party may seek advice of the DAG (Art. 13.14(4)). In this meaning, a DAG is involved indirectly in the DSM. Kim commented that a DAG, although it cannot serve as a DSM, would be established to encourage the participation of civil society during the implementation process of Chapter 13 (Kim 2010, p. 221).

Singapore–EU FTA (April 2018)

Background

Negotiations for a comprehensive free trade agreement between the EU and Singapore were launched in 2007 and finished in 2014. However, on July 10, 2015, the Commission asked, according to Art. 218 (11) TFEU, the CJEU whether the EU independently would have exclusive competence to sign and conclude the FTA with Singapore. The Court indicated in Opinion 2/15 that the EU has exclusive competence for even environmental issues, but the EU does not have exclusive competence for investment-related issues in the FTA.[1] Therefore, the EU and Singapore renegotiated and finally, they agreed on two different agreements, i.e. FTA and investment protection agreement. The former will be concluded by the EU only, and Singapore (European Commission 2018c) and the latter will be concluded by the EU and its member states, of the one part, and Singapore of the other part (European Commission 2018d). The EU and Singapore signed the FTA and the investment protection agreement on October 19, 2018. The FTA agreement between the EU and Singapore is composed of 16 chapters (European Commission 2018a). Chapter 12 is TSD (Art. 12.1-12.17).

The special dispute settlement mechanism

For disagreement on any matter arising under Chapter TSD, the party shall have recourse only to the mechanisms of government consultations and a panel of experts (Art. 12.16(1)). The party is not allowed to apply other provisions, Chapter 15's general dispute settlement and Chapter 16's mediation mechanism (Art. 12.16(1)). There are two stages for the special DSM under Chapter TSD: government consultations and a panel of experts. This framework of the mechanism is the same as that in other EU FTAs.

First, a party requests consultations with the other party, and then consultations promptly commence (Art. 12.16(2)). If a party considers that the matter needs further discussion, that party may request that the Board be convened to consider the matter (Art. 12.16(4)). The Board means a Board on TSD that shall comprise senior officials from within the administrations of each party and shall be established by the parties (Art. 12.15(2)).

Second, a party may request that a panel of experts be established to consider that matter (Art. 12.17(1)). The panel of experts is composed of 3 members from the list of at least 12 individuals, who have specialized knowledge of or expertise in issues regarding Chapter TSD, labour or environmental law, or resolution of disputes arising under international agreements (Art. 12.17(3) and (4)). The panel of experts issues an interim and final report to the parties (Art. 12.17 (8)). This point differs from that in the Korea–EU FTA. These reports shall include findings of facts, the applicability of relevant provisions, and the basic rationale behind any findings and recommendations. In addition, there are provisions setting deadlines for issuing those reports. The final report shall be made publicly available (Art. 12.17(8)). The parties are obliged to discuss appropriate measures to be implemented, taking into account the report of and recommendations of the panel of experts (Art. 12.17(9)). Furthermore, any follow-up to the report and recommendations of the panel of experts shall be monitored by the Board (Art. 12.17(9)). Those things mean that the second stage of the special DSM for TSD shows stricter and more elaborate procedures in order to ensure the implementation of those reports in comparison with the Korea–EU FTA. Those reports are not legally binding, but their implementation method is more strengthened.

Japan–EU EPA (April 2018)

Background

On May 28, 2011, the EU and Japan agreed to start a scoping process to conclude an FTA. The FTA between the EU and Japan is called the Economic Partnership Agreement (EPA). After that, both sides began to negotiate in April 2013 (Nakanishi 2016, pp. 19–20). During the negotiations, the Court delivered the Opinion 2/15[2] regarding the FTA between the EU and Singapore in May 2017. According to the Opinion, the EU has exclusive competence except non-direct investment and investor–state dispute settlement (ISDS). Facing the Opinion 2/15, the EU and Japan decided to divide the EPA into the EPA without investment protection and an investment protection agreement, so that the EU can conclude the EPA alone without the participation of the EU's member states. Both signed it on July 17, 2018, and the EPA entered into force on February 1, 2019 (Nakanishi 2019, pp. 1–15), while they continue to negotiate investment protection agreement because Japan has not agreed with the introduction of an investment court such as the EU requests. The EPA has 23 chapters. Chapter 16 is TSD (Art. 16.1–16.19).

The special dispute settlement mechanism

Although the EPA also has a chapter dispute settlement, the chapter shall not apply to the Chapter TSD (Art. 16.17(1)). Art. 16.17(1) lays down, "*in the event of disagreement between the Parties on any matter regarding interpretation or application of this Chapter*, the Parties shall only have recourse to the procedures in this Article and Article 18.16" (emphasis by author).

There are also two stages of the special DSM: government consultations (Art. 16.17) and a panel of experts (Art. 16.18). One of the remarkable things is the wording regarding the function of the panel of experts. According to Art. 16.18(2), the panel of experts shall interpret the relevant articles of Chapter TSD in accordance with customary rules of interpretation of public international law, including those codified in the Vienna Convention on the Law of Treaties. The interim and final report of the panel sets out the findings of facts, the interpretation or the applicability of the relevant articles and the basic rationale behind any finding and suggestions (Art. 16.18(5)). Art. 16.18 does not provide that a report of the panel of experts is legally binding. However, the report of the panel could partake legal character. The final report shall be made publicly available (Art. 16.18(5)). The parties are obliged to discuss actions or measures to resolve the matter, taking into account the panel's final report and its suggestions and the follow-up actions or measures shall be monitored by the committee (Art. 16.18(6)).

As for the participation of civil societies, each party shall convene a meeting of its new or existing DAG or groups. The Korea–EU FTA also refers to DAGs, but the Japan–EU FTA lays down more details, especially regarding composition, powers and functions. The DAG may on its initiative express its opinion on the implementation of Chapter TSD independently of the party and submit those opinions to that party (Art. 16.15). The parties shall convene the Joint Dialogue with civil society organizations including members of their DAGs. The views and opinions of the Joint Dialogue may be submitted to the committee and may be made publicly available (Art. 16.16). The DAGs and the Joint Dialogue may submit their observations regarding the follow-up actions or measures of the final report of the panel to the committee (Art. 16.18(6)). It also can be found through the relevant provisions that stakeholders are involved indirectly in the DSM. In fact, a request of an involvement of the civil society in the DSM under Chapter TSD was written in the mandate document from the Council to the European Commission before the beginning of negotiations (European Council 2012, p. 13). Environmental NGOs in Japan have not been strong enough to influence governmental policies in comparison with those in the EU countries. These relevant provisions could be a catalyst to strengthen the NGOs. Those relevant provisions are important from the aspect of a democratic environment.

Vietnam–EU FTA (August 2018)

Background

In June 2012, the EU and Vietnam began negotiating an FTA and finished it in December 2015. Facing the Opinion 2/15, the EU and Vietnam renegotiated. The EU and Vietnam also plan to conclude the investment agreement as well as the FTA. The draft FTA (authentic text as of August 2018) has 17 chapters. Chapter 13 is TSD (arts. 13.1–13.17).

The special dispute settlement mechanism

Chapter 13 TSD has its own provisions for dispute settlement procedures. Although Chapter 15 provides for general DSM, Chapter 13 shall not be applied to Chapter 15 (Art. 13.16(1)) and instead Chapter 15 provides a special DSM. Art. 13.15 provides for institutional setup and an overseeing mechanism, Art. 13.16, which provides for government consultations, and Art. 13.17, which provides for a panel of experts. The committee reviews the implementation of Chapter 13. There are two stages for the DSM: government consultations and a panel of experts. This framework is the same as that of other EU-FTAs.

Analysis

TSD chapters are included in the EU FTAs for South Korea, Singapore, Japan and Vietnam. As mentioned earlier, these chapters have similar characteristics as well as the same or similar frameworks and structure, with differences in wording of the text (Nakanishi 2017, pp. 457–468). The EU negotiated with South Korea, Singapore, Vietnam and then Japan, and renegotiated with Singapore and Vietnam after the Court Opinion 2/15. The provisions contained in the text of the Japan–EU EPA are the most precise among those FTAs regarding the special

DSM for TSD. Specifically, there is a provision demonstrating the development towards judicial DSM through negotiations of the FTAs. The panel of experts in the Japan–EU EPA shall interpret the relevant articles of the chapter TSD in accordance with customary rules of interpretation of public international law, although the special DSM is not a judicial one.

While the EU's FTAs agreements have a special chapter on dispute settlement, disputes arising from the Chapter TSD must be resolved pursuant to the provisions from the latter chapter, and not in the former chapter. There are two stages of DSM in Chapter TSD: consultations and a panel of experts. In principle, there are also two stages of DSM under the chapter on dispute settlement; namely consultations (and medication) and the panel of arbitrators. However, the chapter on dispute settlement has more structured and detailed provisions. The primary difference between the special DSM for TSD and the general DSM concerns whether the mechanism is judicial or not, i.e. whether the report of the panel is binding or not. The decisions of the panel of arbitrators in the Chapter TSD shall be final and binding on the parties (Ex. Art. 21.15(8) of the Japan–EU EPA).

The United States' FTAs have a chapter on DSM that includes judicial procedures that apply to the chapters on labour and the environment. In contrast, the EU's FTAs have a chapter on DSM that includes judicial procedures, but the general DSM under the Chapter DSM does not apply to environmental and labour issues under chapter TSD. Marx and others indicate that the complaints procedure under the United States' FTAs is significantly more formalized than under the EU's FTAs (Marx, Ebert and Hachez 2017, p. 51). The Trans-Pacific Partnership (TPP) is an example of this phenomena and is also considered to be a "new-generation" FTA. The United States influenced the text of the TPP, although it ultimately decided to leave the TPP. The new TPP (without the United States) is called the Comprehensive and Progressive Agreement for Trans-Pacific Partnership (CPTPP), the members of which are 11 countries (Singapore, Vietnam, Japan and Canada, which are mentioned in this paper, as well as Australia, Brunei, Chile, Malaysia, Mexico, New Zealand and Peru). The CPTPP entered into force on December 30, 2018. It has Chapter 19 (Labour) and Chapter 20 (Environment). Art. 19.15(12) and (13) for labour and Art. 20.23 for environment enable parties to have recourse to a dispute settlement mechanism including judicial procedures under Chapter 28 (dispute settlement). However, it cannot be assumed that the provisions under the United States' FTAs guarantee higher standards of protection for labour and environment than those of the EU's FTAs. The Chapters on TSD in the EU's FTAs are based on a "promotional" rather than a "conditional" approach (Campling et al. 2016, p. 357). Presumably, it is quite an accomplishment for the EU to incorporate social and environmental values into the EU's FTAs because Asian countries have hesitated to incorporate social clauses into the FTAs (Cf. Garcia and Masselot 2015, pp. 247, 250). In addition, it is generally said that a reason for inclusion of a chapter on labour is to protect the domestic industry in the United States rather than to maintain high labour standards. Anyway, the United States' FTAs have a remarkable institutional point in the DSM.

The EU's FTAs do not establish a possibility of direct participation (allegation) by individuals or NGOs in the chapter on dispute settlement, while some of the United States' FTAs introduce the possibility. For example, the Dominican Republic-Central America FTA (CAFTA-DR)[3] sets a mechanism of a contact point. In this provision, persons of the party can submit communications to it on matters related to the provisions under Chapter 16 (Labour) (Art. 16.4(3)). A party may request consultations with another party regarding any matter by delivering a written request to the contact point (Art. 16.6(1)).[4] In fact, the American Federation of Labour and Congress of Industrial Organizations (AFL-CLO) and other labour unions submitted an allegation to the Office of Trade and Labour Affairs of the US Department of Labour as a contact point.[5] Facing this request, the United States initiated dispute settlement procedures provisioned under Art. 16.6. Further, Chapter 19 (Labour) and Chapter 20 (Environment) of the CPTPP have an article that is entitled "Public Submissions," although the CPTPP does not provide direct participation in the DSM (Art. 19(9) and Art. 20(9)). Any person of the parties can submit opinions regarding its implementation of those chapters. This point is also remarkable.

In the case of the EU's FTAs with Asian countries, civil societies or stakeholders can be involved only indirectly in the Special DSM as mentioned before. In the case of the Comprehensive Economic and Trade Agreement (CETA) between Canada and the EU, Art. 23.8(5) under the Chapter 23 (Trade and Labour) enables the public to submit opinions to the parties on matter related to the chapter. In this point the CETA recognizes the possibility of an allegation by individuals and NGOs in the special DMS under the chapter. However, for the disputes arising under the chapter on trade and labour, the parties cannot have recourse to the general DSM including judicial procedures under Chapter 29 (Dispute Settlement) (Art. 23.11). In addition, Chapter 24 (Trade and Environment) does not provide a direct participation of individuals and NGOs.

As a possibility of participation by individuals and NGOs, they might ensure their interest or rights through the preliminary ruling in Art. 267 TFEU because the EU's FTAs are an integral part of EU law and the CJEU has jurisdiction to interpret them. The inclusion of the participation in DSM by them is desired in the EU's FTAs.

The right to regulate for environmental protection

Background

Environmental nongovernmental organizations (NGOs) (Krämer 2015, pp. 48–51) and consumer protection organizations are active in Europe and participate in decision-making in the EU. The European Commission began to consider public opinion based on a 2001 white paper on European governance (European Commission 2001). After the Treaty of Lisbon, those practices are now regulated in Arts. 10 and 11 TFEU. For example, Art. 10 TFEU provides that every citizen has the right to participate in the democratic life of the EU. The EU institutions must give citizens and representative associations the opportunity to express and publicly exchange their views on all areas of Union action (Art. 11(1) TFEU).

Environmental NGOs in the EU have been concerned about the FTAs between the EU and third countries. Particularly, they are concerned that environmental standards would decrease. Some of them have demonstrated against the FTAs and others have expressed their opinion in the European Parliament.

"The right to regulate" is often discussed in this context. The importance of this right is emphasized by NGOs and consumer protection advocates. The NGOs and consumer protection organizations have expressed concerns about the deterioration of the EU regulatory standards regarding the protection of the environment or social or consumer protection, particularly in negotiations with the United States (Cf. Kim 2018, pp. 313–314). In response, the EU proposed to include recognition of the parties' right to regulate their own domestic and environmental standards (Cremona 2015, p. 355). A draft provision of the TTIP (Art. 2 of Section 2 of Chapter II) lays down, 'the provisions of this section shall not affect the right of the Parties to regulate....

The precautionary principle is outlined in Art. 191(2) TFEU (Cf. Proelss 2016, pp. 35–44) and certain EU measures are based on the precautionary principle. Until now, some conflicts between the EU and the United States in the WTO have related to the EU measures, which are based on the precautionary principle (Forere 2015, pp. 47–48; Reid 2015, pp. 236–238).[6] Taking into account their concerns, the FTAs provide for "the right to regulate," which enables the parties of the FTAs to maintain their standards even for investment issues.

The right to regulate in the Korea–EU FTA

There is a reference to "desiring to strengthen the development and enforcement of labour and environmental law and policies" in the preamble of the Korea–EU FTA. Art. 13.3, with the title of "Right to Regulate and Levels of Protection," states, "(r)ecognising the right of each Party to establish its own levels of environmental and labour protection, and to adopt or modify accordingly its relevant laws and policies, each Party shall seek to ensure that those laws and policies provide for and encourage high levels of environmental and labour protection...".

The right to regulate in the Japan–EU EPA

The European Commission explained in the proposal of conclusion of the Japan–EU EPA in the following way: "like all other free trade agreements the Commission has negotiated, the EU-Japan EPA fully safeguards public services and ensures that governments' right to regulate in the public interest is fully preserved by the Agreement" (European Commission 2018b).

Art. 16.2 of Chapter TSD provides the "right to regulate and levels of protection." The first paragraph of it provides, "(r)ecognising the right of each Party to determine its sustainable development policies and priorities, to establish its own levels of domestic environmental and labour protection, and to adopt or modify accordingly its relevant laws and regulations,... each Party shall strive to ensure that its laws, regulations and related policies provide high levels of environmental and labour protection...." The second paragraph makes clear that the parties shall not encourage trade and investment by relaxing or lowering the level of protection, and thus the parties shall not waive or otherwise derogate from such laws and regulations or fail to effectively enforce them.

The right to regulate in the Singapore–EU agreements

Singapore and the EU divided former FTA into current FTA and investment protection agreement, facing the Court Opinion 2/15, as mentioned above. An investment protection agreement provides for the establishment of an investment tribunal under Chapter 3 dispute settlement.

The right to regulate

The preamble of the Singapore–EU FTA reaffirms that the parties have the right to adopt and enforce measures necessary to pursue legitimate policy objectives, such as social, environmental, security, public health and safety, and promotion and protection of cultural diversity. Based on Art. 12.2 of the Chapter TSD, the parties recognize the right to establish their own levels of environmental and labour protection. The parties must continue to improve those laws and policies, and strive to provide and encourage high levels of environmental and labour protection.

The right to regulate and investment tribunal

Trade and investment are connected to the environment and sustainable development (Viñuales, 2012, pp. 9–18). It means that investors' rights will be limited in order to secure the right to regulate of host states (Reinisch 2017, p. 270).

The EU–Singapore Investment Protection Agreement contains provisions regarding an investment tribunal and appeals tribunal. The right to regulate is related to the EU protection standards, which are set forth in the EU measures. Therefore, it is important to think about how the investment tribunal will treat EU law in resolving conflicts.

"New-generation" FTAs enable individual enforcement via arbitration (in the field of investment) (Cremona 2017, pp. 18–19). This differs from the DSM in the WTO where only states including the EU can take actions. However, in this meaning the investor–state dispute settlement (ISDS) is considered as progressive. ISDS is not an ideal from the viewpoint of democratic legitimacy (Ohler 2017, pp. 227–245). At the European Parliament, there were discussions regarding ISDS, which was related to the US–EU FTA, Transatlantic Trade and Investment Partnership Agreement. The following is the recommendation to the Commission:

> to ensure that foreign investors are treated in a non-discriminately fashion, while benefiting from no greater rights than domestic investors, and to replace the ISDS system with a new system for resolving dispute between investors and states which is subject to democratic principles and scrutiny,

where potential cases are treated in a transparent manner by publicly appointed, independent professional judges in public hearings and which includes an appropriate mechanism, where consistency of judicial decision is ensured, the jurisdiction of courts of the EU and of the Member States is respected, and where private interests cannot undermine public policy objectives. (Cf. Ohler 2017, p. 228)[7]

In light of this, the Singapore–EU investment protection agreement envisages the investment tribunal system like that in TTIP. Art. 3.9 of the agreement provides for the establishment of a permanent investment tribunal. The tribunal is composed of six members, two of which shall be nationals of member states of the EU, two of which shall be nationals of Vietnam and two of which shall be nationals of third countries. The composition means the tribunal is not an organ of the EU. In addition, a permanent appeal tribunal is also established (Art. 3.10). For the EU, especially for NGOs and consumers, it is important to ensure that the investment tribunal respects the EU protection standards.

The right to regulate in the Vietnam–EU agreements

Vietnam and the EU renegotiated the FTA. Both divided the FTA in the FTA and investment protection agreement like Singapore and the EU after the Court Opinion 2/15. The latter lays down the establishment of investment tribunals.

The preamble of the FTA between the EU and Vietnam provides that the parties determined to promote trade and investment under the FTA in a manner mindful of high levels of environmental and labour protection and relevant internationally recognized standards and agreements. Further, as mentioned above, the FTA has a special chapter on TSD. Art. 13.2(1) Right to Regulate and Levels of Protection provides that the parties recognize their right to establish their own levels of domestic protection in the environmental and social areas as they deem appropriate and to adopt or modify accordingly their relevant laws and policies in a manner consistent with the internationally recognized standards. Further, Art. 13.2(2) obliges the parties to endeavour to ensure that their laws and polices (the parties) provide for and encourage high levels of domestic protection in the environmental and social areas and continuously endeavour to improve those laws and policies. It illustrates how the EU and its Asian trade partner, Vietnam, use the FTA to produce new rules. In addition, Art. 13.3 Upholding Levels of Protection lays down, "the Parties stress that weakening the levels of protection in environmental or labour areas is detrimental to the objectives of this Chapter…". The EU stressed the importance of the right to regulate towards Vietnam.

The right to regulate in the CETA between the EU and Canada

Here, the Comprehensive Economic and Trade Agreement (CETA) between Canada and the EU will be discussed to understand the right to regulate better. In October 2016, the EU approved CETA (De Mestral 2017, pp. 438–444).

CETA entered into force provisionally on September 21, 2017. CETA has 30 chapters, including Chapter 22 on TSD, Chapter 23 on trade and labour and Chapter 24 on trade and the environment.

The preamble of CETA provides that CETA preserves "the right to regulate within their territories and the Parties' flexibility to achieve legitimate policy objectives, such as public health, safety, environment, public morals and the promotion and the protection of cultural diversity." The preamble also provides that the provisions "protect investments and investors with respect to their investments, and are intended to stimulate mutually-beneficial business activity, without undermining the right of the Parties to regulate in the public interest within their territories." CETA enables the EU to maintain the right to regulate environmental standards and, at the same time, the provisions of CETA regarding investment will not undermine the right to regulate environmental standards.

Art. 24.3 of Chapter 24: Trade and Environment sets forth the "right to regulate and levels of protection." The parties recognize the right of each party to set its environmental priorities to its levels of environmental protection and to adopt or modify its laws and policies. Further, each party is obliged to ensure that those laws and policies provide for and encourage high levels of environmental protection, as well as to improve such laws and policies and their underlying levels of protection. Art. 8.9 in the chapter on investment provides that the parties reaffirm their right to regulate within their territories to achieve legitimate policy objectives. Bartels expressed doubts, though, about Art. 8.9's legal effect (Bartels 2017, pp. 15–16). He pointed out that by "reaffirming" a right to regulate, Art. 8.9 could be limited to rights that already exist for both parties.

There have been objections to CETA (Cf. Koutrakos 2017, pp. 1–2). For example, citizens and NGOs brought a proceeding seeking a preliminary injunction in the German Federal Constitutional Court (GFCC), claiming that CETA violates their rights under Art. 38 of the Basic Law (Bundesverfassungsgericht 2016). Furthermore, Wallonia of Belgium hindered Belgium's signing of the provisional application of CETA. Therefore, a joint interpretative instrument was also adopted when CETA was signed (Council of the European Union 2016).

The joint interpretative instrument, which clarifies on how the parties want to interpret the rules in accordance with the intent of the treaty drafters, states that the preamble of CETA provides that the EU, its member state, and Canada recognize the right to regulate in the public interest and have reflected it in CETA. Bartels commented that this interpretative instrument, however, does not alleviate his concerns as to the legal effect of the right to regulate (Bartels 2017, p. 16). It is meaningful that the joint interpretative instrument has a specific reference to the right to regulate in "2. right to regulate." Under "6. investment protection," the joint interpretative instrument states that "CETA includes modern rules on investment that preserve the right of governments to regulate in the public interest including when such regulations affect a foreign investment." As for environmental protection, the joint interpretative instrument confirms that CETA recognizes the right to regulate environmental protection and that the EU, its member states and Canada have agreed not to lower their levels of environmental protection in order to encourage trade or investment. It also explains that in case of any violation of this commitment, governments can remedy such violations regardless of whether these negatively affect an investment or investor's expectations of profits. The joint interpretative instrument was indispensable for obtaining the signatures to the provisional application of CETA, as it emphasizes the right to regulate and ensures the right's effectiveness. Further, the DSM under CETA combined with the right to regulate would contribute to its effectiveness, as the concept paper by Frank Gaenssmantel and Chien-Huei Wu indicates, point out the role of actors (government and private litigants) before DSM.

Analysis

New-generation FTAs include not only a specific chapter on TSD but also the right to regulate. The first of the new-generation FTAs, the Korea–EU FTA, also refers to the right to regulate. The clauses that govern the right to regulate in all of the FTAs are similar in principle but have some differences. The EU–Singapore Investment Protection Agreement and the EU–Vietnam Investment Protection Agreement as well as CETA contain provisions for an investment tribunal and refer to the right to regulate the environment. Furthermore, there is a joint interpretative instrument for CETA in which the importance and respect of the right to regulate are emphasized.

The right to regulate environmental standards is one of the characteristics in the new-generation FTAs. Its introduction is owed to the NGOs. The right to regulate has meaning, especially in the context of investment. However, it is uncertain what legal effect the right to regulate will have. It is questionable whether the provisions on the right to regulate is soft or hard law. It is also questionable whether the EU, its member states or NGOs can rely on the "the right to regulate" provisions before courts or tribunals (the CJEU, national courts or the investment court). In order to preserve the right to regulate and protect its intention, it is critical to discern how the investment tribunal can ensure the right to regulate while guaranteeing the EU's highly developed environmental standards in Asian countries.

As a comparison, the right to regulate in the Trans-Pacific Partnership (TPP) will be discussed. In the TPP's preamble, the parties recognize their inherent right to regulate and resolve to preserve the flexibility of the parties to set legislative and regulatory priorities and to protect the environment, including the conservation of living or nonliving exhaustible resources. Chapter 9 of the TPP is a specific chapter on investment. Art. 9.10 provides that certain paragraphs of Art. 9.10 shall not be construed to prevent a party from adopting or maintaining measures, including environmental measures, so long as such measures are not applied in an arbitrary or unjustifiable manner or do not constitute a disguised restriction on international trade or investment. Further, Art. 9.16

provides that nothing in the chapter on investment shall be construed to prevent a party from adopting, maintaining or enforcing any measures, otherwise consistent with that chapter, that it considers appropriate to ensure that investment activity in its territory is undertaken in a manner sensitive to environmental, health or other regulatory objectives. The TPP, thus, recognizes the idea of the right to regulate environmental standards, although the phrase "the right to regulate" is not directly used.

Conclusion

New-generations EU-FTAs are greening Asian countries through new trade rule-making negotiations by introducing a special dispute settlement under Chapter TSD and the right to regulate.

There are special DSMs under the chapters on TSD: consultations and a panel of experts. Disputes arising under those chapters must be resolved under the mechanisms in those chapters. The parties do not have recourse to other means, including the utilization of the chapters on dispute settlement. The EU's FTAs have their own special DSMs under the chapters on TSD. However, those mechanisms are looser and less institutionalized than the general DSMs under the chapters on dispute settlement and the chapters on investment protection that include an investment tribunal. The reports of the panel in the chapters on TSD are not binding on the parties. Those chapters on TSD are based on a "promotional" rather than a "conditional" approach. It can be said that stakeholders are involved indirectly in the DSM under the Chapter TSD. Thus, new trade rule-making plays an important role in managing environmental disputes.

It is remarkable that these FTAs set forth the right to regulate environmental standards as another new trade rule-making. In this respect, new-generation FTAs show great progress in the context of environmental protection, although to ensure the right to regulate needs the contribution by the courts and tribunals including the CJEU and investment tribunal.

The CPTPP as a "new-generation" FTA also has remarkable institutional points regarding environmental protection as mentioned above. The EU's FTAs, the CPTPP and the United States' FTAs have influenced each other and are continuously developing.

Notes

1 Case Avis-2/15 *Accord de libre-échange avec Singapour*, Opinion 2/15 of the Court (Full Court) [2017] ECLI:EU:C:2017:376.
2 *Ibid.*
3 CAFTA-DR is the first FTA between the US and a group of smaller developing economies, Costa Rica, El Salvador, Guatemala, Honduras, Nicaragua and the Dominican Republic.
4 USTR, 'The text of CAFTA-DR: Chapter Sixteen— Labor', available at https://ustr.gov/sites/default/files/uploads/agreements/cafta/asset_upload_file320_3936.pdf.

5 USTR, 'In the Matter of Guatemala—Issues Relating to the Obligations Under Article 16.2.1(a) of the CAFTA-DR', available at https://ustr.gov/sites/default/files/US%20Initial%20Written%20Submission.pdf.

6 As for measures concerning meat and meat products (Hormones), Appellate Body Report on *European Communities – Measures Concerning Meat and Meat Products (Hormones)*, WT/DS26/AB/R and WT/DS48/AB/R of 18 August 1997.

7 European Parliament resolution of 8 July 2015 containing the European Parliament's recommendations to the European Commission on the negotiations for the Transatlantic Trade and Investment Partnership (TTIP), P8_TA(2015)0252, A8-0175/2015, available at http://www.europarl.europa.eu/sides/getDoc.do?pubRef=%2f%2fEP%2f%2fTEXT%2bTA%2bP8-TA-2015-0252%2b0%2bDOC%2bXML%2bV0%2f%2fEN&language=EN.

Bibliography

Barrel, V. (2012) 'Sustainable development in international law: Nature and operation of an evolutive legal norm', *European Journal of International Law*, 23(2), pp. 377–400.

Bartels, L. (2015) 'Human rights and sustainable development obligations in EU free trade agreements', in J. Wouters, A. Marx, D. Geraets and B. Natens (eds.), *Global Governance Through Trade: EU Policies and Approaches*, Cheltenham, UK: Edward Elgar, pp. 73–91.

Bartels, L. (2017) 'Human rights, labour standards and environmental standards in CETA', *Legal Studies Research Paper Series (University of Cambridge)*, paper 13/2017, pp. 1–16.

Bundesverfassungsgericht. (2016) *Im Namen des Volkes in den Verfahren*, available at https://www.bundesverfassungsgericht.de/SharedDocs/Downloads/DE/2016/10/rs20161013_2bvr136816.pdf?__blob=publicationFile&v=5.

Bungenberg, M., Krajewski, M., Tams, C., Terhechte, J.P. and Ziegler, A.R. (eds.). (2017) *European Yearbook of International Economic Law 2017*, Cham, Switzerland: Springer, pp. 438–455.

Campling, L., Harrion, J., Richardson, B. and Smith, A. (2016) 'Can labour provisions work beyond the border: Evaluating the effects of EU free trade agreements', *International Labour Review*, 155(3), pp. 357–382.

Council of the European Union. (2016) Joint interpretative instrument on the comprehensive economic and trade agreement (CETA) between Canada and the European Union and its member states, 13541/16, Brussels, 27 October 2016.

Council of the European Union. (2017) *Directives for the Negotiation of a Free Trade Agreement with Japan*, 15864/12, Brussels, 14 September 2017.

Cremona, M. (2015) 'Negotiating the transatlantic trade and investment partnership (TTIP)', *Common Market Law Review*, 52, pp. 351–362.

Cremona, M. (2017) 'Distinguished essay: A quiet revolution-the changing nature of the EU's common commercial policy', in M. Bungenberg, M. Krajewski, C. Tams, J.P. Terhechte and A.R. Ziegler (eds.), *European Yearbook of International Economic Law 2017*, Cham, Switzerland: Springer, pp. 3–34.

De Mestral, A. (2017) 'Negotiating CETA with the European Union and some thoughts on the impact of mega-regional trade agreements on agreements inter partes and agreements with third parties', in M. Bungenberg, M. Krajewski, C. Tams, J.P. Terhechte and A.R. Ziegler (eds.), *European Yearbook of International Economic Law 2017*, Cham, Switzerland: Springer, pp. 437–456.

Durán, G.M. (2013) 'The role of the EU in shaping the trade and environment regulatory nexus: Multilateral and regional approaches', in B.V. Vooren, S. Blockmans and J. Wouters (eds.), *The EU's Role in Global Governance: The Legal Dimension*, Oxford: Oxford University Press, pp. 224–240.

Durán, G.M. and Morgera, E. (2012) *Environmental Integration in the EU's External Relations: Beyond Multilateral Dimensions*, Oxford; Portland, OR: Hart Publishing.

European Commission. (2001) 'European governance: A white paper', COM (2001) 428 final, Brussel, 25 July 2001.

European Commission. (2006) 'Communication from the commission to the council, the European parliament, the European economic and social committee and the committee of the regions—Global Europe: Competing in the world: A contribution to the EU's growth and jobs strategy', COM (2006) 567 final, Brussels, 10 April 2006.

European Commission. (2009) 'Communication from the commission to the European parliament, the council, the European economic and social committee and the committee of the regions—Mainstreaming sustainable development into EU policies: 2009 review of the European union strategy for sustainable development', COM (2009) 400 final, Brussels, 24 July 2009.

European Commission. (2016) 'Communication from the commission to the European parliament, the council, the European economic and social committee and the committee of the regions—Next steps for a sustainable European future: European action for sustainability', COM (2016) 739 final, Brussels, 22 November 2016.

European Commission. (2018a) 'Annex 1, Annex to the proposal for a council decision on the conclusion of the free trade agreement between the European union and the republic of Singapore', COM (2018) 196 final, Brussels, 18 April 2018.

European Commission. (2018b) 'Proposal for a council decision on the conclusion of the economic partnership agreement between the European Union and Japan', COM (2018) 192 final, Brussel, 18 April 2018.

European Commission. (2018c) 'Proposal for a council decision on the conclusion of the free trade agreement between the European Union and the Republic of Singapore', COM (2018) 196 final, Brussels, 18 April 2018.

European Commission. (2018d) 'Proposal for a council decision on the signing, on behalf of the European union, of the investment protection agreement between the European Union and its member states, of the one part, and the republic of Singapore of the other part', COM (2018) 195 final, Brussels, 18 April 2018.

European Union. (2011) Council decision of 16 September 2010 on the signing, on behalf of the European Union, and provisional application of the Free Trade Agreement between the European Union and its member states, of the one part, and the Republic of Korea, of the other part, OJ L 127, 14 May 2011.

Forere, M.A. (2015) *The Relationship of WTO Law and Regional Trade Agreements in Dispute Settlement: From Fragmentation to Coherence*, Alphen aan den Rijn, The Netherlands: Wolters Kluwer.

Garcia, A. and Masselot, A. (2015) 'EU-Asia free trade agreements as tools for social norm/legislation transfer', *Asia Europe Journal*, 13(3), pp. 241–252.

HM Government. (2017) *The United Kingdom's Exit from and New Partnership with the European Union*, London: HMSO, available at https://www.gov.uk/government/uploads/system/uploads/attachment_data/file/589191/The_United_Kingdoms_exit_from_and_partnership_with_the_EU_Web.pdf.

Kim, H.S. (2010) 'Dispute settlement mechanism of the Korea-EU FTA', *Yonsei Law Journal*, 1(1), pp. 205–228.

Kim, J. (2018) 'Balancing regulatory interests through an exceptions framework under the right to regulate provision in international investment agreements', *George Washington International Law Review*, 50(2), pp. 289–356.

Koutrakos, P. (2017) 'Public disquiet and treaty-making', *European Law Review*, 1, pp. 1–2.

Krämer, L. (2015) *EU Environmental Law*, 8th edn, London: Sweet & Maxwell.

Marx, A., Ebert, F. and Hachez, N. (2017) 'Dispute settlement for labour provisions in EU free trade agreements: Rethinking current approaches', *Politics and Governance*, 5(4), pp. 49–59.

Nakanishi, Y. (2016) 'Economic partnership agreement between Japan and the European Union and legal issues: A focus on investment', *Hitotsubashi Journal of Law and Politics*, 44, pp. 19–30.

Nakanishi, Y. (2017) 'Characteristics of EU free trade agreements in a legal context: A Japanese perspective', in M. Bungenberg, M. Krajewski, C. Tams, J.P. Terhechte and A.R. Ziegler (eds.), *European Yearbook of International Economic Law 2017*, Cham, Switzerland: Springer, pp. 457–474.

Nakanishi, Y. (2018) 'Environmental law', in R. Brinkmann and S.J. Garren (eds.), *The Palgrave Handbook of Sustainability: Case Studies and Practical Solutions*, Cham, Switzerland: Springer, pp. 359–370.

Nakanishi, Y. (2019) 'The economic partnership agreement and the strategic partnership agreement between the European Union and Japan from a legal perspective', *Hitotsubashi Journal of Law and Politics*, 47, pp. 1–15.

Ohler, C. (2017) 'Democratic legitimacy and the rule of law in investor-state dispute settlement under CETA', in M. Bungenberg, M. Krajewski, C. Tams, J.P. Terhechte and A.R. Ziegler (eds.), *European Yearbook of International Economic Law 2017*, Cham, Switzerland: Springer, pp. 227–245.

Proelss, A. (2016) 'Principles of EU environmental law: An appraisal', in Y. Nakanishi (ed.), *Contemporary Issues in Environmental Law: The EU and Japan*, Tokyo: Springer Japan, pp. 29–45.

Reid, E. (2015) *Balancing Human Rights, Environmental Protection and International Trade*, Oxford; Portland, OR: Hart Publishing.

Reinisch, A. (2017) 'The EU and investor-state dispute settlement: WTO litigators going "investor-state arbitration" and back to a permanent "investment court"', in M. Bungenberg, M. Krajewski, C. Tams, J.P. Terhechte and A.R. Ziegler (eds.), *European Yearbook of International Economic Law 2017*, Cham, Switzerland: Springer, pp. 247–300.

Tanaka, Y. (2018) *The Peaceful Settlement of International Disputes*, Cambridge: Cambridge University Press.

Viñuales, J.E. (2012) *Foreign Investment and the Environment in International Law*, Cambridge: Cambridge University Press.

Conclusion

Chien-Huei Wu and Frank Gaenssmantel

This volume set out to explore how policymakers of the European Union (EU) choose between diplomatic, legal and mixed approaches in managing international economic relations with their partners in Asia, and with what effect. To do so, it started from a conceptual framework (in Chapter 1), which proposed to approach this theme with reference to a "logic of choice" and a "logic of constraints." The logic of choice emphasizes that in order to understand international economic relations we must look not only at single courses of action and their specific characteristics but instead place them in the context of a broader set of options amongst which policymakers can choose, on the basis of rational considerations on costs and benefits, ideas about what is appropriate, habit or communicative dynamics. The logic of constraints is intended to take into account that in an environment of multilevel and multi-actor governance, choice is always limited by the international and domestic legal context, established institutions and political structures and dynamics.

In a joint effort, the international lawyers and political scientists involved in this project approached this topic from different perspectives and covered a wide range of thematic subfields and cases. This included, in Part I of the volume, the role of the Court of Justice of the EU (CJEU) in EU–Asia trade disputes (Delgado Casteleiro, Chapter 2), the historical development of EU trade defence measures in the relationship between the EU and China (Eckhardt, Chapter 3) as well as Asian strategies in instances of investment disputes settlement with the EU (Choukroune, Chapter 4). Part II presented analyses of commercial disputes, with a strong focus on the EU's trade relations with China. It covered the solar panel dispute (Gaenssmantel, Chapter 5; Chen, Chapter 6), the contentious issue of export restrictions on raw materials (Wu, Chapter 7) and the still unresolved question of whether or not the EU recognizes China as a market economy for the purposes of trade defence investigations (Hsueh, Chapter 8). Part III of the volume then turned to the negotiation of bilateral agreements, which issues they legalize and how, and what this entails for the future interaction. The chapters looked at the ongoing negotiations between the EU and China on an investment agreement and their implications (Chaisse, Xu and Ji, Chapter 9), recently closed negotiations with Japan (Voogsgeerd, Chapter 10), the long-standing efforts between the EU and India (Roozendaal, Chapter 11) and lastly, more broadly, the theme of environmental provisions in trade agreements (Nakanishi, Chapter 12).

Taking together the findings from the chapters, some general conclusions can be drawn on the cooperative research project as a whole. To begin with, the general legal and institutional framework predetermines the formal policy tools available to policymakers and private actors in particular companies. In this sense, China's and Vietnam's accessions to the World Trade Organization (WTO) mark milestones in that WTO membership, enabling them and their trading partners, including the EU, to refer to the WTO dispute settlement mechanism (DSM) to safeguard their rights and interests. Before accession, they had to rely largely on diplomatic consultation. Alternatively, EU businesses could start trade defence investigations and third-state industries subject to EU trade defence measures, or EU industries not content with the outcome of the investigations could seek recourse from the EU's domestic judiciary, most prominently the Court of Justice of the EU.

These options for private actors remain in place after accession to the WTO, but it is unclear to date whether and to what extent the domestic courts of the EU can offer remedy to affected industries, EU or foreign. On the one hand, the CJEU may serve to constrain the abuse of power of the EU institutions and offer judicial protection to individual economic actors. On the other hand, the Court may wish to maintain the institutional balance and preserve scope of maneuverer for the EU institutions. Moreover, the EU institutions, the European Commission (the Commission) in particular, when negotiating and adopting international trade and investment agreements, may explicitly provide for no direct effects of international agreements and thus prevent individuals from referring disputes arising thereof to the Court.

Beyond the legal and institutional framework, the broader political context has an influence on the choices made by policymakers. In fact, it can constitute a series of heavy constraints on trade policymakers in the European Commission. This concerns first and foremost the political culture of the EU, which discourages the Commission from independent diplomatic initiatives unless explicitly foreseen in the treaties or in legislation. As a result, rather than choosing between diplomacy and law, the Commission officials end up choosing between available legally defined procedures, a choice that is again constrained by the dependence on private actor complaints in the case of trade defence procedures or the Trade Barriers Regulation. Paradoxically, the existence of such formal procedures then may strengthen the hand of the Commission, in that they positively confirm its authority in the concerned policy field and may even create space for diplomatic engagement with its counterparts in instances of legally embedded diplomacy, when procedures include negotiations or consultations.

The only way the Commission can engage in diplomacy in a broader sense is on the basis of a negotiating mandate by the Council of the EU, which is typically given to prepare complex agreements with third parties. Instead of relying on the closely delimited spheres of formal authority as defined in the treaties and legislation, with a Council mandate the Commission is politically authorized to pursue certain goals diplomatically. But even in this case, the limitations for the Commission remain palpable through regular supervision by the Trade Policy Committee but also in frequent instances of contestation, as for example concerning the respective competence of the EU and its member states in the matter, as was the case for the agreements with Singapore and Canada. In any case, it is remarkable that the Commission can only act when its field of action is neatly circumscribed and under explicit checks, meaning that constraints have an enabling effect.

Naturally, political constraints also emerge outside the sphere of established rules, formal procedures and institutional balances. Political movements and popular contestation can have an impact on negotiations and have driven the development of the investment court system. Also, the pattern of lobbying by firms has been changing, in particular in that not only import-competing but also import-dependent businesses are actively attempting to shape policymaking in their favour. This has created a trend towards more politicized trade defence cases.

In case of a dispute, whether a more diplomatic or a more legal approach is adopted also depends on the nature of the issue or subject at stake. Disputes over conventional trade and investment issues are often settled through legal approaches, whereas non-trade concerns or new trade-related issues tend to be addressed through diplomacy. Moreover, some trade issues are legal in appearance but political in nature and thus the help of the legal approach in settling the disputes is limited. The best example is China's market economy status. The Chinese government has challenged the EU in the WTO for its anti-dumping law and practices against Chinese producers, and the latter, when subject to the EU's anti-dumping investigations, often refer to the CJEU and General Court to challenge the determinations of the EC relating to individual treatment and market economy treatment. The ultimate goal is to obtain China's explicit recognition as a market economy by the EU, which is doomed to fail through a legal approach. As a legal concept that originated from political ideology and contains only vague definition, it is unrealistic to expect the CJEU to venture into this highly contested field and resolve the enduring conflict.

The importance of diplomacy in solving disputes over trade-related non-trade issues is not simply the result of policymakers' choice but also reflects the character of related treaty provisions. On the one hand, when we talk about new issues on the international trade agenda, existing treaties are necessarily limited. Legal approaches in resolving trade and investment disputes necessitate a set of clearly defined rules and a mechanism, notably, court-like adjudicatory bodies, to hear the cases, and such provisions are not always applicable to new issues. This means new diplomatic negotiations will be necessary to create the legal basis for addressing them. An example here would be export restrictions. On the other hand, negotiators may also consciously choose not to include such provisions in a treaty, either because their interests or normative stances are not compatible in this regard, or possibly also because they share a desire to avoid legalization. Examples here include labour rights and sustainable development. The divergences in economic interests or normative stances also prompt the EU and its Asian partners to re-evaluate and redesign the investor–state dispute settlement (ISDS) with possible reform through the investment court system.

As noted in Chapter 1, broad consensus among EU member states, and thus a large win-set, facilitates successful diplomacy, while a narrow win-set in combination with disciplined member states that refrain from direct contacts with the concerned third party can strengthen the Commission's negotiating position. However, we have seen a divided EU and member states with an active diplomatic agenda towards third states, both in the context of treaty negotiations and in trade defence measure investigations. As regards new rule-making, the reform of ISDS through the new investment court system and better-defined right to regulate are illustrative examples. Given the divisions within the EU member states, the EU's initiative for new investment rules has only limited success. As regards trade defence measures, the divisions within the EU can politicize disputes and make Council approval for measures proposed by the Commission strenuous.

This divided EU is facing a "legalizing Asia." Asian countries in general and China in particular are increasingly active in the WTO's DSM, and there is a new trend that Asian investors, in particular Indian, refer to ISDS to seek compensation against measures of European governments. This breaks the myth that Asian countries or Asian enterprises are less inclined to legal approaches in resolving disputes. That said, Asian investors' presence in the ISDS comes along with the Asian countries' resentment against it as some Asian countries, notably, India and Indonesia, are terminating their bilateral investment treaties containing ISDS clauses. China's attitude toward ISDS is more ambiguous. It has long been resistant to ISDS; yet, its recent bilateral investment treaties do contain ISDS, which reflects the growth of Chinese outbound investments and Chinese investors' acquaintance with such a mechanism.

In its essence, legalization reflects an agreement amongst the negotiating parties to constrain their diplomatic discretion, by explicitly delineating its boundaries, by binding action to formal procedures and by delegating authority to court-like bodies. At the same time, though, this also implies new modalities for managing economic relations, and, when within the limits of the law, stronger authority, as grounded in law. The established procedures may contain by themselves provision for diplomatic engagement. The selective nature of efforts at legalization and the emergence of new issues on the international economic agenda can lead to another round of diplomatic initiatives towards more legalization. This means that diplomacy and law interact in a cyclical dynamic, in which each one's respective space is constantly redefined. Rather than a clear choice between diplomacy and law to manage international economic relations, this suggests a constant interaction and combination of the two.

The EU, usually represented by the Commission, is a sophisticated player in a legalized environment, but its internal divisions can seriously compromise its effectiveness. The Commission has learned to flourish under the constraints of multilevel and multi-actor governance, and in particular to use to the fullest the formal authority provided to it under the European treaties and law. It also deploys the power of formal procedure towards third states, for example, in the context of trade defence investigations. However, divisions amongst member states and their independent engagement with international partners can weaken the Commission's stance in treaty negotiations and in any setting where member states have a say in the Council, including on trade defence. The EU's Asian partners are catching up in terms of familiarity with and use of legal provisions and formal procedures. Since all of them have less trouble with internal divisions, one should expect to see a shift in dynamics and a more balanced relationship. Be that as it may, the management of economic relations between the EU and Asia is likely to remain marked by complex combinations of legal and diplomatic approaches, with a slow but steady trend towards further legalization.

Index

Printed in the United States
by Baker & Taylor Publisher Services